MW00416158

God
IS MY
Happy
Place

365 DAILY DEVOTIONS
FOR MORNING AND EVENING

BroadStreet
P U B L I S H I N G

BroadStreet Publishing Group, LLC.
Savage, Minnesota, USA
Broadstreetpublishing.com

God Is My Happy Place

© 2021 BroadStreet Publishing

978-1-4245-6232-9
978-1-4245-6233-6 (eBook)

Devotions composed by Rachel Flores.

Design by Chris Garborg | garborgdesign.com
Edited by Michelle Winger with Sarah Eral | literallyprecise.com.

Printed in China.

21 22 23 24 25 7 6 5 4 3 2 1

May God, the inspiration
and fountain of hope,
fill you to overflowing
with uncontainable joy
and perfect peace
as you trust in him.

Romans 15:13 TPT

Introduction

God encourages us in his Word to give thanks in all things at all times. That's not a mistake. When we choose to focus on things we are grateful for, we become happier people. Our satisfaction in life increases. Comparisons cease. Unnecessary pursuits pause. And we begin to notice the little things. The things that matter. Life. Breath. Connection. Kindness. Beauty. This is where we find God—our true happy place.

As you reflect on these devotional entries, Scriptures, and prayers, refocus your perspective and begin to meditate on things that produce life and joy, that bring peace and comfort. Spend the beginning and end of your day with God, experiencing his goodness and being refreshed in his presence. Be encouraged as you take time to ponder how wonderfully unique and abundantly blessed you are.

Evaluate each day in the light of God's truth. From the time you wake up, until the time you fall into bed at night, choose gratitude. Choose satisfaction. Choose your happy place.

All About God

From him and through him and for him are all things.
To him be the glory forever. Amen!

ROMANS 11:36 NIV

"She is very religious; she's always talking about God!" What was meant as an insult was really quite a compliment. Has this ever been said about you? Maybe it has, and it has shut you up. With cheeks flushed, you felt judged and misread by the person you were with. Do not be ashamed. What some meant as harm is really a reflection of the gift God has given you. If you have tunnel vision for Jesus, you are not on the wrong path. The Bible, and this verse in Romans, makes it pretty clear that we are to be all about the kingdom of God!

We are not called to live in a divide of the sacred and the secular, but in all things give God the glory. Not everyone will understand why you choose to make God your happy place and bring him up in areas they don't think he belongs. Don't mind them. You are not too much; God loves how you can see him in all the details of life.

Do you lean more toward dividing sacred
and secular or seeing God in all things?

Because God is the source and sustainer of everything,
everything finds fulfillment in him.
May all praise and honor be given to him forever! Amen!

ROMANS 11:36 TPT

Having eyes for the kingdom of God will make you feel like an outsider. We are told to expect to be hated by the world. But there will even be those who call themselves believers who find you to be too much. A life dedicated to the glory of God is never too much. A heart set on seeking him is exactly where it needs to be. A mouth proclaiming his goodness and mercy so that the rocks don't cry out is speaking what needs to be said.

Well done! God is pleased and delighted in you. He is present in our world: moving and working. To be a person who sees him at work and brings attention to it is exactly what this world needs. You have a mind set on the Spirit. That is to be commended.

Jesus, my mind is set on you. My heart longs for more of you. I see you working in the world around me; thank you! Help me to never be ashamed of the gifts you have given me.

Beyond the Pain

This light momentary affliction is preparing for us an eternal weight of glory beyond all comparison, as we look not to the things that are seen but to the things that are unseen. For the things that are seen are transient, but the things that are unseen are eternal.

2 CORINTHIANS 4:17-18 ESV

Light and momentary? These troubles feel anything but that! you might be thinking. But this verse is written by a man who has been in prison, shipwrecked, beaten, starved, robbed, stoned, whipped, and more. If there was someone who knew about affliction, Paul could for sure qualify as an expert! It just goes to solidify that what he is writing about here is true.

The unseen, eternal glory that is to come is unimaginably good. Incomprehensibly splendid. And on top of that, it's solid. It's not going anywhere. It's more real than any reality you've experienced. It's designed by a good Father who loves you deeply. When things feel hopeless, maybe your hope is in the wrong place. Turn your hope to the unshakeable age that is to come, to our eternal glory with Jesus Christ. That is a sustaining hope that will not disappoint and will afford you much joy in the here and now.

Would you say you have an eternal perspective, or are your eyes focused on now?

Our present troubles are small and won't last very long. Yet they produce for us a glory that vastly outweighs them and will last forever! So we don't look at the troubles we can see now; rather, we fix our gaze on things that cannot be seen. For the things we see now will soon be gone, but the things we cannot see will last forever.

2 CORINTHIANS 4:17-18 TPT

Perspective can be everything. For example, someone in a windowless basement of a house will think it's dark, but the person upstairs can see the sun outside the windows. If we set our eyes above our circumstances, it will change so much for us. Looking up to Christ will fill us with hope no matter how dark a circumstance may be.

Remembering that our time on earth is the journey not the destination, and that our eternal home awaits us, will help us keep our priorities aligned with Jesus and keep us from getting tangled up in earthly affairs. It's helpful to have a fellow believer you can pray over your priorities with and share your perspective so both of you can encourage each other to look to Christ. Who could you reach out to share in the journey of this year with?

God, show me another believer who can help me lift my eyes back to you when times get hard.

Called His Own

*The LORD will not abandon His people on account of His great name,
because the LORD has been pleased to make you a people for Himself.*

1 SAMUEL 12:22 NASB

The Israelites have an extensive history, laid out for us in
the Old Testament. It is often seen as back and forth: the
Israelites disobeying God and God consistently redeeming
them to himself. If you can think of it, it's been done by this
group of people God called his own—idolatry, complaining,
disobedience, murder, lying, sexual immorality, the list goes
on over thousands of years. It leaves you wondering if they
would ever get it right, which is an easy stance to take from
our bird's eye view of reading the Old Testament. It also
makes us wonder if God would ever give up on his people.

The answer to both of those is no; they would never get it right
and God would never give up. If you find yourself shaking
your head at all their shortcomings, it is wise to remember
you are never going to get it right either. The good news is you
don't have to! The glory that is coming to his name by making
a people for himself is the fact that through the Israelites, a
people called the "missionary nation," all other nations could
know God. You can be secure in Jesus, no matter how right or
wrong you get it. Faith in him means you are called his own.

Do you think that you, or someone you know,
has gone too far and God has given up on them?

*For the sake of his great name the L*ORD *will not reject his people, because the L*ORD *was pleased to make you his own.*

1 SAMUEL 12:22 NIV

As we chewed on this morning, it takes pushback against wrong thinking to be free from the lie that we will never measure up to God. People usually swing one of two ways, either trying to work harder for their salvation or giving up completely and accepting the title of unforgivable. The truth is that none of us have to work harder, and none of us are unforgivable. The grace of God is perfect in its mission—to bring God glory.

When we pendulum swing, we either spit on the grace of God by saying it is not strong enough or comprehensive enough to forgive us. If we swing the opposite direction, we try to earn the grace ourselves. This status of being his is a free gift, and it comes with the richest of rewards.

God, thank you for your grace. Thank you for calling me your own. Free me from any swinging back and forth and help me to rest in your grace alone. Help me to forgive those I don't find worthy of your forgiveness and keep me from adding to my salvation, trying to do it in my own power.

Empowered to Hope

May the God of hope fill you with all joy and peace in believing,
so that you may abound in hope by the power of the Holy Spirit.

ROMANS 15:13 NRSV

Think of yourself as a glass. God pours joy and peace into you. When he does that, you overflow with hope. That overflow is noticeable to all around you. They, in turn, acknowledge God, and it spurs them on to believe in him! The cycle starts again in a new believer. This is discipleship made simple.

When you exercise your faith muscle, spending time with Jesus, walking in obedience to him, and reading his Word, God fills you with joy and peace. This joy and peace mixed together release hope. Try and bottle it up, but why would you want to? it's a mixture waiting to be shared with others. When you share what God is brewing in your heart with others, it causes belief in them as well. Isn't it awesome how God wants to use us? Won't you be a vessel for his glory and overflow this morning?

Who can you share God's hope with today?

May God, the inspiration and fountain of hope, fill you to overflowing with uncontainable joy and perfect peace as you trust in him. And may the power of the Holy Spirit continually surround your life with his super-abundance until you radiate with hope!

Who is doing the filling? By whose power is this hope flourishing in us? Is it our own? No! God does the filling. The Holy Spirit provides the power. This is his work! He is not limited by your ability to be productive. He is not prone to measure your days how you measure them. The good, lasting, worthwhile work that he is doing, the glorious fruit that he produces in a person's life, comes from the Holy Spirit!

Stop striving and wearing yourself out achieving things for God. Let him do the work for you; partner with him to see him move. Let us be stripped of our independent ways and built back up so we are dependent on him.

God, will you fill me with joy and peace tonight? Will you let me overflow with your hope? Fill me with your power, work in my life, and let it be contagious to others.

Look to Him

Be of good courage,
And He shall strengthen your heart,
All you who hope in the LORD.

PSALM 31:24, NKJV

Here we are at the start of a new year. The new year often brings fresh hope and a time of seeking vision and direction for the time to come. That is why this verse fits in just perfectly. You are a child of God whose hope is in him. No matter what you face this coming year or what you have planned, you can have strength in all situations by remembering the promises of God toward you.

For every goal you make, find a promise in Scripture that will encourage you. For every path you wish to pursue, use Scripture to make sure it aligns with God's will. It's important that you know God's Word; make that a priority this year too! Whatever you do, start off on a firm foundation of God's Word and turn to him for vision, guidance, and direction.

Do you incorporate the Word of God into your dreaming for the new year? If not, today's a good day to start!

Be strong and take heart,
all you who hope in the LORD.

PSALM 31:24 NIV

To be of good courage means to have the power and
confidence to act according to what you believe. In order to
act on something, you have to know what you believe. There
is a saying: "Stand for something or you'll fall for everything."
It's important that we stand on the Word of God. There are
so many false teachings and wayward paths in the world
today. With the internet and social media, it seems like
misinformation is even easier to spread.

Make it a goal this year to be so familiar with the truth of
God's Word that you will not fall for the lies. God wants you to
walk in the truth. This is how you gain strength for whatever
the year has in store for you.

Jesus, help me to prioritize hiding your truth in my heart this
year. Help me to know your truth inside and out. I want this
to be a year of standing confident in your promises. Thank
you for providing me with your Word!

Listen in the Dark

*"What I tell you in the dark, say in the light,
and what you hear whispered, proclaim on the housetops."*

MATTHEW 10:27 ESV

It is commonplace for us to create a dichotomy in our heads that says God is light, so if there is darkness, God isn't in it. That is understandable, considering all the verses we read that describe Christ as light. However, it's not true. In the psalms we are told there is no place we can go to get away from the spirit of God. In the lowest of lows and the highest of heights, he is there. When your life circumstances feel heavy, dark, and hard, God is there. When you feel weary, exhausted, or broken, God is there.

God speaks in the darkness; it does not hinder him. He sustains you through it, comforts you, and mourns with you. His methods of relating may change, but his presence does not. We must resist the temptation to equate hard times with the absence of God. A happy life in Christ is knowing that in darkness and in light, God is still speaking and moving.

How can you remind yourself that God
is still near when life feels dark?

> *"What I say to you in the dark, repeat in broad daylight,*
> *and what you hear in a whisper, announce it publicly."*
>
> MATTHEW 10:27 TPT

When it's dark, your other senses become keener to compensate for the lack of light. We make ourselves still to hear the whisper of a loved one in the darkness, and it almost feels easier than if you could see them. We are focused on the voice. We should hear the whispers of God so clearly in the dark that we can shout it from rooftops when morning dawns.

This verse is two-fold: first, what we talked about this morning of God speaking in the darkness. Secondly, the fact that what we hear we are supposed to share. Dark seasons are not wasted. Jesus is speaking to you, advocating for you, and building you up, just like in the light. When you reach morning, he wants you to tell others who may be in the dark the things he spoke to you. He wants you to shout and share. Isn't it beautiful that with God, no season is wasted? Tune your ear to hear in the darkness, and if you are in the morning, start to make known what was entrusted to you.

God, thank you that you are ever near. That my happy life is dependent solely on being close to you. You speak in the dark times and in the light, and you waste nothing in my life. Help me to proclaim your truth and goodness to those around me.

Help at Hand

Every time they cried out to you in their despair,
you were faithful to deliver them;
you didn't disappoint them.

PSALM 22:5 TPT

Need a hand? When working on a project, who doesn't like to hear those words? It is a relief when someone offers to share your burden or workload. Jesus doesn't just want to share your burden; he wants to exchange his with you. And do you know how his is described? As easy. Light. Doesn't that sound like relief?

Whatever you are trying to do on your own today, stop and ask God to help you. He is willing and able to take your burden and bring relief and rest. What a friend!

What burden do you need help with today?

They cried to You, and were delivered;
They trusted in You, and were not ashamed.

PSALM 22:5 NKJV

Even the most faithful, loving friends and family will disappoint us. Since we are all human, it is inevitable. However, we serve a perfect God, and he will never let us down. His Scripture is packed full of promises to never abandon you, never leave you lonely, always be faithful to you, and uphold and strengthen you. And that list is just a short one. His promises go on and on.

God gives us relationships with others for many different reasons, but we can't put all our hope on those people. Our true hope can only rest in God. Make sure you have your relationships in their rightful place: God on the throne, with all your trust in him, and people second.

Jesus, thank you that you are faithful; you never let me down. You offer to exchange your burden for mine. Can I do that tonight? I want to lay this down. I need rest. Thank you for being faithful to deliver me. Thank you that you never disappoint and I can always rely on you.

Solid Ground

He lifted me out of the pit of despair,
out of the mud and the mire.
He set my feet on solid ground
and steadied me as I walked along.

PSALM 40:2 NLT

When you were a little kid, did you ever play sinking sand? It is a game that usually involves jumping from pillow to pillow or couch to couch because if you touch the ground, that's sinking sand! As adults we can fall into the routine of living life the same way, jumping from one thing to the next, terrified of failure. Life in Christ doesn't need to be like this though.

No good pursuit or busy schedule is going to save you. A life built on the solid foundation of Jesus Christ is the only thing that will keep you grounded. He is the solid ground, steady and sure, and even if you fail, you can never mess up enough to sink. Be aware of your footing and what you trust in today and pray about if you need to shift to relying on Christ instead of other things.

Is Christ your foundation?

He stooped down to lift me out of danger
from the desolate pit I was in,
out of the muddy mess I had fallen into.
Now he's lifted me up into a firm, secure place
and steadied me while I walk along his ascending path.

PSALM 40:2 TPT

Who are the action words describing in this verse? Christ is lifting. He is setting the psalmist on solid ground. He is steadying him as they walk. The one doing the most in these verses is Christ. We often attempt to do it all in our strength. To get our act together and pull ourselves out of the pit. We try to get our own lives set straight, to bring stability, in our own power.

Why do we strive to do this when the all-powerful God is so near and willing to help? He wants to do things for you. Continue to walk, taking steps of faith, and submit your life to the power of the Holy Spirit to do the rest.

Jesus, will you be my solid ground? I need stability and strength. I want to stop doing it on my own and rely on you. Thank you for your saving power.

Shield around Me

You, O LORD, are a shield about me,
my glory, and the lifter of my head.

PSALM 3:3 ESV

Are you walking through life with your head down just trying to make it through? Some of us call it survival mode. God doesn't want you to just survive in this life; he wants you to thrive! Here God says to us that he is the lifter of our heads. What a beautiful promise.

Lift your eyes for a moment and gaze into the eyes of your Father. Let his kindness break the chains that are weighing you down. Let him build up faith in you, a shield to protect you from the arrows of the enemy. Maybe you've had your shield down for too long now, and the bombardment of lies has caused your head to droop as well. Lift up your eyes! Lift up your shield! Let God restore your soul so you thrive in the life he has called you to.

What is the Lord speaking to you as you ask him
to lift your head and your burdens?

You, O Lord, are a shield for me,
My glory and the One who lifts up my head.

PSALM 3:3 NKJV

You may feel exhausted, but God does not grow weary. You may be at the end, but God is just getting started. You may feel exposed and in need of protection, but God's got the way to wrap you up safe.

This battle that you are in? It belongs to God. Don't try to win it on your own. God is all powerful, and you fight by letting him be your hero and fight for you. You can rest secure knowing that God is with you and he is protecting you. You are safe in his all-encompassing will.

God, will you lift my eyes? Will you show me that my help comes from you? Will you fight my battle? Can you comfort my soul? I need you tonight. Wrap me up safe and don't let me go.

Light of Love

He has delivered us from the power of darkness
and conveyed us into the kingdom of the Son of His love.

COLOSSIANS 1:13 NKJV

God wants to bring all the dark places in you to light and heal them. There are stories and aspects that we will hold tightly to, trying to bury them deep. But God desires for us to be wholly healthy. Your family needs you to be healthy. Your friends need you to pursue light. Your church body needs your testimony.

God is gracious and kind, and he will not force your hand. But if you choose to bring what you're most afraid of to the light, if you are willing to walk through the darkness, you will come out the other side in the most glorious brilliance. He will take the darkest parts of your story, give them light to give you healing and to give others hope. Because when others see and hear about the light in you, they will put their trust in the Lord. Stay tender to God's leading and hold his hand tight through the healing. Let your story be a light in someone else's darkness.

Where is God nudging you to walk through the darkness to get to the light?

*He has rescued us from the dominion of darkness
and brought us into the kingdom of the Son he loves.*

COLOSSIANS 1:13 NIV

Have you ever heard of Seasonal Affective Disorder? Maybe you live in one of the more northern climates and are familiar with the term. It is a term for a type of depression that is caused by winter seasons, with lack of sunlight being the causing factor. There are parts of Alaska that see sixty days of complete darkness. That's two months without the sun! It seems that biologically we are wired for light. Spiritually, we are too. We are made to be at home with Jesus in his kingdom of light. Living in his kingdom brings us to full health and wholeness.

God has rescued you from the dungeon of darkness where you were trapped in your former ways of sin. Days upon days of darkness aren't good for your soul! He longs to let the light revive and heal you. Praise God for his glorious power to save you from the darkness.

God, thank you that you have brought me out of the dungeon and into glorious light! Heal my soul and make me whole in you.

Confident Hope

*Faith is confidence in what we hope for
and assurance about what we do not see.*

HEBREWS 11:1 NIV

The word *faith* can seem so abstract sometimes. It's a word you paint in calligraphy and hang on signs in your house, yet it feels a little ambiguous. So, what does this verse mean? To have faith in God is to stand confidently and take as fact that God exists and he is at work even if we can't see him at work. Our faith doesn't have to stay the same.

If you struggle with the concept of faith as well, take heart that you can grow in it over time. It is a gift from God; step one is asking for it! Step two is acknowledging that you don't have to settle for the same amount of faith you've always had. Ask for more. Step three, let your faith be developed by trusting in God's ways. The ways you can see, and the ways that leave you with whys. All of these steps rely on God. Faith is for the wonderful seasons and downright challenging ones alike. Ask God today to fill you confidently with faith.

How is God building faith in you today?

Faith shows the reality of what we hope for;
it is the evidence of things we cannot see.

HEBREWS 11:1 NLT

Faith is confidence. Do you usually associate confidence with pride? That's because the world shows us that confidence comes from pridefully putting our trust in ourselves. It is a selfish ambition only when the source is yourself. But children of God are called to be confident, and it's actually humble to do so! Confidence is trusting in Jesus.

You have the assurance of who Jesus is and who you are to him. Your identity is completely wrapped up in him, and with Jesus as your source, you can walk out your days full of faith displayed for all to see. The power comes from the one who lives inside of you. Let's dare to live with faith and confidence today.

God, fill me with faith anew. Help me to trust in you. Keep building up faith in me. I love you!

Fullness of Grace

From his fullness we have all received,
grace upon grace.

JOHN 1:16 NRSV

God doesn't waste anything. Do you believe it? Life can leave us high and dry too weary to face another year. The mundane circumstances you live in may seem useless. The trial you went through was too painful and overwhelming. The questions you are asking don't seem to be answered.

God is in the business of making all things new, and in this he doesn't waste one minute of your life. Imagine God as the painter, and you come to him hoping for a beautiful portrait but lacking in supplies. He has everything he needs; he is full of supplies to turn what we offer into the masterpiece canvas we hoped he would create.

What hope arises from the statement
that God doesn't waste anything?

*Out of his fullness we are fulfilled!
And from him we receive grace heaped upon more grace!*

JOHN 1:16 TPT

God is fully qualified. If you've ever interviewed candidates for a job, looked over a stack of applications and resumes, or sat through interviews, you know that the saying, "It's hard to find good help these days" can be true! When looking for employees, it can be difficult to find people who seem qualified with the exact skill set that is needed. And how are we to know that what they write is true?

Jesus is the man for the grace-giving job. Fully God and fully man, he was the only one with the means to conquer sin and death and create the pathway back to God. He's the only one who can give grace abundantly as we need it. How do you know that he is qualified? The Bible is the resume of his love, his character, and his working amongst humanity doing exactly this—handing out grace. Trust in this promise today.

Jesus, thank you for the grace you give. Thank you for being qualified, and for giving your life for me. Thank you for not wasting anything. I need grace tonight. Will you give me more?

Come Again

My life's strength melts away with grief and sadness;
come strengthen me and encourage me with your words.

PSALM 119:28 TPT

When it comes to grief, we often want it to be a one-and-done sort of deal. Wouldn't it be great if it were? We could just say, "Here is my pain, Jesus!" and in one swift swoop, it would be gone. Unfortunately, it doesn't work like that. But Jesus never tires of you. He doesn't get annoyed when you bring your grief again even if it has been years of repetitive coming to him. He doesn't sigh when you ask for his strength to forgive again.

Don't believe the lie that your state is a bother to God. Come again. He wants you to approach repeatedly. He wants to weep with you, hear your sadness, bear your grief, and then when you've been laid bare, he will encourage you and build you back up with his Word. The best way to walk through grief is with Christ. He is a friend who is closer than a brother.

Do you have any hurts you are hiding from Jesus
instead of bringing them to him again?

I weep with sorrow;
encourage me by your word.

PSALM 119:28 NLT

When we are in the middle of grief, things that people say often fall short. Empty platitudes from well-meaning people can be like salt in a wound. For healing balm, the psalmist teaches us to turn to the Word of God. It is living and powerful.

Described as a spring of never-ending fresh water, the Word of God is necessary for your soul. Trite sayings of the world just don't add up in the end; God's Word is relevant to your pain. Ask God to soften your heart and speak loudly through his Word into your sadness and pain today.

Jesus, let your Word be like healing balm to my hurting soul. Teach me to come to you, over and over, and to remember that you don't tire of me. Refresh me in your Word and strengthen me.

Learning to Rest

For God alone, O my soul, wait in silence,
for my hope is from him.

PSALM 62:5 ESV

It seems like society is just speeding up. With the advance of the technological age, coupled with many other factors, productivity and a do-it-all attitude triumph. This is in direct contrast to the command in Scripture for rest. Even our prayer and devotional time can become a to-do list, quickly reading, checking the box, and handing Jesus a checklist of requests. When was the last time you sat in silence in the presence of God?

Our instinct is to fill the void: grab our Bibles, pull out our phones, turn on music. We even have super spiritual ways of avoiding the silence. God is not afraid of the quiet. It takes courage on our part to sit in the silence and wait on God. Rest is the resistance against a world that tells us we must do more to be worthy. Rest is submission to a God who wants us to let him show us our worth. Try it this morning. Take even a few moments to do nothing but wait on God, and let him show you the riches of his mercy.

What hinders you from resting in the presence of God?

My soul, wait silently for God alone,
For my expectation is from Him.

PSALM 62:5 NKJV

Let's not over-spiritualize this. Although prayer and Bible
reading are necessary and good, God invites us into rest in
other ways as well. He is not limited to Sunday mornings
and prayer closets. God has created so many things for us
to enjoy, and each of us is unique. Some will find joy and
refreshment in a long hike in the woods. Others will find
it in a cozy coffee shop surrounded by people. God is not a
merciless dictator, wanting you to live a scheduled and rigid
life of piety. He wants you to delight in life. To enjoy it. To see
the beauty in the world around you.

Rest will never run toward you and make you stop and smell
the roses. You must pursue it. Don't let guilt weigh you down
into thinking taking a long shower or painting a picture are
useless activities that God frowns upon. No, he knows the
beauty of rest, and he wants you to find enjoyment. He does
not require constant productivity. Relax in this truth tonight.

God, thank you that you created a world for us to enjoy. Thank
you for leading me into rest. Help me to learn the spiritual
discipline of silence and rest and to find you there.

Rooted in Goodness

*I would have despaired unless I had believed
that I would see the goodness of the Lord
in the land of the living.*

PSALM 27:13 NASB

This verse is a foundational truth for anyone wanting a
happy life. We must be firmly rooted in the fact that our
God is good. It is his character to be good, and he cannot go
against himself. Our view of God's goodness will completely
shift our lives either to joy-filled living or to despair. Our
circumstances are ever shifting and changing. There are
inevitable things in life that we cannot control, such as death.
The surest footing we have is in Christ. Despair will swallow
you whole if you put your trust in anything else.

Hope in God and know that he is in control. All his actions
toward you are motivated by love, and he will give you joy in
the here and now. The land of the living—that is this moment,
this life. Do you believe God's goodness toward you? Are you
sold on this truth?

Is God good? Write out how or why you know he is.

I remain confident of this:
I will see the goodness of the LORD
in the land of the living.

PSALM 27:13 NIV

How can we experience the goodness of God in our lives?
There are three ways to help foster this. First, have a love for
God's Word. Know it well. Being familiar with the promises
of God will empower you to see him acting, and it will build
faith that he is true to who he says he is. Second, have a right
view of his nature. You know God's nature through his Word.
Culture, upbringing, and experience can sometimes skew our
perceptions of God. We must make sure that how we view him
is in line with how he truly is. Third, live expectant for God to
move and speak.

Do you make space for worship and prayer, or is your life
so busy that those things seem more like extra tasks than
delightful encounters? When you hear God speak, do you
move in faith or let fear hold you back? These areas can help
you experience the power of God in your life and know his
goodness.

God, thank you that you are good! Heal me of any skewed
views of you. Let me see you rightly. Bring me joy in your
presence here and now.

Unload the Burdens

"Come to me, all you who are weary and burdened, and I will give you rest. Take my yoke upon you and learn from me, for I am gentle and humble in heart, and you will find rest for your souls."

MATTHEW 11:28-29 NIV

You've heard the label: Ms. Independent. Maybe you even carry it as a badge of honor. Sometimes it can be positive, but we need to be quick to recognize any pride that may be subtly running in the background. We were not created to be independent loners who have it all together. God created us to be in relationship. First with him, and second with each other. That is how we thrive.

Trying to carry all of life's troubles and the weight of sin ourselves will lead to inevitable failure. You might be able to survive under the pressure for a while, but why? At what cost? In humility, come to Christ and lay it at his feet. Look up at the body of Christ there to help you, and trust God enough to be vulnerable with them. Rest and relationship wait for you when you lay your burdens at Christ's feet.

In what ways is operating independently hurting you?

"Are you weary, carrying a heavy burden? Then come to me. I will refresh your life, for I am your oasis. Simply join your life with mine. Learn my ways and you'll discover that I'm gentle, humble, easy to please. You will find refreshment and rest in me."

MATTHEW 11:28-29 TPT

This yoke that is being spoken of in Matthew refers to the same heavy, wooden device that hung on the necks of animals working in the fields. We all have yokes: trying to live perfectly is the yoke of the law, and living in sin is the yoke of bondage. Even Jesus has a yoke, although it is neither of those.

The yoke of the law or the yoke of sin is heavy and burdensome; it will eventually kill you. A yoke is usually pulled by two animals. Instead of bearing the yoke of the law or sin alone, why not lay it down and share in Christ's yoke? He not only says that his is light, but that he walks next to you the whole way. Who better to be tethered to than Christ our Savior?

Jesus, thank you that you bear my burdens. Show me areas in my life that I am not laying down before you. Walk with me, keep me in step with you, and give me your light yolk.

Even More

God gives us even more grace, as the Scripture says,
"God is against the proud, but he gives grace to the humble."

JAMES 4:6 NCV

It seems like a no-brainer. Stubbornly continue in your own way, not asking for help and foolishly following your pride, and you won't receive grace. Or, humble yourself, ask God for more, submit, and he will give it to you. If it seems so simple, why do we wrestle with it so much? Pride is the hardwiring of our fallen nature. It's the forefront of every sin. That makes it our biggest downfall in drawing near to Christ. God has an abundance of grace available to you, but if you choose to do things your way, he's not going to force you to accept the grace.

Make it a daily practice to come before the Lord and humble yourself. It's as easy as a simple prayer, "Jesus, I choose to submit myself to your will, not my own. Forgive me of pride, show me pride in my life, and humble me in your sight. I need your grace!" God will always answer your plea for grace.

When was the last time you prayed for humility?

He gives us more grace. That is why Scripture says:
"God opposes the proud but shows favor to the humble."

JAMES 4:6 NIV

It is impossible to find yourself with a need for grace greater than God's supply holds. We are asked as believers to walk in this world and not be of this world (Romans 12:2). As we do this, we need grace. Grace is the key. Once we become believers, God isn't allotting us a certain amount until we get our act together. He has an abundance of grace that will never run out.

Do you struggle with repeated sin, beating yourself up when you return to the same action or heart position once again? The question to ask yourself is how did you find forgiveness and grace for it the first time? You came to God and repented! Come again. And again. And for the rest of your life. Humble yourself before God and drink deep of the grace that he gives. Confess your sins and find mercy at the foot of the cross.

Jesus, make me humble before you. Help me not to walk in pride.

Positioned for Rescue

I'm exhausted! My life is spent with sorrow,
my years with sighing and sadness.
Because of all these troubles,
I have no more strength.
My inner being is so weak and frail.

PSALM 31:10 TPT

The psalms can feel a bit like an emotional rollercoaster. This can be reassuring for many of us who feel similarly in our own lives. It makes the psalms one of the more relatable books in the Bible even though David was a king who was pursued by flesh-and-bone enemies, had assassination plots against his life, wars to fight, and a kingdom to run.

The emotions can be the same no matter if you're a barista or a king. Sorrow does not include or exclude based on wealth or position. The point is when David had big feelings, he wasn't bemoaning them to his bestie. We don't see him sending out public decrees through the land. He was at the feet of Jesus pouring out his soul. This is what put him in a position for rescue by the only one who could possibly save him—Jesus. The same is available to you.

Do you air out your soul to others or to God?

I am dying from grief;
my years are shortened by sadness.
Sin has drained my strength;
I am wasting away from within.

PSALM 31:10 NLT

Imagine yourself in a hurricane. It's too late to evacuate on your own and the floodwaters are rising. Do you sit in your house on the floor level, watching TV and hoping someone will find you? No! You go up on the roof and wait for help. You might bring something bright, positioning yourself for rescue by the national guard.

It's the same in our spiritual lives. When life's storms come, it's not helpful to continue on with business as usual, trying to convince yourself, God, and others that you are fine. When the storms come, we need to position ourselves for rescue. We need to move into a posture of prayer and worship. We need to cry out to our Savior. Bottling it all up and pressing on won't change anything. God is faithful to rescue us when our situations seem dire. Won't you humbly submit yourself to his help tonight?

God, I submit myself to you. Life is hard sometimes! The storm swirls around me. Will you rescue me? You are faithful to do so.

Ask Again

Oh, that I might have my request,
and that God would fulfill my hope.

JOB 6:8 ESV

Did Job get it? You know, the one request that he wants to
have fulfilled. Look around at the context: do we even get to
know what this one request is? Perhaps the bigger question
is, does it really matter? What matters is the posture of Job's
heart toward God.

In light of eternity, maybe it's not the subject of our prayers
that holds the most significance, but it is the posture of our
hearts. Do we turn to God in prayer, cry out to him, or have a
heart of submission to his will? If the subject of our prayers
becomes more important than to whom we are praying, we've
made an idol of our will and our desires and cheapened God
to a glorified vending machine. First and foremost, God
wants us to come to him in prayer, with hearts that say, "Your
will be done."

Do you focus more on what you want
than who you are praying to?

Oh, that I might have my request,
That God would grant me the thing that I long for!
JOB 6:8 NKJV

Job is facing so much trial by the time we get to verse six. The heading in one version of the Bible labels this section as *Pressed past limits.* What is the one thing Job is asking for? It's that he might die before he ends up cursing God. Job isn't asking for relief from the trials which is pretty surprising! We've been taught in our culture that God won't give us more than we can handle, but that's not necessarily Biblical.

Job got a lot more than he could handle, and he knew it! When he prayed, he asked to bring glory to God through it all. He prayed that his heart would be soft toward God before he died. He had God in the right focus as the sovereign one, and his life in the right perspective as just a vapor on this earth. God doesn't promise us a suffering-free life, but he does promise to be with us through it all. May we be those who honor God no matter what comes.

Jesus, I want you to be the main focus of my life. No matter what else is going on, may I bring glory to your name above all.

My Sustainer

Preserve me, O God,
for in you I put my trust.

PSALM 16:1 NKJV

When you are canning something, like fresh peaches for delicious jam, you have to listen for the pop. You have to get really still. You pull the jars out of the boiling water, set them on the counter and wait. You wait for the pop. If you hear it, you know that whatever is inside the jar will be preserved. It can sit on your shelf for quite some time, to be enjoyed on a January day when you are cold and in need of some sunshine peaches. But if the jar doesn't pop, the contents won't last long. It's not an extravagant sound, like fireworks. It's subtle, but sure. Like the sound you can make with your lips by smacking them together.

In the same way, we need to get still before God and listen. What are we waiting for? Not a popping sound. We are waiting for the voice of God. This world is noisy and distracting. If we want to persevere until the end, we need to get still on a regular basis. Try and spend five minutes in quiet this morning, not asking God for anything, not singing or even reading, just being still, meditating on who God is, and listening for his voice.

When was the last time you got still before God?

Protect me, God,
because I trust in you.

PSALM 16:1 NCV

Perseverance in the Christian faith is not just about gritting your teeth and pressing onward. That would signify that we are trying to do it in our own strength. To truly persevere we need to fling ourselves onto the only one who can sustain us—Jesus Christ.

Maybe you feel like the weight of your life is too much to bear. Jesus can carry all that weight. He can sustain you through it all. Won't you give it to him tonight?

Jesus, you are my sustainer. I love you so much! You lift me up and carry me in my hardest situations. You are the one who makes me persevere.

He Can Take It

*Cast all your anxiety on him
because he cares for you.*

1 PETER 5:7 NRSV

If you've ever been around a toddler, you'll know that most go through a bag phase. It's a phase where one of their favorite toys is any bag or bucket you can find. They spend their time toddling around on their tiny legs, collecting random artifacts from around the house and placing them in their bag. Temper tantrums ensue if the bag can no longer be carried. What they don't realize is they probably collected more stuff than they themselves weigh! Over the course of their playtime, the load became too heavy.

We operate in a similar fashion. Perhaps we are familiar with this verse about handing our concerns to Christ; maybe we've even prayed and done so recently. Sometimes we are going about our normal routines not even realizing that we are grabbing burdens and holding on to them, weighing ourselves down. Then, we get to a point where we are overwhelmed and we wonder how our bag got so heavy. Casting your cares on Christ is a daily practice. It's an awareness of what you are taking on, and a constant submission to handing it over. When we trust God in this way, we can keep up with what he has called us to.

What do you need to hand over to Jesus this morning?

Casting all your care upon Him,
for He cares for you.

1 PETER 5:7 NKJV

Have you ever worked with someone who micromanages?
Maybe they watch over your shoulder or end up doing the
work they told you to do because it needs to be done a certain
way. It's frustrating, but we can act the exact same way toward
God. We trust him for a while even handing him our cares.
Things seem ok, but then when something happens that isn't
what we want, we snatch our worries back and try to take care
of them ourselves.

If anyone can handle your problem, don't you think it
would be your all-powerful, all-knowing God? Do you not
acknowledge that his ways are higher and better than yours?
Be careful not to be the one trying to micromanage God. He
knows the big picture, the whole story. He's got this. You can
let go.

Jesus, help me to let go of the things I'm clinging to and give
them to you. Help me not to pick them back up again but to
trust in you for my future.

Help Is Here

From the depths of despair, O Lord,
I call for your help.

PSALM 130:1 NLT

There is no such thing as rock bottom when it comes to Christ. You can feel like you are there, for sure, but it will never be far enough that he cannot reach you. When we mess up, we tend to shy away from God in shame. We run the opposite direction and assume that we've done too much—that God can't love us anymore. That couldn't be further from the truth.

Jesus, when he died, descended all the way into hell. That's about as far as you can go! But he didn't stay there. No, he conquered hell, death, and sin, and reclaimed you as his own. He is victorious over all three of these now, and there is no depth too deep that Christ cannot find you and pull you out. Next time you are tempted to turn away from God, turn in to him instead. He's there, waiting, and there is no place he won't go to redeem you.

Do you feel in despair today? Have you turned to God?

Out of the depths I cry to you, O Lord.

PSALM 130:1 NRSV

Maybe you are doing pretty good, so the devotional from this morning didn't touch home with you. But guaranteed, there is someone out there in your world who is feeling pretty despaired right now. When we are doing ok, we need to make sure we are not just living in the comfort of the valley, but that we are on the lookout for those in the trenches.

Maybe you have a friend who is fighting for her marriage, a neighbor who just had surgery, or a mom of littles who is sinking in the mundane.

There are so many different ways people can be in deep despair. Often it's hard to see from the surface level. Pray and ask God who you can reach out to today. Then find a way to encourage that person. A handwritten note, a meal, a visit, the smallest actions can go a long way. While you are connecting, ask the hard questions; how is their relationship with God? Ask if you can pray for God to be near to them.

God, thank you that you are near. You help us when we cry out to you. Please lead me to those around me who need your help.

No Need to Despair

Don't worry, because I am with you.
Don't be afraid, because I am your God.
I will make you strong and will help you;
I will support you with my right hand that saves you.

ISAIAH 41:10 NCV

The subject of these verses is not us, it's God. When he is our source, we cannot fail. It's important to learn that we must shift our focus off ourselves and on to him. We could easily read a devotional from this verse that would make it all about us: how God will make us strong, help us, and lead us away from fear or worry. All of this is true and wonderful. But, the real subject of these verses is God. He is doing all the work, all the heavy lifting.

The real focus is found in the phrase "I am your God." God is our everything. He takes on so many roles in our lives and gives us many great things; we cannot help but be in awe of him. Turn your gaze this morning to God and who he is. Spend time praising him for his glory.

When you read Scripture, do you tend to make yourself the main character or God?

Do not yield to fear, for I am always near.
Never turn your gaze from me, for I am your faithful God.
I will infuse you with my strength
and help you in every situation.
I will hold you firmly with my victorious right hand.

ISAIAH 41:10 TPT

Continuing on with what we discussed this morning, we often tend to take on roles that are not ours to take. Imagine if one actress tried to do every role in a film. It might work for a few monologue scenes, but for a huge production, it would simply fall apart. The same is true in life. We try to take on all the roles that are not our jobs but God's. Then, we wonder why things aren't working out.

It's good to realize our own limits and appreciate that God has none. He can be the one supporting, guiding, crushing fear, and dissolving worry all in the same swoop because he is limitless. We are finite humans, and it would serve us well to take on a more child-like posture of dependency on our Savior instead of attempting to do everything ourselves.

God, I praise you for how powerful and awesome you are. I am in awe of all you do. I confess I try to do a lot of roles too often, making myself out to be you. Will you forgive me? I want to be dependent on you.

Radiant Hope

The Lord alone is our radiant hope
and we trust in him with all our hearts.
His wrap-around presence will strengthen us.

PSALM 33:22 TPT

Late January for some is the coldest time of the year. It's
leaves you hoping to do nothing but sit in front of a roaring
fire, with a steaming mug of coffee in hand, wrapped in the
coziest of blankets. Doesn't that sound lovely? That cozy,
restful picture of warmth is what comes to mind at the last
section of this psalm.

The wrap-around presence speaks of the complete warmth
and peace that comes from Christ. His love toward you
surrounds you in the best possible way. And it's not through
working harder that you get strength; it's being enveloped
in Christ's love and rest that gives you strength for the next
few days. What joy there is to be found in the encompassing
companionship of Christ.

Do you find yourself seeking strength
through resting in Christ or in other ways?

*May your unfailing love be with us, L*ORD*,*
even as we put our hope in you.

PSALM 33:22 NIV

In seasons of winter, we can get a pretty good word picture for hope seeming dim. The view out our windows may be bleak, the air full of a hostile chill, and it gets dark so much earlier. Maybe your outlook on the state of the world would also be described as dim hope. The darkness in the world can feel hostile and overwhelming, leaving our outlooks bleak. It is then that we need to shift our view to Christ, who is our radiant hope.

Radiant light is warm, stunning, and all encompassing. It fills, leaving no area untouched. Our hope is not in any system of this world or for change based on our merit or good doings. Christ is our radiant hope—a light that is unquenchable. He is in control and makes all things new. Praise him for this hope!

Jesus, thank you for your light that brings hope when the world seems dark. Thank you for rest that strengthens and surrounds me. You provide for all my needs; thank you, Lord!

Love Pours In

Hope does not put us to shame,
because God's love has been poured into our hearts
through the Holy Spirit who has been given to us.

ROMANS 5:5 ESV

Most people like to win (there's nothing wrong with that!),
and hope can sometimes feel like a game. It's a gamble really,
to hope, and no one wants to come out on the other side as a
loser after throwing all their eggs into one basket. Shame is
the flavor of the taste of defeat, and nobody is asking to lick
that bowl after it's whipped up.

What do we have though as children of God? We have a hope
that is sweeter than any other. After God's love has been
poured in, after the seal of the Holy Spirit, there is no chance
of you ending up on the losing side. Our hope is a hope that
cannot be defeated, and it makes our lives a sweet aroma—a
delicious taste to those around us. Rejoice that your hope is
everlasting and steadfast.

Have you been afraid to hope
because you might be disappointed?

This hope will not lead to disappointment.
For we know how dearly God loves us,
because he has given us the Holy Spirit
to fill our hearts with his love.

ROMANS 5:5 NLT

Now that you have the confidence of being on the winning side of eternity, what are you going to do with this knowledge? God's love has been poured into you to fill you and for you to pour out. You are a vessel of this hope to those around you. Hope this great and sure should get you excited about sharing with the hopeless world around you.

Don't be fooled by people who seem to have it all together. They said they have no need for Christ, but they really have no idea. If their hope is not in him, then whatever it is in will fail them eventually. As a believer, you have true hope. Share it loudly and proudly with your circle of influence today!

Jesus, thank you for giving us a hope that does not disappoint. Help me to share this exciting, wonderful news with everyone around me, no matter how I view their lives from the outside.

Limitless Love

Your lovingkindness, O LORD, extends to the heavens,
Your faithfulness reaches to the skies.

PSALM 36:5 NASB

Have you ever felt pushed to the end of your rope? You realize you just don't have any more capacity to extend grace or kindness. Often it is a passing feeling, one that simply takes us getting recharged to fix. God is limitless. He never runs out of love for you. He never thinks that you are too much. He is never at a loss for what to do about your sin. He never decides to leave you. He never needs a time of separation from you. His kindness is so extensive, there is nothing you can do to make it end.

Think about the word picture the psalmist paints here. The tenderness and consideration of the Lord toward you extends far beyond what your human eye can see. It stretches to the heavens. The loyalty of God starts at you and is as tall as the clouds. And that's just a human writer trying to express it; his word picture falls short! God's love never does because it is truly limitless.

What does this truth about God's lovingkindness
and faithfulness stir up in you today?

Your unfailing love, O LORD, is as vast as the heavens;
your faithfulness reaches beyond the clouds.

PSALM 36:5 NLT

If you could really get it nestled into your soul that God is
limitlessly tender and compassionate toward you, what would
it change in your life? Sometimes life circumstances speak
otherwise. Maybe we've hoped for something for so long only
to not achieve it, or we lose someone we love, or we enter into
a circumstance that leaves us asking why.

It can be easy to let the tiny seed be planted in your heart that
God is cruel and uncaring toward you. Be on guard against
this. The truth is that he is a tender, loving, considerate God.
What does this truth change about your viewpoint of God?

God, help me to see you as you truly are. Help me to know
your true character and to trust you. Thank you for your
lovingkindness.

Always Good

The Lord is good to those whose hope is in him,
to the one who seeks him.

LAMENTATIONS 3:25 NIV

You know how you can hear about a restaurant and how great a particular dish is from others, but it's not until you taste it for yourself that you really know? You have to experience the meal, chew it up, and let it fill you in order for you to also to be able to factually proclaim to someone how good it is. You run a risk when you go partake of the meal, however. You risk it not being as good as you thought; you do risk being let down.

This analogy pertains to God's goodness as well. There is a risk when we hope. When we choose to partake of hope, we risk being let down by whatever it is we are hoping in or for. Is God really as good as everyone else has said he is? As the Scriptures proclaim he is? The only way to really know is to hope in him—to take a risk and find out. Here's a little secret though, God never disappoints. He is good, but don't settle for taking everyone's word on it! Taste and see, and find out for yourself this morning.

Have you tasted and seen that the Lord is good?
Have you experienced it for yourself?

The LORD is good to those who depend on him,
to those who search for him.

LAMENTATIONS 3:25 NLT

Do you find it curious at all that this verse about the goodness of God being available to us is found in the book of Lamentations? A lament is a passionate expression of sorrow and grief. The book was more than likely written after the destruction of Jerusalem by the Babylonians near 600 BC.

How is a book about the goodness of God written by a people who has seen their land captured, city burned, and people destroyed or hauled off into slavery? Surely their circumstances speak otherwise. No, let it be even more encouraging to you. God's goodness is not circumstantial; it remains forever.

God, I am in awe that your goodness is not based on the circumstances of life around me. You are good! I want to experience your goodness.

New Life Coming

To all who mourn in Israel,
he will give a crown of beauty for ashes,
a joyous blessing instead of mourning,
festive praise instead of despair.
In their righteousness, they will be like great oaks
that the LORD has planted for his own glory.

ISAIAH 61:3 NLT

This is the great exchange. Close your eyes and picture it. Picture yourself surrounded by ashes. Imagine all the dirt and sorrow that such a picture entails. Then imagine Jesus cleansing you, giving you a crown, your surroundings changed to a beautiful flower garden instead of an ash heap. Next, imagine yourself in mourning. Maybe you've already met with grief; many times in our lives on earth we will experience mourning. Then, picture Jesus blessing you, like a father gives a joy-filled toast at a wedding.

Imagine yourself in the depths of despair, when Jesus walks in and turns your response into the most joy-filled praise. Picture yourself among the Sequoias on the California coast: the 200-foot giants that grace the forests of that region. Imagine the awe and the majesty you feel being there. That's your future in Christ. Praise him for the new life that is coming for you today!

What does picturing these things stir inside your soul?

To console those who mourn in Zion,
To give them beauty for ashes,
The oil of joy for mourning,
The garment of praise for the spirit of heaviness;
That they may be called trees of righteousness,
The planting of the LORD, that He may be glorified.

ISAIAH 61:3 NKJV

Let it be known, God is in the business of restoration. It's one of the very things he does best. God is not satisfied with leaving us in our current state. You could also say he is not satisfied with just removing our sins from us, though that is an awesome victory he has won for us! He wants to make all things new. He wants to restore and redeem.

What area of your life needs this promise today? There is no area too difficult, no sin too deep, no life too far gone for God not to restore it. Won't you ask him to move in your life today?

God, will you restore to me what has been stolen? I long to see your restoration power in my life.

Everything I Need

"The LORD is my portion," says my soul,
"therefore I will hope in him."

LAMENTATIONS 3:24 ESV

When having guests over, or perhaps even just feeding your own family, it's wise to take into account portions. Some come to the table hungry every time, and you learn that you need to have more food available for them. Others come and peck around, maybe dissatisfied with what's being served or just not as eager to eat. When someone comes who is hungry, it's pretty inevitable that they will get more food. As they should!

Tying this to our passage today, the Lord is your portion. Are you coming to the table hungry, or distracted and peckish? If you're hungry for the things of the Lord, he is faithful to give you more. Consider your stance today. If you're hungry, tell God. Ask for more. I think it delights him to give to those who are hungry for more. If your posture is different, try searching your heart to see what ways you could be filling your appetite with things that won't sustain your soul.

Are you feeling hungry for the things of the Lord today, or are you full on less fulfilling things?

I say to myself, "The L<small>ORD</small> is my inheritance;
therefore, I will hope in him!"

L<small>AMENTATIONS</small> 3:24 NLT

A life of thankfulness leads to a life of contentment, and a life of contentment is a life of happiness. The very title of this devotional shows that if you picked it up, you want to be someone whose happy place is God! We can find everything we need in Christ. Learning to become happy includes learning thankfulness. Even scientific studies have shown the intense benefits of being thankful. As Christians, we double that because our thankfulness is grounded in truth.

Learning to be thankful for the small, everyday gifts of God, the daily portions he sustains you with, fills you with contentment for your current life. If you are full of contentment, isn't that the definition of a happy life? Try jotting down five things you are thankful for right now (be specific!) and start a year of growing into a content, happy, child of God.

Jesus, thank you for these five things. Thank you for all your gifts. Create in me a renewed hunger daily for the things that are of your kingdom.

Hope Is Here

I rise before dawn and cry for help;
I put my hope in your words.

PSALM 119:147 NRSV

Here you are. Sure, it might not be before dawn, but you've opened this devotional at the end of this month and you're sitting here, expectant. Maybe it's still dark outside, or it's late enough that you could have brunch. No matter the situation, opening this up and soaking in Psalm 119 shows you are a someone with a similar heart to the psalmist: one who puts their hope in the Word of God.

You know that in order to live, you need his Word. It's better than a fresh cup of coffee, more sustaining than a hearty breakfast. It's encouraging just to be here in God's Word at this moment. Everything you need for life and godliness is available to you here. Open it up, soak it in, and ask His Spirit to guide you today.

Do you fight off guilt about what time of day
you spend in God's Word? Pray about that today.

I rise before the dawning of the morning,
And cry for help;
I hope in Your word.

PSALM 119:147 NKJV

In life, no matter what stage or circumstance you find yourself in, hope is present. It's as simple as crying out in prayer. As simple as opening God's Word and meditating on it. The more you ingest of God's Word, the healthier you get. You can never have too much. The more you read it, the more it gets committed to memory.

When you have it in your memory, you can access hope more often no matter where you are. It disposes of the lies you've previously believed. It squelches the fears you've let grow for too long and uproots bitterness that has gotten so deep. It calms anxieties that threaten to overrun you and provides wisdom when you feel fresh out. And it does so much more. Seek health in your spiritual life by actively seeking out God's Word.

Jesus, let your Word take root in my heart. Expel the lies that I've taken in and let truth flourish! And with truth, hope. Let hope arise in me anew.

Love Covers Everything

He has brought me to his banquet hall,
And his banner over me is love.

SONG OF SOLOMON 2:4 NASB

We use banners a lot at parties to declare things. Sometimes they are as simple as a banner that states "Happy Birthday!" Other times, more intimate and personalized messages can be conveyed. Banners are usually large, very visible when you walk into a room, and are able to be read by all. If the banner says, "Happy birthday, Jane!" you know how to interact with Jane—by wishing her a happy birthday!

Beloved, God's banner over you is love. Written over you is his endless love. It is your status and your truth. You are loved by God. This is far better than any earthly love. It knows you to the depths of your soul, inside and out, and still loves. This is what God thinks of you, "That is the one I love." Anyone who comes near you should be able to see it. Because love is God's banner over you, you can let it shine through you today.

How can the truth of God's love change your day?

He escorts me to the banquet hall;
it's obvious how much he loves me.

SONG OF SOLOMON 2:4 NLT

Imagine yourself with a large banner written over you that says, "Loved by God!" You're in a big celebration hall. But you showed up in rags. Sitting under that banner wouldn't you feel a little self-conscious? We often approach our relationship with God this way. He says that we are loved, pure, and cleansed by the blood of his Son, yet we still think we are sitting in rags, completely out of place. Self-conscious in our state, we fail to believe that what the banner says is true.

We must reshape our thoughts to see ourselves how God sees us. We must cling tightly to the truth of Scripture and how God sees us instead of falling back into the lies. If you are a child of God, you are bought with a price; you are redeemed. Can you see yourself how God sees you?

God, it amazes me that you would put a banner of love over me. You love me deeply. Thank you for this truth! Help me to see myself how you see me.

He Sees Me

Those in need shall not always be crushed.
Their hopes shall be fulfilled, for God sees it all!

PSALM 9:18 TPT

We've all been there. It's not a good feeling to be overlooked or go unnoticed or underappreciated. The loneliness that settles in can feel like it has suppressed all hope or joy. Though we cannot expect to never experience this from other humans, we can expect to never experience it from God. God turned away from Jesus on the cross so that he never has to turn away from you.

Even in your lowest of states, your messiest of problems, or just your mundane life, he sees you. He notices your struggle. He sees your pain. He delights in your rejoicing. Having the Holy Spirit living in us means we have God as our constant companion. If you woke up today feeling crushed, take heart. God sees you with eyes full of love and compassion and his ear is leaning toward you, wanting to hear what you have to say. Won't you open up to him?

How do you need to be seen by God today?

The needy will not be ignored forever;
the hopes of the poor will not always be crushed.

PSALM 9:18 NLT

To be seen is to be known. A longing we all have in some way or another is to be known. With our strengths, weaknesses, quirks, flaws, a sign of a deep relationship is that we feel known by those who have seen it all. Do you feel known by God? What is holding you back from being known? Though God is all-knowing, he is also a gentleman. He will not force his way into places you refuse to open up to him. Perhaps it's your whole life in general.

Jesus is standing at the door, knocking, but your belief is what opens the door. Your submission to the Holy Spirit is what lets him see in the closets, the cupboards, the basement of your heart. The encouragement is that he's not here to criticize, he's here to renew. What a beautiful hope that is! Pray to God, submitting yourself to him, and let him know and renew you from the inside out.

Holy Spirit, I submit my life to you. Come in and remodel! Make me more like you. Heal the broken parts of me, restore to me the things that sin has stolen. Thank you for your kindness and for the hope that I can be in relationship with you.

Never-ending Help

Do not worry about anything,
but pray and ask God for everything you need,
always giving thanks.

PHILIPPIANS 4:6 NCV

Humans seem to have a default mode of worrying or fixing. When we need something, we either spend our time worrying about it or trying in our own power to fix it. Here in Philippians, it's telling us the kingdom's way to do things. Pray. It takes spiritual discipline to make prayer our default, but it is something we can grow in over a lifetime.

God is able to meet every need you have. Physical, spiritual, emotional, financial—he's got it. The lack is not on his end, it's on ours for not asking. Imagine you had a child and the child was hungry. You're sitting at the table with the food already made, but the child keeps trying to make his own food out of wood blocks. That's crazy, right? That's how we often act around God. What do you need today? Confidently ask him.

What do you need today? Can you ask God for it.

Don't worry about anything;
instead, pray about everything.
Tell God what you need
and thank him for all he has done.

PHILIPPIANS 4:6 NLT

The third section of this verse is just as important as the first two. The verse tells us not to worry, to pray and ask God for our needs, and lastly, to give thanks. Always. Constantly. Does it feel a little overwhelming when you see the word *always*? Paul is simply stating that we can choose to have a lifestyle that breathes thanks to God or the opposite.

If you want happiness in Jesus, gratitude is the sure-fire way to get there. Gratitude is the opposite of worry; it shows that we confess God as being in control. It is a form of worship that will unlock countless benefits in your life and the lives of those around you. Every time you find yourself latching onto something to worry about, flip it around, find gratitude in it, and pray about it. Watch your life change!

Jesus, thank you for providing for all my needs. Help me grow in the discipline of having gratitude.

Everlasting Life

These things I have written to you who believe in the name of the Son of God, that you may know that you have eternal life, and that you may continue to believe in the name of the Son of God.

1 JOHN 5:13 NKJV

Some of us have been raised believing that faith in Jesus is a one-time deal. You hear the gospel, say the sinner's prayer, and that's it! You've gained your ticket to heaven, and you can go on living however you please. That is just a partial truth. Upon hearing the gospel and feeling the conviction of the Holy Spirit for sin, it is as simple as praying to Jesus to save you. But then, God is not done giving you grace with that one-time transaction. You must continue to believe.

It doesn't mean that you can slip up and lose your salvation if you have a rough day, but God wants you to continue to apply his grace to your life daily. Coming to faith in Jesus should change your life, and then continue to change it until you die. Faith is an ongoing process of changing your worldview to be eternally minded.

Are you continuing to believe and apply grace?

*I've written this letter to you who believe in the name of
the Son of God so that you will be assured and
know without a doubt that you have eternal life.*

1 John 5:13 TPT

John is writing to his audience to reassure them. He wants to
share the truths from his letter because perhaps the church
was having a hard time continuing in their faith after they
first heard the gospel. When you first believe in Jesus, there
is an excitement and a newness about it that inspires you. But
as the years go by, doubts can grow and continuing to live in a
godless world can take its toll. You may start to wonder about
the faith you found.

It's important to be in God's Word, praying to find
encouragement and perseverance. It's also important to have
spiritual mentors in the faith who can help you when times
get tough. Who can remind you to continue to believe just like
John did with the recipients of his letter. If you don't have
anyone, pray about who you could ask to partner with you in
faith tonight.

Jesus, thank you for the assurance of salvation. Help me to
grow in faith and to continue to believe.

Met By Mercy

Let us come boldly to the throne of our gracious God.
There we will receive his mercy, and we will find grace
to help us when we need it most.

HEBREWS 4:16 NLT

When someone has a history of being short with people, angry, frustrated, or mean, we would tend to avoid approaching that person with things. Maybe we would walk on eggshells and make sure we came at what seemed to be the most ideal time. The same tiptoeing around is true of relationships with people who lie a lot or who are manipulative. The bottom line is that there is no trust in the relationship, so, in reality, there is not a good relationship.

Think about your relationship with God. Do you view him as angry, always needing to approach with hesitation? Maybe you think of him as manipulative, and you're unsure if he has your best interest in mind. What lie about the character of God is holding you back from entering into his presence? If something is making you hesitant to come to him, you can be sure it is a lie. Search your heart today, ask God to reveal to you what lies about his character you may be believing.

Prayerfully ask what is holding you back
from the throne room of God today?

Let's approach the throne of grace with confidence, so that we may receive mercy and find grace for help at the time of our need.

HEBREWS 4:16 NASB

Once we identify what might be keeping us away, we can overcome that lie by drenching it in truth. Scripture is full of tools to help you rightly align your thinking. Then, it's like walking into a surprise birthday party. What joy awaits you in the presence of God! Abundant mercy, rivers of grace, buckets of joy, an atmosphere of love. Where else would you want to be? God is eager to meet with you.

Think about having coffee with a friend whom you haven't seen in a long time but you dearly love, or welcoming home a child or loved one who has been gone for a while. These feelings are just minor tastes of how God feels toward you. And what is waiting for you is everything you need for life. Do you need mercy? It's there. Do you need love? It's there. Do you need grace? It's there. Do you need strength? It's there. Everything you could possibly need is available to you from your loving Father. Approach, ask, and receive.

Father, thank you that we can come boldly to your throne. Help me identify any lies that are holding me back from you, that are misconstruing your character. Thank you for providing everything I could ask for or need.

Rewards

Do not throw away your confidence,
which has a great reward.

HEBREWS 10:35 NCV

The parable of the pearl of great price, the story of the treasure hidden in a field, these are stories Jesus told to illustrate the importance of what he was buying for us on the cross. Our very great reward is eternal life, a life free of sin and forever united with Christ. This promise is worth everything; the disciples displayed that they knew this because most of them gave up their very lives for it.

Jesus says we can gain the whole world and lose our soul, or it can be the opposite. This reward is worth losing our very lives over. It is the most prized treasure. If all this is true, what would you give it away for? A few nights of pleasure? A comfortable and secure physical life? Jesus gave it all for us, what will you give for him? The reward is great, but the cost is high. Count the cost and choose to follow Christ. You will never regret it.

Are you living all in or are you holding
onto other perishable rewards?

Don't lose your bold, courageous faith,
for you are destined for a great reward!
HEBREWS 10:35 TPT

Is Jesus enough? This morning you were asked to count the costs. Did you find the cost too much to bear? If you feel like other things are alluring you in life, that maybe Jesus is asking too much of you, take some time to really dwell on the reward. The price might feel high: security, family, status, wealth. It's not guaranteed that you will lose these things, but everyone does lose something. The question is, do you see that Jesus is better?

Jesus is worth it. He is higher than anything you can lose. Maybe you are having a hard time reckoning with that truth. Take some time alone to contemplate the cost that Jesus gave to bring you into his kingdom, the glorious nature of what he promises you when you follow him, and the wonder of Jesus himself—your very great reward. Let God minister the reassurance of who he is to your heart tonight.

Jesus, thank you. You are my great reward. You died on the cross and paid the highest price for me. Comfort me. Where I'm having a hard time letting go, show me your patience, your goodness, and your glory.

Calmed by Comfort

When anxiety was great within me,
your consolation brought me joy.

PSALM 94:19 NIV

On a computer internet browser, you can have many tabs open at the same time. Each tab can hold a different website. Browser brain is when your brain feels like it is doing that exact same thing—tabs and tabs of cares, worries, anxieties all running and taking up space at once. Some people have also called it popcorn brain: the analogy there being worries popping up in your brain constantly. Whichever visual picture you choose, the point is that it can be overwhelming!

In these times we can choose two paths of comfort. The first is to remember past experience. If you've been a believer for any length of time, you have already encountered God's faithfulness in your life. Look back and remember. He has never failed you or abandoned you, and he won't start now. Secondly, remember his promises toward you in his Word. He has promised to heal you, to be near to you, to redeem and restore you. And that's just a few examples! These two forms of comfort can be the consolation that closes all the browsers and stops the popcorn, leaving you with peace of mind.

How has God been faithful to you in past experience?
What is one promise of God you can cling to today?

Whenever my busy thoughts were out of control,
the soothing comfort of your presence
calmed me down and overwhelmed me with delight.

PSALM 94:19 TPT

It is one thing to be at rest, it is another level to have joy. Biblically speaking, joy can be described as the confidence that God is in control of your life so you know everything will be ok. It's also choosing to praise him for this fact and his character. It takes determination to find a heart of praise after you've been attacked by anxiety. But when gratitude and admiration for God take the forefront of your thoughts and what comes from your mouth, then anxiety has no choice but to be silent.

Don't go to sleep tonight recounting all of your anxious thoughts. Instead, list off what you are thankful for, what you find amazing about God. Take control of your thoughts and find the shared joy that the psalmist speaks of.

God, thank you that you are in control. Help me to quiet my thoughts this evening; remove anxiety from me. I thank you for all you have done in my life.

Steady Love

Let your steadfast love become my comfort
according to your promise to your servant.

PSALM 119:76 NRSV

What is the value of a promise in today's culture? In our culture, promises seem to be broken often and without much regard. Vows for marriages, friends who don't follow through, business partners who skim on the facts, politicians saying lofty things we know won't happen. You can probably even think of a personal time you have not kept your word. Who can be trusted?

Thank God that his ways are not our ways. God has made many promises to us, and they are backed by his perfect character. This is what the psalmist banks on for comfort. How does he know what the promises of God are? They are presented to him (and to us!) in Scripture. The psalmist knows God will have resolute love toward him because God said so in Scripture, and loyal love is in his very character. Trust in the promises of God today; he won't let you down!

What promise of God will you cling to today?

*Comfort me with your love,
as you promised me, your servant.*

PSALM 119:76 NCV

It's hard to find a word in our English language that describes steadfast love. What does that mean? Steadfast love is a characteristic of God that is stated over and over again in Scripture. It's important that we understand its depth so we can receive the same type of comfort that the psalmist gained. Steadfast love is the Hebrew word *hesed*. It is a loyal love, a love that is based on a promise that will never be broken.

When it says in Scripture that nothing can separate us from God's love, this is what it means. When it says that there is nowhere you can go to hide from God's love, steadfast love is the reference. He will never give up on you. Nothing can keep you from him; he is pursuing you with a love that cannot be broken. The love of God—his loyal, powerful, unbreakable love—may it support you in your daily life.

Jesus, thank you for your unbreakable, unstoppable, loyal, faithful love. What a promise! Help me to dwell in it this evening.

All I Need

God will never give you the spirit of fear,
but the Holy Spirit who gives you
mighty power, love, and self-control.

2 TIMOTHY 1:7 TPT

Perhaps you don't consider yourself afraid of much of anything. And on the surface, that may be true. Fear, like the enemy, likes to disguise itself. Anxiety is fear of future things. Anger is fear turned inward. Doubt is fear of making the wrong choice. Depression can be fear of the past. Perfectionism is fear of failure.

Fear can be the driving force behind addictions: a root in relationship problems. Do any of these ring a bell? You can already identify where fear comes from: the enemy! Now if you can identify it as fear, you can disarm its power in your life. The Holy Spirit does not want you to live in fear, and he gives you all you need to kick it to the curb and live an empowered life in God.

Do any of these things stand out to you
that you did not think of as fear before?

God has not given us a spirit of fear,
but of power and of love and of a sound mind.

2 TIMOTHY 1:7 NKJV

Naming something as fear helps us see that God does not want us to live like that; these things are not from him. God wants you to live in the freedom of his love by his power. How do we fight the enemy? Read Ephesians, chapter six. Our battle is not with flesh and blood. We fight by prayer, by being in God's Word, by praising.

God is more powerful than any fear you could have, and he is more than able to break the chains of fear that are enslaving your life. Won't you let him bring you freedom today? Identify your fear, hand it over to Christ; let him protect you and praise him!

Jesus, thank you that you do not give us a spirit of fear. Thank you for giving us power over fear. Tonight, I hand these fears over to you. Keep me in perfect peace; keep my mind set on you.

Living Water

"He will be strong, like a tree planted near water
that sends its roots by a stream.
It is not afraid when the days are hot;
its leaves are always green.
It does not worry in a year when no rain comes;
it always produces fruit."

JEREMIAH 17:8 NCV

The imagery here is stunning and memorable. It brings to mind John 4:13-15 and Revelation 21:6 where Jesus refers to himself as the living water. Think of yourself as the tree, and Jesus as the water in these verses. In order to live a vibrant, fruitful life, you need to be rooted in Christ.

You do not draw from outside resources (like the rain in this verse) for strength and sustenance; you draw from the living water. You do not fear outer circumstances that could wilt you (like the heat) because you draw from living water. You choose to find your support in Christ. Those who are rooted in Christ choose to prioritize the things that bring them into deeper relationship with him.

How do you need to move your focus from external fears, worries, and outward things, and prioritize your relationship with Jesus as your source?

"They will be like a tree planted by the water
that sends out its roots by the stream.
It does not fear when heat comes;
its leaves are always green.
It has no worries in a year of drought
and never fails to bear fruit."

JEREMIAH 17:8 NIV

When you read this verse, it cannot be an earthly image that comes to mind; it is a supernatural picture. No earthly tree (even if it is near water) has no need for rain, always produces fruit, is resistant to scorching heat, has a brilliant green color year-round, and is strong enough to last for centuries. It sounds like something out of a storybook! That's the point.

Your life rooted in Christ is supernatural. God has given you everything you need to flourish as long as you keep him as your direct lifeline. Practically doing this looks like being a Christian who knows how to pray, reads the Bible and uses it as the source of absolute truth, and allows the body of Christ to be a sharpening tool. Stop trying to fix symptoms and get to the root. Root yourself in Jesus and let him take care of the rest.

I want to be a tree rooted in you, Jesus. I want to live a life that flourishes and blesses those around me! Show me where in my life I need to lean more into you; dig out my earthly roots and let me draw from you as my only source.

Not Done Yet

Rejoice in hope,
be patient in tribulation,
be constant in prayer.

ROMANS 12:12 ESV

A prayerless life is spiritual suicide. So, why do surveys show that it is one of the most neglected spiritual disciplines amongst believers? We are exhorted several times in Scripture to remain in prayer. Here in Romans it says our prayers should be constant. In the Old Testament, God was only accessible through priests and sacrifices or on less frequent occasions when an angel or God himself appeared or spoke. Since Christ's resurrection, we have been given the gift of the Holy Spirit and have full access to the throne of God.

What is holding us back? Here are three things to consider: 1) you feel discouraged; you've prayed in the past and haven't seen anything happen, 2) prayer is not a priority; even good things can become idols if we are not seeking first his kingdom through prayer, or 3) you have a lack of belief; do you really believe God is near and wants to have a relationship with you through prayer?

Consider these three reasons. Which one resonates most with you as a reason for prayerlessness in your life?

Rejoice in our confident hope.
Be patient in trouble
and keep on praying.

ROMANS 12:12 NLT

These words by Paul seem simple enough when etched at the top of this page, yet putting them into practice is something else entirely! It's important to see that our rejoicing, patience, and consistent prayer all point to the fact that God is not done yet. He is still working and moving in our world, redeeming and creating.

Our hope is in the fact that this world is not our home; our home is eternal. Our patience can be maintained because we our earthly life is the journey not the destination. Our constant prayer keeps us connected and in relationship with our God who is at work. He will keep us in tune with what his plan is and what he is doing when we spend time seeking him.

God, you aren't done yet, and I praise you for that! Help me to be patient in hard times. To find joy in my eternal hope. Thank you for listening to me. Connect me with what you are doing in the world around me right now.

Led by Love

"I will bring the blind by a way they did not know;
I will lead them in paths they have not known.
I will make darkness light before them,
and crooked places straight.
These things will I do for them and not forsake them."

ISAIAH 42:16 NKJV

We are a people who have been treading down the paths of sin, destruction, and death for our whole lives leading up to Christ. It was the only way we knew, as horrible, painful, and dark as it was. But Jesus came onto the scene, and he had a new way: a straight new path full of light. What a change! This new life in Christ is uncharted territory for us. We don't know how to live in the light which is why we need to rely on him to teach us.

How wonderful that God says he will bring us on this journey, light the way, and be with us for every step! As one who used to dwell in darkness, the unfamiliar law of love will seem intimidating at times. You might be waiting for the other shoe to drop, for God to reject or abandon you. But this new way is a path led by love itself. He will not leave you and he will gently teach you to live according to his will.

What promise of God has become your light?

I will lead the blind by ways they have not known,
along unfamiliar paths I will guide them;
I will turn the darkness into light before them
and make the rough places smooth.
These are the things I will do;
I will not forsake them.

ISAIAH 42:16 NIV

Are new things scary to you? Fear of the unknown can hold you back from the glorious things God has planned for your life. In Isaiah, the talk about going on new paths implies leaving old ways behind. Our walk with God is meant to be just that—a walk, not a standstill!

Don't let fear weigh down your feet and rob you of what God has planned. He is trustworthy, and he will provide for you. He will light your path and be with you every step of the way. With a guarantee like that, how could you not get moving?

Jesus, thank you for bringing me out of darkness into glorious light. Thank you that your ways are light and truth. Teach me your new ways; help me not to be afraid but to follow you as you lead me in love.

Perfect Father

You did not receive a spirit of slavery to fall back into fear, but you have received a spirit of adoption. When we cry, "Abba! Father!" it is that very Spirit bearing witness with our spirit that we are children of God.

ROMANS 8:15-16 NRSV

Abba. It's the Aramaic word used for Father, more specifically, *my* father. Used by children and adults alike, the word drips with intimacy. Using it shows familiarity, vulnerability, and a deep sense of trust. Do these words seem foreign to you when referring to God? Some of us grew up with very rigid fathers: relationships void of the words above. Others grew up in a stoic and rigid religion, without the warm familiarity of a loving, kind father.

Both of these upbringings can significantly impact your relationship with God. But you have an advantage: the Holy Spirit living inside of you. By simply saying in prayer, "My Father!" the Holy Spirit unlocks that level of intimacy with God to show you desire a childlike relationship with him. Try praying this way, and rest in the care you receive from your loving, kind Father.

What kind of fatherly care do you need today?
Ask for it in prayer.

The Spirit you received does not make you slaves, so that you live in fear again; rather, the Spirit you received brought about your adoption to sonship. And by him we cry, "Abba, Father." The Spirit himself testifies with our spirit that we are God's children.

ROMANS 8:15-16 NIV

There are many benefits of being a child of God. First of all, you have complete security. If you were just a servant, you would be expendable. But as God's child, there is nothing that can separate you from his love. You can live without fear of losing relationships. You also have authority. Servants don't have authority in a household, but those who belong to the family do.

As a child of God, you have been given authority over sin. This entire world was created by your Father and it belongs to him. You can walk confidently in life because of this. You also have his family name: a status given to you in the spiritual world that implies to whom you belong. All of this and more are the joys of being a child of the king. Rejoice in these truths and walk in confidence!

Father, thank you for bringing me into your family. The riches of what that entails are endless. I cry out to you for my needs. Thank you for hearing me and for drawing me in close.

Daybreak Is Coming

Do it again! Those Yahweh has set free will return to Zion
and come celebrating with songs of joy!
They will be crowned with never-ending joy!
Gladness and joy will overwhelm them;
despair and depression will disappear!

ISAIAH 51:11 TPT

In the winter, it gets dark early and stays dark longer. This leaves many of us longing for daylight. This physical longing reminds us that we will live our whole earthly lives longing for Jesus to come back. More sure than the breaking of the next day, than the promise of spring after a long winter, is the surety of Christ's return. And when he does, what promises are in store for you? One of them is joy! Never-ending joy.

All the darkness that weighs you down in this world will be lifted. All the despair—poverty, racism, abuse, corruption—will be gone. Depression and anxiety will be no more. We are given joy as our constant lifestyle. Does it seem too good to be true when you look at the day's headlines in comparison? In Christ, it's not. It's a fact. Be encouraged today by our coming hope.

Do you have the joy of the Lord today?

Those the LORD has rescued will return.
They will enter Zion with singing;
everlasting joy will crown their heads.
Gladness and joy will overtake them,
and sorrow and sighing will flee away.

ISAIAH 51:11 NIV

In regard to attire, a crown is not necessary. It's not practical or functional. It is above and beyond adornment, usually reserved for royalty. You are a child of the king; the crown is yours in Christ. When we are Christians, we can take off the old rags and adorn ourselves in the new attire that reflects kingdom living—the cloaks of joy.

When you are adorned with the joy of the Lord, it outshines despair to the point of making it disappear completely. The darkness cannot be upheld against such strength. This joy is not the superficial happiness we so often try to grab through material possessions. It cannot be bought. It is a gift from the King. Won't you put on your crown today?

Father, thank you that I am your child. In you I am a new creation. Crown with me with joy today. May my life reflect and glorify you.

Peace in Provision

Let the peace of Christ rule in your hearts,
to which indeed you were called in the one body.
And be thankful.

COLOSSIANS 3:15 NRSV

Peace, happiness, and thankfulness are all interwoven. Do you remember that your Father in heaven has said he will provide everything you need? Why do we so often choose to walk the path of fear and worry when it comes to provision? We must train ourselves along the path of thankfulness if we want peace to rule.

Thankfulness is expressing that you trust God and noticing all the ways he is meeting your needs in this moment. Worries about finances and the future can loom large, but they are just a threatening cloud of smoke that you can blow away with the winds of thankfulness. What do you already have? What has God gifted to you? What can you be thankful for? All of these questions can help you choose gratitude and find peace that sustains your spirit in uncertain times.

Write out answers to the three questions above
and give thanks to God this morning.

Let the peace that comes from Christ rule in your hearts.
For as members of one body you are called to live in peace.
And always be thankful.

COLOSSIANS 3:15 NLT

Wanting more is not always a bad thing. We all hope to describe our lives as abundant and full. God has given you everything you need and will continue to provide for you. Unlock the perspective of abundance with the key of thankfulness. When thankfulness spills from your lips, it lights up in technicolor what is already present in your life—the abundance of God.

We can choose to see everything in grey, living our lives complaining and worrying. Or, we can live in full-blown color posturing our hearts in thankfulness. If you've ever wondered where the abundant life that you've been promised is, maybe it's right in front of your eyes. Pick up the lens of thankfulness and let God show you the beauty in your life.

Jesus, thank you for providing for me! Thank you that you go before me and behind me. You have given me all that I need. Help me to see my life through the lens of gratitude tonight.

Needy

Blessed is he whose help is the God of Jacob,
whose hope is in the Lord his God.

PSALM 146:5 ESV

Women are sometimes famous for trying to do everything by themselves. They fight to juggle career, health, relationships, kids, social life, etc. which is strongly encouraged by the culture, and the perception is that those who do, achieve it all by themselves. But this is not how Christians are called to live. God wants us to bring our needs to him. He's perfectly ok with us being needy because that is when we depend on him. Contrary to what we think, that's how we thrive!

A Christian who is needy for God is a Christian who then finds help in the God of the universe who always comes through for us. You can never fail! Though the world tells you that being needy is a bad thing, you live by the upside-down kingdom rules of Christ that say needy is necessary. It takes humility, but the same God of Jacob who led the Israelites miraculously out of Egypt is the God who is ready and wanting to help you too.

What need should you bring to God today?

Those who hope in the Lord will be happy and pleased!
Our help comes from the God of Jacob!

PSALM 146:5 TPT

Just like we tend to try and do it all ourselves, we can also swing the other way and look for help from everyone but God. You can identify this by answering a few questions. When you are stressed, where do you turn? Do you binge eat, scroll endlessly, exercise an extra hour, have another glass of wine? The basic question is what do we turn to in order to alleviate pain? This doesn't just mean physical pain: pain can be relational or emotional from basic life stresses.

To live a blessed life, we must turn to God first and foremost. He is the only source that our strength can come from. He is the only help that can actually work through our problems and redeem them. All other solutions might bring temporary relief, but long term they are fruitless. Try to identify some things you turn to instead of Christ. Repent, and turn to Jesus next time instead.

Jesus, you are who my hope is in! You are my strength, and I praise you that you always come through for me. Help me to not turn to other things or my own strength but to let you be my help.

Eagerly Waiting

If we hope for what we do not see,
we eagerly wait for it with perseverance.

ROMANS 8:25 NKJV

Hope and waiting go hand in hand. If you hope for something, once your hope is fulfilled, you no longer need to hope; you get to move onto the joy over it coming to fruition. Our entire Christian life is to be spent in hope, which means it will also be spent waiting. Our hope is in our coming King and the future glory. We are sojourners on this earth.

There is something happening even when it seems like nothing is happening. God is moving in the waiting. He is sharpening your character and producing good fruit like humility, trust, and perseverance. In the gospels, the disciples hope Jesus will stay longer, and Jesus repeatedly told them that he would be going away. He walked out the plan the Father had for him, and then it was time to go. God has a plan for humanity and is not willing that any should perish. Jesus will come back when that plan is complete. In the meantime, we grow in character and loving anticipation of his return.

Are you hoping and waiting for Christ's return?

Because our hope is set on what is yet to be seen,
we patiently keep on waiting for its fulfillment.

ROMANS 8:25 TPT

Christ is coming back. That's a fact we can pull from Scripture. Does this affect your day-to-day life? It's very easy to get caught up in our plans and agendas so we stop living for our future life. Living for the age to come means that we live with an awareness that Jesus is coming back. Our priorities and time will play out differently because we are focused on eternity. We realize that our time on earth is like a breath, so we focus on what truly matters.

This impacts our priorities because our goals do not have to do with worldly success, financial security, or fleeting pleasures, but rather preaching the gospel, using the gifts God has given us, and leaving a legacy of hope in Jesus. Do you have an eternal mindset? What would you change if you knew Jesus was coming back next week?

Jesus, thank you that you have promised to return, and you keep your promises. Thank you for developing my character in this time of waiting. Help me to have an eternal perspective. Come soon, Lord Jesus!

More than Imagined

Return to your stronghold, O prisoners of hope;
today I declare that I will restore to you double.

ZECHARIAH 9:12 NRSV

Have you suffered great loss? The Scripture today brings
to memory the story of Job. Job lost his children, his
possessions, his health, and his livelihood. But there is a
Scripture near the end of the book of Job (42:10), that says
the Lord restored to Job double.

Here, we have a prophecy by Zechariah to the people of
Israel who had been in captivity in Babylon for 70 years. The
Lord is also promising back double. God loves to restore.
Redemption is one of the largest themes in the Bible. Making
things new is what God is all about. What's beautiful is that he
doesn't just make it right, he goes above and beyond. Past our
wildest dream and expectations, God restores double. Isn't he
amazing? If you have suffered a loss today or look around your
life wondering how it could possibly change for the positive,
take heart. God is in the business of restoration and he does
more than we could ever imagine. Trust in him!

What do you need to ask God to restore today?

Come back to the place of safety,
all you prisoners who still have hope!
I promise this very day
that I will repay two blessings for each of your troubles.

ZECHARIAH 9:12 NLT

Our enemy is out to do nothing but steal, kill, and destroy. Living in sin will always lead to these things in your life. But living for God will always end in more. Have you heard the saying, God gives and takes away? This phrase is in a few popular hymns and Christian songs today. The lyrics derive from the beginning of Job (Chapter 1). Though the Lord does take away, when he gives, he gives back more. Living according to our own pride and sin, however, will always leave us destroyed and empty handed.

When the Lord takes, he doesn't mean to leave you empty handed. He will restore your heart. He is a good Father, and he wants to heap blessings on your plate. What's even more amazing is the destruction we cause in our own lives because of our sin. God can restore that too, more than you could ever think. Isn't he good? Blessed be the name of the Lord!

God, I praise you that you are the God of restoration. You are a good Father!

Sustained by Peace

You will keep in perfect peace
those whose minds are steadfast,
because they trust in you.

ISAIAH 26:3 NIV

Has God given you a dream that seems insane to everyone around you? Consider the countless people in the Bible who received their vision alone. Mary, the mother of Jesus, is one who comes to mind. God could have sent the angel to speak to her and Joseph when they were together, but instead he spoke to her alone. And then, she had to carry the vision alone. No one else saw that angel until Joseph too got a visit.

It can be difficult to have a dream that God has placed on your heart that no one else understands. It takes perseverance to hold onto a promise God has given you in the secret. Keep your mind focused on him, not on those around you and what they say. Let God take care of changing other people's hearts and moving the pieces into place. You remain in peace, eyes locked with the one who gave you the promise.

Has God spoken something clearly to you
that you haven't told anyone else because of fear?

You, LORD, give true peace
to those who depend on you,
because they trust you.

ISAIAH 26:3 NCV

This world is full of great opportunities. So many, in fact, that we have even coined a term for people who don't like to miss out. FOMO stands for *fear of missing out*. It's a real thing not just for the younger generation trying to decide which social event to attend, but for many of us. When we have FOMO, we keep saying yes to opportunities that may seem great and line up with what God wants us to do, but they cause strain on the things God has already asked us to do. Here's the test: are you saying yes out of fear, or are you saying yes in peace?

God's peace can be a perfect indicator as to which category the yes falls into. Will your current calling to your family suffer? Will you lay aside that creative endeavor God told you to pursue because this one makes money? Will you take on another volunteer role at your church even though God clearly told you to be in a season of rest? Put your yes to the test. What is its underlying motive, fear or faith? God's peace can help you answer that question tonight.

Jesus, help me to not live in FOMO, but in your peace. Help me to be focused on what you have called me to.

How Long

How long must I worry and feel sad in my heart all day?
How long will my enemy win over me?

PSALM 13:2 NCV

The Christian life is a known victorious one. yet these are hard questions that the psalmist is uttering. Maybe you've spoken them in prayer out loud too. Or maybe you've been too afraid. Is there a place for our doubts in Christianity? Can a believer even ask questions like this? There is plenty of room for your "how longs"!

God does not want us to stuff our doubts, fears, and questions down deep, putting on a good outward front. When he died for us on the cross, he died for our whole selves. He wants to redeem you. That means even the doubting you. Even when you feel angry about a situation. That means even the girl who is crying out "Lord, help my unbelief!" Unbelief, doubt, questions, fears—God is big enough to handle them all; he is not intimidated by them. Stop hiding them today; instead, let God shine his light on them and bring healing.

Do you tend to live in a style of Christianity
that does not welcome doubts or questions?

You, Lord, give true peace
to those who depend on you,
because they trust you.

PSALM 13:2 TPT

We stated above that the Christian life is a victorious one. It seems contradictory to the second question the psalmist asks though, doesn't it? Christianity is a long game. That means that though Christ has won the victory over sin and death on the cross, there is still a lot coming. There is still the sanctification of all the saints. There is still an enemy who seeks to distract and distance us from God.

While the enemy might win the short battle, are you in this for the long haul? Are you submitting to God so you can be presented as full and complete in the end? Don't let small setbacks knock you off course. Continue to persevere in Christ tonight.

God, thank you that you are big enough with my doubts, fears, and questions. Will you meet me tonight? Will you quiet my fear with your love?

Constant and True

*Jesus Christ is the same yesterday
and today and forever.*

HEBREWS 13:8 NASB

Change is inevitable—from the often-overlooked changes like night turning to day or winter melting to spring, to more personal, unexpected changes. Change can bring good things: excitement, joy, or a feeling of accomplishment. But it can also bring heartache and loss. When change leads to worry, and worry grows into fear or helplessness, we need to ground ourselves in a solid fact. Jesus never changes.

The character of the God you see presented in the Bible is the same character you talk to today. All that mercy, compassion, strength, grace, and love? It didn't run out. God is the same, and his promises toward you are just as strong. They are your sure footing when the quakes of change rock your world.

What change are you facing today,
and what promise do you need to stand firm on?

Jesus, the Anointed One, is always the same—
yesterday, today, and forever.
HEBREWS 13:8 TPT

As Christians, we are asked to change. The process of sanctification is the change God brings to our daily lives and character as we grow to become more like Jesus. In this way, change is a good thing! Wouldn't it be frustrating though, if what we were asked to change to was forever changing as well? If you are running a race, and someone keeps moving the finish line, you are going to get frustrated and probably quit!

When we are running our Christian race, it doesn't change. The Holiness of God is the same, and he is moving all of us as believers toward glorification and being reunited with him. The process will look different in each of our lives, but the end goal is the same.

God, I praise you for being unchanging, for being steady. Help me when change comes to trust in you. Help me to submit to you along this road of sanctification.

Wait on Him

> As I thought of you I moaned,
> "God, where are you?"
> I'm overwhelmed with despair
> as I wait for your help to arrive.
>
> PSALM 77:3 TPT

What is the opposite of waiting? Action. When it doesn't feel like God is showing up, we can take matters into our own hands and spring to action. When God seems inactive, our desires for control rise up and we begin to work on the situation in our own ways. This is not a good idea! It's like when you watch those shows where instead of waiting for backup the person bursts into the situation all alone, usually resulting in a worse situation.

Don't make matters worse by springing to action on your own. Waiting for God might feel like you are doing nothing, but it is the best thing you can do when you need help. God can accomplish more in a quick minute than you could in years of labor. Don't make the mistake of taking matters into your own hands. Wait on the Lord, wait for his help, and let him be in control.

Do you tend to do things on your own or wait for God?

I think of God, and I moan,
overwhelmed with longing for his help.

PSALM 77:3 NLT

Waiting doesn't mean not communicating. While you are waiting, if you're getting antsy, up your prayer life. Get into the nitty gritty of it with God. He is big enough to handle all your emotions, doubts, and fears, so let him know what they are.

Don't the experts say that one of the most important aspects of a good relationship is communication? Communicate with God. Tell him the depths of your soul. And then trust that he cares, and he is moving on your behalf. He's working even when you can't see it.

God, I need your help. I don't like to wait. I don't the feeling of not being in control. Help me continue communicating with you, letting you know how I feel and listening for your perspective to help me in the waiting.

My Constant Companion

Surely your goodness and love will be with me all my life,
and I will live in the house of the LORD forever.

PSALM 23:6 NCV

When you first wake up in the morning, it can be hard to keep the swirling storm of to-dos at bay while you try to read your Bible and pray. Just like a professional runner, you can get really good at starting your day shooting out the gate, running hard from the stress that threatens to overtake. Do you know what is chasing you, pursuing you faster and harder than any to-do list or stress could? God's blessings.

God's blessings of love and goodness are hunting you down, and they aren't going to stop. Ever. When God feels silent, his love is on the move. When there is too much to do, his goodness is coming for you. When you feel alone, his presence is near. God wants to bless you not just on good days. His love is running after you every single day.

How can you let God's blessings catch up with you today?

Surely goodness and mercy shall follow me
All the days of my life;
And I will dwell in the house of the LORD
Forever.

PSALM 23:6 NKJV

We can often be in pursuit of something—a new career, raise, spouse, child—a better life in some fashion. Most people believe in working to make your life, or the lives of those who come after you, better. What would it change if you knew the truth: that God's good life is chasing after you? That you don't need to pursue it as much as you need to pursue him.

Pursue Christ alone, and the good life will overtake you. Run hard after Jesus, and his goodness and mercy will catch you by surprise. Make Jesus the one true goal in your life, and you'll wake up one day seeing that you are living a blessed, full life. What a beautiful truth! How do you need to change your priorities to run after Jesus tonight?

God, the imagery of your goodness and mercy overtaking me is beautiful. Help me to stop the rat race and pursue the only good thing—you!

Father of Compassion

Praise be to the God and Father of our Lord Jesus Christ,
the Father of compassion and the God of all comfort.

2 CORINTHIANS 1:3 NIV

It's good to have compassion on others. We all know this. We've read about it in our Bibles, and we try to be compassionate toward those in our influence. Even the most compassionate people, however, usually give out compassion on their terms. It's just instinct. For instance, say someone in your family is sick. Of course you feel the compassion to take care of them. However, they don't listen when you tell them to do certain things to get better. Then, your compassion fades, and you don't want to help them anymore. This is compassion on your own terms.

If you see a poor person on the side of the road asking for money, do you only give them food you have in your car? Do you give them nothing? Do you only give if they have kids with them? Your compassion is once again limited by your terms. We serve a God of limitless, boundless compassion. He doesn't withhold his love because it is who he is. It's a part of his character. His compassion knows no boundaries. How amazing!

How have you experienced God's boundless compassion?

All praises belong to the God and Father of our Lord Jesus Christ.
For he is the Father of tender mercy and the God of endless comfort.

2 CORINTHIANS 1:3 TPT

In the same way that we desire God's compassion to never run out, we are asked to model that same kind of compassion to others. Did you recognize any conviction in your heart over how you have limited your compassion? If so, prayerfully work through changing to become more like our limitless Father.

If he abundantly gives us compassion, then we need to model him and also give it without boundaries. Then the love of Christ will be boldly displayed.

God of compassion, thank you that you are compassionate toward me. I love you! Help me to model your compassion to those around me.

Practicing Patient Trust

Be still in the presence of the LORD,
and wait patiently for him to act.
Don't worry about evil people who prosper
or fret about their wicked schemes.

PSALM 37:7 NLT

Where your vision goes, your feet follow. It's a tip given to new drivers, it's a saying amongst runners, and it's true in our Christian lives as well. We must be careful not to fall into the trap of comparison. If our eyes are focused on others, we will miss what God has for us. It's very easy to get caught up in looking at that person on social media, or that particular person at church, or our best friend, or even a movie star, and comparing their lives to our own. Every single time, we find ourselves coming up short.

When our eyes are focused on Christ, other people can run at their own pace, and it doesn't change ours. They can win awards, and it doesn't deter us from claiming our own. We are so focused on God that we don't notice those who aren't running and seem to be having a rather nice time eating wings on the sidelines ("the evil who prosper"). The point is, keep your eyes on Jesus. He is the only one your eyes need to be on.

What is distracting you from keeping
your eyes on Christ today?

Be still before the LORD, and wait patiently for him;
do not fret over those who prosper in their way,
over those who carry out evil devices.

PSALM 37:7 NRSV

The world moves at a fast pace; it can be easy to feel like you are being left behind. You look around you and wonder why it seems like evil people are getting ahead in life, and you are stuck. We already spoke this morning of the need to not compare, but we also need to let go of the need for speed.

God's ways are not our ways. He can accomplish more in two minutes than you could hustle to achieve your entire life. It's important that you stay focused on the good things that truly matter: being in the presence of the Lord, waiting for his leading, and listening for his voice. We don't need to move at the same pace as everyone else, we need only be still and wait on God.

God, thank you for leading me. Help me to keep my eyes focused on you. I don't want to look to the right or the left.

Freedom Is Mine

The Lord is the Spirit,
and where the Spirit of the Lord is,
there is freedom.

2 CORINTHIANS 3:17 NIV

This passage in Corinthians is explaining to its readers the difference between the old covenant, also known as the law, and the new covenant we have in Christ. Its joyful proclamation of freedom is in regard to the throne of God. Moses had to have a veil over his face to even think of approaching God.

Because of Christ's work on the cross, we have full access to God. No veil, no rituals, the sacrifice has already been made and we have complete freedom. Because of this, God has full access to our lives, transforming us to shine brilliantly in this world. Don't let fear or shame hold you back anymore; boldly live in freedom and approach the throne of God with rejoicing this morning.

Do you feel like there are a lot of hoops
to jump through to get to God?

The Lord is the Spirit,
and where the Spirit of the Lord is,
there is freedom.

2 CORINTHIANS 3:17 ESV

Let's further explore this concept of freedom before God. Before you became a believer, sin is what separated you from God. Upon believing in Christ's work on the cross and resurrection, you have been justified. This doesn't mean that now you will never sin. It means your status before God is in his Son; he sees you without sin in Christ.

When you feel ashamed to approach God, or insignificant, or like you don't have the right things to say, this is where you need to stand on God's Word. Remember who he is and how he feels about you. The love of the Father is the freedom of a wide-open field; he's just waiting for you. He wants to hear what you have to say. He cares about the smallest detail, and that openness in relationship is the true flood of freedom you need.

Jesus, thank you that your work on the cross tore the veil and gave me freedom before the throne of God. Thank you that your love pours out in this way to me.

Not Finished Yet

There is hope for a tree, if it is cut down,
that it will sprout again,
and that its tender shoots will not cease.

JOB 14:7 NKJV

Are you familiar with the Biblical concept of pruning?
A gardener knows that many plants produce fruit best if
someone is cutting away the dead or overgrown branches.
This can leave the plant looking barren and stripped for a
time, but in the long run, it produces the best (and most)
fruit. Jesus speaks specifically on this process in John 14.

Each of our pruning processes will be unique because we are
all unique human beings. But God is the same; he is always
good, and he always wants to produce the best fruit in us.
Pruning isn't an easy process; it is often painful. It comes in
the form of suffering and things you don't like. But God is
so faithful, and he is not finished with you. Trust the master
gardener that all the pruning is for his glory, and for your good.

What area of your life feels like it is being pruned right now?

If a tree is cut down,
there is hope that it will grow again
and will send out new branches.

JOB 14:7 NCV

God cutting things out of our life is rarely enjoyable. Often, he is exposing our sin by pruning our hearts which is a painful process. God isn't out to get you or hurt you; on the contrary. He wants to restore to you the thing sin has stolen from you. He doesn't want to cut you down; he wants to build you back up. He wants the tender shoot to sprout again. Sin leads to death, and he wants to get rid of anything in our lives that leads us to death. He wants to make us holy, as he is holy.

God knows what he is doing. When all you know is the sin you have lived with for so long, won't you trust God who has known only goodness, holiness, and beauty, to restore you and make you like him? You can trust him. He is good.

God, thank you for pruning me even when it is hard and it hurts. Please make me holy like you.

Never Alone

Behold, the eye of the LORD is on those who fear him,
on those who hope in his steadfast love.

PSALM 33:18 ESV

As the most connected generation to ever live, it is ironic that loneliness is one of the top things that plagues us. As Christians, we have the answer to the problem. In the Bible, the *eyes of the Lord* often refers to God's intimate knowledge of our lives. Take heart as you battle loneliness with the fact that you are never alone; God knows you. He is near you.

There are so many things that try to connect us more in life, that try to heal the wound of loneliness, but none will ever be sufficient. Only a relationship with the God who sees us will heal that wound in our hearts. Once we come to know this, we then need to share the truth with the world around us. You are known and loved by the Creator of the universe. He cares so deeply for you.

How can you share truth with others
who desperately need it today?

The LORD watches over those who fear him,
those who rely on his unfailing love.

PSALM 33:18 NLT

Loneliness can drive us one of two ways. It can either take us closer to God or further from him. When our hearts are in despair, we tend to want to isolate even further. We must not give in, allowing the lie of God's indifference to win. Let loneliness drive you deeper toward God. Ask him to turn his face toward you, to show you himself, to speak to you.

When you feel abandoned by others, tell God about it. He is near; the Bible promises that. If the Bible says it's true, then everything else is a lie. Stand on the promise of Scripture today and draw near to God.

God, when I'm feeling lonely, will you turn your face toward me? I run into your open arms. Thank you that your words are solid and true. The Bible tells me that you are always near, and that your eyes are on me. I choose to believe it.

Still Hope

You are my hope; O LORD God,
You are my confidence from my youth.

PSALM 71:5 NASB

What does it really mean that God is our hope? Hope is considered one of the primary virtues of Christianity, along with faith and love. Without hope, however, the other two cease. God is the origin of our hope. It comes from him. Jesus is the reason for our hope. He died on the cross and saved us from our sins. The Holy Spirit is the source of our hope. The Holy Spirit is where we draw our hope from.

If something is not found in and powered by God, it can do us no good. This may seem like circular reasoning, but it is so beautiful because with God being the origin, reason, and source of our hope, none of that is worked out in our own strength! The pressure is off us and on God. He will never fail; he is faithful to deliver. What a God we serve!

Do concepts like hope, love, and faith seem abstract to you? How can you make hope practical today?

You are my only hope, Lord!
I've hung on to you, trusting in you all my life.

PSALM 71:5 TPT

Most people have hopes: I hope my team wins the big game, I hope they have my favorite food, I hope my grandpa comes to visit this year. Their hope is more of a wish or a strong desire. The wording should be different because our Christian hope does not act like this; hope is not like a wish. Our hope is a strong confidence that is unbreakable and unshakeable.

We have the hope that we will live in eternity with God, and this is as solid of a fact as they come. Let's separate out the terms in our head so we know that we can wish for things on earth that may or may not happen, but our hope is so solid in Christ that it's not a wish; it is a reality.

God, thank you that you are hope. You are my confident expectation. I believe and trust in the strength of your faithfulness. Will you fill me with confidence today in the hope of my future? Show me who to share this hope with.

Wonderful News

"The blind see again, the crippled walk, lepers are cured, the deaf hear, the dead are raised back to life, and the poor and broken now hear of the hope of salvation!"

MATTHEW 11:5 TPT

When was the last time you turned on the news to see a headline like that? Probably never! Our current headlines are filled with just the opposite. That is because they proclaim the works of man, and the Scriptures show the headlines of God's kingdom. That's good news! Today, instead of opening your phone and scrolling through the endless headlines of the world which are guaranteed to bring you into a state of anxiety, depression, or despair, open up God's Word and take in the headlines of the kingdom first.

This good news is not just the reality for believers when Jesus walked the earth. The good news of the kingdom is for us today. Now, the hope lives in you and is carried by you to the world. Be a newsie today with the amazing opportunity to shout the message of Jesus that smothers the darkness of this world.

Who do you need to encourage
with the message of Jesus today?

"The blind see and the lame walk; the lepers are cleansed and the deaf hear; the dead are raised up and the poor have the gospel preached to them."

MATTHEW 11:5 NKJV

Maybe today's verse leaves you confused because the joyous news Jesus proclaims doesn't seem to be reality. The fact is our verse today is in response to a question that John the Baptist asked his followers to ask Jesus. Why couldn't John just ask Jesus himself? Because he was in prison at the time. John didn't seem to care about his current circumstance, asking Jesus when he would be released or if perhaps he could loan him some money or visit him. John was focused on the mission God had given him to prepare the way for the coming Messiah.

Maybe you are in the same boat, wondering how the gospel can be good news when yourself or others might not be experiencing good news. God is not unaware; he is in control. Stay on mission with what God has called you to do.

Jesus, thank you that you are the Messiah so many have longed for. Let your kingdom come on earth as it is in heaven! Make me a bright light to share your good news with anyone I come in contact with no matter my circumstances. My hope is in you.

Lifted Up

Be humble under God's powerful hand
so he will lift you up when the right time comes.

1 PETER 5:6 NCV

He's going to squash you like a bug. That may be the first picture
that comes to mind when you think of putting yourself under
someone's hand. If that's your thought, it is far from the truth.
The mighty hand of God is not a force with which to squash
people, but a hand of protection. Consider yourself lowly
under God's protection and shelter, and he will exalt you.

God has not positioned himself against you, waiting for you
to mess up. God wants you to live your life in submission to
his will. He is a good Father with a good plan, and though it
might seem against the grain in our world to live in humility,
the glory that is to come is worth it. You have everything to
gain and nothing to lose—a loving Father in your court and his
protection all the way. Humble yourself before him today.

Do you view God as waiting for you to mess up?

Humble yourselves therefore under the mighty hand of God,
so that he may exalt you in due time.

1 PETER 5:6 NRSV

The right time is when Jesus returns and you are brought into glory with him. Then he will lift you up. To be looking forward to this and hoping for this is called having an eternal outlook. To live like this takes perseverance. Do you find yourself longing for glory now? You are tired of the mundane, of maybe not being noticed in your service, or of watching seemingly evil people live well while Christians suffer.

God is not unaware. He asks you to submit yourself to his plan now and reap the benefits in eternity. He knows what glories await you if you can trust in him. Do you trust him?

God, thank you that you are so powerful. Thank you that your posture toward me is one of love not anger. Humble me in your sight. Give me an eternal perspective of what is to come and help me to continue to wait for that time.

Dwelling Place

God's dwelling place is now among the people, and he will dwell with them. "He will wipe every tear from their eyes. There will be no more death or mourning or crying or pain, for the old order of things has passed away."

REVELATION 21:3-4 NIV

Kind of like an onion, Scripture has layers of revelation. Something that is prophesied about or seen in the Old Testament can come up again and be fulfilled in the New Testament also holding meaning for future events. These things can reveal overarching themes about God's character. One of these themes is that of dwelling.

In the Old Testament, we first see God's desire to dwell with his people by the intimate nature of the walks in the garden with Adam. Then, there was the tent and the temple with the people of Israel where the glory of the Lord dwelled and the priests met with God. It wasn't a perfect system, but it was what they had, and it allowed the people to dwell with God while he maintained his holiness. Sin separated man from God, but he still desires to dwell with us.

Do you recognize how sin separates us from God's holiness?

I heard a loud shout from the throne, saying, "Look, God's home is now among his people! He will live with them, and they will be his people. God himself will be with them. He will wipe every tear from their eyes, and there will be no more death or sorrow or crying or pain. All these things are gone forever."

REVELATION 21:3-4 NLT

The New Testament tells us that Jesus came to dwell among his people. The term used is to literally pitch his tent. He left heaven and took on our human form to pitch his tent with us. He became flesh; how much closer can you get? This shows the great lengths that God was willing to go to restore that intimate dwelling he had with mankind before sin.

When Jesus died, the temple was no longer needed. The veil was torn, and God came to dwell with mankind. The Holy Spirit now dwells inside of you. This will be how we dwell for the current age. And then in eternity, God will dwell with his people fully. We will be in full communion, in our glorified bodies, one with God as Jesus is one with him. The theme of dwelling with God meets completion. Isn't God's faithfulness to fulfill his plans and his desire for us amazing?

God, thank you for revealing your plan to dwell with us. Thank you for never giving up on it and pursuing us.

In His Sight

Humble yourselves in the sight of the Lord,
and He will lift you up.

JAMES 4:10 NKJV

Kneeling in a garden, you can see an entire other world.
Seeds are doing the slow work of becoming plants, towns of
bugs and pollinators are busy at work, and mountains of soil
create new landscapes. It's such a miniscule part of our big
world, and you, with your knees in the dirt, are tending to
it. This is what comes to mind when considering the word
humility.

To be humble is to get low. When you get down into a garden
and you see all the details, it's mind blowing to think that God
is aware of even this small plot of dirt and its happenings.
How much more is he aware of his children on whatever size
plot of dirt they occupy. Sometimes the louder life seems,
the lower we need to get. It's good to feel small amongst it all,
knowing how big God is. If you are feeling unseen, remind
yourself of the truth: he does see you, and he cares.

How do you like to acknowledge your humble estate?
Try doing that today.

*Be willing to be made low before the Lord
and he will exalt you!*

JAMES 4:10 TPT

Doesn't it seem like everyone is seeking a platform? We know that a platform is used to make you higher, to amplify your voice. Maybe that seems nice: to have massive amounts of people noticing you and listening to you. Perhaps you view yourself as small and insignificant. To truly succeed in life, a platform is not what you need. You need to get low.

Practicing the art of humility before God is the only true way to succeed. He has given you a voice and placed you where you are for a reason. You have to believe that he will use you. Hustling to find that spot is not the way. Prayerfully come before God acknowledging that you want to do things his way and get low before you ever will truly rise up.

Jesus, teach me humility today. Thank you for seeing me. Help me seek first your kingdom and not my own platform. Use me where you have placed me today.

Freed by Love

He delivered us from such a deadly peril, and he will deliver us.
On him we have set our hope that he will deliver us again.

2 CORINTHIANS 1:10 ESV

God is not in the business of one-and-done. His promises don't expire; he doesn't grow weary of deliverance. It delights him to save you. He wants to help, and he is waiting for you to call on him. You don't need to live in fear of calling out to him again, wondering if he is tired of you or hoping he will show up. He is faithful. He never tires; he never grows weary. He will deliver you every single time you call on his name.

There is so much power in the name of Jesus to bring freedom from fear and darkness. When you feel oppressed, all you need to do is whisper his name and he will deliver you. He has overcome death and sin, and he sits victorious. Call out to him to deliver you every time you need it.

Do you feel shy asking God for deliverance again?
Step out in courage; he is near!

He did rescue us from mortal danger,
and he will rescue us again.
We have placed our confidence in him,
and he will continue to rescue us.

2 CORINTHIANS 1:10 NLT

If you crack open your Bible and continue a few verses in 2 Corinthians 1, Paul says something interesting. He thanks the church in Corinth for their prayers which were essential to deliverance. The church in Corinth was a part of the deliverance of Paul and his companions—an essential part!

God moves through the prayers of his people. Just as he wants us to cry out to him, we are also to cry out for each other. Working together and lifting up each other's burdens as the body of Christ pleases him. He loves to answer his children, and there are so many in your circle of influence who need your prayer. You could be asking for deliverance for them right now. Join in their cry, and watch God move mountains!

God, thank you for delivering me. You never abandon me. You deliver me over and over again. Show me others who need your power to move in their lives, so I can lift them up in prayer too.

I Am Covered

You bless the righteous, O Lord;
you cover them with favor as with a shield.

PSALM 5:12 NRSV

If life is a battlefield, God's got you covered. You may think of favor as material prosperity or unending health, but that is not what the psalmist is talking about. A right view of this verse understands that life is a battle. We are in a very real war against the enemy of our souls, but we are protected by the favor of God.

When the enemy tries to steal from you, God's got you covered. When he tries to lie to you, you have access to all of God's truth. When he is out to destroy you, God will defend you. Favor is not money and possessions; it is protection. We serve a very real and powerful God who shields you from the enemy's attacks. Know that you are covered and protected as you go into your day.

How have you seen God's protection over you in the past?

Lord, how wonderfully you bless the righteous.
Your favor wraps around each one and covers them
under your canopy of kindness and joy.

PSALM 5:12 TPT

The Romans carried shields that were rectangular in shape:
large enough to cover a human body. When in formation,
the Roman army would set one shield vertical and then an
adjoining shield over the top, creating almost a box to protect
the army. There was no way any arrows of their enemy could get
through when they created this formation with their shields.

The enemy has arrows flying straight toward you; what
protection will you use? No shield of your own strength will
do. God has you covered. He has the whole body of Christ
armed with shields, so when you join in prayer or fellowship
with other believers, you join the shields to create an
impenetrable force. With God on your side and his people
next to you, you are safe from the enemy's arrows. Stop using
your own shield and abide in the protection of the Almighty
God today.

God, will cover me with your favor? Will you help me to find a
body of believers to join in the fight side by side? Thank you for
protecting me. I praise you for being strong and able to save.

Made New

Put off your old self, which belongs to your former manner of life and is corrupt through deceitful desires, and to be renewed in the spirit of your minds, and to put on the new self, created after the likeness of God in true righteousness and holiness.

EPHESIANS 4:22–24 ESV

Paul makes a distinction between life before Christ and life after. He is not asking us to simply replace sinful lifestyle with a moral lifestyle or obviously bad deeds for seemingly good deeds. He is telling us that when we become Christians, we are handed a new life in Christ. A difference should be present.

In verse 17, Paul talks about life before Christ and how people have futile minds. This means they are living with no regard for God or his ways. They are self-focused and living with no thought to eternal consequence. He mentions that this is a thought pattern.

Do you live as if God exists?

You were taught, with regard to your former way of life, to put off your old self, which is being corrupted by its deceitful desires; to be made new in the attitude of your minds; and to put on the new self, created to be like God in true righteousness and holiness.

EPHESIANS 4:22-24 NIV

Paul tells us to renew our minds. Victorious and happy living in Christ starts with the spirit transforming our minds. We don't just clean up the outside to look pious by doing moral things like attending church. We need an inside-out kind of transformation, and the Holy Spirit is the one with the power to do it.

Renew your mind by taking God's Scripture and chewing on it. This means memorizing it, reading it, and most importantly, applying it practically. This is how you pursue righteousness and holiness: by submission to the Holy Spirit. Renew your mind through the power of God's Word. When your mind is transformed, your outward actions will follow. Put on your new self today, taking into account God and his life-changing Word.

God, thank you for empowering me to put off my old self and put on righteousness. I am made in your image. Renew my mind by the power of your Word.

Peace Is My Portion

*My people will live free from worry
in secure, quiet homes of peace.*

ISAIAH 32:18 TPT

Isaiah is a book of prophecy. Often in the Bible there are layers of prophecy, where the prophet says what will happen to Israel in tandem with future things that will happen through Jesus. This verse shows one of those layers. Though the prophecy is primarily about the people of Judah, it applies to when Christ returns as well.

We have a peace-filled existence to look forward to. Right now, we are at peace with God. The circumstances of our lives may not always seem peaceful, but we have a future hope of peace. Rejoice now that your salvation and peace with God are secure.

Can you confidently say you are at peace with God?

My people will live in safety, quietly at home.
They will be at rest.

ISAIAH 32:18 NLT

One of the prominent themes of the Bible is how God desires
to be with his people. In the book of John, for instance, we are
told over and over to abide in him. When we abide in Christ,
he is our peace. Those who dwell in Christ find their peace
in Christ.

Though your circumstances may be tempestuous, you
can know that Christ is in control. Though people and
relationships in your life may be trying to stir the pot, you can
seek wisdom from Jesus for how to respond. If anxiety attacks
or worry looms, you know to settle into Christ, your safety.
Are you residing in a dwelling of peace?

Jesus, be my home; be my peace. Thank you for being a
safe dwelling place. Thank you that I am at peace with God
through your work on the cross.

Immeasurable Goodness

To him who is able to do immeasurably more than all we ask or imagine, according to his power that is at work within us, to him be glory for ever and ever! Amen.

EPHESIANS 3:20–21 NIV

What does *immeasurably more* look like in your life? The abundant goodness spoken of here is not a one-size-fits-all kind of order. We are God's children, and he delights in each one of us. He made you unique, and his goodness and mercy toward you will be unique as well. We tend to look to the right and to the left, trying to measure what we have next to what others have to see if what God has given us is good enough. In doing so, we miss the unmeasurable.

As your good Father, God knows exactly what you need. He knows what will bring you immeasurable joy, he knows what hopes to fulfill, he knows you personally better than you could know yourself. He is the God of the impossible, of the immeasurably more—the God of the beyond abundance.

What would immeasurably more look like in your life? Ask for it today.

All glory to God, who is able, through his mighty power at work within us, to accomplish infinitely more than we might ask or think. Glory to him in the church and in Christ Jesus through all generations forever and ever! Amen.

EPHESIANS 3:20-21 NLT

Now that you have spent the day pondering what *immeasurably more* to ask for, how have you seen it already in your life? The last half of the verse gives us another key aspect: to God be the glory. Do you recognize the more he has already done? We must learn to be people who can recognize the more, so we shout his praise the loudest.

Give all credit where credit is due—to God alone! By doing this, you can spur others on to ask for more and to find the wild riches of grace that are available to any who call on his name. What an honor!

God, I want more of what you have for my life. I want to give you all the glory. Thank you for what you have already done.

Safe Space

The Lord also will be a refuge for the oppressed,
a refuge in times of trouble.

PSALM 9:9 NKJV

Safety is a basic human need. It is ingrained in us; our
bodies have ways of keeping us safe without us even asking!
Sometimes we consciously pursue safety at all costs. If we live
in the right neighborhood, have the right job, go to the right
school, then we will be secure. Though it is not bad to take
care of ourselves, we need to make sure we are not making
safety a god in our lives. Sometimes our pursuits swing too far
on the pendulum, forsaking faith to pursue what we think will
keep us secure.

The only true refuge and security is a life found in Christ.
When you are in submission to the Holy Spirit, you are safe.
God has the bird's eye view on your life; he knows it all.
Choosing to wrap yourself in worldly securities to preserve
your soul is more dangerous than choosing to let God be your
security.

Is God your refuge, or do you find safety in other ways?

The LORD is a shelter for the oppressed,
a refuge in times of trouble.

PSALM 9:9 NLT

Many struggle for control of their lives. The feeling of being vulnerable is not welcome, so we strive for perfection to compensate. Perfectionism can be a warning sign that we are finding our security in our ability to control and not in Christ. It's not healthy and it fails to unlock the life that God wants for us.

We must learn that God has so much grace. He is not expecting us to be perfect, and he doesn't ask us to have it all together. He wants us to give him control, to let him be our safety and protection, allowing us to live a wide-open, joy-filled life in Christ.

God, I give you control. Be my safe place. Remove the idol of perfectionism and false security from my heart today.

Wisdom's Path

Know that wisdom is thus for your soul;
If you find it, then there will be a future,
and your hope will not be cut off.

PROVERBS 24:14 NASB

Earlier in this chapter of Proverbs, it tells us to eat honey.
Why? Because it's good for us, and it's delicious! Honey was
plentiful in the land at the time, and it was considered to be
strengthening, nourishing, and refreshing. But the point the
writer made was a comparison between honey and wisdom.
Wisdom is good for us; it strengthens, nourishes, and
refreshes our souls. Doesn't that sound like a happy life?

Where do we get this wisdom? The Word of God! Starting
out your day right here in the book of Proverbs is the perfect
spot. It is considered the book of wisdom. As you read God's
Word daily, you will notice the change in your soul and in your
appetite. The wisdom you receive will be so delicious you will
start to crave the good, wise things of the Lord more than the
quick meals of the world.

Do you have an appetite for God's wisdom?

Then you will perceive what is true wisdom,
your future will be bright,
and this hope living within will never disappoint you.

PROVERBS 24:14 TPT

The other interesting thing about honey in the Bible is that it was used for medicine, for healing. It was known that the one who consumed honey would live a longer life with less disease. Doesn't that comparison work perfectly for the Word of God too?

God heals us through his Word. His words are like medicine to our souls; we need it to survive. The life we live when it is directed by God's wisdom is a real, abundant life: full to the brim! The benefits of being immersed in wisdom are endless. Let God's Word heal you and be a balm to your soul this evening.

God, thank you that you give us the Bible, full of wisdom and truth. Let your Word guide me, heal me, and refresh my soul.

Not the End

Let not your heart envy sinners;
but continue in the fear of the LORD all day.
Surely there is a future,
and your hope will not be cut off.

PROVERBS 23:17-18 ESV

Don't be fooled by what you see paraded in front of you. The movies, social media, magazines, can all declare to us what wonderful lives are being lived by those who don't fear the Lord. The deception is quite convincing, and it can leave children of God envious; they feel they are missing out.

Don't buy into it. Their happiness is fleeting and their moment temporary; our God promises us a hope and future that is everlasting. He has an inheritance in store for us that is beyond anything anyone can possibly imagine. The goodness that is to be found in the presence of God is soul quenching and bone satisfying: the deepest reality of happiness. Trust in God, and keep your eyes focused on an eternal perspective.

Do you need to repent of envy this morning?
How can you refocus on an eternal perspective today?

Don't envy sinners,
but always respect the LORD.
Then you will have hope for the future,
and your wishes will come true.

PROVERBS 23:17-18 NCV

What does it mean to continue in the fear of the Lord? Let's paint two pictures to help us gain a deeper understanding. Imagine a storm. It's a fierce storm with wind howling, rain, thunder, and lightning—the works. It's powerful. There are two different scenarios. One, you are on a hike in the middle of a field when you see the storm coming. Suddenly you realize you are vulnerable, and it very well could be the end of you. In the second scenario, you are in your home. You see the storm coming, but you know your shelter is sufficient to not only protect you, but you can actually enjoy its grandeur.

The storm in our story is like God: a mass of his holiness, power, justice, and wrath all in his glorious self. If you're not sheltered in him, it should be a terrifying kind of exposed fear. But when you are found in him, safe and secure, you can enjoy the storm rather than fear it.

God, you are majestic. You are great. You are worthy of awe and fear. Thank you that I am sheltered in you and can enjoy the richness of who you are. Show me your glory; give me an eternal perspective that doesn't fade.

Held Together

He's the hope that holds me and the Stronghold to shelter me,
the only God for me, and my great confidence.

PSALM 91:2 TPT

There are many things you can place your hope in that will
let you down. We tend to do it all the time. We place our hope
in political candidates, our career, our spouses, our health,
our financial status, our achievements and accolades, our
presence on social media, our friendships; the general list
could go on and on and each of us could probably write our
own specific list as well.

Not all of these are bad things to hope in or for. God is not
upset at you if you hope to get that promotion, be married,
or desire to have friendships. The difference lies in lining
up your life with hope that cannot be shaken. It's the fact that
your first and most prominent hope is in Jesus—a hope that
can never disappoint. It is from this hope that all other hopes
can flow.

Is your first and most prominent hope in Christ today?

He is my refuge and my fortress,
my God, in whom I trust.

PSALM 91:2 NIV

We've all had those moments or seasons where we feel shattered. Everything seems to be falling apart and there are just too many pieces to try and put back together. Often these shattering moments can be an exposure for the question of what we truly rely on to hold our lives together. If everything has fallen apart, were we relying on our own strength to hold it together?

The psalmist talks of a life that is held together by Christ. That life may have been in pieces, but his confidence was in the fact that God had it under control. Could you say that about your life? If your life falls apart, will you still say God has it under control? Do you believe he sustains you and is holding you together? You will find your happy place in God when you are sustained by him and you trust him to hold your life in his hands.

Jesus, thank you that you have my life. You are not unaware. You hold me together. I submit my life to your power and declare you as my hope, my source, my everything.

Living Hope

Blessed be the God and Father of our Lord Jesus Christ, who according to His great mercy has caused us to be born again to a living hope through the resurrection of Jesus Christ from the dead.

1 PETER 1:3 NASB

Have you heard of the term *false hope*? False hope refers to having confidence in something that is not true. It is based on ignorance. How can you be sure that your faith in Christ is not just false hope? Has the fear ever arisen that you are dedicating your life to a lost cause? If so, quiet those fears with fact. The hope you have in Christ is based on the character of God and the work of Jesus. He died for your sins, overcame death, and rose from the dead. He is alive today; he is your living hope.

It is not just wishful thinking or false hope because it is backed by the entire character of God. Your salvation is sealed by God himself. Throw your life into living for Jesus; it's not a lost cause but a sure and living hope—one you can bet your life on.

How does the concept of Jesus being your living hope encourage you today?

All praise to God, the Father of our Lord Jesus Christ. It is by his great mercy that we have been born again, because God raised Jesus Christ from the dead. Now we live with great expectation.

1 PETER 1:3 NLT

We are in the season of Easter, the best celebration for the Christian faith. The beginning of spring and the celebration of Christ's resurrection fit so well together. Nature shows us the emergence of life from death. It will display the removal of the barren trees, the weary ground, the dreary and tedious nature of winter, and burst forth with the joy, color, and warmth found in spring.

Here, Peter sums up the whole of Easter quite well in his sentence in chapter one. Resurrection is the theme: life from death—hope! But this living hope is not something to be celebrated only in March and April; it should come to us daily. Jesus being alive then and now means he is alive through our day-to-day lives. Each day we have access to this living hope: a continuous spring that never fails. No matter how the season falls, we can have spring anew every morning because Jesus is our living hope.

Jesus, thank you for dying on the cross; I praise you and rejoice that you are alive! What an encouraging truth.

Unwavering Love

The LORD takes pleasure in those who fear him,
in those who hope in his steadfast love.

PSALM 147:11 NRSV

God has created some pretty amazing, wonderful things, wouldn't you agree? Take just the slightest interest in nature and you will find this planet perfectly positioned from the sun, seeds that burst forth to become glorious flowers, snow-capped peaks, intricate bugs that change colors, majestic animals that strut across the horizon. There are so many details, so much beauty and wonder.

Even with this world bursting with the wonder, majesty, and creativity of God, he takes the most pleasure in you—sitting on your couch in your pajamas, nursing a cup of coffee with a messy bun. Jesus even stepped down from all the grandeur of heaven (opulence you cannot begin to imagine) to pursue you. To save you. To meet with you on that couch. God takes pleasure in you. Welcome him this morning and bask in his love.

How does the truth of God delighting in you
change your outlook today?

The LORD delights in those who fear him,
who put their hope in his unfailing love.

PSALM 147:11 NIV

How do you know if you fear God? Have you ever wondered
this before? The verse today says that the Lord takes pleasure
in those who fear him; do you qualify? Obedience is the
outward evidence of fearing the Lord. When God makes
something clear to you in Scripture or through prayer, you
obey. You forsake your own way and will and follow what
he says. It won't always make logical sense, but this type of
submission shows God that you trust his plan, knowing that
his way is far better than ours.

Whatever you face today, choose to listen to what God says
and obey. There is much in store for those who fear the Lord.

God, thank you that you look on me with delight! Out of all your
creation, you stepped down and became human to bring me
back to yourself. Help me to obey you as you speak to me today.

All Access Pass

This hope we have as an anchor of the soul, both sure and steadfast, and which enters the Presence behind the veil.

HEBREWS 6:19 NKJV

If you have ever been out boating, you know the importance of an anchor. Whether you're fishing or hanging out with friends, when you find a good spot for your boat, it's impossible to keep it there without an anchor. Without the anchor, you just drift, aimless and without control.

Jesus is an anchor for your soul. Without him, you will find yourself drifting in a sea of doubt. He secures you in the certainty of his truth. If you're drifting in a sea of unforgiveness, he can lead you to the quiet waters of forgiveness and grace. If you are floating through waters of bitterness and hurt, let Jesus secure your heart in a bay of healing waters and remove those weeds from your hull. You need Jesus. Won't you cry out to him for security this morning?

What area of your life do you need to be held sturdy and firm in truth?

We have this hope as an anchor for the soul, firm and secure.
It enters the inner sanctuary behind the curtain.

HEBREWS 6:19 NIV

Have you ever scored backstage passes to a concert? Many of them promise all-access, meaning you can look around at parts of the stage that fans normally aren't allowed and meet people you otherwise would not see. It is a special privilege given to only those with a pass.

Jesus has scored for us the all-access pass to the Father. Prior to Jesus' death, there was a veil that hung in the temple that separated the Jews from the presence of God. Only on certain occasions was the priest allowed to go behind the veil. When Jesus died on the cross, the veil was torn from top to bottom. We now have complete access to the Father. Isn't that amazing? There is so much to explore—the riches of his grace are immeasurable. Won't you come into his presence and discover him today?

Jesus, thank you that you tore the veil, giving me full access to the Father. Thank you for being the anchor of my soul. Keep me from drifting through waters of uncertainty. I want to stay close to you.

All Things with Love

Love bears all things,
believes all things,
hopes all things,
endures all things.

1 CORINTHIANS 13:7 ESV

1 Corinthians 13 is often read at weddings, and why wouldn't it be? The entire passage is about love. This doesn't mean though, that those who aren't in a romantic relationship can skim by the chapter. It's not just for weddings. The world presents an idea of love every day; it's a love driven by attraction and emotional response. It's a feeling that can come and go, with people falling in and out of love. It's conditional and has terms that will at some point fail.

Paul had to lay out for the Corinth church (and for us!) a real definition of love: love for a spouse, fellow Christian, mom, child, neighbor, or stranger. What does Godly love look like? Love puts up with anything, looks for the best, trusts God, and keeps going to the end.

What kind of love are you aiming for?

Love never gives up,
never loses faith,
is always hopeful,
and endures through every circumstance.

1 CORINTHIANS 13:7 NLT

Remember the tall order of love we considered this morning? How can we possibly fulfill that? There is good news and bad news. The bad news is you can't fulfill it. The good news is that the power of the Holy Spirit can help you fulfill it. Without him we cannot truly love anyone, at least not in Godly fashion. And what is love, if not the pure, God-honoring kind?

On your own, you are powerless to love in this way. But the Holy Spirit can empower you to do all things with love. He can help you to persevere in loving that sibling that has hurt you. He can empower you to keep looking for the best in your spouse. He can show you how to offer patience and mercy to that person you disagree with often. He is the only way you can truly love your fellow human. Won't you ask him to strengthen you in love tonight?

Holy Spirit, empower me to love even the most difficult people. Fill me with your love.

My Strength

On the day I called you, you answered me.
You made me strong and brave.

PSALM 138:3 NCV

Do you consider yourself a courageous person? What exactly is it that makes a person courageous? How do you know that when opportunity arises, you will act with bravery and not shrink back in fear? God offers to make us into brave people. Being brave will look different for each of us. We are all unique people and God empowers us all in different ways.

Being a person of courage does not mean that you never hear from fear again. On the contrary, brave people often hear fear, but they choose to trust God and walk in courage instead of listening to the lies. God has given us an entire book full of truth to throw in the face of fear. When fear tries to tell you one thing, recall Scripture and tell it another.

How can you use Scripture to combat fear this morning?

When I cried out, You answered me,
And made me bold with strength in my soul.

PSALM 138:3 NKJV

God making us strong and brave doesn't happen in one
step. If it were like that, we would probably give in to the
temptation to think that we don't need God anymore! This
strength and courage becomes who we are when we draw it
straight from the source. It is only in God that we can face
whatever life throws our way. It is only from God that we can
quiet the nagging voice of fear and walk in courage.

Resist the temptation to think you may have arrived and
don't need Christ anymore. Bravery and strength are
characteristics of someone who is completely dependent on
God, not independently going about life alone.

God, will you give me strength and make me brave? Help me
to know your Word and use it to quiet the voice of fear.

Help Me

It is good that one should hope and wait quietly
for the salvation of the LORD.

LAMENTATIONS 3:26 NKJV

The name of the book alone should give us a hint as to how hard times are: lamentations. Lamentations are a passionate expression of grief and sorrow. And rightly so, as the devastation of Jerusalem was fresh and its people had been taken into exile. Most of us have a hard time imagining or relating to such a plight. Here in chapter three is the theological highpoint of the book. Hope and wait are coupled together and repeated over and over.

The hope is in God's love and goodness. It is a confident expectation that this is not the end, that God has not abandoned his people. And he didn't. They expressed their deep grief and sorrow, and then they expressed the hope that remained. There is always hope, no matter how deep your sorrow, how obvious your plight, or how wide your grief. Hope is found in the Lord.

Where do you find hope in hard times?

It is good to wait quietly
for the LORD to save.

LAMENTATIONS 3:26 NCV

Waiting on God in silence is expressed many times in the Bible. It's this idea that God is so good, so great, so holy, it brings us to silence in awe of him. When was the last time you fell silent in the presence and magnificence of God? He has not changed. He is just as awe inspiring now as he was in the Old Testament. We must be the people who notice it. Who sit in silence before God and meditate on his goodness.

Silence does not come easy to us. We live in a very noisy world. Televisions, phones, social media, and radios all make for great distractions. We can live at a fast pace with the noise level on high and never realize that silence is what we need to bring healing. Being in awe of God is what will make hope arise in us. We can even fill our lives with spiritual noise and miss out on the grandeur of God. Embrace silence and awe this evening.

Jesus, I come to you and sit in silence. I am in awe of you. Let hope arise in me.

A Higher Perspective

I pray that the eyes of your heart may be enlightened, so that you will know what is the hope of His calling, what are the riches of the glory of His inheritance in the saints.

EPHESIANS 1:18 NASB

Your eyes are pretty useless when you are sitting in a pitch-black room, aren't they? You can have 20/20 vision, but without light you aren't going to see a thing. This is kind of what Paul is talking about in Ephesians. The eyes of our heart need the light of the Holy Spirit in order for us to have proper perspective. It's interesting that Paul writes this section of Scripture to believers: wouldn't you think that they are already full of light? Believers need daily light. We need God to show us more and more of his light.

When you are saved, you are secure. Imagine being in a dark room your whole life and then someone shines a light straight into your eyes; it would overwhelm you! God is merciful. He walks us along a journey of getting our sight back. He heals and enlightens our souls in a process, showing us more and more of his glory as we mature.

Are you practicing daily walking in the light?

I pray that the light of God will illuminate the eyes of your imagination, flooding you with light, until you experience the full revelation of the hope of his calling—that is, the wealth of God's glorious inheritances that he finds in us, his holy ones!

EPHESIANS 1:18 TPT

We hear so much about our callings. We are told to seek them out, find them, and pursue them with all our hearts. But what about God's calling? This calling that Paul speaks of is one of deep intimacy with the Father. He has chosen us, called us, before the foundations of the world, to walk in intimacy with him.

We receive so many things when we become believers: forgiveness, redemption, a seat at God's table, a heavenly home, authority, a position in his family, the list goes on. What does God receive? He receives you. You are his inheritance. Let that sink in. He knew the cost when he saw you, and he said you are worth it. Meditate on the deep love of God tonight.

God, your love for me amazes me. Open the eyes of my heart; fill them with light.

Revelation's Light

Your faith and love rise within you as you access all the treasures of your inheritance stored up in the heavenly realm. For the revelation of the true gospel is as real today as the day you first heard of our glorious hope, now that you have believed in the truth of the gospel.

COLOSSIANS 1:5 TPT

The promises of God are a guarantee; they aren't going anywhere. Your inheritance is a sure thing. Believing in Jesus is not a bait-and-switch tactic or a gimmick with a catch. When you choose to follow him, Jesus says that his promises toward you are a done deal. And who is more faithful than God? His reputation of keeping his promises and being faithful proceed him. This is a truth that cannot be shaken or stolen and doesn't get destroyed or old and broken with time.

The glorious truth of trusting in Jesus is just as wonderful on day 1,000 as it is on day one. Isn't that good news? Let this news bring you hope. Let your faith and love rise up in your soul as you consider the sure foundation that you stand on. Let your mouth open in praise to the Creator and in exclamation of this truth to those around you.

Has the gospel message become old or stale to you?
Ask God to refresh your faith today.

You have this faith and love because of your hope, and what you hope for is kept safe for you in heaven. You learned about this hope when you heard the message about the truth, the Good News.

COLOSSIANS 1:5 NCV

Have you ever wondered what the promised inheritance is? We have established that it is imperishable and cannot be taken from us. We've also seen that it is a gift from God since we are adopted into his family. But what exactly is it?

There are many aspects to it. We will inherit the fullness of our salvation, meaning we will be united with God forever.

We will inherit the kingdom of heaven and the whole restored earth. New Jerusalem is full of the glory of God. It's a city that we will reside in. The Bible also tells us there is honor, glory, and a place at the table of God. Our inheritance is more than we can ever imagine. What a God we serve who gives us such good gifts!

God, thank you that you adopted me into your family and call me your child. Thank you for giving me an eternal inheritance.

Forever Faithful

The Lord always keeps his promises;
he is gracious in all he does.

PSALM 145:13 NLT

We are presented with so many characteristics of God in Scripture. One that is spoken of often is the compassion of God. How is it that we have a mental picture of God that depicts him as distant and even cruel? It is the great lie of the enemy to downplay the compassion of God toward us. If he can convince us that God is aloof and does not care—a man with a grey beard in the sky letting evil run its course—then he wins. If he can skew our understanding of who God is, then he will succeed.

If you soak yourself in the truth of Scripture, you will be told again and again of the gracious, loving, merciful, compassionate God you serve. This is the truth. You must rebuild your idea of who God is. It comes from reading the truth of his Scripture and by living with him. When you see the faithfulness of God active in your daily life, it builds credibility. Try writing down the ways you see God being compassionate. This can help when the enemy attacks with lies again. You serve a loving God; open your eyes to see this truth today.

How have you seen God's compassion toward you recently?

You are faithful to fulfill every promise you've made.
You manifest yourself as kindness in all you do.

PSALM 145:13 TPT

Let us follow in the footsteps of our God and Savior and be people who also keep our promises. As we grow in Christ, we seek to become more like him. One of the ways we can do this is by striving to be people of our word. When we keep our word to someone even when it hurts, that's integrity.

Our world is full of leaders who lack integrity, who back out on promises and lack faithfulness to the things they say. Let us be slow to speak, but quick to keep our word when we do. By doing so, we display the greatness of the God we serve. We stand out amongst those who lie and cheat to get to the top and we show how kingdom living is the best way.

God, help me to live with integrity. Thank you that you are full of integrity and always keep your promises.

My Refuge

The LORD is good, a refuge in times of trouble.
He cares for those who trust in him.

NAHUM 1:7 NIV

We sing about it often: God is our refuge. What does that really mean to us? When you hear the word *refuge*, what do you picture? A building with tall walls and locked gates? A cave that protects from the storm? Many people have a different picture, but the point of a refuge is typically the same: a refuge is a safe place. When the Bible says that God is our refuge, it means that he is our safe place.

We can understand protection when it comes to our physical bodies easily, but what about protection that is spiritual? Often, we can build up walls of defense and ways to protect ourselves that rely on ourselves instead of letting God protect us. We might label it as being self-sufficient, introverted, extroverted, or any number of harmless traits, but deep down that's just a fancy label for attempting to protect our own souls. What we need is to say goodbye to these faulty refuges and invite God to be our only one.

Ask God to show you where you are protecting yourself
instead of letting him be your refuge.

The LORD is good,
a strong refuge when trouble comes.
He is close to those who trust in him.

NAHUM 1:7 NLT

Self-defense mechanisms are ways of keeping control. We
may have been hurt in some manner in the past, so we take
control of protecting ourselves. We show God that we trust
him by asking him to identify the areas in our lives that we
are trying so desperately to care for ourselves, and we let him
take over.

God truly cares for you, and he wants no harm to come to
you. He is strong and mighty—the ultimate safe place for us.
Once you learn to let God be your refuge, you can be more
vulnerable and authentic in your relationships with others.
You no longer try to guard yourself, which brings incredible
freedom and opportunity for the gospel to spread.

God, will you be my refuge? Show me the areas I'm protecting
myself in and teach me how to let go.

Hidden in Love

You are my hiding place;
You shall preserve me from trouble;
You shall surround me with songs of deliverance.

PSALM 32:7 NKJV

Did you enjoy playing hide and seek as a kid? It seems like the most prized role in this game is to be the one who finds the very best hiding place: quietly behind a door, deep under a pile of blankets, squished into an obscure crevice. As adults, we don't usually play the game, but we sure come across times we wish we could hide.

In the beginning verses of Psalm 32, it seems David's sin makes him want to hide. And doesn't sin work like that? It covers us in shame that makes us want to hide in so many ways—like David, like Adam and Eve. The only hiding the Father wants you to do here is in his love. That's the safe kind of hiding: the kind where you know you are going to win.

When you sin, do you usually hide in shame
or repent and hide in love?

You are my hiding place;
you protect me from trouble.
You surround me with songs of victory.

PSALM 32:7 NLT

As believers, we do not need to hide in shame. We can follow
the steps of David, repenting for sin and being made free
from it in Christ. If we confess sin, we get to walk in the light.
We get to be free; we don't have to carry around shame. You
will hear the voice of condemnation telling you to keep quiet.
It says God doesn't love you and could never accept you back
for what you have done. That is a lie!

Happiness is found by the one who lays out all their
wrongdoings in the light at the foot of the cross. It is there
that you will hear this joyous melody of deliverance and find
freedom in the fact that Christ has taken the punishment for
you. You are fully loved.

Jesus, thank you for your work on the cross! I confess my sin
to you. I repent. I want to walk in your freedom. Help me to
live in the light. Hide me in your love.

Tower of Strength

The name of the LORD is a strong tower;
the righteous runs into it and is safe.

PROVERBS 18:10 NASB

When you become a believer, it is like insurance against anything bad happening to you again, right? Wrong. We often get our desire for worldly safety mixed up with our definition of God's grace and blessings. God is good, but life with him is not always safe—in our definition of the term. The need to feel safe is a basic human instinct. When left to its own devices, it can grow bitterness in our hearts toward God when we don't perceive ourselves as being protected by him.

A life in Christ is safe because you can trust God; he has conquered death and promised us victory. The Holy Spirit lives inside you to guide you in unsure circumstances. You have peace that is unshakeable, and he is the God of restoration, working to make all things new.

Which of these promises do you need
to dive more into today?

The name of the LORD is a strong fortress;
the godly run to him and are safe.

PROVERBS 18:10 NLT

Flowers start as seeds. To become the beautiful blooms
we see and admire, they must break through again and
again. They break through the seed shell, the soil, and then
withstand elements that work to harm them. Even things we
know are good for a flower to grow—sunlight and water—in
the wrong amounts can be deadly.

Jesus tells us in Matthew how he keeps an eye on
flowers. How much more does he care about you and
your development, keeping you safe through trials and
distractions, through times of breakthrough and hard
periods, so that you bloom? He is your strong tower; don't be
discouraged by the elements. Trust the safety of Christ.

Thank you, Jesus, that you are a safe place to me. I can run to
you for protection. In all of life's situations, keep me hidden
in you.

My Caretaker

The LORD is all I need.
He takes care of me.
My share in life has been pleasant;
my part has been beautiful.

PSALM 16:5-6 NCV

The role of caregiver often falls on the shoulders of women. They are typically viewed as being more nurturing, an attribute given them by God and even mentioned in Scripture. It looks different for different people. You could be caring for an elderly parent, your children, or other children. You could be helping a friend or spouse with a chronic illness. Maybe you are a doctor, nurse, or mental health specialist, and caretaking is your profession.

There are many different roles for caretaking, but who is taking care of the caretakers? It's often overlooked that those giving out compassion and support also need it themselves. You might be so busy you don't even notice, but you are in need of care as well. What do you need? It's ok to ask for your needs, especially from the Lord who wants to take care of you.

What do you need today?

LORD, you alone are my portion and my cup;
you make my lot secure.
The boundary lines have fallen for me in pleasant places;
surely I have a delightful inheritance.

PSALM 16:5-6 NIV

Maybe you don't find yourself in a caretaking role right now.
We all have people around us in need though. Next time you
visit the sick or a friend in need, take notice of those caring
for them as well. Maybe you'll hear about someone in church
through the prayer line. Who is caring for the caretakers?

God works through his people, and he has asked us to share
in one another's burdens. One way we can do this is by
noticing those who are already carrying a burden and support
them as well. Maybe it's the spouse of someone with cancer or
a mom of new kids. Who could you reach out to and care for
this week?

God, help me to notice those around me who need care. Fill
me up as a caretaker so I can better care for others. Thank you
that you take care of all my needs.

Fighting for Me

The LORD your God is the one who goes with you to fight for you against your enemies to give you victory.

DEUTERONOMY 20:4 NIV

Not many of us are in a physical battle as Israel found itself in when this promise of God's presence was first given. The promise is still applicable to us today, as all of us are in a spiritual battle against the enemy of our souls. The Lord is the one to fight for us. He will go with us and give us the victory. All of it is done by God! We don't need to fight, strive, or push to succeed. We can't work our way into victory.

What we can do is pray. We can take up the sword of the Spirit and praise. This is how we fight—through worship. God does the rest. He is on the offense and the defense for us. There is victory to be found in this life in whatever stronghold or dark place you are facing. Start praying and praising God today, asking him to move on your behalf and watch the victory come!

Do you tend to try to fight your own battles
or let the Lord fight for you?

The LORD your God is He who goes with you,
to fight for you against your enemies, to save you.

DEUTERONOMY 20:4, NKJV

Another beautiful promise we reap from this verse is that
we will never show up for a fight alone. God is with you!
When the Israelites spied out the promised land, they let
fear take them captive because they saw how big the enemy
was. The spies came back and reported this to the people,
and everyone cowered. But Joshua and Caleb did not. They
reported on how big their God was and that he was going into
battle with them so they had nothing to lose.

With God on your side, every battle is victorious, and you
are never alone. Don't let fear try to hijack the victory that is
waiting for you.

God, thank you that you don't leave me to fight alone.
Thank you that you go in front of me and you fight for me.
What a promise!

Entwined

Here's what I've learned through it all:
Don't give up; don't be impatient;
be entwined as one with the Lord.
Be brave and courageous, and never lose hope.
Yes, keep on waiting—for he will never disappoint you!

PSALM 27:14 TPT

We all go through seasons of waiting. We sometimes are very aware of our waiting season, as we cannot get off our minds whatever it is we are waiting for. Other times it is just running the background of life. We wait for important and unimportant things, sometimes patiently and sometimes not so patiently. It is in the waiting season that we can really grow our patience muscles and learn to get to a place where we can say we aren't in a hurry.

We know that God is working and moving on our behalf; we know that he is in charge. When we can rest in those truths, we display an attitude of patience. We show that we are hoping in God, not hoping in the timeline. God will never disappoint us. Long seasons of waiting can be hard, but we must know that God is doing things in his time which is often different than ours. We can pout, get frustrated, and complain about the timing, or we can live with open hands to our Savior.

What are you waiting on?
How can you trust God with the timing?

Wait for the Lord;
be strong, and let your heart take courage;
wait for the Lord!

PSALM 27:14, NRSV

Waiting places can also feel like very still places which is something we may not like. We seem to be accustomed to a very busy pace. Stillness can feel like emptiness and lack of accomplishment. That is where faith comes in. In the stillness, there is so much happening. Growth is not an overnight thing but a process that takes time.

When you plant a seed, eventually you will see the harvest, but there is a lot of underground work that can't be seen—work that is done while you wait. It seems like nothing, but establishing those roots is so important for the plant to flourish. Don't discount the quiet, still times. Instead, press in deeper to Jesus. Entwine yourself with the Lord, and trust in him.

Jesus, help me to be patient in the waiting. Teach me to draw closer to you in the stillness.

Promises Kept

Sustain me according to Your word, that I may live;
And do not let me be ashamed of my hope.

PSALM 119:116 NASB

Do you find it hard to trust? Without careful tending, the older we get the harder it is to trust both people and perhaps even God. In the Bible one prominent characteristic of God is that he is trustworthy. This means that he is reliable. He makes promises, and he keeps them. There are over 8,000 promises of God in the Bible. It is full of information about his character, his feelings toward us, how he wants to help us, and so much more!

The way to live an abundant life, full of happiness, is to be held up by these promises, to know what they are, and to live your life by them. God cares about every detail of your life. If you take one shaky step forward in faith, know that he is trustworthy to hold you up. That's how your faith builds! One step at a time away from fear into abundance.

What promise of God are you clinging to today?

Lord, strengthen my inner being by the promises of your word
so that I may live faithful and unashamed for you.

PSALM 119:116 TPT

Another beautiful aspect of the Bible is that as we read the stories of people who came before us, in the Old and New Testaments, it shows that God is trustworthy. You cannot help but see that he is tried and true throughout Scripture. Time and time again when his people turn their back on him, he restores them. He never gives up on them, never abandons the plan to restore all of humanity to himself.

He followed through on his promises to the extent of humbling himself to the lowest of fashions, suffering and obediently going through with death on the cross. His resurrection three days later shows he is faithful by defeating death and making a way for all of us to be restored to him. Dig into God's Word, and let it bring up thankful remembrance in your heart that God is steadfast.

God, I praise you for all the examples you have given me in Scripture of how you are trustworthy. I stand on your promises today.

Healing for My Heart

For you who fear my name,
the sun of righteousness shall rise
with healing in its wings.

MALACHI 4:2 ESV

At the very beginning of spring, life starts to burst forth from the earth. Winter days can be marked as cold and dark, often more gray and shorter than the other days of the year. This can leave many of us dreaming about tropical vacations just so we can catch a glimpse of the sun! The sun does more than make a vacation enjoyable. It gives us vitamins, and lack of sun can damage our health. The sun gives off energy, and without it there would be no life on earth.

These are all the reasons why the word picture the prophet paints is so glorious. The Son of righteousness brings us healing. Without Jesus, we have no life at all. He is our strength and source. He has come to us offering true life and healing. What a wonderful picture of the love our Savior has for us! By diving into the Scriptures this morning, you know where you get health and the source of life. Let Jesus shine his face upon you this morning and worship him.

How has Jesus brought you health and life
in a season of darkness?

For you who revere my name,
the sun of righteousness will rise with healing in its rays.

MALACHI 4:2 NIV

Spring is a time of rejoicing. The new flowers, the melting snow, the gradual increase of daylight and warmth. Isn't it great that Easter falls into this season? The work Jesus did on the cross causes great rejoicing. Jesus has risen from the dead; the sun of righteousness has risen with healing in his wings!

This is a great reason for us to celebrate! Just like we bask in the newness and wonder of spring, let the resurrection of Christ bring joy to your heart.

Jesus, you have risen; I praise you for this fact! Thank you for bringing me life and light.

My Firm Hope

"Let not your heart be troubled; you believe in God, believe also in Me. In My Father's house are many mansions. I go to prepare a place for you. And if I go and prepare a place for you, I will come again and receive you to Myself; that where I am, there you may be also."

JOHN 14:1-3 NKJV

Traveling can be a draining. It doesn't matter if you are traveling by plane or car, there can often be unexpected hiccups that are taxing. It's so nice to know that when you get to your destination, there is a place ready for you. Maybe it's your family's cabin, already outfitted and perched on a quiet lake, or maybe it's simply a hotel room that has the bed, warm water, and solitude. The point is, you find rest in the fact that no matter what happens along the trip, when you get there, a safe place is waiting for you.

We are sojourners, or pilgrims, in this world. We are on a journey with many bumps and hiccups along the way; we all know that! But what rest and reassurance we gain from the fact that Jesus is preparing a place for us. A place that is with him—a safe place. When life's journey feels tempestuous, take hope in the fact that Jesus has gone ahead to prepare a place for you.

What comfort do you take in knowing that Jesus has a room waiting for you in his Father's house?

"Don't worry or surrender to your fear. For you've believed in God, now trust and believe in me also. My Father's house has many dwelling places. If it were otherwise, I would tell you plainly, because I go to prepare a place for you to rest. And when everything is ready, I will come back and take you to myself so that you will be where I am."

JOHN 14:1-3 TPT

In Jewish times, the groom would often prepare a place in the father's home. The extended family would live in the extra rooms. In the same way, Jesus has gone to prepare a place for us in his Father's home. This is the place we are to dwell forever with him.

What a beautiful picture of being welcomed into the family of God! Jesus gives us the reassurance that the Father has completely accepted us by allowing Jesus to come prepare a place for us. We are part of the family, welcomed and loved. There is no need to operate like an outsider anymore. Welcome to the family!

Jesus, thank you for preparing a place for me! Thank you for being safe. Father, thank you for welcoming me into your family. Let this hope encourage me tonight.

A Home

A father of the fatherless and a judge for the widows,
is God in His holy habitation.
God makes a home for the lonely;
He leads out the prisoners into prosperity.

PSALM 68:5-6 NASB

This verse calls out very specific things about God. He is a father for those who don't have one, a judge for widows who need justice and an advocate, a homemaker for lonely people, and a leader of prisoners into a new life. What do you need today from God? He is on the lookout. What you need is possible if you just ask today. You are his child and he is available to you.

You aren't using God or trying to take advantage of him by bringing your needs before him. Several times in the Bible, he specifically instructs believers to ask for what they need. So, what do you need God to be in your life today? A comforter, advocate, justice bringer, kind father, or close friend? You serve a mighty God who is able to meet all your needs! Bring them to him this morning.

What do you need today?

To the fatherless he is a father.
To the widow he is a champion friend.
To the lonely he makes them part of a family.
To the prisoners he leads into prosperity until they sing for joy.
This is our Holy God in his Holy Place!
But for the rebels there is heartache and despair.

PSALM 68:5-6 TPT

In the book of John, the word *abide* is used sixty times. When something is repeated in the Bible, it should make us pay attention! The concept being spoken of in this psalm is the same as the concept of abiding. God wants us to make our home in him—to abide in him. What makes a place a home? The amount of time you spend there and your comfort level are both factors.

God wants to be a part of your daily life: the ins and outs, the highs and lows. It shouldn't be a guilt trip, where you beat yourself up if you don't have a one-hour quiet time with Jesus every day. Think of it more like you and God abiding together instead of two ships passing in the night. He also wants you to be comfortable with him. You don't have to dress up or present yourself in a certain fashion to come to him. Be encouraged today as you find God so very near.

Father, thank you that you are all I need. Today you gave me what I needed; you showed up. I want to abide with you. Abide in me tonight.

Champion Defender

He alone is my safe place;
his wrap-around presence always protects me.
For he is my champion defender;
there's no risk of failure with God.
So why would I let worry paralyze me,
even when troubles multiply around me?

PSALM 62:2 TPT

What would you attempt if you knew you could not lose? God has a plan for your life that from your perspective might include some pretty risky things. You'll be asked to step out of your comfort zone, to persevere in hard times, to count the cost of being a believer. Are you willing? The amazing thing is that if it's God's plan, he is on your side. And if God has your back, there is no way to fail.

God is in the business of restoring all things; even things we see as failure he can redeem for victory. That's a risk-free situation! Fear will try to hold you back with lies about God. Turn to his Scriptures; everything he has promised will come to pass. You have a rock-solid footing when you are living in Christ. What is he asking from you today that you are holding back from?

Is fear holding you back from stepping out in faith?

He is my rock and my salvation;
he is my fortress, I will never be shaken.

PSALM 62:2 NIV

Have you ever heard that worry is faith going in the opposite direction? Faith is expecting God to be true to his promises and to act in line with his character. Worry expects and believes the worst. The psalmist makes it pretty clear that worry is not beneficial to us; he describes it as paralyzing. When circumstances arise that cause us to feel paralyzed, when worry sticks our feet to the ground and makes us gaze more at ourselves than at Christ, when troubles replay over in our heads and make us unable to act, we need to remember where our help comes from.

God has a great track record. He is always good, he always shows up, and he always comes through. He is perfectly just and abundantly righteous. He knows what is best for you; he will never leave you. Don't let fear make you live your Christian life crippled. Cry out to God for more faith; stand up and walk in the promises he has given you.

God, I want to believe; help my unbelief! Quiet the worry in my head and help me to step out in faith in your promises and in what you have spoken to me. Thank you that you are all-powerful and you cannot fail.

Restored by Peace

The LORD is my shepherd, I shall not want.
He makes me lie down in green pastures;
he leads me beside still waters;
he restores my soul.

PSALM 23:1-3 NRSV

The world wants to tell you that what is most important is taking care of yourself. It says that your self-care is all up to you, and to feel better in life you just need to get away, get a manicure, get a massage, or take a trip to the mall. Though these things are not bad, they fall short, as most of our attempts at self-care will.

Instead, look to God to supply all your needs. Turning to your good shepherd is the best self-care gift you can give yourself; it's the only one that will truly heal and refresh. Jesus is waiting to whisper to you, "In me, you will never lack." There is only one that can bring you to waters that will make you never thirst again and bread that will make you never hunger. Only one can restore our soul—Jesus.

How can you let God care for you today?

The Lord is my shepherd;
I shall not want.
He makes me to lie down in green pastures;
He leads me beside the still waters. He restores my soul;
He leads me in the paths of righteousness
For His name's sake.

PSALM 23:1-3 NKJV

You've already chosen to let God care for you by picking up this book. It shows that you place a priority on reading his Word. Good job! There are many important things asking for attention but being in his Word and in prayer are the most important. Continue to persevere in this, dwelling in his Word and praying.

Instead of hitting snooze in the morning, grab that cup of coffee and your Bible. Sleep is important, but Jesus is better than that extra fifteen minutes every time. It can be hard to ask for help, but those who find God as their happy place embrace dependency on God. Asking him for what you need is the action that shows the posture of your heart. And you want the posture of your heart to be turned toward the Father.

Jesus, lover of my soul, the one who cares for me, I turn my heart toward you. Will you feed me, give me a drink, and help me to be satisfied in you.

Not Far Away

The LORD is near to the brokenhearted
and saves the crushed in spirit.

PSALM 34:18 ESV

Feeling lonely or isolated can be one of the worst feelings in the world. Sometimes we are physically alone, which makes sense to us why we would feel lonely, but other times even in crowds the feeling can creep in. Some of us isolate to avoid pain, and others are removed because of grief or depression.

None of these scenarios, or others you can name, are walls too great to keep the Lord away. He's in the business of breaking down any barrier that keeps him from his children. When you are feeling lonely or isolated, remember that he is not far away. He is the friend that sticks closer than a brother. If the walls feel too high, simply cry out his name. That prayer has enough power to bring down the walls.

Do you view the Lord as being near you today?

The Lord is close to all whose hearts are crushed by pain,
and he is always ready to restore the repentant one.

PSALM 34:18 TPT

A big sign in the clouds would be easier. A clap of thunder and a flash of lightning right when we finish our prayer would be great. A supernatural move of God in nature would be easier than relationships with other people. People can be hard, and even if loneliness is what is plaguing us, it can often seem better than being vulnerable with others. If God is so near, why can't he just make his presence known in other ways?

Often, God is reaching out to you through others. He created us to be in relationship with him and with people. He regularly works through his people to encourage, strengthen, and comfort. While a bolt of lightning might seem more reassuring of his presence to you, he might be trying to communicate his nearness and bless you through others. Don't be so closed off from his people that you miss the gift he's trying to give.

Jesus, thank you that you are near to me. You show your nearness through nature, through other people, and in so many ways. Help me when I'm feeling lonely to cry out to you and to look for the gift of relationships that I might be closed off to.

Rock of Salvation

My God is my rock. I can run to him for safety.
He is my shield and my saving strength,
my defender and my place of safety.
The LORD saves me from those who want to harm me.

2 SAMUEL 22:3 NCV

Most of us are not living like David, the king of an entire
nation and a fugitive at one point in his life. For him, those
who wanted to harm him was likely an extensive list. For us,
hopefully not even one person comes to mind! The reality is,
whether you have a list like David's or a blank piece of paper,
you and David have a common enemy: Satan.

Working against you to keep you from the goodness of God,
the father of lies wants to harm you. Once you can identify
this, and recognize his attacks, you begin to fight the battle
that is not against flesh and blood but against the enemy of
your soul. The beauty of this is what David tells you about
God. You can run to him for safety. He is your shield, your
strength, and your defender. There is no need to fear with
God acting in these ways for you.

Do you take into consideration the enemy of your soul,
or do you see people as your enemies?

My God is my rock, in whom I find protection.
He is my shield, the power that saves me,
and my place of safety.
He is my refuge, my Savior,
the one who saves me from violence.

2 SAMUEL 22:3 NLT

We are told that David would hide in caves as he was on the run from Saul. We imagine him lying in wait behind rocks as he came close enough to Saul that he could cut a corner from his robe. To say the least, David was a man very familiar with rocks. He could appreciate their ability to conceal him from the elements and from his enemy.

This can bring us comfort as we think of God as our rock. He shelters us from the harsh elements of life. When life feels harsh and unforgiving, we should turn to God to be our safe place. We can pour out our souls to him, trust him, and find rest from all that is around us.

God, I praise you that you are a safe place to me. Thank you that I can tell you all my troubles, that you are reliable, and that your Word is true. Defend me against the enemy; be my rock.

Make It Clear

Don't hide yourself, Lord, when I come to find you.
You're the God of my salvation;
how can you reject your servant in anger?
You've been my only hope,
so don't forsake me now when I need you!

PSALM 27:9 TPT

Perceptions of God versus who God really is can throw us off track. We collect ideas about God or who we want him to be from our experiences, relationships, and interactions with the church, to name a few ways. Sometimes we even try to fit God into a box of our own making, labeling him in a certain fashion. All of these can be harmful to our view of God.

It's so important to read your Bible to find out who God truly is, and how he responds toward you. The Bible, accompanied by honest prayer, can bring so much clarity when our emotions or experiences are telling us something else. These two things combined are like turning on the defrost when your car is all foggy; suddenly, clear views are intact and it's much easier to drive safely.

What negative or wrong views of God are keeping
your vision foggy today? Pray for insight.

Do not turn your back on me.
Do not reject your servant in anger.
You have always been my helper.
Don't leave me now; don't abandon me,
O God of my salvation!

The psalmist petitioned God by acknowledging his character. He speaks of the God of his salvation, the God who has been his only hope. These past experiences with God are how he relates to God. Not all of our past experience teaches us negative things about the character of God. In fact, in many other places in the Bible we are called to be people of remembrance.

To be a person of remembrance is to be someone who recounts what God has done and gives him acknowledgement and praise for it. This act of worship helps to build faith during hard seasons. Let faith rise up in you this evening, and as you go to sleep, remember a time when God was your salvation or your hope. Pray a prayer of thanksgiving as you go to sleep with this sweet memory and confidence in your God.

Jesus, thank you that you give me your Word that reveals your character. I want to remember all the ways you have been my hope in the past.

Called by Divine Love

*His divine power has granted to us everything pertaining to life
and godliness, through the true knowledge of Him who called us
by His own glory and excellence.*

2 Peter 1:3 NASB

It's become popular to post Scriptures on signs and stickers.
You can see them hanging around people's houses, maybe
even your own. On the internet, verses are thrown on top
of beautiful scenic photos or written in calligraphy across a
white background and shared.

We put the promises of God on plaques, memes, and
bumper stickers for display, but do we ever use them? Do we
practically allow what God has given to change our everyday
lives, or are they just cute farmhouse décor? Peter writes that
we have been given everything we need for life from God—a
gift. The question is, do we use it?

How can you practically apply God's Word
to your life to change something today?

Jesus has the power of God, by which he has given us everything we need to live and to serve God. We have these things because we know him. Jesus called us by his glory and goodness.

2 PETER 1:3 NCV

Jesus is sufficient. A great temptation is to live with a Jesus-plus mindset. Jesus plus wealth. Jesus plus good health. Jesus plus my favorite self-help book. Jesus plus hustling hard. But Jesus is sufficient for our lives; he has given us all we need for a victorious life. True knowledge of him is what will transform us. The Holy Spirit making us more Christ-like is what will change us.

What are you trying to add to Jesus today? Instead of adding, bring what you need to him in prayer. Let him guide and direct you, transform and change you. He may be leading you to a certain relationship, a new church, or a business venture. He may be asking you to give something up. It's not that Jesus won't use things like hard work, counseling, medicine, or a relationship to answer your prayers. It's the fact that you cannot add that thing to him. He is the source, the leader, the provider of everything you need. Turn to him for sufficiency today.

Thank you, Jesus, that you are sufficient for me. You have given me everything I need.

Overcome with Peace

*"I have said these things to you, that in me you may have peace.
In the world you will have tribulation. But take heart; I have
overcome the world."*

JOHN 16:33 ESV

There are two uses of the preposition "in" in this verse. *In Christ*, for he is the one speaking here, and *in the world*. These two statements do not have to exist separately; if you are in Christ, it doesn't imply that you are not in the world and vice versa. In fact, if you are reading this, you are in the world. You are alive. What does Jesus say will be guaranteed to us while we are alive? Tribulation, or troubles. That should at least reassure us that troubles do not mean that we are doing something wrong or lacking in faith. Jesus said we would have them.

But to be in Christ is not a guaranteed matter. This is the part of the verse where we come into play. To be in Christ means that God no longer sees our imperfections. Once we have come to faith in Christ, our debt is cancelled and our relationship is restored.

Can you be found in Christ today?

"Everything I've taught you is so that the peace which is in me will be in you and will give you great confidence as you rest in me. For in this unbelieving world you will experience trouble and sorrows, but you must be courageous, for I have conquered the world!"

JOHN 16:33 TPT

If we are in Christ, what are we told by Jesus that we have? Peace! But how can Jesus tell us we are going to have troubles and also peace? Can the two statements coexist? Yes, because your troubles and tribulations are based on circumstances, and your peace is not.

Your peace is guaranteed no matter what storm is swirling around you because you have peace with God. Now that your standing before God is righteous, peace for your circumstances is available because you have the Holy Spirit living inside of you. You have access to the wisdom of God. You have his power in you. Everything you need to continue in the world, in trial, in hard times, in bleak circumstances, is available to you in Christ. What a promise!

Jesus, thank you that though I am in the world, I can also be in perfect peace because I am found in you.

A Better Gift

*"I am leaving you with a gift—peace of mind and heart.
And the peace I give is a gift the world cannot give.
So don't be troubled or afraid."*

JOHN 14:27 NLT

Have you ever wanted something so badly but decided to try the knock-off version instead? Maybe you settled for an off brand and it just didn't measure up? Imagine asking for a specific new car for Christmas, and instead getting a used clunker? That's the picture you should get when you imagine us as believers settling for the world's version of peace over Christ's.

The world offers peace in so many different packages, and they all look quite alluring. We are offered peace in financial security, self-care, having a spouse, more material possessions, a high status, or a squad. The world's peace comes wrapped in all different boxes, but none measures up or compares to the real deal—the peace that Christ gives us. Why do we so often seek out peace in the counterfeits when we have the Holy Spirit who can fill us with the real deal?

How do you settle for counterfeit peace?

*"Peace I leave with you; my peace I give you.
I do not give to you as the world gives.
Do not let your hearts be troubled and do not be afraid."*

JOHN 14:27 NIV

A lot of fear can come to us because of the unknown. Try as we might to plan and account for unknowns, none of us can know what the future holds. One phone call, one diagnosis, a few careless words can change so much. You may not know for certain what is ahead of you, but you can know for certain who is beside you.

The gift Jesus left us all with is peace. Peace himself gave us his Spirit of peace to be with us all the time. When we have certainty in our hearts over this, fear has to flee. Peace is with you, so there is no need to worry, no need to latch onto troubles that haven't even happened. With the Holy Spirit, you can conquer fear of the unknown and face the future with confidence.

Jesus, thank you that you are our peace. You give us peace that cannot be matched by the world. Help me to dwell on that peace, and to live without fear of the unknowns in life.

Always with Me

Those who love me, I will deliver;
I will protect those who know my name.
When they call to me, I will answer them;
I will be with them in trouble,
I will rescue them and honor them.

PSALM 91:14–15 NRSV

There is great power to be found in the name of Jesus. For those who profess Christ as Savior, we will come against the spiritual forces of darkness in our lives. When times get dark, let light burst forth; proclaim his name. It doesn't have to be a big lengthy prayer or a certain ritual, and you don't have to be in a specific place. Anytime, anywhere, when darkness tries to overtake you, fight back. Simply speak his name.

There is power in the name of Jesus, for it is recognized in the spiritual realm as the name of the one who is victorious. He stripped death of all its power and set free those in darkness. The darkness knows his name and trembles. Do you know the power in his name? Jesus knows his own and never abandons them. Call out to him in your time of need.

What power have you found in the name of Jesus?

I will rescue those who love me.
I will protect those who trust in my name.
When they call on me, I will answer;
I will be with them in trouble.
I will rescue and honor them.

PSALM 91:14-15 NLT

Psalm 91 can be great comfort to those in hard times. The promise that God will deliver us, protect us, answer us, and be with us in trouble are very reassuring. Another beautiful aspect of this verse is that God goes above and beyond. Doesn't it feel like enough that he would deliver and save us? But he doesn't stop there. He goes on to honor us. To restore us. To make new what sin broke. He could have just saved us, plopped us into safety, and left us there. That would have been enough.

Our God is a God of abundance who goes above and beyond. He is working in our lives to restore what was stolen. He wants to honor you. It seems like a fairy tale! God sees you in your lowly estate, rescues you, and then builds you back up to show you honor. All praise be to God!

God, thank you for saving me and for showing me honor. Your work is amazing!

Can't Stay Away

Those who go to him for help are happy,
and they are never disgraced.

PSALM 34:5 NCV

You aren't going to walk away from an encounter with the living God dissatisfied. Unlike when we turn to imperfect people for help, God is perfect in every way, and he never changes. He is powerful enough to overcome any circumstance, wise enough to decipher any problem, and loving enough that he will serve you by helping.

In the gospels, Jesus displayed his love by serving those around him. For example, on the night before he was murdered, he took out a towel and he washed the disciples' feet. The character of Jesus does not change, and he is one with God the Father and the Holy Spirit. Therefore, the Holy Spirit who lives inside you displays his love by helping you. What are you in need of this morning? If you want to pursue a happy life, accept the serving love of Jesus this morning.

Will you let Jesus help you this morning?

Gaze upon him, join your life with his, and joy will come.
Your faces will glisten with glory.
You'll never wear that shame-face again.

PSALM 34:5 TPT

Have you ever felt like you have outstayed your welcome? Maybe you've been in a time of great need and you know you leaned on someone for help maybe a little too much. These kinds of situations can make us feel like a burden or a bother and deter us from asking for help in the future.

Humans have limitations, that is true, but God doesn't in this matter. His love toward you is never ending. You could come to him for help every second of the day for the rest of your life, cast every anxiety on him, lean completely on him, and he would never grow weary of you. What a blessing! In fact, doing those things is exactly what God asks you to do: rely and lean and ask for help all of your days. Don't believe the lie that you've asked too much, or you're a burden to God. He welcomes and delights in you, and he desires you to draw near.

Jesus, thank you for the example you gave me in Scripture of servanthood. Thank you that you do not grow weary of me, but you show me your love by helping me. I want to rely completely on you; I ask for your help unashamed tonight.

A Gentle Reminder

"Are you weary, carrying a heavy burden? Then come to me. I will refresh your life, for I am your oasis. Simply join your life with mine. Learn my ways and you'll discover that I'm gentle, humble, easy to please. You will find refreshment and rest in me."

MATTHEW 11:28-29 TPT

Have you ever met someone and discovered they are completely different than you had perceived them or heard about them from others? Sometimes we can really misjudge character and find out that a person is far different than we expected. This also happens with God. We may have heard things about him our whole lives and formed an opinion about who he is without ever really meeting with him. Perhaps we heard he is always angry, just waiting to smite us from heaven. Our perception might have been that he is aloof, just an old man in heaven taking tickets and letting the world do its own thing.

It's important to search your heart and find out how you have misjudged God. Then, you can fill in the gaps of your understanding with the truth of his Word. Take this passage, for instance. How does Jesus describe himself? As gentle, humble, and easy to please. Does this align with your view of him? if not, realign your thoughts with the truth of Scripture.

How does Jesus' description of himself align with or oppose your current view of him?

> *"Come to me, all you who are weary and burdened, and I will give you rest. Take my yoke upon you and learn from me, for I am gentle and humble in heart, and you will find rest for your souls."*
>
> MATTHEW 11:28-29 NIV

Geographically speaking, an oasis is a fertile spot in a desert. It's the place we see in cartoons and movies that the characters dream about and sometimes imagine as they are dragging their parched, weary bodies under the hot sun through the relentless desert.

If you are carrying a heavy weight, that description above may be exactly how you feel, and an oasis is exactly what you need. But you don't need to reach a certain spiritual point on your journey or jump through any fancy hoops to get there. Right here, right now, Jesus is offering to refresh your life and be an oasis for you. Set your load down; it's time to drink deep.

Jesus, thank you for being gentle and kind. Will you align my thinking of you with your true character? Be an oasis to me this evening.

Hopeful in the Spirit

This is no empty hope, for God himself is the one who has prepared us for this wonderful destiny. And to confirm this promise, he has given us the Holy Spirit, like an engagement ring, as a guarantee.

2 CORINTHIANS 5:5 TPT

The same Spirit which raised Christ from the dead, which parted the seas and led the Israelites across, which hovered over the new believers in the upper room as a tongue of fire before they spread the gospel like wildfire, is the Spirit that lives in you! Let that sink in. You may be feeling defeated, but you have this Spirit inside of you. This is the Spirit of life that will raise your mortal body at the time of resurrection and has spiritually brought you to life right now. You used to be dead in your sins, but now you are alive in the Spirit.

The benefits of this life are already playing out in your life, the promises of God are available to you. Why operate as a dead person any longer, bound to sin and hustling in your own strength to get by? Submit to God and let the Holy Spirit work in your life to find the abundant, truly life-filled reality that is available to you.

What evidence of a Spirit-filled life do you see in yourself?

This is what God made us for,
and he has given us the Spirit
to be a guarantee for this new life.

2 CORINTHIANS 5:5 NCV

When you became a believer, several things happened. The grace of God was applied to your life, as you became justified before God, and at peace with him because of Christ's work on the cross. God the Father now views you through the sacrifice of his Son, Jesus, and he sees you as holy. You also are indwelled with the Holy Spirit. He is like the evidence of the promise that God has made to believers to make them holy as he is holy.

The Holy Spirit desires to do a sanctifying work in your life. Sanctification is an ongoing process of your life being in submission to God. As you walk with God, releasing your grasp on your life and your need to be in control, he guides and leads you and makes you more like himself. The fruit of the Spirit becomes evident in your life, and those around you can see something different because you are led by the Spirit and not by your flesh. What an amazing work he is doing!

God, thank you that you gave me the Holy Spirit as a seal. Thank you, Holy Spirit, for the sanctifying work you are doing in my heart. I submit my life to you God and ask you to continue to make me holy.

Set Free

*"If you abide in My word,
you are My disciples indeed.
And you shall know the truth,
and the truth shall make you free."*

JOHN 8:31-32 NKJV

We would like freedom to be defined as the ability to do whatever we want, whenever we want. That definition probably does not sound like what you know about the Bible, does it? Many view the Bible as an impossible book of rules, a high bar you will never quite reach. However, restricting yourself to the truth of God's Word actually releases you into true freedom.

God the Father is good; it is who he is. He knows how to empower and guide us to live in joy and victory. What the world views as restrictive, we view as healthy boundaries. We see the loving hand of a father, a good father, guiding his children through a dark world where an enemy wants to destroy them. And one way he does this is through the truth of his Word. Aligning your life with God's Word is not outdated or confining; it's the path that leads to the most joy.

How have you been listening to the lie
that the Bible is too restrictive?

"If you continue to obey my teaching, you are truly my followers. Then you will know the truth, and the truth will make you free."

JOHN 8:31-32 NCV

What does it mean to abide? Jesus uses this word over and over in the book of John. Think of it as *home*. You are to be at home in the Word of God. It's pulling up a chair, getting your comfy clothes on, grabbing a steaming cup of tea, and throwing your hair in a messy bun kind of home. To be at home in the Word of God is to know it in and out. To know something, you need to spend a lot of time in it.

When you call a place home, you know which board squeaks when you walk up the stairs. You know the perfect temperature to make a room comfortable; you can walk its layout with your eyes closed, and you feel at peace there. Abiding in the Word is exactly like that. You can approach Scripture in a lingering fashion, to study deeper. You could approach it more shortly, like the single verses given in this devotional to dwell on all day, or perhaps even memorize it. However you go about it, make yourself at home in God's Word!

Jesus, thank you that you are the Word. Thank you for providing me with a home to be safe in, a guide on this journey, and for giving me truth. Give me a hunger for your Word and for truth and help me learn to live in your freedom.

Never Left Alone

Those who know the LORD trust him,
because he will not leave those who come to him.

PSALM 9:10 NCV

Your reputation precedes you. Reputation can be important. You might choose a professional based on the reviews of friends, or act differently in situations based on what you've heard of those around you. The reputation of the Lord is clear throughout the Bible, and partly stated right here in this psalm. Have you heard? You can trust the Lord. He's as loyal as they come. All the people who trust him? They turn out just fine.

Can you hear the whispers and the shouts about God throughout the ages? The testimony of his reputation is being spread through the Scripture, by nature, by the church; he is trustworthy. Let it build faith in you to hear them. And when faith arises, you too can give testimony to his reputation. The Lord is faithful; he will see you through!

Do you believe that God is loyal?

May everyone who knows your mercy
keep putting their trust in you,
for they can count on you for help no matter what.
O Lord, you will never, no never, neglect those
who come to you.

PSALM 9:10 TPT

It takes humility to admit we need help. We desire to live joy-filled lives so we must come in humility to the Lord. When we come to the Lord for help, he is loyal. He is willing and able to meet all our needs and lift us up from your burdens.

The key is to come. Jesus is a gentleman, knocking at the door to your life. The door only has a handle on the inside; the hinges swing outward. This means that you must respond; he will not force his way inside. Come to Jesus, open the door, and find that you will never be without help again.

Jesus, thank you for being loyal to me. I respond to your invitation to come, and I open the door. Humbly I ask for you to lead and direct me in my life.

Source of Healing

Do not be wise in your own eyes;
fear the LORD and turn away from evil.
It will be healing to your body and refreshment to your bones.

PROVERBS 3:7-8 NASB

It happens a lot in families: parents see their kids getting ready to do something crazy, and they know that it will end badly. But the children, full of pride, insist that it's going to be fine. If left to their own devices, it usually goes as the parent predicted—badly! The children are demonstrating being wise in their own eyes. This phrase drips with pride.

To be wise in our own eyes is to forsake the counsel around us and the leading of the Lord. It seems like our culture is really into celebrating those who are wise in their own eyes. Believing that the Bible is not true, lacking morality, creating relative truth, and focusing on being politically correct instead of Biblically sound are all the cries of the petulant child insisting on their way. If we act out of the belief that we know better, our wisdom and knowledge will fail us. Let us be people whose own opinions, knowledge, and feelings don't get in the way of truth.

Ask God to search your heart and see if you have
any areas of being "wise in your own eyes."

Don't think for a moment that you know it all,
for wisdom comes when you adore him with undivided devotion
and avoid everything that's wrong.
Then you will find the healing refreshment
your body and spirit long for.

PROVERBS 3:7–8 TPT

Healing and refreshment are beautiful words. These are the promises in store for you as you turn from your own wisdom and toward the wisdom of the Lord. It is not easy to embrace humility and admit that you are wrong. Don't let shame sneak in after you repent; it's hungry to drag you down. Instead, recognize what a good and blessed thing it is that you have the opportunity to repent and turn!

How wonderful is the Lord that he longs to share his wisdom with you. His promise to you for turning from your wisdom is not punishment; it's freedom! Doing things your own way does not lead to a healthy life; it makes you sick and can lead to death. Let God restore you tonight, tending to you in your sickness and loving you back to health.

Jesus, thank you that you give me the opportunity to repent. Heal me tonight. May I not be wise in my own eyes but follow after your wisdom only.

Lasting Appeal

The world and its desires pass away,
but whoever does the will of God lives forever.

1 JOHN 2:17 NIV

Our world is full of opportunity at every turn. It's pretty exciting, isn't it? We live in a time of options, and it can be a beautiful thing. Each of us are given one life but a myriad of choices. You decide how your days are lived out, what you pursue, and who you spend time with. John is appealing to you to choose wisely. There are so many passions and pursuits you could take that aren't worthwhile because they don't honor God. There are even things that seem good on the surface but lead to an empty life.

As children of God, we want to use our lives to pursue things of eternal value. That's the measuring stick we use when choosing what opportunities to take. How will this decision measure up in light of eternity? Material goods and worldly success are passing away. People always have eternal value, and loving God by serving others should take a high priority. Take a step back and analyze your life this morning.

Are your pursuits lasting, or are they temporary?

This world is fading away, along with everything that people crave. But anyone who does what pleases God will live forever.

1 JOHN 2:17 NLT

We can use busyness as an ally in our quest to do great things for God. When we do this, it's very easy to miss out on God himself. Like we mentioned above, sometimes even good things get in the way of eternal things. When we fill our schedule with endless acts of service, committees and activities, we can neglect God in the busyness. Suddenly, we have become more his employees and less his children.

Do you know that God wants a relationship with you? To just sit with you. And that's enough. God gives us tasks and asks us to serve others of course, but when we are running on empty and focused on those things, how do we wait on God as he has asked? How do we pray and get to know him more through his Word? What happened to God commanding us to rest? We can't pick and choose. Don't let the busyness of good deeds keep you from the best thing—just being with God.

God, help me to slow down and prioritize you. Show me what things in my life don't have eternal value and help me to live in your will.

Until the End

*"Teach them to obey everything that I have taught you,
and I will be with you always, even until the end of this age."*

MATTHEW 28:20 NCV

The disciples had the pleasure of walking with Jesus through his entire earthly ministry. Some of them may have even known him longer. For three or so years he was a constant companion, traveling with them, eating with them, teaching them. Then he said he was leaving. Can you imagine their panic? How could things ever be the same when God himself had been walking amongst them, and no longer would? I'm sure it confused them when Jesus said he would be with them always. He promised the Holy Spirit, who did come, and the disciples did not seem to complain about it! Instead, with the power of the Holy Spirit they turned the world upside down.

Maybe you've daydreamed about what it would have been like to actually walk with Jesus and wondered at how much easier things might be if you could see his face or touch his hands—like Thomas who needed to see Jesus in the flesh before he believed. We are called to believe but not without anything to back our belief. We also have the gift of the Holy Spirit, who is fully God, inside of us. There is nothing Jesus did that the Holy Spirit cannot do. He is with us! What will that change in our lives today?

Do you realize you have the Holy Spirit with you always?

"Teach them to faithfully follow all that I have commanded you.
And never forget that I am with you every day,
even to the completion of this age."

MATTHEW 28:20 TPT

When we study God's Word and let it sink into our souls, the
Holy Spirit uses it to remind us of truths we need to hear.
Maybe you are having a rough time, and you feel like God
is being unfair or you don't understand why something is
happening. When you voice those thoughts in prayer, backed
up by his Word, the Holy Spirit may bring to mind another
Scripture. This isn't coincidence, it's God speaking through
his Word!

Listen up. Grab a hold of Scripture and never let go. Listen to
all of Jesus's teachings.

Jesus, thank you that you did not abandon us but you gave us
your Word and the Holy Spirit to help guide us. This brings us
incredible comfort, peace, and joy in the precise moments we
need them. You are such a good God!

Through Everything

Even if my father and mother abandon me,
the LORD will hold me close.

PSALM 27:10 NLT

It's startling when you realize that not everyone you know thinks the same as you. It can be especially hard if those people are supposed to be the closest ones to you and the most supportive. Jesus knew that those who chose to follow him would face a great cost. He knew that it had the ability to even divide families, as he says in Matthew 19:29. Interestingly enough, Jesus' own family did not believe he was the Messiah for a very long time. So, Jesus was very familiar with the heartache that comes from choosing God over family.

Though the pain is high, take comfort that Jesus has been there, and he is with you through it. He knows what it is like to watch those you love choose not to follow God and pick a path of destruction instead. He knows the loneliness and heartache that can come on those who choose to forsake all for him. He promises to be near to you in this pain. Won't you let him draw you close this morning?

How can you still love those in your family
who don't believe in Christ?

If my father and mother leave me,
*the L*ORD *will take me in.*

PSALM 27:10 NCV

The of following Jesus is high. There's a lot to give up: family, friendships, position, wealth, doing things our way. But there is so much to be gained. Though it will be hard on this earth to let go of the things Jesus asks us to, he is faithful to stay near to us.

There is a great and lasting reward for those who follow Christ. No matter what sacrifice you have given, rest assured that Jesus can empathize with your loss. He doesn't tell you to count the cost and get over it. He knows the pain of letting go. But he also knows the beauty to be found in communion with your heavenly Father. Won't you trust him along this road of letting go?

Jesus, thank you that you are not unaware of my needs, and you can empathize with me. Be near me today.

Into His Heart

It is impossible for God to lie for we know that his promise and his vow will never change! And now we have run into his heart to hide ourselves in his faithfulness. This is where we find his strength and comfort, for he empowers us to seize what has already been established ahead of time—an unshakeable hope.

HEBREWS 6:18 TPT

Honesty is important to any relationship. But there isn't a human on earth that can say they have never told a lie. We tell what we call small white lies ("No, you don't look like you've gained weight," "Yes, I love this casserole!") or sometimes even bigger lies that cause damage to our relationships. At times we even lie to ourselves, convincing ourselves we are fine when we are really in pain, or telling ourselves to do something, saying it will be ok when we know it won't.

What a difference there is between us and God. God cannot lie. It's impossible. It's against his very nature. So, if God cannot lie, then you can hold true everything he has written in his Word! His promise to never leave you? Absolute truth. His promise to keep you until the end? One hundred percent. There's no fudging the lines or backing out of a promise with God. What he says he does, and it's who he is. God will always be honest with you.

What does it change for you knowing that God cannot lie?

God has given both his promise and his oath. These two things are unchangeable because it is impossible for God to lie. Therefore, we who have fled to him for refuge can have great confidence as we hold to the hope that lies before us.

HEBREWS 6:18 NLT

When we lie, it shows that we are trusting in ourselves to get us out of whatever situation we are in. When we speak truth, no matter what, it indicates that we are hiding ourselves in the faithfulness of God.

We can't control the outcome of every situation in our lives, and sometimes we use lies to help with that. Telling a lie can be a way of telling God that you don't trust him enough to get you out of a tricky situation. Are you going to run to refuge in God or try to hide in your lies? You get to choose.

God, help me to be honest. Help me to trust you. Thank you that you are trustworthy, merciful, and true.

Something that Lasts

All flesh is like grass and all its glory like the flower of grass.
The grass withers, and the flower falls,
but the word of the Lord remains forever.

1 PETER 1:24-25 ESV

Those of us made in the image of God bear flesh while we are on this temporary earth. Our flesh will pass away, but our souls are eternal. Young and old, humans die at various times. But our glory is like the flower. Our earthly doings may leave a legacy for a few hundred years, but they are not eternal either. We can write great books, produce awesome films, compose amazing music, construct complex buildings, and run large companies, but whatever legacy we make isn't eternal.

The Word of the Lord remains forever and finds its source in God. God is forever. Things that bring him glory and honor remain forever. Loving your neighbor well has eternal value, as does humbly serving your family, being faithful to your spouse, fighting for justice, and defending the fatherless. What kind of legacy are you leaving? Choose the legacy of God today.

When you analyze your life, what kind of legacy
do you think you are leaving?

All people are like grass,
and all their glory is like the flowers of the field;
the grass withers and the flowers fall,
but the word of the Lord endures forever.

1 PETER 1:24-25 NIV

How can you ensure you are leaving an eternal legacy? There are a few steps. First, make sure you are walking in the fear of the Lord. It all starts with your relationship with him. It is most important that you are spending time in the Word and praying. Walking in the fear of the Lord means having a heart that leans toward God's understanding and away from your own. Next, Recognize the needs in the world, and take prayerful action. God has created you with unique gifts, placement, and ability to make an eternal impact on this world.

If you step out of your bubble and look at the world around you, you will be quick to find where God needs you to move. Are you excited? Step out in faith and let God move through you.

God, what do you want me to do? I'm all ears. Help me to step out in faith and begin an eternal legacy for your glory.

Face like Flint

The Lord GOD helps Me,
Therefore, I am not disgraced;
Therefore, I have set My face like flint,
And I know that I will not be ashamed.

ISAIAH 50:7 NASB

We need to have grit! Grit is the relentless pursuit of a goal—no giving up. You might see it referred to in the Bible as steadfastness or perseverance. There are many examples of people in the Bible who had grit: Noah, facing the scorn of his community as he built that boat on dry land; Joseph, stuck in an Egyptian prison while he waited on God to move on his behalf; Moses, leading the Israelites through the desert for forty years. The list could go on, but you get the point. They all had grit, so how can you?

Grit is often formed through fire, in the flames of adversity. We all have hard times; we all have trials. It's not a question of if we will have an opportunity, it's what we will do with it. Let the hard times strengthen and shape your faith, developing you into someone who leans hard on God and continues no matter what. Let it make you have a face like flint.

How does this morning's devotion
change your perspective on trials?

The Lord Yahweh empowers me, so I am not humiliated.
For that reason, with holy determination,
I will do his will and not be ashamed.

ISAIAH 50:7 TPT

The confidence of the writer comes from one source: God. He can say with full confidence that he will not be humiliated; he doesn't have to fear shame because God is reliable. God will not let you down or fail you. This rock-solid promise is so helpful when you are facing hard times and trying to build grit in your life.

No matter what lies the enemy throws your way, you can continue on because you know the truth: God will never let you down. With this firm foundation, you are unstoppable! Praise God for his reliability and love today.

God, thank you that I can rely on you and your promises. I pray you will use every hard situation in my life to build grit in me.

Love Meets Me

Fill us with your love every morning.
Then we will sing and rejoice all our lives.

PSALM 90:14 NCV

Many of us take time to start our mornings with a full mug of coffee or tea. You being here this morning, in this devotional, means you're also taking time to fill your soul. What is the key to a good life? It's this right here—being filled with God's love every morning. Just like our morning beverages, we need it fresh every day. Most of us empty our coffee mugs every morning and our spiritual mugs every day.

If you are living a life for God, you are constantly pouring into those around you, which is a great thing! But those who pour out need to be filled up again. When you start your days in your strength and skip out on God's Word, you start on empty. Most people don't like cold, old coffee either. If you set your mug down and forget about it, do you pick it up a few days later and drink it? Usually not. When the coffee gets cold and old, it usually gets thrown out. Bring your cold heart before the flame of God every day and ask him to fill it afresh.

How can being filled with God's love everyday transform your life?

Oh, satisfy us early with Your mercy,
That we may rejoice and be glad all our days!

PSALM 90:14 NKJV

It's hard to operate on an empty stomach, and it's hard to have joy when you're running out of steam as well. As children of God, we want to be the people the psalmist describes here: those who sing and rejoice and praise God all through our days. We can't operate on empty though, and joy doesn't magically appear. We need to be filled by God in order to live a life full of joy.

God has asked us to pursue rest, or Sabbath; it's one of the many ways he fills us up. Are you living your life at high speed seven days a week, or are you honoring God by taking a day to rest, focus on him, and let him fill you with joy?

God, teach me to rest. Teach me Sabbath rest. Fill me with your joy and love anew tonight.

Light of Wisdom

The teaching of your word gives light,
so even the simple can understand.

PSALM 119:130 NLT

Do you ever find yourself engrossed in a good book, so much so that you may have not realized it had gotten dark? Then someone, usually a mom, comes in and flips on the light and chastises you for trying to read in the dark! Your eyeballs must have been thankful because suddenly all those words became so much easier to read.

This is the picture we get from this verse. We are like children trying to read a book in the dark, and wisdom (through the Holy Spirit) is the light that suddenly makes it so much easier. The Bible can be overwhelming at first take. Good for you that you are here today, seeking wisdom and light. The Holy Spirit will illuminate his Word and bring you understanding. Trust in him!

Do you find yourself avoiding the Bible
because it seems hard to understand?

Learning your words gives wisdom
and understanding for the foolish.

PSALM 119:130 NCV

Because of the Holy Spirit, you are fully capable to be a vessel of light to those around you. Maybe you don't consider yourself a teacher, but with his power you can bring the understanding of God's Word to those who are living in darkness. It's as simple as sharing the passage you read this morning with a coworker, talking about what God is showing you, or finding ways to drop God's wisdom into conversations. Social media is an easily accessible way to share light in a dark place.

God will give you the inspiration of the how; be faithful to respond. You might not carry the title of teacher or preacher, but as a Christian full of the Holy Spirit, you can share his light with the influence he has given around you.

God, help me to bring the light of your wisdom into every situation I face. Give me the boldness to speak directly and the grace to do it in love.

Always Reliable

The Lord is faithful, who will establish you
and guard you from the evil one.

2 THESSALONIANS 3:3 NKJV

Who is the evil one? The enemy is Satan. It's important to know some facts about him. He is not God's peer or equal in any way. Only God is eternal, omnipresent, omniscient, and omnipotent. It's important to make this distinction because we can be taught misleading things about the enemy and think he has qualities that only God possesses.

The beautiful thing is, the all-knowing, all-powerful, ever-present God is full of love toward you. He offers to protect you from the one who seeks to destroy you. Whose side do you want to be on? It's a choice you make every day by either humbly submitting to God, opening the door to his protection and guidance in your life, or pridefully trying to defend and care for yourself.

In what ways do you try to protect yourself
that you could submit to Jesus instead?

The Lord Yahweh is always faithful to place you on a firm foundation and guard you from the Evil One.

2 Thessalonians 3:3 TPT

The evil one has other names in Scripture as well. He is called the father of lies in John 8:44. There is absolutely no truth in him. He longs to mislead you with false information regarding God and God's Word. He tries to construct false truths about your reality and the circumstances that surround you. He is the accuser, constantly pointing out your failures and sins, trying to cripple you in shame. He is the tempter, asking you to fulfill passions in ways that dishonor God. The name Lucifer means "shining one." It's easier to deceive with things that are attractive, things that may seem shiny and good yet dishonor God.

As a Christian, Satan cannot destroy you. But he can work hard to deceive you and make your time on earth unproductive for the kingdom of God. Be aware that there is an evil one working against you. Take refuge in your relationship with God, your all-powerful King who is always there to protect you from anything the evil one tries to throw your way.

Thank you, God, that you are all-powerful, a mighty protector of those you love. Be a refuge to me. Make me alert and on guard to the attacks of the enemy. Protect me from deception.

Never Forgotten

God will never forget the needy;
the hope of the afflicted will never perish.

PSALM 9:18 NIV

We all have times in when we feel alone, forgotten, or maybe even abandoned. Our earthly relationships will fail us in some manner and leave us with these feelings. The promise here, and in so many other spots in Scripture, is that God will never forget us. He doesn't leave, forget, or abandon us. What a promise!

When we find ourselves in these lonely positions, may they spur us on to call out to God. May they move us to seek comfort in him, discover his compassion toward us, and hide in the refuge he offers. When our human relationships fail, it can be an opportunity for us to discover these attributes and more about God. It can strengthen us and cause us to be closer to God. What we might see as a failed relationship, we can take as an opportunity to draw closer to the one who will never abandon us.

Does loneliness drive you into
the arms of your Savior or elsewhere?

He will not ignore forever all the needs of the poor,
for those in need shall not always be crushed.
Their hopes shall be fulfilled, for God sees it all!

PSALM 9:18 TPT

Loneliness plagues this generation that is supposed
to be more connected than ever before. With so many
opportunities for instant human interaction, why is
loneliness an issue? Our souls were made to be in union with
God. When we aren't in relationship with him, our human
connections can only sustain us so much. Our priorities are
out of line when we rely on those around us to cure us of the
deep loneliness in our souls.

It is not the job of your boyfriend, best friend, pastor,
roommate, husband, or anyone else to meet your need for
loneliness. That can only be met in Christ. When loneliness
arises in you, let it be the red flag that sends you running to
God. Don't try to fulfill those needs in other manners with
other things. Pay attention to your soul and find refuge in
God alone.

God, I need you. Be near me when I feel lonely. Help me to
know I am never alone.

All Seen

In hope we have been saved,
but hope that is seen is not hope;
for who hopes for what he already sees.

ROMANS 8:24, NASB

There are t-shirts out there that say, "I just don't feel like
adulting today." They comically express the feelings of those
who don't want to do grown-up things. Maybe someone
has said to you in protest, "But I don't feel like it!" This is
usually a child's response when you ask them to do something
responsible. As Christians, we also operate out of these
emotionally charged sentiments, and trusting solely in
feelings is a dangerous road.

Are you a Christian? Better yet, do you feel like a Christian?
Feelings can be tricky and fickle. One day you feel like
reading the Bible, another you don't. One day you feel saved,
the next you don't. It can be a tempestuous ocean, tossing you
about from one feeling to the next. But God is a solid rock,
and he is where your confidence and hope can live. He is
never changing, unlike your feelings. If your hope is in God,
he has declared you saved. Trust in the unshakeable truth of
God rather than your feelings.

How do your feelings deceive you about God?

We were saved in this hope,
but hope that is seen is not hope;
for why does one still hope for what he sees?

ROMANS 8:24, NKJV

We need to turn to Scripture if we want to know who God is.
Many of us base our view of God off our feelings and hearsay
from others. But if we are to truly know God, we must turn
to his Word. We don't trust in God because of how we feel.
We trust in God because he is trustworthy, because he is who
he says he is! This reliability makes it easy for us to have
confidence in our salvation.

If you are doubting your salvation, dive into finding out who
God is and how trustworthy he can be. Let it increase your faith
and your hope even though you cannot physically see him.

God, help me to trust in you, and not in my feelings. My hope
is in you! Thank you for salvation. I will hold tightly to your
Word and the promises it contains.

Great Acceptance

"The Spirit of the Lord is upon me, and he has anointed me to be hope for the poor, freedom for the brokenhearted, and new eyes for the blind, and to preach to prisoners, 'You are set free!' I have come to share the message of Jubilee, for the time of God's great acceptance has begun."

LUKE 4:18-19 TPT

These are the words of Jesus quoting the prophet Isaiah, speaking to us the best news we could ever hear. This is the gospel—the time of great acceptance is here. God is not willing that any man should perish, and so the time has come for us to proclaim the gospel to the ends of the earth: to bring hope where there is none, to bring freedom to those in bondage, to preach loudly the news that Jesus Christ died on the cross, rose again, has conquered death, and now offers us resurrection life and peace with God.

Just as Isaiah proclaimed in the Old Testament that it was coming, and Jesus in the New Testament that he brought it, he has asked us now to proclaim his good news to all.

You have the best news in the world.
Who will you share it with today?

*"The Lord has put his Spirit in me,
because he appointed me to tell the Good News to the poor.
He has sent me to tell the captives they are free
and to tell the blind that they can see again.
God sent me to free those who have been treated unfairly
and to announce the time when the Lord will show his kindness."*

LUKE 4:18-19 NCV

What does it mean to you to be accepted by God? In the Old
Testament, the Israelites were the nation chosen to display
to the world the goodness of their God. Because of what
happened with Adam and Eve in the garden, sin separated
mankind from God. God still moved amongst his people, and
his presence even resided in the temple for a while. He gave
them the law for right living and to show them their need for
a Savior. He desired to be in relationship with all mankind,
and he made Israel the missionary nation.

But then, at the appointed time, Jesus came. He made
everything right. He brought us back into right relationship
with God. He built the bridge between God and man. Now
God has asked us to be missionaries to the world. To share his
life-changing message that it is possible to dwell with him.
This acceptance by God is for anyone who believes in his Son.
Who is God asking you to share this with today?

God, thank you that you have accepted me and drawn me
near. Help me to share your great news with others.

He Is Powerful

"Let us praise the Lord, the God of Israel, because he has come to help his people and has given them freedom. He has given us a powerful Savior."

LUKE 1:68-69 NCV

This section of Scripture is the beginning of a prophecy by Zechariah, John the Baptist's father. Zechariah and his people had been waiting centuries for the promised Messiah. Those who loved God listened to the Scripture and tried to watch for the signs. Zechariah himself became a part of the fulfillment of prophecy by being the father of John, the one who prepared the way for Jesus.

From the beginning of time, God had a plan to bring redemption to mankind. He worked through many different people and periods, and in just the right time, Jesus came. Our God is an all-knowing, all-powerful God who is not unaware of even the smallest details of humanity. He appointed and saw the tiny baby John born to Zechariah, and he sees and cares about the tiniest details of your life. He is powerful enough to work big miracles and also move in small ways. Won't you praise him for this today?

How do you need to see God's power
at work in your life today?

> *"Praise the Lord, the God of Israel,*
> *because he has visited and redeemed his people.*
> *He has sent us a mighty Savior*
> *from the royal line of his servant David."*

LUKE 1:68-69 NLT

Have you ever been inclined to think that God is an angry old man, sitting up in heaven just waiting to send people to hell? Along life's road we often gain misconstrued ideas about who God is. We must turn to the truth of his Word and allow it to reshape our vision into rightly seeing God. In Luke, it says he came to his people. God humbled himself and took the form of a man to help his people.

Jesus become fully man so that you could be restored to right relationship with God. This simple verse tells a plain truth that everyone needs to hear: God has come to help us, to give us freedom. His goal is not to smite and destroy. He is not callously hanging out in heaven, enjoying our suffering. The God of Christianity is the only true god who enters right into our suffering and desires to give us freedom in him.

Jesus, thank you that you humbled yourself even to death on a cross, to bring me into freedom. Change my skewed views of you and give me right vision.

Never Give Up

One day Jesus told his disciples a story to show
that they should always pray and never give up.

LUKE 18:1 NLT

This phrase is given right before Jesus tells the parable of the persistent widow. But what does it mean to pray and never give up? We could change a couple of things about our prayer life. First, God needs to be our plan A. Often we come to him after we've tried to gain what we are asking for by our own means. Prayer cannot be our secondary source; it needs to be our first response. That is the first marker of persistence. Secondly, there seems to be a stigma about repetition when it comes to prayer and worship, but Jesus himself is asking people to repeat their prayers here.

To never give up means you bring your requests to the feet of Jesus over and over again. It's not annoying to God; it's exactly what he has asked from you.

What have you prayed for but given up on?
What do you need to pick back up and be persistent in?

*Jesus told his disciples a parable to show them
that they should always pray and not give up.*

LUKE 18:1 NIV

When you persist in prayer, it can't be guaranteed that you
will get what you prayed for. There is a guarantee though
that talking to him constantly and asking him tirelessly can
only lead to a deeper and more intimate relationship with
him. Isn't that the ultimate win? Though we do not have the
promise that our persistent prayers will for sure change
things, they will for sure change us. We might even notice
a shift in how we are praying, or a deeper longing for the
presence of our Savior more than whatever we are asking for.

Persistent prayer is a win for you, because it brings you closer
to Jesus. Don't give up when things don't go how you planned.
Keep praying, keep seeking, and know that God is faithful to
reward you.

God, I want you to be my plan A. Stir my heart toward you.
Help me to be persistent in prayer. Keep me in a place of
longing for fellowship with you. You are good and you are
faithful. I want to remember those attributes as I lay my
requests before you.

Don't Turn Away

O Lord; give ear to my pleas for mercy!
In your faithfulness answer me, in your righteousness!

PSALM 143:1 ESV

In this communication age, there are many different avenues for trying to get hold of someone. Text messages, phone calls, e-mail, social media, and good old-fashioned letter writing as well. Sometimes, the number of messages from all different spots can be overwhelming, and some are missed or forgotten. Another way to word this verse is to say that God is reliable with his answers.

When you talk to God, he is listening. He is responding. He might make you wait, but he hasn't let your prayer slip through the cracks. You can count on God to answer. He wants to answer your prayer and he will blow you away with his response. Miracles, healings, chains broken, freedom, there is nothing too big for God. What are you waiting for? Make known your requests to God today.

In what ways do you remember God's faithfulness
to your previous prayers?

Lord, you must hear my prayer,
for you are faithful to your promises.
Answer my cry, O righteous God!

<small>PSALM 143:1 TPT</small>

Have you ever poured out your heart to a friend, only to
realize they weren't actually listening? That can be a painful
thing to go through, and it causes you to lose trust in your
friendship, doesn't it? God will not turn away his ear from
you. He is always listening. Day or night, a long-winded spout
or a short-breathed whisper, he is listening.

You can trust God to care for you well. As you become more
like Christ, pray that he will help you be the kind of person
that listens well and doesn't turn away from those in need.
You can reflect his trustworthy character to others every day.

Jesus, thank you that you are listening. You are faithful to
hear me. You are powerful, willing, and able to move in my
situations. You care about the smallest details of my life. Help
me to become more like you and to be a friend who listens
well. Help me teach others about bringing their needs to you.

Comforting Words

The precepts of the LORD are right,
giving joy to the heart.
The commands of the LORD are radiant,
giving light to the eyes.

PSALM 19:8 NIV

Have you ever tried to find your way in a dark room? Especially in an unfamiliar home, the moving is slow and you are very likely to bump into something. Life can often feel like walking around in a dark room. The only true source of light to guide you is God's Word. The world's wisdom will promise you light but you will end up following shadows and mirages.

Only the Word of God has the rock-solid backing of being pure truth, given by our good Father who has a plan for your life. Stop turning to the wisdom of the world to guide you. Find truth and light to face all of life's decisions, crossroads, and worries in the Bible.

What area of your life feels like
you could use light in it right now?

His teachings make us joyful and radiate his light;
his precepts are so pure!
His commands, how they challenge us to keep close to his heart!
The revelation-light of his word makes my spirit shine radiant.

PSALM 19:8 TPT

True happiness is only found in the light. Jesus is the light; in him there is no darkness at all. Even the night is like day to him. The interesting thing is, in the Bible it says that Satan can masquerade as an angel of light. Take legalism, for example. A legalistic person thinks they are doing many good deeds and are pleasing to God, but their good deeds trying to work for their righteousness are really, filthy rags.

We can get so caught up in good deeds that we miss God altogether. The only way to know him is to continue to dive into his Word and see his character. The true light will shine into your life and illuminate any falsehood. And the best part is, God's Word will bring joy to your heart. This removal of darkness in your life will bring you true happiness.

God, thank you for the gift of your Word and its power. Help me to hide your Word in my heart, to know it more, and to find joy in all you say.

His Delight

The LORD your God is with you,
the Mighty warrior who saves.
He will take great delight in you;
in his love he will no longer rebuke you,
but will rejoice over you with singing.

ZEPHANIAH 3:17 NIV

Could you use a little encouragement this morning? Did you know that Jesus is rejoicing over you, and he takes great delight in you? He is just waiting to encourage you and love you in your moment of need. Oftentimes, we act like we are employees of God instead of his children. We do our duty for him, checking all the boxes, but we fail to realize that he delights in us!

God loves you immensely, and he is not looking for an employee to do all his heavy lifting. He sees you. If you need encouragement, turn to Jesus today. Pray for it. Meditate on the fact that he delights in you, and he is dancing over you.

Have you been working hard as God's employee
and not enjoying the delight of being his child?

The LORD your God is with you;
the mighty One will save you.
He will rejoice over you.
You will rest in his love;
he will sing and be joyful about you.

ZEPHANIAH 3:17 NCV

Does it make you feel needy if you want encouragement? If God is rejoicing over you, don't you know it's a song that you need to hear? He gets pretty specific in Scripture about his feelings for you, going to such great lengths as sending his Son to die on a cross so he could be reunited with you.

God is big enough to handle your needs of love and affirmation. He delights in meeting those needs, sometimes through his Word, sometimes through the voice of the Holy Spirit, sometimes through other people in our lives. God created you with a need to hear his voice and know his love, and he will meet that need. In the same way, don't be afraid to speak encouragement to others as well. God wants to use you to let others know that he delights in them—that he sees them. You get to share in the joy of spreading God's love! What a gift.

Jesus, thank you that you delight in me. I need to hear your song and feel your love. Will you meet me here with encouragement tonight?

Feet of Jesus

*Come, let us bow down in worship,
let us kneel before the LORD our Maker.*

PSALM 95:6 NIV

When you hear the term *worship*, you probably picture a more western setting of people standing in front of chairs or pews, facing a stage, singing along with the music. Perhaps some have their hands in the air, some have their eyes closed. When we read this passage in psalms, it might make you pause and wonder when is the last time, if ever, you bowed down to worship? The Hebrew word for *worship* literally means to bow down.

Sometimes your body will long to follow the positioning of your heart and you may have the urge to bow down. But you can also think of this in the broader sense of making it a life posture to bow before the Lord. A heart that is bowed down is humble and reverent. In fact, this heart posture is more important to God than any outer showmanship. Remember, God cares most about your internal, eternal being.

Search your heart today.
Do you live in a posture of humility before God?

Come and kneel before this Creator-God;
come and bow before the mighty God,
our majestic maker!

PSALM 95:6 TPT

To be reverent and kneel means to acknowledge that you
are lesser, and whatever you are bowing before is of utmost
importance. We must be careful not to bow our knees to
material things, relationships, status, or power. Those are
just a few of the idols that we exalt today.

When your knee is bowed only before God, you acknowledge
him as Creator and ruler of all. He is the king of your heart,
and your will is submitted to his. You trust that he knows
best. Are you this kind of person? If you are, you will find true
happiness serving your king.

Jesus, be the king of my heart! I kneel in humble submission
to you today. To you be all the glory and praise and honor.

Always Learning

Wise people can also listen and learn;
even they can find good advice in these words.

PROVERBS 1:5 NCV

One of the marks of a mature Christian is having a teachable spirit. What does it mean to be teachable? A teachable spirit always has a hunger for learning and growing. There is an air of humility and a willingness to be taught through demonstration and correction. You easily admit that you don't know it all while confidently holding onto good doctrine. Being unteachable means you will not learn from others. You bristle at confrontation and get angry when corrected. It's your way or the highway. You know you are right and everyone else should know that too.

It's obvious from these descriptions which kind of person pleases God. The question is, how teachable are you? Prayerfully consider your life this morning, your attitude toward others, and your willingness to hear correction.

Would you consider yourself teachable?

Let the wise listen and add to their learning,
and let the discerning get guidance.

PROVERBS 1:5 NIV

What do you do if you find yourself with an unteachable spirit? Good news! All is not lost for you. You can change and grow in wisdom. The problem at its root is pride. If you find yourself avoiding accountability in your life because you don't think anyone else knows better than you do, or you justify away your actions when confronted, that's pride. If you don't think you need God's Word for wisdom, and you spend hardly any time in it, that's pride.

A proud heart does not like rebuke, it does not receive correction from God or from the people God uses. But all hope is not lost. You can pray today and ask God to forgive you of your pride and make you teachable. You can confess that all that you have and know is a gift, and apart from God you have no good thing. Thankfulness is a great way to cultivate a heart of teachability, and a teachable heart is essential to a life of deep meaning and joy.

Jesus, make me teachable. Remove any pride that sits on the throne of my heart and take over instead! Make me sensitive to your conviction, open to your Word, and humble in confrontation. I want to be wise, mature, and open to your correction.

Great Expectation

All praise to God, the Father of our Lord Jesus Christ. It is by his great mercy that we have been born again, because God raised Jesus Christ from the dead. Now we live with great expectation.

1 PETER 1:3 NLT

Jesus is alive! This is not just something we stick on banners and sing about at Easter. Jesus being alive is a fact that should change our daily lives. Not only is Jesus alive, but if you are reading this sentence, so are you. You are alive and breathing on this created earth with a purpose. What's even better is that if you believe in Christ's resurrection and defeat of sin and death, you have life forever!

Having eternal life means you are more than just breathing. You have been given a true, abundant life in Christ right here, right now. You are living with hope inside you that cannot be tarnished, shaken, or taken away. Are you ready to have an abundant day?

Who do you need to share the wonderful news
about eternal, abundant life with today?

Praise be to the God and Father of our Lord Jesus Christ! In his great mercy he has given us new birth into a living hope through the resurrection of Jesus Christ from the dead.

1 PETER 1:3 NIV

This great expectation we have is also referred to as a living hope. What does that mean? It's not fleeting hope like, "I hope my team wins!" which is something that is uncertain but desired. No, we have a living hope which is certain. The Holy Spirit is our seal for salvation, the guarantee to the promise that nothing can separate us from the love of God.

Jesus has gone to prepare a place for you, and you will be in joyful union for eternity. This is the kind of hope that has the power to transform how you live. This promise is also too good to keep to yourself! Pray tonight for people to share this living hope, this great expectation, with.

Jesus, lead me to people who need your hope. Thank you for being my living hope! Thank you for your promises. I rejoice in your love.

Good Father

"Don't worry. For your Father cares deeply
about even the smallest detail of your life."

MATTHEW 10:30-31 TPT

Worry is a thief, and this generation is being robbed blind.
Do you realize what is being stolen from you? The smallest
moments as a whole make up your life. When you succumb
to worry, you lose your life. But you do not have to live in the
poverty of worry. You serve an all-powerful, all-knowing
God cares so deeply for those small moments. He wants to
tend to the moments that are being stolen by anxiety and
redeem them. He can change all those circumstances that are
haunting you.

Supplication is asking for something, and your Father has
asked you to ask! The action that your mind takes on worrying
can be flipped on its head and redeemed if you turn it into
prayers to the Father. And then, watch as God moves mightily
in your moments and your life is transformed by the power of
God, marked by the abundance that comes when you cast your
worries on God.

What is worry robbing you of?
How can you flip it on its head to become supplication?

"The very hairs on your head are all numbered. So don't be afraid; you are more valuable to God than a whole flock of sparrows."

MATTHEW 10:30-31 NLT

Have you ever wished for some extra help? Someone to carry some of the load: a maid or a cook perhaps? Maybe your longing is deeper than just physical help and you want someone to care about the things you care about. God is a good father.

What characteristics come to mind when you think of a good father? Jot some of them down. The Father cares for you, and he offers to carry your burdens, to share in your life, and to listen to you. Isn't he wonderful? When you feel like you are starting to unravel because of worry, remember the one who knit you together in the first place. Let him share in your life and find comfort in the care of a good father.

Father God, thank you for caring for me. Thank you for knitting me together. Free me from worry! I cast my cares on you.

More Mercy

Do not, O LORD, withhold your mercy from me;
let your steadfast love and your faithfulness
keep me safe forever.

PSALM 40:11 NRSV

There are many different ways to preserve foods. Most have to do with changing the temperature, such as freezing or boiling. Some you need to add vinegar or other liquids to when canning. The point is food doesn't just stay the same forever. Without techniques or special ingredients, your food goes rotten.

This sentiment here about being safe has the same feel as preserving something. Your life may seem rotten without the two things that preserve it: God's love and faithfulness. They are what keep you fresh and away from the deterioration of the world.

How have you seen God's faithfulness preserve you?

Lord, don't hold back your love or withhold
your tender mercies from me.
Keep me in your truth and let your compassion overflow to me
no matter what I face.

PSALM 40:11 TPT

There are three characteristics of God mentioned in this passage. His mercy, his love, and his faithfulness. The Lord does not hold back mercy; there is an abundance waiting for us to dive in. We can't let shame hold us back. His steadfast love refers to a covenantal love; God does not break his promises. He does not abandon or turn his back; he has promised his love toward you.

How have you seen his covenantal love played out in your life? It's important that we remember that we look back and articulate, to ourselves and others, how God has been faithful to us. It's very encouraging to your walk with Christ and others.

Jesus, thank you for your mercy, love, and faithfulness! Bring to my mind the great works of your hand in my life, that I may praise you and proclaim them to all.

Carried by Grace

In all their affliction He was afflicted,
And the angel of His presence saved them;
In His love and in His mercy He redeemed them,
And He lifted them and carried them all the days of old.

ISAIAH 63:9 NASB

There is a famous novel where the hero, stranded on a deserted island, sees the footprint of a man and rejoices greatly because he knows he is not alone. This is how it is for us as believers. In this world full of sin and heartache, we need the presence of another to encourage us.

We have the presence of the living God with us through it all to encourage us. What a gift that God doesn't just send an angel, but he himself promises to be with us through it all! The footprint of God is already on any path we are getting ready to tread. He has gone before us, and he has experienced all the temptations and suffering that we may face. Our guide is Christ. His way is gentle, and he will comfort you with his loving care and tender mercy.

How does Jesus being with you encourage you today?

When they suffered, he suffered also.
He sent his own angel to save them.
Because of his love and kindness, he saved them.
Since long ago he has picked them up and carried them.

ISAIAH 63:9 NCV

There is a famous poem about walking with Jesus that describes two sets of footprints on a beach. When only one set is to be found, that was the time that Jesus carried the person he was walking with. What a promise we have in Isaiah, and put into the words of that poem, that Jesus will carry us in his grace through the hard times.

If you are weary today, lean on him. If you don't feel like you can go on, let Jesus offer you grace and rest, and come into his arms. He is not bothered by your need; he welcomes you.

God, thank you that you are near. You carry me when I feel like I can't go on. You are not burdened by me. Your grace, love, and mercy never run out. Thank you that I am never alone.

In Perfect Faithfulness

L<small>ORD</small>, you are my God;
I will exalt you and praise your name,
for in perfect faithfulness you have done wonderful things,
things planned long ago.

I<small>SAIAH</small> 25:1 NIV

Imagine planning a surprise vacation for someone you love. Being that you are a person of the details, you plan it all out perfectly. You plan the meals and an adventure that they would delight in. You buy the tickets, make sure they have the perfect attire for the climate, and pack every minute with something they would enjoy. Every detail is covered. You have to wait, but finally the time comes for the trip. What a gift!

God has wonderful things planned for you. He's been in the details and had it all planned out for a long time. For you. Just like the vacation you planned for your friend, God has had you in his mind and has been delighting in the wonderful things that are to come for you. Do you see how special you are to him? Do you see how much he loves you? Rejoice in his goodness this morning.

Have you asked God what wonderful things
he has planned for you?

I will exalt you and praise your name forever,
for you have done so many wonderful things.
Well-thought-out plans you formed in ages past;
you've been faithful and true to fulfill them all!

ISAIAH 25:1 TPT

God did exactly what was expected of him—in perfect faithfulness. What did he do? Wonderful things! What are you expecting from God? Are you waiting for the other shoe to drop or for something bad to happen? If so, you are thinking wrongly of God.

He's not planning long-ago ways to punish and smite you or to hurt you. He's planning wonderful things like how to restore you to himself, how to make you more like Jesus, how to redeem your life, how to make things new, and how to bring healing! God is faithful to his goodness toward you. Believe it.

Jesus, change my thinking. You are good! You have wonderful things planned. Help me to trust in your thankfulness.

Kindness Given

The Lord GOD is like a sun and shield;
the LORD gives us kindness and honor.
He does not hold back anything good
from those whose lives are innocent.

PSALM 84:11 NCV

Have you ever read passages in the Bible like this one that contain promises that seem to have conditions? For instance, here it says, "He does not hold back anything good," and the condition seems to be "from those whose lives are innocent." This can lead us on the train of thought, *Well, is my life innocent? I guess not because I've sinned*. So is God holding back good things from you? How do you remedy this? On and on our train of thoughts go.

Here is the answer to quench all those questions and fulfill each of the conditions—in Christ. In Christ, you are innocent. In Christ, God sees you as completely whole. In Christ, he is not holding back any good thing from you. What a relief! You qualify for every promise of God simply because you are found in Christ. Rejoice in this fact today and latch onto the promises that are yours!

Which promise of God do you claim as yours in Christ today?

The Lord God is a sun and shield;
the Lord bestows favor and honor;
no good thing does he withhold
from those whose walk is blameless.

PSALM 84:11 NIV

Will you receive the kindness of God this evening? We can be our worst critics, our greatest enemies. God wants to meet you this evening with kindness. How can you accept it tonight? Maybe it looks like putting down your work and resting. Maybe it's taking a walk, asking for forgiveness, allowing room for you to take up space.

If God in his infinite wisdom can forgive you and show kindness, why would you pridefully refuse to give it to yourself? Let down your guard tonight and let God minister to your heart, drenching it in kindness and reviving your soul.

Jesus, thank you for your kindness. Thank you for not holding back any good thing from me. Help me to let down my guard and accept your kindness and love. Refresh my soul and revive me again. Thank you that in you all the promises of God are available to me.

He Calms My Soul

He awoke and rebuked the wind and said to the sea,
"Peace! Be still!" And the wind ceased,
and there was a great calm.

MARK 4:39 ESV

As you read this, you may be under the dark, threatening clouds of a storm. You may be feeling the wind tearing at you. You may also be mirroring the reaction of the disciples and asking, "Jesus, where are you!?" Take heart; he is near. Peace in your soul will not come from the absence of the storm, but from the presence of God. You may be wondering if he is asleep, but he is not.

The Bible says in 2 Corinthians 13:5 that Christ is alive in you. He is awake, he is alive. All you need to do is cry out for him. Wait and listen for his voice. Let him speak to the situation that threatens to overtake you right now. Let his presence calm your soul.

If you aren't experiencing a storm right now, can you think of a friend who could use this encouragement today?

*He got up, rebuked the wind and said to the waves,
"Quiet! Be still!" Then the wind died down
and it was completely calm.*

MARK 4:39 NIV

Storms aren't always the turbulent, intense scene that the
disciples experienced in the book of Mark. Sometimes
storms are just an unrelenting shower, soaking us through
and leaving us chilled to the bone. One isn't worse than the
other, but both create a need for the calm comfort of our
Savior. The drizzle may be less noticeable than the fury,
but it's an ache in our souls that we just can't shake, the
persistence of situations that doesn't seem to let up. Those
who grieved with us may have moved on and we can't seem to
join them.

Jesus is near to you in these moments. Christ is your peace.
There is nothing too small or too persistent that he is unable
to be the peace for. His peace does not run out. He will be by
your side through it all. Bring your heart before the warmth of
his presence and comfort this evening.

Father, in relentless drizzles and crazy storms, you are the
one who can calm my soul. Be near me tonight. I need you.

Truth that Remains

The very essence of your words is truth;
all your just regulations will stand forever.

PSALM 119:160 NLT

The postmodern mindset of our current world says there is
no truth. Some may stretch it farther to say there is truth,
but it cannot be known. Christians must hold to a completely
different worldview and say that there is truth, and it is the
Word of God. Why is it important to believe that the Bible is
truth, and it is inerrant? Because the Bible is a reflection of
God himself. In John 1, Jesus says he is the Word. If the Bible
was written by God, it must be perfect because God is perfect.
God cannot make mistakes; it goes against his character and
who he says he is.

The truth of God's Word will stand forever. You can build your
life upon the foundation of Christ as the Word because it is
unshakeable and eternal. God has given you the most solid
thing to stand upon. Aren't you thankful for this truth today?

How does the Bible being without error change your life?

The entirety of Your word is truth,
And every one of Your righteous judgments endures forever.

PSALM 119:160 NKJV

The Bible must be taken as a whole. We cannot try to become the judge of Scriptures by picking apart the text, holding fast to our favorite verses about love and peace and disregarding things we see as unnecessary or difficult. It is prideful to approach the Bible this way, as though we can judge the thoughts of God. It is good to remember that we are human, and God's ways are so much higher than ours. If the Bible is wrong on topics that we don't like, how can we trust that it is right on topics we do, like God's eternal love and faithfulness?

When you start to tear apart the Bible, it becomes a foundational trust issue. You don't trust the ground he has asked you to stand on, so you quickly find your own path. Walk in humility before God, holding his holy Word as the only ground on which you can stand. Present your heart before God declaring that you trust him. The Word became flesh, and you can live on the rock-solid truth of his Word.

God, thank you for your Word. Your Word is truth. Help me to build my life on the foundation of truth and trust you even when I don't understand what I read or it feels confusing to me. Give me wisdom and understanding.

Peace at Every Turn

The Messiah has come to preach this sweet message of peace to you, the ones who were distant, and to those who are near.

EPHESIANS 2:17 TPT

Driving down a road full of curves can be thrilling and also terrifying! Fear comes from not knowing what is around the next bend. When driving, it is a healthy fear that causes us to use caution and slow down. Life can also be like that curvy road; you just don't know what will happen on the next day, in the next moment. Past wreckage or surprises can cause you to want to not continue down the road at all, and fear of what's next can lead you to be controlling or overly cautious, unwilling to step out in faith.

If you struggle with these realities, what you need to do is get out of the driver's side. You are not meant to know the whole road. You aren't created with that capacity! Get out of the driver's seat and let Jesus, our infinite and loving Savior, take the wheel. He knows what's ahead of every bend and turn. When you let him be in control, you're in for an adventure, but one that comes with the assurance that you will never crash.

Is Jesus in control and at the wheel in your life today?

*He came and preached peace to you who were far away
and peace to those who were near.*

EPHESIANS 2:17 NIV

The message of peace in Christ is a truth that Christians need to latch onto. It's not a secret that we need to keep to ourselves. If you take a look at the headlines, or maybe even just your own neighborhood or work environment, you can see that this world needs a message of peace. It is hungry and starving on the rigid diet of unrest and discord that it feeds on every day.

You have the Holy Spirit living inside of you and the same message that the Messiah came to preach: peace on earth. It is a sweet, satisfying message, one that will heal the hunger of this world. Don't keep this truth to yourself. Everyone needs to hear this message that peace has come in the form of a man. Share the news today.

Jesus, thank you that you are peace to all. Take the wheel in my life; I give you control. Help me to preach the gospel of peace to those near and far.

Secret Strength

I know what it is to be in need, and I know what it is to have plenty. I have learned the secret of being content in any and every situation, whether well fed or hungry, whether living in plenty or in want. I can do all this through him who gives me strength.

PHILIPPIANS 4:12-13 NIV

Self-help book after self-help book promise you the secret to the life you've always wanted. They keep getting published. If you just pay a small fee, or use this product, or join our program, we promise it will change your life! You've heard it before. They can be rather alluring, don't you think? Who doesn't want to be in on a grand secret that can make life better? But none of those man-made methods will satisfy.

Paul writes the secret right here: a timeless truth that trumps them all. Do you want to know the secret to contentment? You find it in Christ. That's the secret. If you are abiding in Christ, you can live content in poverty and in wealth. You can live content through trials and in joyous moments. You can be satisfied in any circumstance because your rock and refuge are Christ. It's not a trick, not a gimmick, not a "but wait, there's more!" kind of ad. It's really this simple: abide in Christ and God will give you everything you need.

Do you tend to keep searching for another secret to life?

I know what it means to lack, and I know what it means to experience overwhelming abundance. For I'm trained in the secret of overcoming all things, whether in fullness or in hunger. And I find that the strength of Christ's explosive power infuses me to conquer every difficulty.

PHILIPPIANS 4:12-13 TPT

Sometimes we can become so familiar with a Scripture that we gloss right over it. This verse in Philippians is a prime example because it has been taken up as a banner in secular and church culture. You see it plastered all over coffee mugs, signs, football helmets, and sports displays. Does the Word of God grow old or lose power if we overuse it or see it taken out of context? The answer is no. God's Word does not fail. It does not grow old or become outdated; it endures forever.

If your instinct is to say, "Oh, I know this already. There's nothing new here!" Pray over the Scripture. Ask God to use it in your life. Meditate on it. Do a word study in the original Greek or Hebrew. God's Word doesn't get stale like old bread. He wants to use Scripture, even those you've heard a million times, in your life today. Be open to the Spirit giving you fresh life from this verse.

God, thank you for your Word that doesn't fade or grow old. Help me to abide in you, and let your Word be fresh manna to my soul.

Right Relationship

The kingdom of God is not eating and drinking,
but righteousness and peace and joy in the Holy Spirit.

ROMANS 14:17 NASB

This passage is a lot less about food and a lot more about good relationships. Paul is writing to the church that is having conflict over meat sacrificed to idols and observing certain festivals and holidays. They seemed to be very focused on what their brothers and sisters were doing or not doing more than they were focused on Christ! They weren't even necessarily intent on helping their fellow believers find freedom in Christ, but on judging them.

Jesus summed it up quite well: love God and love your neighbor as yourself. If you place petty things like food (or fill in the blank for your modern-day alternative) at the forefront of God's priorities, you are quite out of touch with what God really deems important. Your task at hand is to single-mindedly serve Christ. When you do this, that's the kingdom of God on earth. It's not your job to be the Holy Spirit for other believers. It is your job to be a conduit of peace, joy, and righteousness in the lives of those around you.

How can you better serve Christ by pursuing right relationship with those around you?

The Kingdom of God is not a matter of what we eat or drink,
but of living a life of goodness and peace and joy in the Holy Spirit.

ROMANS 14:17 NLT

There are so many verses in the Bible about how to live in
relationship with other people. It's pretty important to God.
We are his body, all of us together, and he cares deeply about
how we treat one another. He doesn't want us to live alone.
The body of Christ can be a beautiful thing when it doesn't
turn to worldly wisdom and judge each other but walks
according to God's kingdom and lifts one another up.

There are many reasons why some could be considered
weaker. Maybe they are new believers in Christ. Perhaps
encouragement is needed to exercise spiritual muscles.
There might be a lack of solid teaching or legalism that
causes sickness. Whatever the case, we are not to be like wild
animals, ready to devour the weak. We are led by the Holy
Spirit to prefer our brothers and sisters and serve them.

Jesus, your Word brings so much wisdom for how to live in
right relationship with others. Help me to prefer my brothers
and sisters in Christ—to encourage them and lift them up.

Filled with Kindness

The LORD is righteous in everything he does;
he is filled with kindness.

PSALM 145:17 NLT

Most have heard the glass half empty or glass half full analogy. Maybe you have even used it to describe yourself. A glass half full person is someone who is optimistic or hopeful. A glass half empty person might be viewed as cynical, pessimistic, or even prone to complaining. When you think of a glass that is full of water, it means that there is enough.

Do you ever find yourself grumbling against the Lord? Giving into a scarcity mindset that causes you to feel poor? The Lord is full of kindness. God is not holding out on you, bestowing favor on others and leaving the scraps for you. He isn't leaving your glass half full of his abundance. Circumstances may leave you feeling like his kindness has run dry; comparison to others can leave you feeling like it's been used up on everyone else. Neither is true! Truth says that God is full of kindness, and there is enough for you.

Do you see areas in your life that feel
like God is holding out on you?

You are fair and righteous in everything you do,
and your love is wrapped into all your works.

PSALM 145:17 TPT

In Galatians, there are nine fruits of the Spirit. One of those in the list is kindness. Do you ever find yourself with a shortage of kindness, wondering how you will be able to muster up one more day, or even one more moment, of being kind? Maybe your struggle is with a neighbor, co-worker, child, church member, or spouse. Perhaps kindness is even difficult to extend toward yourself.

Whatever the relationship may be, the fruit of the Spirit, like kindness, is not something you can muster up on your own. You can try it for a while, but why try harder when you have access to full kindness? Why keep trying to make a fire when you're standing next to an eternal flame? God is full of kindness, and it is his Holy Spirit that lives in you. Only as a Spirit-filled believer, whose life is submitted to Christ, can you find the kindness to face those difficult life relationships.

I praise you, God, for you are full of kindness toward me! As a believer, I am full of your Spirit and have access to the kindness I need to relate well to those around me. I submit myself to you, acknowledging the abundance of your kindness and asking you to empower me in kindness toward others.

Look No Further

Since we have been justified by faith,
we have peace with God through our Lord Jesus Christ.

ROMANS 5:1 ESV

This verse is good news that demands to be shared. You can hear the cries everywhere from people who are looking to find peace with God. It's a cry for help that we have the answer to. Our souls are made to be in union with God. When sin entered the world, we were separated from God, and the peace of walking with God was shattered. But when Jesus came, he built the bridge back to God. With his death and resurrection, he made a way for us to have peace with God again.

No longer is there separation; no longer is there a debt to be paid. We have reconciliation with God. This is the best news! If you're reading this and have been a believer for a while, you might be thinking it is old news. Pray for God to refresh the beauty of this message in your heart today. Pray for him to show you who you need to share it with because some people still don't know that what they've been looking for has already come.

How can God refresh this truth in your heart today?

Since we have been made right in God's sight by faith,
we have peace with God because of what Jesus Christ our Lord
has done for us.

ROMANS 5:1 NLT

Do you know what the term fire-and-brimstone preacher means? It's a harmful style of preaching that constantly tells people God is angry with them and waiting to smite them. Whole generations have grown up on this, maybe even you yourself.

God is not at war with you. "Peace with God" in the original Greek, is not a mistake. This word implies a movement— peace toward God. Imagine yourself able to move toward God as he welcomes you. Jesus made the way for God to welcome you home. He is not against you or at war with you. It is sin that separates us from our loving Father, and it's time to be welcomed home.

Jesus, thank you for welcoming me home! Thank you for drawing me near to you. Thank you for peace!

Unchanging One

Answer me, O LORD, for your steadfast love is good;
according to your abundant mercy, turn to me.

PSALM 69:16 NRSV

God never acts outside of his character. He is in perfect sync
with himself. The psalmist is petitioning God on behalf of
his character. He is acknowledging that God always keeps in
step with his nature. Abundant mercy, endless compassion?
That is who he is, and he never changes. Maybe you've heard
a reputation of God that seems otherwise. That God is up in
the sky, angry and ready to strike. That he is distant and aloof,
with no concern over what is happening on earth.

Make sure the things you are hearing about God, and the
reputations you believe align with Scripture. God's Word
doesn't change, he doesn't change, and who he says he
is in Scripture is who he is. That's how he acts. God is
compassionate toward you. He is overflowing with mercy
when you need it most. Turn to the unchanging one today and
ask him to alter your wrong perceptions of who he is.

Do you ever act out of incorrect perceptions of God
instead of trusting who he really is?

Oh, Lord God, answer my prayers!
I need to see your tender kindness, your grace,
your compassion, and your constant love.
Just let me see your face, and turn your heart toward me.
Come running quickly to your servant.
In this deep distress, come and answer my prayer.

PSALM 69:16 TPT

Have you ever been afraid to approach someone, unsure of how they will react? That fear is unnecessary and misplaced when it comes to God. Mercy and grace—that's how he will react. Let's approach God boldly and unedited, asking for the things we so desperately need.

There is no need to cower in the corner or find the right moment. You don't need to walk on eggshells like so many do when approaching earthly fathers. God the Father shows up with kindness in his eyes, mercy in his hands, and grace on his lips. Uninhibited prayer will open the wild, expansive view of the Father moving and working in your world. Stop holding back. What do you need to bring to him today?

God, help me to see you as you truly are. I come to you for unlimited mercy and compassion.

Covered by Covenant

*I know that you will welcome me into your house,
for I am covered by your covenant of mercy and love.
So I come to your sanctuary with deepest awe
to bow in worship and adore you.*

PSALM 5:7 TPT

God is on the move. He doesn't make promises or covenants and then not keep them. He doesn't promise you that life will be all unicorns, rainbows, and gold-covered walkways. He convicts us of the areas we need to work on. He gives his commandments to follow, like loving him and our neighbors. He also makes big promises, like sending Jesus to die on the cross to save us from our sins. We can count on him to keep his promises.

Just as the psalmist writes, God has promised to welcome into his house all those who believe in him. That's what is meant by the promise of mercy and love. God made a promise to you, one full of mercy, one deep in love. That promise is for you to dwell in his house with him forever. No wonder the psalmist came with awe and adoration! Let your approach be the same.

Do you know that God keeps his promises?

I, by your great love,
can come into your house;
in reverence I bow down
toward your holy temple.

PSALM 5:7 NIV

Like a VIP to a most exclusive party, Jesus has you covered for entrance into his Father's house. In Christ, you are clothed in mercy and love. God no longer sees you dressed in your filthy rags of sin, but you have put on the new, perfect garment of Christ.

You are white and pure, wearing the righteousness of Christ. You have full access to the Father, and your Father has full access to everything you need. Won't you approach him tonight and ask? Come into his sanctuary and worship. Feel the beauty of his presence, the warmth of his love, and know that you are cherished by him.

Jesus, I adore you. Thank you for making a way for me to come into the presence of God. I worship you. I stand in awe of you. Your mercy is so deep. Thank you for it. Your love covers me. My heart overflows with gratitude and worship toward you tonight.

Priceless Treasure

How priceless is your unfailing love, O God!
People take refuge in the shadow of your wings.
They feast on the abundance of your house;
you give them drink from your river of delights.
For with you is the fountain of life;
in your light we see light.

PSALM 36:7-9 NIV

What do you own that is priceless? This means irreplaceable, of great value. Another way to say it is if you had to evacuate your home quickly, what would you take? What would you grab in a fire? This is a small test to show you what material possessions you consider priceless. Family photos, heirlooms, important documents often top people's lists. The word *priceless* used in the psalms holds a similar concept. It is something worth giving everything for—it's irreplaceable. The subject is not a material good though; it's the unfailing love of God.

Try as you might, with idols and other pursuits, to fill the void in your life, there is nothing that replaces the need you have for God's love in your life. You are empty without his love. The best news is you don't have to earn his love. It's a free gift. The most priceless, valuable thing in all the universe is a free gift for you. How amazing!

God's love is free with no strings attached.
What does that knowledge stir up in your soul?

How precious is your unfailing love, O God!
All humanity finds shelter
in the shadow of your wings.
You feed them from the abundance of your own house,
letting them drink from your river of delights.
For you are the fountain of life,
the light by which we see.

PSALM 36:7-9 NLT

We like to put valuable things on display when we feel like we have the right amount of security for them. In museums lie all sorts of valuable artifacts that are protected by security guards, alarms, and cameras. We want to share the wonder of a Monet or the beauty of a sculpture by Michelangelo. You may hear some say that the beauty of these pieces deserve to be seen and known by the world.

With the priceless gift of God's love, it's too good to keep locked away. The world needs to see it. The world will be changed by seeing the love of God displayed through his disciples. The world longs to get its hands on such a priceless treasure. Don't hide his love anymore. Put God's love on display in your life.

God, your love is extravagant and priceless. Thank you for it! Help me to show it to the world.

Everything Is Covered

They shall neither hunger nor thirst,
Neither heat nor sun shall strike them;
For He who has mercy on them will lead them,
Even by the springs of water He will guide them.

ISAIAH 49:10 NKJV

If there is one thing we all know we can't control, it's the weather. We work hard to try to predict it, but sometimes it just rains on your wedding day, or it's perfectly sunny when you have to work inside all day. You can't control the weather, but you know who can? God. So, what's the point? Do we start praying for God to hold off on the storms so we can go swimming? Though you most certainly can pray for those things, the point is that we serve a very powerful, very in-control God. There is nothing happening on earth that is outside his scope of vision, beyond his reach of intervention.

The same God that has storehouses of snow and names every star is the God who is working in your life. Next time you're feeling like your situation is utterly impossible, take a step outside and observe the weather. Consider what you could do to change it. Then, remember the fact that your loving Father is the one in control of it all. He's got the weather, and he's got you.

What comfort do you receive from knowing
that God is mighty and in control?

They will never be hungry or thirsty.
Neither scorching sun nor desert wind will hurt them,
for he, the Loving One, will guide them
and lead them to restful, renewing streams of water.

ISAIAH 49:10 TPT

You can choose two paths: your way or God's way. When walking through hard times, these options are in front of you. God has the bird's eye view; he knows the best path, he knows what is coming, he knows when you will need relief and where you can find it. He's an excellent guide. Trusting in your own plans seems unwise next to this knowledge, doesn't it? Don't you want a sure guide?

Some of the most relaxing vacations are packages that are called all-inclusive. This means you go to a spot, pay one price, and everything is covered. It's relaxing because you don't have to take care of all the details or worry about the stress of careful spending. In the same way, you can entrust your life to the all-inclusive God. He's the perfect guide and he has taken care of all the details. You just have to trust him.

God, I give you my life. I entrust it to you. Be my perfect guide.

Refreshed

He saved us, not on the basis of deeds which we have done in
righteousness, but according to His mercy, by the washing of
regeneration and renewing by the Holy Spirit.

TITUS 3:5 NASB

It's hard to keep your white clothes and sheets white, isn't
it? Don't worry, this is not the beginning of an attempt to
sell you laundry detergent. It's just a relatable fact most of
us know. You can buy the whites brand new, and they are
lovely, fresh, and clean. Over time, it's hard to keep them
that way. Similarly, our righteousness is referred to as dirty
rags elsewhere in Scripture. Titus writes here that it's not by
those dirty rags that we are saved; that would never work. It's
according to the mercy of God that we become washed and
renewed. We are washed of any past sins we have committed.
That's the washing. And we are given a new life by the Spirit.

You are washed and you are new. You no longer wear filthy
rags. You have fresh, white linens handed to you by Christ.

What excites you most about having
a new life by the Holy Spirit?

He saved us, not because of the righteous things we had done,
but because of his mercy. He washed away our sins,
giving us a new birth and new life through the Holy Spirit.

TITUS 3:5 NLT

We do not in any way deserve to be born again. Like we said
this morning, all we have to offer is filthy rags. That's our own
righteousness; imagine what our sin life must look like! We
don't deserve it, but what does Titus say moves God to give
it to us? His mercy. In his passionate expression of love and
forgiveness on the cross, God through Jesus showed us mercy
when we deserved none. His love is loyal, meaning he did not
abandon us or jump ship when we chose sin. Instead he put
into motion a plan to restore us to him.

God is going to renew and restore all of creation. Creation
waits in great anticipation for that day. He has started the
process with us now because he is so merciful toward us.
As you become more like Christ, thank him for his mercy to
hand you a new life.

Jesus, thank you for my new life! Thank you for washing me
and renewing me. You are so kind!

Watched Over

The Lord keeps you from all harm and watches over your life.
The Lord keeps watch over you as you come and go,
both now and forever.

PSALM 121:7-8 NLT

On Memorial Day weekend, most local swim places open for the summer. The pools hire their lifeguards to watch over the waters. These lifeguards will sit up and keep their eyes always on the water and the swimmers. It's important that they do because from where they sit, they can see danger better than the swimmers down below.

In the same way, God is watching you. He's not keeping his eyes trained on you because he's waiting for you to slip up. He's not watching you because he is writing down all your mistakes to critique you later. No, God is your loving Father, keeping his eye on you to protect you much like the lifeguard. He has the bird's eye view of your life and doesn't want harm to come to you. God is watching out for you because he loves you.

What reassurance do you get from the fact that God is looking out for you?

He will keep you from every form of evil or calamity
as he continually watches over you.
You will be guarded by God himself.
You will be safe when you leave your home
and safely you will return.
He will protect you now,
and he'll protect you forevermore!

PSALM 121:7-8 TPT

If God is always watching over us, this can clue us in to another encouraging thought: God cares about the little details of our lives, and he's there for them. When we are washing dishes, God can meet us there. When we are driving a 30-minute commute, he will meet us there. Just as much as he is with us and near us in dangerous situations, he is right there with us in the mundane as well.

As much as we need God at our lowest spots, we also celebrate him at our highest. He is present for the sweatpants and t-shirts kind of days as well. Our constant companion, our faithful friend, God cares for our whole lives. Won't you praise him in your face cream and pajamas and tonight?

God, I am so thankful that you watch over me all the time. Thank you for caring for me and being near to me.

I Look to You

To you I lift up my eyes,
O you who are enthroned in the heavens!

PSALM 123:1 NRSV

Who are you looking to in life for care? For support? For guidance? We all look somewhere for our needs to be met. We might rely only on ourselves for everything. We may look to our friends to support us emotionally. We could look to a boss, pastor, coach, or parent and rely on them to guide us in life. We all turn our eyes somewhere; the question is where?

Turn your eyes only to God. He is the source of everything you need. Yes, he will use your friends and leaders in your life. But your first turn must be upwards. You must lift your eyes to God first and foremost. Before you scroll through your phone or lower your eyes to your to-do list, lift your eyes to God and meet his gaze.

Do you turn your eyes upward every day?

Unto You I lift up my eyes,
O You who dwell in the heavens.

PSALM 123:1 NKJV

If you lift your eyes to God, you will find him looking at you. God says that those who seek him will find him. The key is who is doing the searching. This is not like a massive game of hide and seek. You need to be seeking, but God is not hiding. He is waiting to lock his gaze with yours.

In this intimate moment with your Savior, you will find exactly what you need for the day ahead. Why turn to other sources for help and direction when you have Jesus waiting for you? The King of the universe wants to meet with you. Don't turn away from him. Listen to what he has to say. Lift your eyes and stay right here awhile.

Jesus, I lift my eyes to you. King of the universe, I seek you.

Focused Attention

We don't focus our attention on what is seen
but on what is unseen. For what is seen is temporary,
but the unseen realm is eternal.

2 CORINTHIANS 4:18 TPT

We talked yesterday about focus—about how we need to lift our eyes to Christ. Today, the theme continues showing us what to turn our attention to. In life, there will be many things that cry out for our attention. Some of them are valid physical things that need to be done, like laundry and dishes. Sometimes, it will be TV or social media, which could be qualified as more of a distraction from what matters. We should be kingdom minded. There is no set list of what is temporary and what is eternal; throwing laundry only in the temporary category and prayer in the eternal doesn't always work.

Specific categories will be different for everyone, but the heart of the question is the same: what is going to last? Investing in human relationships and in your relationship with God will last. Building earthly wealth and success? That's temporary. It takes discernment to start living your life for what is eternal over what is temporary. Ask God to grant you discernment this morning as you make decisions for your day.

Can you think of some examples of choosing
the temporary over the eternal?

We don't look at the troubles we can see now; rather, we fix our gaze on things that cannot be seen. For the things we see now will soon be gone, but the things we cannot see will last forever.

2 Corinthians 4:18 NLT

Another thing that is temporary is trials and hardships. God promises that they will not last forever. He promises to see you through them. Sometimes they can feel like walking through an unfamiliar dark room. You can't see anything and you keep bumping into things! In these times, God grabs you by the hand and leads you.

When your attention has shifted from peering into the darkness and trying to discern things for yourself to holding tight to the one who can see, you will do much better. Your attention should be focused on God and the future glory. That is eternal, unfading, and never changing. Let go of focusing so intently on your current circumstances and focus your eyes on Christ.

Jesus, help me to focus on you. I want to meet all the God-appointed moments you have for me—the eternal ones that will last. Help me to have discernment to see.

Keep Going

*I have fought the good fight,
I have finished the race,
I have kept the faith.*

2 TIMOTHY 4:7 NCV

Do you admire people who are really into running? Maybe you are an avid runner. There is a lot to be learned from the sport of running that can be used as a metaphor for the Christian life. Here, Paul is likening our Christian life to a race, not because we are competing against one another, but because to run a long race it takes endurance.

Endurance is an important character trait that you grow in as you allow the Holy Spirit to do his sanctifying work in you. There is a shift in your life when you realize that being a Christian is not just a prayer you pray, but a lifetime race that requires you to keep pace with the Holy Spirit. He's not a crazy task master though; he's the perfect coach, gently working with you to become more like Christ.

Do you think endurance is a trait you possess
or need more of?

I have fought an excellent fight.
I have finished my full course
and I've kept my heart full of faith.

2 TIMOTHY 4:7 TPT

When a person first starts running, it's a common mistake to just take off as fast as you can. But you must learn, when training for marathon running, to find a pace. That is why you will often see playlists that have "bpm" next to them (beats per minute). The bpm helps the runner to align their pace with the music so they can achieve their goal.

In the same fashion, we need to find the rhythm of the Holy Spirit in life and keep pace with him. Trying to race ahead and hustle your way through life will leave you weary. On the other hand, if you are lagging behind, complacent in your journey, you may need to pick up the speed a bit. Pray and ask the Holy Spirit to align your pace with his today.

Holy Spirit, thank you for being my guide in life. Align my pace with yours. Help me keep in step with your rhythm as I run the race in front of me.

Choose Kindness

*Be kind to each other, tenderhearted, forgiving one another,
just as God through Christ has forgiven you.*

EPHESIANS 4:32 NLT

Kindness is a new buzzword. But what does it really mean? A person who is kind is full of empathy. They show consideration for others and are quick to be moved with compassion. Jesus was kind; God the Father is kind. The interesting thing about kindness is that it's not about us. To be kind involves being in a relationship with other people. Then, most of the actions related to being kind are dealing with how you treat others, and your level of concern for their circumstance.

Elsewhere in Scripture, it says that people will know that we are disciples of Jesus by our love for one another. A good indicator of love is kindness. Do you treat others with kindness? Do you give only to expect back in return? Are you humble, seeking to serve those around you? This is the way of Christ, and it should be your way as well.

How can you show kindness today?

Be kind and loving to each other,
and forgive each other just as God forgave you in Christ.

EPHESIANS 4:32 NCV

We are often taught by the world that in order to live a happy life, we need to look out for number one—ourselves. We need to take care of ourselves, gain more possessions for ourselves, and protect ourselves from others. But in God's kingdom, it's the opposite. He asks us to look out for the needs of others because he has looked out for our needs. He asks us to serve in kindness, because he has served us that way.

Jesus modeled what it looks like to be kind and tenderhearted toward others. He met people in their brokenness and loved and served them. We are not above our servant Savior and must learn to humble ourselves to show others the love of Christ. In order to live a happy life, do it God's way. Serve others. Love deeply. Be kind. Forgive your enemies and those who hurt you. That's the road to happiness.

Jesus, teach me to be kind and to love like you. Thank you for your example.

A Better Way

The word of the LORD is upright,
and all his work is done in faithfulness.

PSALM 33:4 ESV

We are told to follow our truth. Prominent leaders encourage people in the ideology of self-truth; if it works for you, it's true. This is a false hope that is leading many people astray. The Word of God is our source of truth. It should be the final say in how we view the world. It affects all aspects of our lives: the choices we make, our reactions, our relationships. If we base all of these things on the Bible, we have a steady footing for life. If we define truth as whatever feels good or works best for us in the moment, our ship is sure to sink.

Living your life in the freedom God gives is the best way to live, but it's also the most unpopular way. You can count on God to lead you rightly, and that the work he does in your life is for the best outcome of eternal glory with him.

Do you live your life based on what God says,
or on what you feel?

God's Word is something to sing about!
He is true to his promises, his word can be trusted,
and everything he does is reliable and right.

PSALM 33:4 TPT

Everything God does will be consistent with his character. Never will there be a forgotten moment, a slip-up, a person whose life slips through the cracks. When we say that God is faithful it means that he is who he says he is; he is loyal. People will inevitably let us down and disappoint us because no one is perfect. But God is. Perfectly trustworthy, perfectly loyal, perfectly aligned with himself to never go against who he says he is in his Word.

Are your views of God based on what others have said to you, or do you dig into his faithful Word for the truth? If there is an area you are struggling with regarding your view of his character, try looking up verses today that tell you who he truly is.

God, you are faithful and true; your Word is a firm foundation. Thank you for giving me your Word. Help me to know you better by finding your true character in your holy Scriptures.

God's Goodness

Do you despise the riches of His goodness, forbearance, and longsuffering, not knowing that the kindness of God leads you to repentance?

ROMANS 2:4 NKJV

We are more prone to use punishment, threats, and nagging as a way to get people to change. Kids, spouses, employees, it's just the way things have been done. This is obvious by how we view God as well. Do we see his desire for us to turn from our sins out of fear that he will punish us, the Bible as a nagging list of rules, or only hear verses about conviction as threats? God's kingdom is the upside-down kingdom, and he has a whole different way of doing things. He is a good God and uses his kindness to lead us to repentance. But just because he is a kind God doesn't mean he is a pushover. His kindness is like the firm hand of a father, grabbing our hands and leading us away from death and toward life.

Why is repentance such a great thing? When the Father shows us the things we are doing that will lead to death, repentance means we turn away from those things and turn toward life. He is kind to forgive us, to accept us every time we ask for forgiveness. What a good God we serve!

Do you notice God's kindness most,
or do you notice nagging, anger, and threats?

Don't you see how wonderfully kind, tolerant, and patient God is with you? Does this mean nothing to you? Can't you see that his kindness is intended to turn you from your sin?

ROMANS 2:4 NLT

When we are confronted with God's kindness, it changes our lives. We realize that we can do nothing to save ourselves. It is his pure kindness and goodness that leads us to repentance, and his mercy that saves us. We should be in awe of this grace, this free gift that we don't deserve. It should be humbling to be the recipient of this gift.

When all these realizations crash into you, change follows. You want to change because you see how good he is. How much better his ways are. How truly amazing his grace is. God empowers you to become more like him, and the sanctification process continues. Feel the sorrow of repentance but also the joy at a Savior who loves you so deeply.

God, thank you for your kindness. Thank you that you lead me in higher ways; show me what I need to repent of.

In Not Of

"My prayer is not that you take them out of the world, but that you protect them from the evil one. They are not of this world, even as I am not of it. Sanctify them by your truth; your word is truth. As you sent me into the world, I have sent them into the world."

JOHN 17:15-18 NIV

If you've grown up in Christian circles, you've probably heard the phrase of not being of the world. In Christian culture we work very hard to train our kids to reject everything that has to do with the world. It seems that either we work very hard to remove ourselves from the world, and reject it completely, or we dive in, ignoring the warnings in the Bible about participating in sinful things. Is there a happy medium?

Should you be hiding your love of music or current events or things that could be considered "worldly"? God did tell us to not be of the world, but he didn't want us so removed that we never come close to someone who needs Jesus. He sent you to the place that you are to reach those around you and gave you specific interests for a reason.

How can you use what you are interested in to bring glory to God?

"I'm not asking you to take them out of the world, but to keep them safe from the evil one. They do not belong to this world any more than I do. Make them holy by your truth; teach them your word, which is truth. Just as you sent me into the world, I am sending them into the world."

JOHN 17:15-18 NLT

Jesus didn't want us to be taken out of the world or to end up in hiding. He wanted us to be protected from the evil one and sanctified in truth. We cannot live hiding away from evil.

If you don't know one person who doesn't know Christ, maybe it's time to come out of hiding. God has given you a mission of spreading the gospel. He has placed you in this particular spot and place in history for a reason. He has given you gifts and talents to encourage the body of Christ and to lead others to him. What are you doing with this? Hiding away, attempting to be holy? Or are you allowing God to sanctify you while you tell as many people about him as you can?

God, thank you that you put me here. Show me who you want me to reach out to with your love!

Strength for Today

"Be strong and courageous. Do not be afraid or terrified because of them, for the LORD your God goes with you; he will never leave you nor forsake you."

DEUTERONOMY 31:6 NIV

Be strong and courageous. This phrase can be found over and over again in the stretch between Deuteronomy and Judges. It is a time in the Bible when the Israelites were finally approaching the land that had been promised to them. Are you in a spot where you are approaching something that has been promised to you? A dream that you have persevered in for years? Maybe at the end of this stretch of endurance you are feeling weak and run down. This whole way God has been with you; you can think back and remember his faithfulness.

Keep going! He is so near to you, ready to give you strength for this moment. No matter how insurmountable the trials in front of you look, God has not brought you this far to abandon you. He also has not set you up for failure. He will give you exactly what you need; just keep moving forward in faith.

What has been promised to you that you are persevering in?

"Be strong and brave. Don't be afraid of them and don't be frightened, because the LORD your God will go with you. He will not leave you or forget you."

DEUTERONOMY 31:6 NCV

What does it mean in the most practical of terms to find strength in the Lord? Sometimes we can read or hear these verses, or commonly quoted phrases, but then there will be a gap between the phrase and its real-life fleshing out. To walk in the strength of the Lord, practically speaking, means to acknowledge to God that your strength is insufficient. Ask him for help in what you are facing, persevering in that dream or just facing the mundane daily tasks.

Actively expect God to give you help as you go through your day. The help will not empower you to do things against his will, but he will empower you to live according to his kingdom's ways. You also have to take action to see that strength worked out. Praise him for his strength. Write down or acknowledge all the ways you have seen God move on your journey so you can remember.

God, fill me up with your strength. Help me to persevere in the things you have put on my heart to do. Let it be obvious in my life that I would have never succeeded but for your strength. Thank you for never leaving me.

Alive in Christ

God, being rich in mercy, because of His great love with which He loved us, even when we were dead in our transgressions, made us alive together with Christ (by grace you have been saved).

EPHESIANS 2:4-5 NASB

A life separated from God is no life at all. Do you believe that? God did not ask his Son to die on the cross, take the full weight of humanity's sin, conquer death, and rise again so we could live a life of endless rules and religion. Yet so often, that's what people think! No, our good God went to those great lengths so we could live free and alive in him. There is no limit to the joy, goodness, safety, connection, and love for a Christian.

After becoming Christians, we often let all that fade into the background as we continue to try and fulfill the law or do good deeds to earn our salvation. We measure our quiet times in minutes, we feel guilty about lack of prayer, we dutifully go to church, and on the outside our lives look quite good. But striving for our lives in Christ and checking off religious boxes is futile work. Rest in the sacrifice he already made, and you will find bountiful life in him.

Do you feel trapped in religious duty today?

God still loved us with such great love. He is so rich in compassion and mercy. Even when we were dead and doomed in our many sins, he united us into the very life of Christ and saved us by his wonderful grace!

EPHESIANS 2:4–5 TPT

You may be wondering how you can be dead to sin if you still sin every day. Becoming a believer in Jesus does not mean you will never sin again. It means the process called sanctification is at work in you. Sanctification is the lifelong process in a believer of becoming more like Christ. When you first become a Christian, you're justified. This means that God now views you as not guilty of your sins through the lens of Jesus and his work on the cross. Jesus is perfect, and the Father sees you in Jesus, thereby looking at you as perfect as well.

The more you let go and submit to the Holy Spirit, the more alive in Christ you become. Dying to sin is a daily occurrence. You allow the Holy Spirit to work in and change your life. So, don't be discouraged if you find yourself feeling like sin is still alive and kicking. Continue to submit to the Holy Spirit, trust in his promises, and remember his faithfulness to redeem you.

God, thank you for your abundant mercy! Thank you for your great love and power to save. Free me from any legalistic pursuits I may be trapped in and help me to become more alive in you.

Tender Mercy

His unforgettable works of surpassing wonder
reveal his grace and tender mercy.

PSALM 111:4 TPT

A memorial is a specific place that helps us remember a person or event. Sometimes there is a statue, other times it's art or a building that is named after someone. God's works throughout the world are memorials to his grace and his mercy. The Bible is full of them, but it doesn't contain all of them. God continues to work throughout history, displaying mercy and bestowing grace on us. There are many who have gone before us whose lives inspire us to remember God's mighty works.

Every person's life is like a message. What is yours communicating about God? Let us be children of God whose lives are beacons of God's grace. When people hear our stories, may they know that the Lord is merciful toward those who call on him. Your life can cause remembrance of the goodness of God in others. Won't you share with someone today how he has worked in your life?

What is a story of God's grace or mercy
that you could share with the world?

He has caused his wonders to be remembered;
the LORD is gracious and compassionate.

PSALM 111:4 NIV

You can tell a lot about an artist's life from their work. It is said that art comes from a person's soul, so it is difficult to create things that are not a reflection of where you are as a person or who you are. Some artists may have very difficult lives, and you can see it in their paintings. Others might have met great joy at one point, and you can hear it in the symphony they wrote shortly after. Perhaps it is even as simple as an author spending more time in nature than most, so their poetry pulls from that experience.

God's works mentioned here, the ones of great wonder, reveal his character, his history to us. What's on display is grace; what's noticeable is mercy. What a God we serve, he is unlike any other.

God, I praise you for the mercy and grace you have shown me in my life. Help me to share it with others.

What Matters Most

Three things will last forever—
faith, hope, and love—
and the greatest of these is love.

1 CORINTHIANS 13:13 NLT

It's been commonly said when people get to the end of their lives they don't wish they had spent more time at work, pursuing money or success. The number one regret is time not spent in relationship. Of all the things we dedicate our lives to, may it be said that we were those who pursued the eternal treasures of faith, hope, and love.

Faith in Christ is the foundation that brings you into eternal life. Hope is fuel that reminds you to keep eternity in focus. And love is your greatest calling, spending a life loving God and doing the sanctifying work of loving your neighbors. Perhaps you have a hard time seeing significance in your day-to-day life. A life spent dedicated to the love of God and learning how to love those around you is a life full of eternal treasure.

How does this verse change what you prioritize in life?

These three remain: faith, hope and love.
But the greatest of these is love.

1 CORINTHIANS 13:13 NIV

Spending the day dwelling on this verse and the question presented above hopefully made you think about your priorities. It's unbelievably easy to get side-tracked and caught up in worldly pursuits. Sometimes it's not even the blatantly sinful things that derail us, but things we see as good.

Even good things distract us from faith, hope, and love. We can get caught up in our to-do lists and not take the time to love our neighbor. We can look to a political party or leader for hope instead of Christ. We can get our faith wrapped up in trying to name and claim good things for ourselves and muster up faith instead of laying it at the foot of the cross. The key to our pursuits is that they are centered on eternal values and on Christ.

Jesus, show me what areas of my life I'm not submitting to you. Show me how I may have gotten sidetracked by worldly things or even good things. Be at the center of my life and pursuits once again.

Coming Back Home

Let the wicked forsake their way,
and the unrighteous their thoughts;
let them return to the LORD, that he may have mercy on them,
and to our God, for he will abundantly pardon.

ISAIAH 55:7 NRSV

Have you ever watched videos of homecoming soldiers? All over the internet there are heartwarming videos of soldiers being reunited with their loved ones. The most emotional ones are the total surprise versions, where the people are not expecting their soldier to be home yet. Bottle up all that love and emotion, and it wouldn't be even a drop in the overflowing rejoicing that happens when we come home to our heavenly Father. We aren't talking death coming home, but the time when we turn from evil and run toward Christ.

When you come to faith, you come to the most warm, loving, safe home you could imagine. Shame hopes to block our homecoming, to cripple us into thinking we are unforgivable and keeping us in darkness. But the mercy of God has no limit. He is the willing Father waiting in anticipation. Let's get our homecoming party started today and find joy in his mercy!

Are there parts of your life where shame
is crippling you from receiving mercy?

The wicked need to abandon their ways,
and sinful ones need to banish every evil thought.
Let them return to Yahweh,
and they will experience his compassionate mercy.
Yes, let them return to God,
for he will lavish forgiveness upon them.

ISAIAH 55:7 TPT

When we humble ourselves and come to Jesus for forgiveness, he looks us in the eyes and tells us we are forgiven, to go in peace. And that is the final word. Shame for sin is rightly placed at the foot of the cross. When we walk away, we might be tempted to listen to lies, "You don't deserve forgiveness!" "You'll never change!" "God remembers how awful you've been." "You need to do more work before you can really be forgiven." Couldn't we all write down a list of lies? But that is exactly what they are—lies.

Isaiah tells us God loves to pardon abundantly. This is an overflowing, never-ending, no-strings-attached kind of mercy. Don't confuse shame that brings you to repentance with ongoing shame that separates you from his mercy.

Jesus, thank you that you abundantly pardon! You are rich in mercy and you freely give it when I ask. Protect me from the wrong kind of shame, the kind that tries to make me earn my salvation or tells me I can't be with you. I return to you; thank you for your mercy.

Holy Help

The LORD will fight for you,
and you shall hold your peace.

EXODUS 14:14 NKJV

"Hell hath no fury like a woman scorned." Has this phrase ever been used to describe you, or perhaps when you read it you nod your head in solidarity? If so, our verse here in Exodus should give you pause for reconsideration. Who does it say is going to fight our battles? The Lord. He, unlike us, is perfectly merciful and perfectly just. He, unlike us, can be angry and not sin. The foundations of his throne are both righteousness and justice.

God has the capability to unconditionally love both you and the one your fury may be aimed toward. When the instinct rises up to destroy your enemies, to scorn, to seek revenge, turn instead to your perfect, just Father. Lay your grievances before him and let him fight your battles.

Is there a battle you are fighting right now that you instead need to be still and let God fight for you?

The LORD will fight for you;
you need only to be still.

EXODUS 14:14, NIV

When reading the second half of this verse, close your eyes
and picture yourself holding a gift, completely at peace. Be
sure to picture this peace not attached to the settings around
you, but just you and the gift. This is your status in Christ:
perfect peace. Now picture yourself in different settings,
maybe a metaphorical storm or a place that always brings you
unrest. Does your stance change? Do you become anxious?
Have you lost the gift? What is snatching your peace?

Peace is a gift that is not based on circumstances; it's based
on your confidence in Christ. Identify what areas your peace
is being snatched from you—a particular friendship, family
relations, world events, marriage trouble, artistic pursuits,
career issues, your motherhood—and prayerfully analyze if
you are letting God fight for you. If you are swinging your
fists, you may be dropping the gift of peace that has been
handed to you.

Jesus, restore peace to me. I don't want to fight my own battles
anymore. Help me to know when to find shelter in you. I want
to be still and let you fight for me. Thank you that you care
about every detail of my life and that you are just and righteous.

Heard

Hear the voice of my pleas for mercy,
when I cry to you for help,
when I lift up my hands toward your most holy sanctuary.

PSALM 28:2 ESV

Let's do a little word study. The word *hear* in this passage is the Hebrew word *shama* which means "to listen." It is stated here in an imperative form, or with the very strong plea to urgently ask God to consent. But the psalmist is not being demanding of God, he is yearning for God's mercy. This is a loud plea for help. In the last part of the verse, the psalmist lifts up his hands. The words and body language of this psalm show that the psalmist wants to be heard. If you read on, you'll see that his prayer is answered, and he starts praising God.

It's ok to come to God full of emotion—loud voice, hands raised, deep feeling—in your prayers. You aren't being demanding or annoying. God created us as human beings with thoughts and feelings, and he is big enough to handle all of them. When you are full of emotion and need God, don't hold back. Cry out to him!

Do you feel safe enough in your relationship with God to bring all your emotions to him?

Hear the sound of my pleadings when I cry to You for help,
When I raise my hands toward Your holy sanctuary.

PSALM 28:2 NASB

There are times when we feel like God is silent. Many people refer to this as a desert season or the wilderness. Don't let times like those discourage you from crying out to the Lord. It is common for times of seeming silence to make us draw away from God. You may think since he didn't answer before he won't now either. We see in the Psalms though, that the psalmist is persistent. He doesn't give up or shy away from God. He recognizes God is bigger than perceptions, bigger than emotions, bigger than circumstances.

God is near even if you think he is silent. He hears you even if lies tell you he doesn't. Trust in the truth and what you know of God's character and don't pull away from him because of what you perceive. You have been heard! Continue on in prayer.

God, thank you that you hear me and know me, and you answer my prayers. Thank you that you're big enough to handle all of me. Help me draw near to you and not be shy.

Shining Star

Do everything without grumbling or arguing, so that you may become blameless and pure, "children of God without fault in a warped and crooked generation." Then you will shine among them like stars in the sky as you hold firmly to the word of life.

PHILIPPIANS 2:14-16 NIV

There are ways the world operates and ways the kingdom of God operates. The epistles are great resources for finding out what some of those ways are. Here in Philippians, just a couple are pointed out. No grumbling, no arguing. What small things, yet what a big difference! The words that come out of our mouths matter. When we sound just like everyone else around us, bickering about useless matters and complaining about circumstances, then we don't stand out in the least. These types of words are like clouds covering over what is supposed to be our bright witness.

When we use our words to give thanks, to find joy, and to seek peace, the clouds are parted and we shine. We stand out from a world that can do nothing but tear down, and we bring glory to God. Let's be bright stars in our atmospheres today, using our words to bring the glorious light of Christ to a dark world.

Do you struggle with complaining or arguing?
How can you use your words to bring God glory today?

Live a cheerful life, without complaining or division among yourselves. For then you will be seen as innocent, faultless, and pure children of God, even though you live in the midst of a brutal and perverse culture. For you will appear among them as shining lights in the universe, offering them the words of eternal life.

PHILIPPIANS 2:14-16 TPT

How does arguing keep us from bringing glory to God? When we have conflict, often our pride can rear its ugly head. We dig our heels in, convinced that we are the only one with the answer. But God wants us to humble ourselves. To put right relationship before being right. To humbly admit our sin and ask for forgiveness quickly. This is how we shine. This is how we become peacemakers, which Jesus tells us are blessed in his kingdom.

When you try to create peace, you are demonstrating how God made peace with us and how we make peace with each other. Next time you are quick to jump to your own defense, be quicker to ask for forgiveness and humble yourself. Let God do a bright work in and through you.

Jesus, help me not to argue and complain but, in humility, shine your glory to those around me.

Endless Kindness

May God himself, the God of peace, make you pure, belonging only to him. May your whole self—spirit, soul, and body—be kept safe and without fault when our Lord Jesus Christ comes.

1 THESSALONIANS 5:23 NCV

God is holding onto you. God wants to completely sanctify all of you—your whole self. It is a journey that you will take over your entire lifetime as a believer. It is a process that is done by God alone. God will guard and preserve you. He is holding onto you. He is working in your life to make you pure and blameless.

Glorification is the completion of sanctification, and it will happen when we are reunited in Christ. Until then, we walk this road of sanctification, being kept on the straight path by our gentle Savior. How reassuring that this is not our job, for by our own human strength and willpower it could never be achieved. Rest in the promise that God is keeping you, guarding you in the way of holiness today.

How does this promise bring rest to your soul?

May the God of peace make you holy in every way, and may your whole spirit and soul and body be kept blameless until our Lord Jesus Christ comes again.

1 THESSALONIANS 5:23 NLT

Our lives are not our own. When we become believers, we give our lives to Christ. It may sound like a metaphor, but it needs to be literal. We now belong to him. Our bodies, our spirits, our souls are his. This means there is no angle of your life that God doesn't want to be involved in or he doesn't care about. He cares about your body, which is to be submitted as a living sacrifice to him. He cares about your mind, which is to be renewed. He cares about your soul, which he had his Son go through death on a cross to save.

God wants to redeem every inch of your life. Won't you submit your whole life to him tonight and see the wondrous work he does?

Thank you for keeping me, Jesus. I submit my whole life—body, mind, and spirit—to you tonight.

Made Complete

Rejoice, be made complete, be comforted, be like-minded,
live in peace; and the God of love and peace will be with you.

2 CORINTHIANS 13:11 NASB

This is the final section in the second letter to the Corinthians written by Paul. As he is wrapping up his letter, he gives a few short pieces of wisdom. It makes sense that he would tell them to rejoice and to live in peace, but what does it mean to be made complete? Other translations say, "strive for full restoration." What does that look like in our lives? Striving for restoration is the equivalent of seeking to live in health.

God is working toward restoring you and all of creation. The work of the Holy Spirit in your heart makes you more like Christ, but God wants you to be whole in all areas of your life. This looks different for each person but could include taking care of your physical body, going to counseling for emotional help, and reading your Bible and praying. Think of your whole self when pursuing restoration. It's no good if you focus on your body but ignore your soul or focus on your mind and forget about your body. You will never be fully restored until heaven, but here on earth let God work his restoration power in you.

How can you pursue health?

Rejoice. Aim for restoration, comfort one another,
agree with one another, live in peace;
and the God of love and peace will be with you.

2 CORINTHIANS 13:11 ESV

A lot of these commands that Paul gives have to do with
seeking health for yourself, but mainly in relationships with
other people. We are told to be united, to live in peace with
one another. This is often easier said than done! God has
created us to be in relationship with other humans, so doing
it all on our own will never do.

We need to be in community with others to really be seeking
holistic health. It's not easy, but when we focus our attention
on letting the Holy Spirit empower us to live in peace and
unity with others, there is joy to be found.

God, help me to be restored completely. Show me areas of my
life you want to restore here and now. Help me to live in peace
with others.

No More Walls

He himself is our peace, who has made us both one and has broken down in his flesh the dividing wall of hostility.

EPHESIANS 2:14 ESV

It's a timeless activity practiced by people groups all over the world and from the beginning of time: we really like to build walls. We separate ourselves out with the people that we feel are most like us. Maybe they look like us, believe like us, live near us, or share in some common interest. Though you would expect division and walls amongst those who don't know Christ, the church still struggles with it too.

Paul writes about breaking down the walls that cause animosity and division in the body of Christ. For instance, how are we letting walls of gender, economic status, or race keep us from fellowship in the body of Christ? Jesus addresses all of these walls. Gender is covered in John 4 with the story of the Samaritan woman, economic status is mentioned in James 2, and race is addressed in the gospels with Jesus interacting with people from many different races and commanding the disciples to take the gospel to the ends of the earth. The point is, tear down the walls and seek unity in Christ, to the glory of God.

Are you choosing to erect or stand beside any walls that are causing division in the body?

He himself is our peace, who has made the two groups one and has destroyed the barrier, the dividing wall of hostility.

EPHESIANS 2:14, NIV

Sometimes the walls seem impossible. They are far too high and wide and old to come down. The beauty is it is Jesus who is the wall breaker. The work Jesus did on the cross broke down the barrier between man and God, and it breaks down the barriers between mankind.

It says here that God has made us all one group with a new, unheard-of way of doing things. The unity that is to be found in the body of Christ is mind blowing. Let's display the amazing power of God to the world by walking in agreeance with our Savior, the one who brings down walls.

Jesus, thank you that you bring down the walls that divide us. I want to live like you; help me not to live with walls of hate that separate. Bring unity to the body of Christ, regardless of race, gender, or economic class.

Overflowing Affection

We were all baptized by one Spirit so as to form one body—
whether Jews or Gentiles, slave or free—
and we were all given the one Spirit to drink.

1 CORINTHIANS 12:13 NIV

There comes a point in your life when you look around and realize that not everyone believes and thinks the way you do. If you grew up as a believer, this can be alarming and unnerving. *How could so-and-so call themselves a Christian and yet believe differently in this matter?* It doesn't seem to make sense. What we must realize when this arises is that humility is required on our part toward the relationship. We are not all created the same, not all brought up the same, and we aren't at the same marker in our journeys. But that doesn't mean we should only surround ourselves with people who are.

Believers have unity in the Spirit of God. It is the same Spirit that lives inside of you that lives inside of the other church member whom you might not agree with. We are all given the same Spirit and by living in love and humility toward each other we put on display the beauty that God intended for the body of Christ to show.

How can you humbly approach a difficult relationship today?

Some of us are Jews, some are Gentiles, some are slaves, and some are free. But we have all been baptized into one body by one Spirit, and we all share the same Spirit.

1 CORINTHIANS 12:13 NLT

Our verse today is not calling for a blanket unity absent of truth. Unity is a morally neutral thing; you can be united in both evil or good. If we in unity choose to forsake Scripture and pursue sin, that is not good unity. The source of our unity must be the Spirit of God who cannot deny himself. Our unity must align with the character and values of God. There are boundary lines we must hold when it comes to things like sin. But there are boundary lines we can remove as well, like specific preferences in worship style.

The Holy Spirit will guide you if you humble yourself in these matters. The goal is to love others as Christ has loved you and be a witness to the world around you of what living in unity regardless of petty differences actually looks like.

Holy Spirit, thank you that you unify us across lines that we normally draw to separate ourselves: across ethnicities, cultures, denominations, and genders. Help me seek unity with the body of Christ and glorify you.

Greater Reality

Preach the word, be ready in season and out of season;
reprove, rebuke, and exhort with complete patience and teaching.

2 TIMOTHY 4:2 NIV

This verse is not reserved for pastors and Sunday school teachers. Every believer is asked to share the Word of God with others. Some seasons it may feel like a given. How could you not share the Word of God as it burns inside of you? Other times it does not come as naturally. We can find ourselves in a season of busyness with to-do lists miles long. Our day-planners are full, leaving no time for us to think of talking about the Word of God with anyone. We barely see the clerk at the checkout line or our kids as we drop them off at activities. Our friends get a quick text, or our neighbors a wave as we move on. And on top of it, in this technological age we are quick to pick up our phones to fill any down time we may find.

The Holy Spirit wants to move mightily through you. Make sure you are ready by slowing down enough to truly see those around you as God sees them and to not be so busy that you are unprepared to seize the opportunity he has for you to share the good news with this world.

You have joy; who can you share it with today?

Preach the word of God. Be prepared,
whether the time is favorable or not.
Patiently correct, rebuke,
and encourage your people with good teaching.

2 TIMOTHY 4:2 NLT

The Word of God is like a multifaceted diamond. We aren't
given it for one sole purpose. Here, Paul lists several ways
the Scriptures are beneficial to us and others. Did you get
an opportunity to share his Word today? To reprove is to
challenge. Who do you know that needs to be challenged by
God's Word? To rebuke is likened to chastising. The Word of
God convicts us when we stray from truth. Are you prepared
to share the sometimes hard message of the gospel? It's never
fun to confront someone in sin, but when done in love and
humility it could be the very word they need to turn their soul
from death.

The Word of God encourages. This is the easy one! What
promise of God could you share to encourage someone? A life
without Christ is hopeless and dark indeed. Use the Word of
God to bring light to dark places this week as you encounter
your community.

Jesus, help me to see the opportunities in front of me to share
your Word and to have confidence as I speak it to the world.

Victory

*Every child of God defeats this evil world,
and we achieve this victory through our faith.*

1 JOHN 5:4 NLT

Life can sometimes feel like the rush to a gate at the airport. You are clambering along with all your bags, moving as quickly as you can. Glancing to the side you see people working less with just as many bags yet going significantly faster than you! How is that possible? Looking down, you see they are on a moving sidewalk while your feet reside on solid ground.

In life, if you glance to the right or the left it's easy to fall into the comparison trap. It seems like everyone else is getting ahead and you are being left behind. The truth is that, as a believer, you get ahead by faith. Victory has already been won for you! You have a loving Father who has a plan for you. Keep in submission to him, and he will lift those heavy bags and get you where he wants you to go (where he gets the most glory!) right on time.

What area of your life are you spending too much time comparing and not enough submitting to Christ?

Every child of God overcomes the world,
for our faith is the victorious power
that triumphs over the world.

1 JOHN 5:4 TPT

Do you feel like you were born into this world with your boxing gloves on, always needing to fight? It's time to put those away. As a child of God, you don't have to fight and scrap. It is no longer necessary for you to pull yourself up by your bootstraps to find worth and favor in this world. Your worth is found in God!

As a child of God, you are on the winning team. Everything Christ has defeated has been done for you. In Christ, by faith, you are the victor. Stop striving to prove your place in this world and rest in your identity as a child of the King.

Jesus, thank you that you defeated this world. You descended into the grave and you have victory over death and hell. As your child, I too am a victor. Forgive me for comparing my journey to others. Help me to find rest in my identity as your daughter. Be my source.

He Is Coming

"I will make all my goodness pass before you and will proclaim before you my name 'The Lord.' And I will be gracious to whom I will be gracious, and will show mercy on whom I will show mercy."

EXODUS 33:19 ESV

The passage beckons us to come and have genuine dialog with God. God has become frustrated with the people of Israel because of their idolatry with the golden calf. He talks about destroying the people of Israel, and Moses pleads with him not to, saying that this would not bring glory but shame to God's name. God agrees and doesn't destroy them. The people repent, and Moses asks God to forgive them. God does, but says he isn't going with them to the Promised Land. Again, Moses argues with God. He says the people shouldn't even go to the Promised Land if God doesn't come, and then asks God to show his glory.

What's fascinating about this whole passage is it seems that God invites Moses to have a genuine conversation about himself, his character, and his behavior. It appears that God wants a relationship with Moses. He shows special, gracious favor to Moses. In the same way, God invites you to argue with him, to ask questions, and to bring doubts. He wants to reveal his character to you. One willing to engage in conversation is what he is looking for.

Have you thought about this story in this way before?

> *"I will cause all my goodness to pass in front of you, and I will proclaim my name, the Lord, in your presence. I will have mercy on whom I will have mercy, and I will have compassion on whom I will have compassion."*

EXODUS 33:19 NIV

Referring back to the story of God and Moses, God is not a far-off deity waiting to smite us all. He is not a dictator looking to rule with an iron fist and a compassionless heart. He is full of mercy and compassion, and wants to have fellowship with his people, with you.

God wants to answer your questions, take into consideration your needs, and know your thoughts. Will you approach him tonight?

God, it amazes me that you care what I think. That you hear my prayers and want to know me and for me to know you. Show me your glory like you did Moses. I want to be your friend.

Generations

Know that the LORD your God, He is God, the faithful God who keeps covenant and mercy for a thousand generations with those who love Him and keep His commandments.

DEUTERONOMY 7:9 NKJV

We like products that last. Companies often boast about the longevity of the things they sell, and we read reviews and do research to make sure what they promise is true. Who wants to buy a new car, only to have it break in a year? Who wants to invest in a house, only to have the foundation crumble in a few months? We marvel at structures like the pyramids that have lasted for thousands of years. We put value in things that last.

God is the master at this. Faithfulness is the name of his game, longevity of integrity he is completely proficient in. A thousand generations. Some people calculate that to be over 25,000 years; that's older than even our earth! His mercy toward you will never run out. His promise-keeping is a sure thing for all eternity. What a God we serve!

How does the faithfulness of God inspire awe in you this morning?

Understand, therefore, that the L{\scriptsize ORD} your God is indeed God. He is the faithful God who keeps his covenant for a thousand generations and lavishes his unfailing love on those who love him and obey his commands.

DEUTERONOMY 7:9 NLT

When you start to dwell on and try to comprehend how God keeps his promises, it really blows your mind. It makes statements like, "He is faithful in his promises toward you," take on a whole new meaning. These promises are set before the foundation of the world. That's quite a long time!

God has a history and a reputation older than time itself of never breaking his promises. You can count on God. You can put your full weight on what he has promised you. When you face discouragement and doubt, turn to his covenant keeping to reassure you and bolster your faith. Know it in your bones, know through and through, that God cannot go back on his Word. What a most reassuring thing!

God, you are amazing. Your covenants are firm and solid. This is wonderful news! I am in awe of you.

So Good

LORD, answer me because your love is so good.
Because of your great kindness, turn to me.

PSALM 69:16 NCV

Think back to different scenarios that you have described as so good. Perhaps it was a delicious home-cooked meal. Maybe a compelling film, a long hike, a steaming cup of coffee, or a well-placed conversation. So good. These memories should evoke feelings of warmth and attachment. Can you, do you, think of God in the same manner? When someone brings up the things of God, do you think "so good" or do you cringe a bit?

Over time, it is easy to become cynical toward God. Perhaps our prayers are not answered the way we thought they should be, suffering comes, or we are hurt by his people, the church. It is a slow process sometimes, yet it drains out the "so good" in our relationship with him. Search your heart. How could cynicism be stealing your view of so good in regard to God's love?

Answer the question above, and prayerfully ask God to show areas that you have developed cynicism in.

Answer me, O LORD, for your steadfast love is good;
according to your abundant mercy, turn to me.

PSALM 69:16 ESV

Take a moment to read through the beginning of Psalm 69 before you arrive at today's verse. The psalmist is in a dark place! Things do not seem to be going well for him. This communicates to us two important factors. First, the Christian life is not a guaranteed easy life. We are told that there will be suffering and hardship, so we should not be surprised or angry with God when life turns that way.

There is a break in the clouds. What two qualities does the psalmist mention? Steadfast love and abundant mercy. When life gives us grief, sorrow, or difficulty, we get through it by remembering the true character of God—his steadfast love and overwhelming mercy.

God, thank you that you are loving and merciful toward me— abundantly so. Thank you that I can rely on your character to be true even when suffering comes my way. Help me to cling to your goodness. I repent of the areas I thought of today that I have become cynical in. Renew my heart in your love.

Measuring Sticks

*Do you not realize this about yourselves,
that Jesus Christ is in you?*

2 CORINTHIANS 13:5 ESV

Many of us go through life trying to measure up. It could be put on by our parents, teachers, coaches, friends, or even ourselves, but at some point we all grab a hold of a measuring stick and try to see what we are worth. Sometimes we exceed the standards. Other times we use the sticks to flog ourselves, beating ourselves up with shame when we don't measure up. You might even see the Bible as a measuring stick: an impossible standard of God that you will never live up to. That is true; on our own we could never measure up to God's holiness. But the good news is, in Christ, we do.

When God looks at you, he sees Christ's righteousness which measures up completely. You are good enough because of Jesus. You achieve things because of Jesus. Jesus has met the goal and exceeded the standards, so you don't need to try to be perfect anymore. Praise God for this freedom in him!

Do you see yourself as measuring up in Christ?

Haven't you already experienced
Jesus Christ himself living in you?

2 CORINTHIANS 13:5 TPT

This morning we talked about how when we measure up, it's because of Christ. We are whole in him. This takes the pressure off of us and has the potential to free us from shame. If we grow and change and become more sanctified, it's not by a work we have done, it's because of Christ. It's the Holy Spirit moving in us.

What peace comes when you realize you don't have to hustle anymore to live up to God's standard. What freedom you are rewarded with when you choose to let Christ be enough. It also frees you from the bondage of finding your identity in others. When you measure up in Christ, you don't need the other measuring sticks anymore. Burn them and live free in Christ!

Jesus, thank you that I measure up in you! Thank you that in you, I am whole and complete.

Led by Truth

Guide me in your truth and teach me,
for you are God my Savior,
and my hope is in you all day long.

PSALM 25:5 NIV

What is truth? Pilot asked Jesus this question during his trial. Philosophers throughout the ages have each come up with their own brand of truth. Truth is what God has to say about a matter which he communicates to us through his Word. As a child of God, you have a book full of answers at your disposal. How do you walk in truth? You can start by reading it.

Every day, allow God to align your decisions, ambitions, thought patterns, and actions with his truth. You can use the Bible as your lens for how you see the world, bringing every circumstance into focus instead of blindly following your own desires or the loud opinions of others. Become a studious explorer, hungry to know the character of God as he presents himself in his Word. Being guided in truth is a path of unspeakable joy. Try it!

Do you view the Bible as the standard of truth in your life?

Lead me by your truth and teach me,
for you are the God who saves me.
All day long I put my hope in you.

PSALM 25:5 NLT

When someone says they will guide you, what comes to mind? Imagine you are in a jungle in a foreign country. You don't know the language, the layout, and you have no map. All you have is a local guide. You are essentially trusting this person with your entire wellbeing, trusting they know the lay of the land and the right way to go.

The Holy Spirit was sent to be our guide through life and through Scripture. The Bible might seem like an overwhelming landscape of rules and stories, but it is really a love letter with a map to redemption and peace etched inside. Follow your guide on the scarlet trail of the love of God for you through this book, and you will find the treasure of happiness along the way.

God, thank you for not leaving me here without a guide. Thank you for sending your Holy Spirit and providing me with your Word, which is truth! Guide me in your truth; teach me to view the world through the lens of your absolute truth.

Hemmed In

The LORD is near to all who call on him,
yes, to all who call on him in truth.

PSALM 145:18 NLT

If things don't turn out the way we have planned, does
that mean that God hasn't answered our prayers? We can't
simplify our life and prayers and God like that. When we do,
we put God in a box—where he does not belong. God is not
our great genie in the sky, granting wishes or denying them.

A red flag in this area would be if you move on and forget
about God when he answers your prayer until the next time
a request pops up. Prayer is a part of your relationship with
God. It strengthens your faith, exposes your weaknesses, and
leads to real communion with the Father. God won't always
answer your prayers the way you think he should or even in
the time that you want. Come to God with expectancy to grow
in a relationship instead of demanding your own way.

Do you see a red flag in your prayer life at all?

You draw near to those who call out to you,
listening closely, especially when their hearts are true.
PSALM 145:18 TPT

God is near. He hears your prayer. He is listening to your requests, empathizing with your feelings. The idea that God is aloof and doesn't care could not be further from the truth. We must learn to trust that he hears us. Life circumstances may make it seem like he turns a deaf ear. But he is so close there is no way he cannot hear you.

Do you hear God? Are you drawing closer to him? The lie is that if life doesn't go the way you want, then God is distant and can't hear you. The truth is he has a plan in mind that is far better. Trust him in it.

God, I trust you. I draw near to you even when things don't go my way.

Miracles of Mercy

*Lift your hands and give thanks to God
for his marvelous kindness
and for his miracles of mercy for those he loves!*

PSALM 107:8 TPT

The concept of a fresh start is something we usually get around January first. There are new planners with clean blank boxes to fill. A whole calendar, empty. The magical wonder of a fresh year ahead can almost be felt in the air. Like a fresh blanket of snow, the year is laid out before us, clean and full of anticipation. But here we are, halfway through a year, on an ordinary day. The snow has melted. Most of the magic has faded, and the planners have been filled with things crossed off and things left unachieved. Dates made and appointments broken.

Wouldn't it be a miracle to have that new feeling every day? God's mercy is brand new every morning, laid out like the calendar, it miraculously can be fresh for you every day. For those God loves, there is no ending to the newness, to the joy that comes when you experience his mercy new every day. The Psalmist is right; lift your hands and give thanks to God, for his mercy is new and miraculous.

What mercy can you thank God for today in your life?

*Let them give thanks to the L*ORD *for his unfailing love*
and his wonderful deeds for mankind.

PSALM 107:8 NIV

Have you ever wondered what the difference is between grace, mercy, and all the other benevolent terms we read in the Bible? Grace and mercy can feel like the same thing. While grace is the free and unmerited favor of God, mercy comes is more about forgiving a grievance that is typically punishable. God had every right to give us the sentence we deserved for our sins. Instead, he chose to show us great mercy.

What's amazing is he didn't just stop at not punishing us for our sins. He went above and beyond to restore us to himself. He showed us mercy, and then he took interest in us as individuals and chose to adopt us into his family. He always does abundantly more. Praise him!

God, I praise you for showing me such miraculous mercy. You have gone above and beyond, and I am eternally grateful.

God's Terms

It depends not on human will or exertion,
but on God, who has mercy.

ROMANS 9:16 ESV

No matter how hard you try, it's never going to work. That's not exactly the encouraging devotional thought you wanted to start this day, is it? Don't close the book though. Even after we become believers, the age-old lie of Jesus plus something else tries to take us off track. We think we can do it all, try harder, and find that "enough" that we long for. If we just read our Bibles more, it would be enough. If we said yes to volunteer at one more thing at church, prayed more, or visited the sick more, it would be enough. If we had a successful business venture, an excellent marriage, a social-media-worthy lifestyle, it would be enough. If we could just stop sinning in that particular way, it would be enough.

From legalistic pursuits to outright sinfulness, with simply good things in between, anything you try to add to Jesus for identity, salvation, and worth will never work. But that's good news! Jesus is enough, so in Jesus, you are enough as well. Be encouraged. You don't need the effort. You don't need to be enough. You don't need to try harder. Let it be inspiring to know your hard work doesn't need to work because he is working for you.

How have you been trying to be enough without Christ?

Again, this proves that God's choice doesn't depend on how badly someone wants it or tries to earn it, but it depends on God's kindness and mercy.

ROMANS 9:16 TPT

Mercy received feels like a dip in a cool lake on the hottest day of the summer. You have a floatie nearby, and the mix of sunshine and cool lake water keeps you at the perfect temperature the whole day. Bliss.

As you thought today about the ways you try to exert your own effort to be enough, repent of the ways you've been doing things in your own effort. Take a dip in the cool lake of mercy that is offered to you, and praise God for the blissful peace that will wash over your tired soul.

Jesus, thank you for being enough. Thank you for making me complete. I repent of all the ways I keep trying harder to prove myself and earn my way. Help me to find bliss in your mercy.

Give Thanks

Oh, give thanks to the LORD, for He is good!
For His mercy endures forever.

1 CHRONICLES 16:34 NKJV

This section in 1 Chronicles is a section of praise to God. The whole part is a long song, and it can also be found in parts in the Psalms. In Psalm 136, for instance, the phrase "his mercy endures forever" is repeated often for all of the twenty-six verses. It seems the psalmist wanted us to remember, doesn't it? Once we become believers, we don't automatically stop sinning. It's not like a court system, where a judge gives mercy to a defendant but then tells that defendant to never do it again or else they are going to jail. That would mean the judge's mercy runs out, and often rightly so.

God's mercy never runs out. He doesn't get fed up with you when you sin and say, "Well that's it! I'm done with you!" His mercy endures. It goes on and on past all you could imagine. When you love the Lord, you don't want to sin, but you are right in the middle of the journey of sanctification. Don't let shame and condemnation whisper the lies that his mercy has run out on you. His mercy endures forever. Give thanks for this wonderful news!

Have you thanked God recently for his mercy?

Give thanks to the LORD, for he is good;
his love endures forever.

1 CHRONICLES 16:34, NIV

What comes to mind when you hear this word *endure*? Often, we think of enduring as putting up with something, pushing through something hard or miserable. You endure a car ride with a difficult person. You endure a job you don't really like. You endure a workout. But what if pushing through nasty circumstances is not what God is trying to convey here?

Doesn't endure also mean to last for a very long time? Instead of getting the idea that God is simply putting up with you, gritting his teeth and tolerating you, what really aligns with the rest of Scripture about the character of God is that he lasts. With you, his mercy lasts forever. God has a long-term commitment to you. He's in it for the long run; never giving up, never quitting, his mercy endures forever.

God, your kindness toward me is astonishing. Thank you for your mercy! Thank you that it endures.

Good Gifts

*Grace, mercy and peace will be with us, from God the Father
and from Jesus Christ, the Son of the Father, in truth and love.*

2 JOHN 1:3 NASB

What makes a good gift? Often it is the thought behind it. It's
the personal nature of the gift, showing that a person knows
you well, that makes it such an excellent gift. We all long to
be known and loved in spite of our failures. God is a Father
who gives us good gifts. He knows us personally; he loves us
deeply. This makes his gifts extra special.

His grace, mercy and peace is for everyone. But wouldn't you
know that he tailor-makes it for you as well? He gives you the
exact grace you need when life is overwhelming. He extends
oceans of mercy when you feel condemned. He weighs you
down in peace when you feel like you're swirling in a storm.
Just like the trials you face are unique to you so the gifts of
God are individually designed. Praise God that he knows you
so intimately!

What gift do you need from God today?

God our Father and Jesus Christ, his Son, will release to us overflowing grace, mercy, and peace, filled with true love.

2 JOHN 1:3 TPT

The truth hurts. We get that saying ingrained in us and it makes us almost afraid of the truth. In 2 John, the author views the truth as a very good thing. He is excited to hear that the church he is writing to is remaining in the truth and growing in it. He uses the word several times and admonishes the people to stay in the truth.

Don't believe the lie that you should fear the truth. Jesus uses the word *truth* to refer to who he is—the way, the truth, and the life. Think of what you know of the character of God and see if that aligns with what you feel about truth. Jesus is the truth, he loves you, and he wants you to grow in truth.

Jesus, thank you that you are the truth. Help me to grow in truth. Thank you for knowing me. I am grateful for all the good gifts you give.

Keep Me Close

I have tried hard to find you—
don't let me wander from your commands.

PSALM 119:10 NLT

What makes God hard to find? Is he playing a cosmic game of hide-and-seek with us when we need him the most? If you have felt this way, you are not alone. From David in the psalms all the way to some of our great modern theologians, the question of why God seems hard to find has been uttered from the lips of many.

This might help. Take time to remember the mercy of the Lord in your life so far. Remember his great deeds, the times he has answered prayer, when he has felt close. You can't base your relationship with God completely on feeling, one day feeling close to him and the next not. Though it is hard when he feels distant, our first step is to remember all of his moving and working in our life up to this point.

What do you remember today that God has done in your life?

I seek you with all my heart;
do not let me stray from your commands.

PSALM 119:10 NIV

Another thing we can do when God feels far away is dive
deeper into his Word. Or, as the psalmists puts it, don't
wander from his commands. The devil would like nothing
more than to convince you that God does not care about you.
He wants you to believe the lie that God has abandoned you.
When faced with lies, you must go to the source of truth,
God's Word.

Meditate on who God says he is, and how he says he will act
toward you. He says he will never leave you. He will be near;
you will never be alone. Look up Scriptures, memorize them,
take them to heart, hold onto them. Prayerfully remind God
of his Word by praying these Scriptures back to him. When
you seek God with your whole heart, he will be found. God is
faithful! You are not alone.

God, thank you that you are true to your Word and you have
remembered me in the past. Be near to me today as I seek you.

Gracious God

*In Your great mercy You did not
utterly consume them nor forsake them;
For You are God, gracious and merciful.*

NEHEMIAH 9:31 NKJV

"That's just how she is." Have you ever heard someone say
this about someone else? It's a conclusive statement, lacking
in faith that the person will ever change if referring to a
negative characteristic or full of wonder if it's positive. It's
as though we could sum up a person's entire personality and
life with a short description. While it might not be best when
describing someone else, it's awesome when describing God.
Who is God? He's always gracious and merciful; that's just
who he is!

When we sum someone up with one comment to someone
else, that person tends to then only see that characteristic
in the person. It's like when you are shopping for a car and
you hope to buy a certain type, suddenly you see that same
car everywhere. You notice it; they stand out. Nehemiah
is describing God and what stands out about him in this
passage. He uses the words *gracious* and *merciful*. That's just
who he is! Praise him for this today.

How would you sum up God?
How do you think others sum you up?
Do you reflect the character of God?

Because your mercy is great,
you did not kill them all or leave them.
You are a kind and merciful God.

NEHEMIAH 9:31 NCV

When dwelling on this question today, perhaps you had a hard time because you've never had to sum up God in a few words. Maybe you don't spend a lot of time talking about God in your daily life. No one's ever asked, and you've never offered. God's graciousness and mercy deserves to be shouted from the rooftops. It's a knowledge and an experience too good to keep to ourselves.

You must share with others who God is. Ask God to make a desire for others to know his character something that burns within your soul. You know an amazing God who has extended abundant mercy and never-ending grace toward you. Share it!

God, you are amazing! Your reputation precedes you. Help me to share your good news of mercy and grace with others.

Abundance

*God is able to bless you abundantly,
so that in all things at all times, having all that you need,
you will abound in every good work.*

2 CORINTHIANS 9:8 NIV

What is a poverty mentality? It's when you believe you are inferior, inadequate, and lacking in resources. It doesn't have much to do with the amount of money you actually have, but it's a mindset about yourself and your life. Some ways it plays out in daily life is in how we struggle with insecurities, have low self-esteem, or always worry about lacking.

We must break this mentality. God is a God of abundance, and you are his child. He has everything you need, and he will provide for you. That's the promise of this verse; cling to it! He has all the provision, the skills, the mercy, anything you need. He gives abundantly so you can abundantly thrive in a world that is greatly lacking. What do you need? Ask him for it this morning!

Do you suffer from a poverty mindset?
How does it hinder you from living in abundance?

God will generously provide all you need. Then you will always have everything you need and plenty left over to share with others.

2 Corinthians 9:8 nlt

God is able to provide for you. That's what this Scripture says. He has every ability and inclination toward blessing you. He will open up the heavens and let it rain down on you. He is able. So, when you are hoping to abound in every good work, when you have family needs, ministry needs, relational needs, provision needs, God is able. Say those words! Let them be the loud promise that quiets every doubt a poverty mindset tries to plant.

Do you want to abound in your calling? God is able. Ask. Do you want to know your true identity? He has abundance for that. Do you need more? He's got it. He's not handing out sparingly or holding back. This is a wide open, generous festival of giving. What do you need? Receive it from Jesus today.

God, I am amazed by you! Thank you for your abundance toward me. Here is what I need tonight. Please break the poverty mentality in me and help me to ask you for all I need.

Never Abandoned

I had said in my alarm,
"I am cut off from your sight."
But you heard the voice of my pleas for mercy
when I cried to you for help.

PSALM 31:22 ESV

Did you ever get lost in a store as a kid? One minute you are right there with a parent, and the next time you turn around, they're gone! It's a pretty frightening experience at a young age, one that can help us relate to what the psalmist felt. If you're a kid and you get lost, it causes alarm. It gives you a slight taste of what being abandoned feels like.

Abandonment ranks high on the list of fears in people's lives, and it causes many to live in ways that ensure they won't be abandoned or left behind again. God will never abandon you. He will always hear you when you call out to him. You will always find him when you seek him. These are guarantees! God's Word is full of promises like this. You are his child, and he will never let you out of his sight no matter how far you might wander.

Have you ever felt abandoned?
How can God's promise to not abandon you encourage you?

I spoke hastily when I said, "The Lord has deserted me."
For in truth, you did hear my prayer and came to rescue me.

PSALM 31:22 TPT

It's not natural for most of us to ask for help. We try to push through and do things on our own, proudly wearing the badge of independence. Asking for help takes humility. Did you know that humility in the kingdom of God is like gold? It's a quality to be admired and sought after.

We need to be humble enough to ask for help—from others and from God. Here is David, king of an empire, a mighty warrior who has killed wild animals, and he's crying out to God for help. His heart is postured in humility. Let us be like David, so no matter how fierce we think we are, we are just as humble and quick to ask God to help us.

God, I need you. I need your help. I'm prone to wander; keep me close. Help me to be humble and to accept help from others.

Resurrection Life

If while we were still enemies, God fully reconciled us to himself through the death of his Son, then something greater than friendship is ours. Now that we are at peace with God, and because we share in his resurrection life, how much more we will be rescued from sin's dominion!

ROMANS 5:10 TPT

Don't we all just want some peace? From the myriad of songs, poems, books, movies, speeches, and organizations all dedicated toward it, it's safe to conclude that peace is a high pursuit of mankind. Religions are built around trying to find the answer on how we can appease the gods. Do you know that following Jesus is the only way to peace with God? And the beauty of it all is that there is not one thing you do to earn it.

God wanted peace with you, so by his Son, Jesus, dying on the cross and rising again, your belief in this truth gives you the unchangeable status of being at peace with God. No need to work harder, to outweigh your good with your bad, or keep charts and lists, Jesus' work on the cross is the bridge that brings you peace. You can never revisit this truth too much or remember the cross too often. Thank God for your status before him today.

Do you find yourself skimming fast past the truth of the cross, like a story you know too well? Ask God for new appreciation of Jesus' work on the cross today.

*If while we were enemies, we were reconciled to God through the
death of his Son, much more surely, having been reconciled,
will we be saved by his life.*

ROMANS 5:10 NRSV

Now that we are at peace with God, what does this resurrected
life spoken of in Romans look like? Two important factors
come to mind. First, full access to God. You can approach
God anywhere, anytime, about anything. Big or small, bring
it to the throne of God. He wants to know your cares and
concerns. He wants to answer your prayers. He wants to be
in relationship with you. The resurrected life is that of full
communion with the most Holy God.

Second, sharing in his resurrected life means being in
submission to his sanctifying work in your life. That means
allowing the Holy Spirit to have full access to your life, to
make you more Christlike. What a beautiful thing it is to be
living life by the power of God!

God, thank you that you made a way for me to be at peace with
you. I submit my life to your power. Do your work in my heart
today.

Here for Sinners

Jesus said to them, "It is not the healthy who need a doctor,
but the sick. I have not come to call the righteous, but sinners."

MARK 2:17 ESV

What kind of state were you in when you came to Christ?
Some of us grew up in the church, and some did not. Some
of us have extensive outward lists of sins that might make us
feel like we don't quite fit in at church. When church becomes
more of a pageant of the holiest of people, and less of a
hospital for the broken and needy, there might be a problem.
If you have what would be considered a broken and beat up
past, don't hide it when you come to church. Don't get so
caught up in trying to clean up to please those around you that
you miss your appointment with the doctor—Jesus.

We can get the wrong impression that if people can't handle
the wounds and pain we bring to church, then God can't
handle them either. That he would rather us get dressed
up and pretend like we have it all together. Nothing could
be further from the truth. God sent his Son to heal the
brokenhearted, to tend to those who are sick, and to redeem
those in the bondage of darkness. If you are in need of God,
you belong at church. Don't hide anymore.

Do you feel the need to keep up appearances at church?

Jesus overheard their complaint, he said to them, "Who goes to the doctor for a cure? Those who are well or those who are sick? I have not come to call the 'righteous,' but to call those who are sinners and bring them to repentance."

MARK 2:17 TPT

Don't believe anyone who tells you they aren't broken. Without Jesus, every single one of us is. Some seem to show it more externally, and others try to tidy it up and keep it to ourselves. Do you need God? If you can answer a wholehearted yes to that question, then great! You are humbly showing your submission to Jesus which is exactly what he is looking for.

You belong in the body of Christ, scars, past, and all. Jesus wants to work in your life to heal you, but he doesn't work to clean you up for show. Remember that. He will use your story for his glory. You can count on it.

Jesus, thank you that you came for sinners like me. Thank you that you have redeemed me and you are working in my life.

For Sensitive Souls

*Put on then, as God's chosen ones, holy and beloved,
compassionate hearts, kindness, humility,
meekness, and patience.*

COLOSSIANS 3:12 ESV

There is a disease called congenital analgesia. Those with this condition cannot feel physical pain. That might sound like a blessing to you, but it is actually not a good thing. People who cannot feel pain are more likely to die from smaller injuries because they cannot feel the warning signals of pain that come before the problem becomes life threatening.

Some of us believers might consider ourselves sensitive. Maybe you are, and maybe you see it as a bad thing instead of a gift. God has given some of us the gift of a compassionate heart. You might be known as the feeler of the group. This is beneficial to the body of Christ. Without you, the body would be in pain and not even know it, which could lead to serious harm. When we use our compassionate hearts and sensitive nature to perceive the needs of the body of Christ, we please God. Don't shy away from your calling!

Do you wish you weren't so sensitive?
How can you see it as a gift?

You are always and dearly loved by God! So robe yourself with virtues of God, since you have been divinely chosen to be holy. Be merciful as you endeavor to understand others, and be compassionate, showing kindness toward all. Be gentle and humble, unoffendable in your patience with others.

COLOSSIANS 3:12 TPT

Maybe you view your sensitivity as a weakness. The question is, who made you that way? God did! He made you in his image. He gave you these gifts. Does that make God weak? Certainly not! We serve a compassionate, feeling God who is far from weak. He gave you these gifts because he knows our body of believers needs them to be strong.

So, put on your compassion. Speak out of kindness. Serve in humility. You are beloved by God, and you are needed in the body of Christ. Don't shrink away from feeling all the feelings he has given you. Love deeply, knowing that your heavenly Father is proud of you.

Jesus, you care deeply. Help me to care deeply as well and show me how to use my gifts.

Constant Comfort

*Your words have comforted those who fell,
and you have strengthened those who could not stand.*

JOB 4:4 NCV

Sometimes, we know when we should turn to the Bible for comfort. We grab our Bibles and suddenly have no idea where to begin. It's so big, with so many chapters, so many different forms of writing. How is a person supposed to know where to start or where to find comfort? If you need comfort right now, turn to Psalms or the book of John. But here is an even better tip; don't wait until your moment of need to crack the book open.

Daily Bible reading is important. Your soul is a storehouse for what you consume. If you consume the Word of God daily, even sections that might not make sense at the time, then you are storing nutrients for your soul later. Then, in your moment of need, the Holy Spirit will have a vast array of nutrients to draw from and to bring you comfort. Don't get caught up on where you should start; just make sure you are digesting God's Word daily. It has so many benefits for your life!

Do you have a hard time finding where to start in the Bible?

Your words have upheld him who was stumbling,
And you have strengthened the feeble knees.

JOB 4:4 NKJV

God's Word is so powerful. It is so useful to our lives. We cannot set aside or dismiss this gift God has given us. God's Word can give us strength when we fall. The words of the enemy beat us up when we fall, and they shame and condemn us. That's how we know that those words are not from God. God's words lift us up, lead us to repentance, and strengthen us.

If you are feeling beaten down and low, identify the words that you are listening to. Make a list of all your negative thoughts and share them with a trusted friend. Have that friend point out the lies to you and replace them with the uplifting truth of God.

God, help me not to listen to lies. Let your Word come alive to me; store it in my soul. Comfort me with your Spirit.

Holy Exchange

"Blessed are the poor in spirit, for theirs is the kingdom of heaven.
Blessed are those who mourn, for they will be comforted."

MATTHEW 5:3-4 NIV

What does it mean to be poor in spirit? Jesus is not talking about an economic poverty here, though he does have a lot to say about the economically poor in the Bible. No, he is referencing those who have spiritual poverty, and in this case, that poverty is a good thing. This spiritual poverty is about being humble.

Humility is foundational to our Christian faith. It means that we come to Jesus broken, aware of our spiritual need and sin, and emptied of all pride. This is the posture of a believer. Jesus blesses those who come to him in this way of poverty, because then we experience a deep dependence on God. When we are broken and humble, it is then that we can experience the true blessings that God has in store for us.

How does this change your understanding
of being poor in spirit?

"God blesses those who are poor and realize their need for him, for the Kingdom of Heaven is theirs. God blesses those who mourn, for they will be comforted."

MATTHEW 5:3-4 NLT

We often associate the term "blessed" with the term "happy," but those who mourn don't seem to be happy people. Isn't this beatitude contradicting itself? The true prosperity Jesus is referring to is not a physical prosperity, but rather a spiritual one. Being blessed isn't about being happy; it's about having spiritual wealth. But what are they mourning? Jesus is talking about those who grieve over their sins.

In the Old Testament, when the people returned to the land to rebuild the walls with Nehemiah, they found the book of the law. They asked Ezra to read it, and when he did, they mourned over their sins. Our sins should grieve us. This aligns with the humility presented by Jesus. Realizing our need for God, and having conviction and mourning over sin, is the path to a blessed life.

Jesus, help me to be poor in spirit and to mourn for my sins. I want to be dependent on you.

Way of Peace

"Because of the tender mercy of our God,
With which the Sunrise from on high will visit us,
To shine upon those who sit in darkness and the shadow of death,
To guide our feet into the way of peace."

LUKE 1:78-79 NASB

This verse is a part of a prophecy that Zechariah gave when he was filled with the Holy Spirit after bringing his newborn son, John the Baptist, to the temple. From birth, John the Baptist was given a very specific ministry to prepare the way for the coming Messiah, Jesus. Today's verses are about Jesus. What a beautiful description we have! At the time, there had been 400 years of silence among the people of Israel. It was like living in a dark night. But now, with Jesus about to be born, the sun was rising.

Have you ever watched the sunrise? Slowly, the blackness that engulfed you fades as brilliant colors welcome the dawn of a new day. That's how Jesus entered the world. We, living in darkness, in the shadow of death, now see the light. Brilliant colors are all around because new life has come to us. Praise God!

How has Jesus woken you from a dark night in your life?
Tell someone this glorious testimony today!

> *"Because of God's tender mercy,*
> *the morning light from heaven is about to break upon us,*
> *to give light to those who sit in darkness*
> *and in the shadow of death,*
> *and to guide us to the path of peace."*

LUKE 1:78-79 NLT

This word *peace* is brought up time and time again when Jesus is talked about. Rightly so, because one of his four prophesied titles in the book of Isaiah is "Prince of peace." Jesus himself is our peace. By dying on the cross, he has won for us the prize of peace with God.

Once, our sins alienated us from God. The great divide had existed since Adam and Eve, and nothing could bridge the gap until Jesus. By dying on the cross and taking the punishment for our sins, peace with God is now ours. This peace cannot be stolen from you; it is yours. Jesus has come to lead us in the way of peace with God, which is life changing. Won't you follow him today?

Jesus, lead me in the way of peace.

Drink Deep

*"I am the Alpha and the Omega—the Beginning and the End.
To all who are thirsty I will give freely from the springs
of the water of life."*

REVELATION 21:6 NLT

Most of us have easy access to water. If we are thirsty, we go to
our tap and fill up a cup, or we stop at a store and buy a bottle.
Have you ever had to go a long period without water? Imagine
going on a hike and running out of water halfway. By the end,
you would be hot and quite thirsty! What little water you had
left you wanting for more.

There are times in our life when we are left wanting more.
More love from a spouse (or perhaps a spouse in the first
place), more money, more recognition at work, more friends,
more material possessions. We can follow the way of the
world and try to achieve these things, put our hope in them,
and make them quench our thirst. But their ability to satisfy
will always run out. We will always want more. When we put
our hope in Jesus and turn to him to fulfill our needs, we
will be satisfied. Only he has the power to quench our thirsty
souls. Only he can fulfill our true needs and deepest desires.

Instead of Jesus, what have you been turning to
when you are thirsty?

"It is done. I am the Alpha and the Omega, the Beginning and the End. To the thirsty I will give water without cost from the spring of the water of life."

REVELATION 21:6 NIV

Water has become trendy. There are so many different kinds now: fancy bottles, water with caffeine, flavored waters, water from Himalayan springs, water from mountain wells. These kinds of water are not free. Funnily enough, they often don't satisfy in the same way that just plain, clean water does. This is what the world's offers are like. Often, the lies that we face are close to the truth but twisted or doctored, like water with caffeine.

To be satisfied, you do not need Jesus plus anything. You just need Jesus. He offers to satisfy you for free. Don't listen to the tempting offers that say you need Jesus plus money, Jesus plus marriage, or Jesus plus world travel to have a better life. You just need Jesus. Drink deep of his gift, without all the flashy add-ins, and be truly satisfied.

Jesus, I need only you. I want to drink deep from your well today. I am thirsty; quench my thirst.

Marvelous Mercy

Magnify the marvels of your mercy to all who seek you.
Make your Pure One wonderful to me,
like you do for all those who turn aside
to hide themselves in you.

PSALM 17:7 TPT

How does a magnifying glass work? It is a curved outward lens that refracts the light, making the light bend together and tricking your eye into seeing a larger image. It's cool science, but what does it have to do with Jesus? We need to magnify Christ in our lives. If you look around your world and wonder at the evil around you, then it is time for you to make Christ big.

The psalmist writes about making the marvels of God's mercy larger to all who seek him. He's not saying to lie about them, but rather to point them out. Draw attention to the mercies of God. God is working in our world. God is working in our lives. It's happening; we just often miss it with our normal vision. We need to put on lenses that look for and magnify the mercies of God in our life and not the problems, issues, and evils around us. These lenses will change your life, and you will see the world in a whole new way!

What mercies in your life can you magnify
and share with others today?

Wondrously show your steadfast love,
O Savior of those who seek refuge
from their adversaries at your right hand.

PSALM 17:7 ESV

Does our need to magnify Christ mean he is small? Absolutely not! Neither is his work in the world small. Christ has already been magnified by God. He is sitting at the right hand of the Father, a place of highest honor. Angels surround the throne, chanting "Holy, holy, holy." In Psalm 95:4 it says, "In his hand are the depths of the earth; the heights of the mountains are his also."

Christ is no small thing that needs our help. We don't magnify him because he is small; we magnify him because our limited, sin-stained vision is small. We need to magnify him to see how awesome and wonderful he is. Then, we need to magnify him to share him with the world.

Jesus, help me to magnify you in daily life. I lift you up. You are glorious!

Ready Relief

Blessed be the God and Father of our Lord Jesus Christ, the Father of mercies and God of all comfort, who comforts us in all our affliction so that we will be able to comfort those who are in any affliction with the comfort with which we ourselves are comforted by God.

2 CORINTHIANS 1:3-4 NASB

Have you heard the phrase "filled up to be poured out?" It means that we cannot give to others unless we are first filled up. Imagine trying to serve someone water out of an empty pitcher. You aren't going to get any, and neither are they! Even the mundane day-to-day parts of life can be draining. We need to fill up on God before we tackle our day and whatever lies ahead.

What are you in need of today? Courage? Comfort? Mercy? Patience? Perseverance? Hope? Perhaps you are just need a listening ear. God has what you need this morning. Don't be afraid to ask him for it in prayer.

What do you need this morning?

Praise be to the God and Father of our Lord Jesus Christ, the Father of compassion and the God of all comfort, who comforts us in all our troubles, so that we can comfort those in any trouble with the comfort we ourselves receive from God.

2 CORINTHIANS 1:3-4 NIV

Would you describe God as nurturing? Here in Corinthians, he is the God of comfort. Over and over, Scripture says that he is full of compassion and empathy, willing to comfort and guide us. If you have ever thought of yourself as too tender or too sensitive, take heart in knowing that your nurturing nature is a reflection of God. That's his image shining in you. It is a gift he has given you to share with others as well.

You are called to be like Christ, to comfort and to love like he does. Don't harden yourself to the world; be the vessel he has called you to be. Allow God to use the afflictions and the hurts you have experienced to bring empathy and compassion to those who otherwise might not receive it.

God, thank you for how you made me. I should nurture others the way you nurture me. Help me to be bold in this, that I might receive comfort from you and bring comfort to those around me.

Wonderful Wisdom

The wisdom from above is first pure, then peaceable, gentle, open to reason, full of mercy and good fruits, impartial and sincere.

JAMES 3:17 ESV

Just as "The Road Not Taken" by Robert Frost talks about two roads splitting, James presents to us two roads for community living. Community living refers to any situation you share with other people. You have your church community, school, neighbors, extended family, friendships, work relations, etc. He gives us two types of wisdom—earthly and godly.

Earthly wisdom is full of jealousy and selfish ambition, a very "me-first" attitude that elevates the self above others. Godly wisdom begins with a holy life, and it shows itself by getting along with other people (and not just people you like). It is gentle and merciful, treating all people with dignity and honor. Self-examination is key in a happy life with Christ. Which road have you taken? Do you operate out of worldly wisdom that leads to failed relationships? Or do you follow the road of godly wisdom, which harvests a thriving community that is living right with God?

What areas of your life need more godly wisdom?
What steps can you take to add it?

The wisdom that is from above is first pure, then peaceable, gentle, willing to yield, full of mercy and good fruits, without partiality and without hypocrisy.

JAMES 3:17 NKJV

If you love lists, this passage is for you. James is not giving us a lofty theory; he presents the practical and tangible outcome of a person who lives in godly wisdom. To examine your life, the decisions you make, and the way you interact with those around you, this verse is a helpful guide. Are you a person with a submissive heart to the Holy Spirit, praying for him to make you pure and holy, as Christ is? God our King is also peaceful; though he has every right to be harsh and penal toward us in our sins, he is gentle and kind toward us instead.

Think of the vast forgiveness you received through Christ on the cross. Are you extending the same to others? Do you give out the gentleness you wish to receive from others to others? Do you have a teachable, correctable spirit, or are you stubborn? Do you share the same measure of mercy that you receive from God? These are questions you can ask yourself to see Holy Spirit's fruit grow in your relationships.

Holy Spirit, search my heart. See if there are places where I am living according to the wisdom of the world and not of God. Help me to live with godly wisdom for my community.

You See Me

You do see! Indeed you note trouble and grief,
that you may take it into your hands;
the helpless commit themselves to you;
you have been the helper of the orphan.

PSALM 10:14 NRSV

Every heart longs to be seen, known, and understood, yet the vastness of our thoughts are unnoticed or unavailable to those around us. Perhaps this is how God intended it to be. He is the only one who can see the wholeness of who we are, and he doesn't walk away. He witnessed our unformed frames. He knows our thoughts and deepest longings. He is present in every seemingly hidden moment.

You may feel disregarded, unnoticed and underappreciated by the world. Let these feelings be the grace that draws you closer to the one who fulfills the longings of your soul. Let his seeing heal your heart.

How have you felt unseen recently?
How can you invite God to heal those areas of your life?

LORD, surely you see these cruel and evil things;
look at them and do something.
People in trouble look to you for help.
You are the one who helps the orphans.

PSALM 10:14, NCV

Let the mundane day-to-day motions not be wasted, instead using them as whispers of worship for your heavenly Father. Share the eyesight of God as you take delight in the ordinary moments. Let joy morph to praise in the smallest details of his handiwork. He has ordained every one of them, and he is present for each of them.

We often recognize God in the highest moments, and we draw near to him in the troubles and the grief. What is there to say of the simple moments that we are told don't matter? There isn't a moment he has missed. These ordinary times come with the temptation of feeling sidelined in God's story, but we are not being benched. This is an invitation to experience an intimate level of relationship with God.

God, I am amazed at how personal you are. Your eyes have not missed a minute of my life. I praise you for seeing me when I feel overlooked, for knowing me so deeply. You bring healing to my soul by showing up in my most private moments, good and bad. You are here for them all, and you never stop loving me.

It's Time

Sow for yourselves righteousness;
Reap in mercy;
Break up your fallow ground,
For it is time to seek the LORD,
Till He comes and rains righteousness on you.

HOSEA 10:12 NKJV

Have you ever planted a garden? You find a plot of land and till, turning the soil until it is broken and ready for seeds. Then, you select your seeds, some sunflowers, and plant them, burying them in the soil. Water, sunshine, patience. Soon, little green sprouts start to come up and you find yourself happy with a large zucchini plant.

Wait, what? That's not how it should go! If you plant sunflower seeds, what do you expect to grow? Sunflowers! This principle is applicable to life too. Plant righteousness in your life. Breaking ground is like the breaking and humbling a hard heart. It is never too late. Humble yourself before the Lord. Let him plant the righteousness of Christ in you. If that is what is planted, that is what you will harvest. What will you do with the garden of your heart this morning?

What have you been planting in your heart lately?

Plant the good seeds of righteousness,
and you will harvest a crop of love.
Plow up the hard ground of your hearts,
for now is the time to seek the LORD,
that he may come
and shower righteousness upon you.

HOSEA 10:12 NLT

At this point, it seemed like it was too late for Israel. They had been given opportunity after opportunity, and they just kept rebelling against God and not following his ways. They hardened their hearts against him time and time again. But in this beautiful verse, God says there is still time. Even if it is like a late October day, with frost already on the ground, you can still plant, and God will still harvest. God never gives up on us.

Is there someone in your life you have prayed over for a long time, someone you want to meet the Lord? Do they seem like that late October day, a day when it seems no one should plant and nothing will grow? Don't give up hope because God has not. Continue to pray that God will harvest a crop of righteousness in their life.

Jesus, thank you for working in my heart. Sow righteousness in me.

No Fear

Even though I walk through the darkest valley,
I will fear no evil, for you are with me;
your rod and your staff, they comfort me.

PSALM 23:4 NIV

Psalm 23 is a beloved psalm, read over and over for generations. In this section, the psalmist says that he is walking through the darkest valley. If our shepherd is good, why would he lead in that direction? Why not keep us in green grasses and by still waters forever? Why not stay in the sunshine and comfort of the stable?

Deep, dark valleys will come, even to Christians—especially to Christians. Darkest valleys are a part of life. The question is, who is leading us through them? Are we stumbling around in the dark, hoping to find our way? Or are we trusting Jesus, the Good Shepherd, to lead us? We can't pretend the darkness doesn't exist, shutting our eyes and dwelling only on the comforts and the good times. We must go forward. We can keep going without fear because Jesus is near. He will never abandon us, and he knows the way. He is the light. Cling to him. Keep going.

How can you let Jesus lead you through hard times today?

Lord, even when your path takes me through
the valley of deepest darkness,
fear will never conquer me, for you already have!
You remain close to me and lead me through it all the way.
Your authority is my strength and my peace.
The comfort of your love takes away my fear.
I'll never be lonely, for you are near.

Psalm 23:4 TPT

What is the meaning of the rod and the staff? A shepherd used his rod to count the sheep in the morning and night, to make sure that all of them were accounted for. Jesus has an intimate interest in your life, and if you wander, he will search for you. He notices if you go missing. The rod also defended the sheep in times of danger. The shepherd stands between his flock and the wild beasts, like David fighting off the lion and the bear. Your Good Shepherd stands between you and the enemy.

The staff was used to guide sheep to things like clean water and green pastures. Jesus wants to guide you. The staff could also rescue sheep. If a sheep fell into a pit or down the side of a mountain, the staff could retrieve them. All of these parallels remind us that our Good Shepherd cares for us.

Jesus, help me to follow you without fear. May your rod and staff comfort me. Thank you for being the Good Shepherd.

He Still Heals

"I have seen what they have done,
but I will heal them.
I will guide them and comfort them
and those who felt sad for them.
They will all praise me."

ISAIAH 57:18 NCV

Standing in line at the grocery store, you can glance over and see the papers full of scandal headlines. These stories are meant to shock readers. Papers promise all the details, and headlines are written to try and pull us in. We want to know the shocking details for ourselves.

Let's talk about the scandal of grace. With the description given above, *scandal* probably isn't a word you want associated with your beliefs or your church. But what Isaiah is preaching here, and what Paul preaches in Romans 9, is scandalous indeed. The good news of God's grace is so good, it has to be scandalous. The fact that Jesus, perfect in every way, lived a sinless life before becoming sin for us, is shocking. At least, it should be. That's the beauty of grace! Read this headline: Sinner doesn't get what she deserves because of the righteousness of Jesus Christ! What a headline, what a love, what a Savior.

Does your understanding of grace shock you?

*"I have seen their ways, but I will heal them;
I will guide them and restore comfort to Israel's mourners."*

ISAIAH 57:18 NIV

There is nothing you can do that God doesn't know about. The first line in the verse above tells us that God saw what Israel had done. He knows the depravity of our hearts, the depths of our sin, the strength of our chains. He loves us anyway. He wants to redeem us unto himself in spite of our sins. He sent his Son to die (that scandal we discussed this morning) to rescue us from sin's grasp once and for all.

Let's use our lives as testimony so that the last line rings truth: They all will praise me. Let God use your sinful past as a testimony of his grace and love, of how he can save. There are others out there in darkness and bondage who need to hear your story to know that God's grace reaches deep enough to grab them too.

God, thank you for saving me from my sin. Thank you for the scandalous grace you gave me. Help me to use my life as a testimony to your goodness, so that others who are trapped may be free as well.

My Life's Song

My loving God, the harp in my heart will praise you.
Your faithful heart toward us will be the theme of my song.
Melodies and music will rise to you, the Holy One of Israel.

PSALM 71:22 TPT

Praise is an intrinsic part of life. You hear the roar of a crowd when their team wins. The audience applauds after a brilliant play or musical performance. There are cheers at the dining room table when you win your favorite board game. Families hoot and holler when graduates walk across a stage and when newly married couples kiss.

We are created to praise. We praise what we support, value, and love. So why do we let embarrassment, pride, or lack of understanding rob us of showing God that he is our number one? Audible praise is a sign of a healthy inner spiritual life. Even if you don't consider yourself musically talented, praise is a gift to God that glorifies him and edifies yourself and those around you. Try it this morning. Crank some worship music and praise the Lord, beginning your day in the exuberant presence of God!

What can you praise God for this morning?

I will praise you with the harp
for your faithfulness, my God;
I will sing praise to you with the lyre,
Holy One of Israel.

PSALM 71:22 NIV

Praise gives us access to God. It's not just the fifteen minutes or song set before the main act of the preacher comes to the stage. Praise is how we turn our hearts into fertile ground for the seeds of God's Word. It's a tilling of the ground of your heart. We often come before God with hearts that are cold and distant, frozen by all the cares and worries we carry. But when we praise God, when we shift our focus to his glorious attributes, we prepare the soil of our heart. We bring fresh nutrients to the surface, and we make a planting ground for good things to grow.

This isn't restrained to the time right before someone else preaches a sermon for you. Praise will till your heart before you dig into this devotional in the mornings, while you drive down the road, and while you wash dishes in your kitchen. We have ample opportunity for God to work in our lives. Praise him!

I praise you, God, with my whole life! I praise you for the gift of this day, for waking me up and giving me purpose, and for never leaving me. You are faithful! May I sing my song to you all the days of my life.

Joyful Freedom

I prayed to the LORD, and he answered me.
He freed me from all my fears.
Those who look to him for help will be radiant with joy.

PSALM 34:4-5 NLT

Joy feels wild and unrestrained, so how can Christ followers be joyful when the Bible is full of restraints? When we view God's freedom as a list of "do this, don't do that," we aren't seeing the freedom found in Christ accurately. True freedom has boundaries, and they are good. We have a good Father who knows what is best for us. He leads us to wide open pastures of grace, pointing us toward abundant living.

Yes, God has guidelines, but these guidelines are life-giving and full of joy. Taken without submission to the Spirit and the power of God, they will seem like nothing but a burden. The voice of the enemy loves to focus on the "can't" rules. He wants to manipulate you to see God's leading as restrictive and rigid. You then find yourself in bondage, depressed about what you can't have, rather than free in the joy of God's will.

Which inner voice is free of fear and insecurity,
full of joy and trust? Which direction truly sets you free?

I cried to God in my distress
and he answered me. He freed me from all my fears!
Gaze upon him, join your life with his, and joy will come.
Your faces will glisten with glory.

PSALM 34:4-5 TPT

Can you think of a more perfect pair than freedom and joy?
It's hard to have one without the other. Think back to stories
of liberation, like the Israelites leaving Egypt, Paul and Silas
escaping prison, or countless times throughout history when
oppressed people were set free. What joy is found!

You were once in bondage to sin. You were under the
oppressive rule of death. Before Christ, you were a slave to
sin. Now, in Christ, you have been set free. See your chains,
now open and scattered on the floor. Look at your oppressor,
fleeing at the sound of Jesus' name. See the open jail cell,
the door broken by your Savior. With these truths before us,
how can we keep our feet from dancing, our mouths from
praising, our joy from overflowing into exuberant worship
before our God?

Savior, thank you for freedom. Thank you for joy in your
presence! Help me to trust in your freedom.

At All Times

*May the Lord of peace, himself, give you peace at all times
and in every way. The Lord be with all of you.*

2 Thessalonians 3:16 NIV

There are many verses regarding peace in Scripture, and they can encourage us. God himself is peace, and he became man and dwelt with us. The angels could sing about peace on earth because peace himself was coming down to earth.

Now, the Holy Spirit dwells inside of you. He is peace, and he produces his fruit of the Spirit, peace, in you. You bear this fruit by dwelling in fellowship with peace himself. This peace is not based off this shifting changing world or man's ideas and thoughts. God is unchanging and unshakeable, and the peace he offers is the same. Let us stop trying to achieve peace through this world and instead look through our spiritual eyes, believing that he will sustain us through all circumstances.

Where do you need peace today?

May the Lord himself, the Lord of peace,
pour into you his peace in every circumstance
and in every possible way.
The Lord's tangible presence be with you all.

2 Thessalonians 3:16 TPT

We are shaped by what we eat. If you are on a steady diet of
fast food, your shape is going to change, and you will probably
experience some unhealthy side effects. If you eat healthy
food, it will form you and change you for the better. Our
minds operate in a similar fashion. If you are constantly
listening to angry music and shows, then you will be more
prone to responding in anger.

This is also how our souls operate. If you spend time in God's
Word, with the countless number of verses about peace, your
soul will be shaped by peace. It will transform how you relate
to God and to others. The more time you spend in God's
Word, the more time you spend dwelling on promises of
peace. This is a major way that God brings peace. His Word,
dwelling inside of us, reminds us of who he is. Meditate on
his promise of peace this evening. Write his words on your
heart and let peace form your soul.

God, thank you for being my peace. Thank you for giving me
peace anytime, anywhere. Let your peace form my soul and
change me as a person.

My Defense

I will sing of Your power;
Yes, I will sing aloud of Your mercy in the morning;
For You have been my defense
And refuge in the day of my trouble.

PSALM 59:16 NKJV

Have you ever felt sorry for the poor guy that has to carry the flag in battle, or the band that accompanies the army? It seems like they are easy targets. Wouldn't they rather have a weapon in hand than an instrument? In a physical battle, that would make sense. But in our spiritual battles, our praise is our weapon. The soldier singing and worshiping God is the one most fit for battle.

Praise is our weapon. It is both a spiritually offensive and defensive weapon. When we praise God, we invite him into the situation. We display our faith in who he is. We choose to sacrifice our feelings about the event, which are often hopeless and subject to despair, and instead sing about who God says he is. In this way, we overcome our own feelings too. When we praise and call out to Jesus, the enemy has no choice but to retreat. There is power in your praise. Sing out your song of victory this morning!

How can you fight with praise today?

As for me, your strength shall be my song of joy.
At each and every sunrise, my lyrics of your love will fill the air!
For you have been my glory-fortress,
a stronghold in my day of distress.

PSALM 59:16 TPT

In Scripture, there are several examples of praise as a spiritual line of defense. Look up Acts 16, with Paul and Silas in prison, or in 2 Chronicles 17 about King Jehoshaphat. Something about the song of God's people is powerful against the enemy. How can you practically apply this to your life?

First off, when you feel under attack, turn up that worship music and praise. You don't need the help of a radio; sing the doxology or your favorite hymn. Secondly, in your daily life, try to incorporate more worship. Let songs of praise and worship shape your day and your household. In your quiet times, begin with a song. Let the songs clear out spiritual deadness, purify your soul, and carry your heart into the presence of God. It doesn't matter if you don't think you can carry a tune. God's not asking you to become the next pop star. He's looking at the posture of your heart.

God, I praise you! Put a new song in my heart to sing my defense. Remind me to fight my battles with praise.

Ancient Path

Be mindful of your mercy, O Lord,
and of your steadfast love,
for they have been from of old.

PSALM 25:6 NRSV

Many animals, like deer and cows, walk the same paths. In wide-open, overgrown fields and through dense forests, you can find paths made by these animals. They walk the same path over and over again, which beats down the brush and creates the walkway. This can make the animal easier to find because they are sure to return.

Before the beginning of time, God created the ancient path of mercy and covenant love. God has walked this path with humanity, from Adam to the present moment. Over and over again, God displays these characteristics to us. Are you wondering where God is, how to find him? Look to the overflowing mercy, walk the path of faithful love, and you will find him there.

Can you trace the path of mercy and faithfulness
in your life back to God?

Remember, O Lᴏʀᴅ, Your tender mercies and Your lovingkindness,
For they are from of old.

Pˢᴀʟᴍ 25:6 ɴᴋᴊᴠ

Why do you think the psalmist asked God to be mindful or remember something? Does this imply that God forgets? God doesn't forget, especially about mercy and faithfulness. They are part of his very character. So, what is he getting at here?

Sometimes, life's circumstances can make us feel like God has forgotten mercy or walked away from faithful love. Hard times make us question, and God is not afraid of these questions. He is secure enough to handle our questions. In turn, he reminds us that he has never stopped being faithful, and he could never walk away from being merciful. Often, when we think God has forgotten, it is we who have forgotten him. May we find fresh discovery of God's mercy and love tonight.

God, you are always faithful, you are always merciful, you are full of love toward me. It's who you are! It's in your very nature. You cannot turn to another path. Thank you for the beauty of these realities. Remind me of who you are when I forget and try to take a different path.

New Levels

He who sits on the throne said, "Behold, I am making all things new." And He said, "Write, for these words are faithful and true."

REVELATION 21:5 NASB

When you look at the world, it feels like all hope is lost. A glance at the TV will reveal urgent news reports of global pain. You might catch up with a friend who tells you they have cancer. Social media can become a tornado of bickering. Taking it all in, you might wonder why God doesn't finish it all now. Despair can settle in as you look out on the barren landscape.

Listen to the King's proclamation of hope. "Behold, I am making all things new." Don't be fooled by how things appear. You can miscalculate the outcome of the world if you base it off news reports and your grandma's social media page. Our broken, fallen state is not too much for God. He is not unaware; he is not overwhelmed. He hasn't surrendered, and he isn't wondering what should happen next. Behold! Look and see God moving among us. Look and see what he is doing. The ending already planned, and the victory is won. Let hope bloom in you.

How does focusing on the despair of the world
make you doubt God's Word?

The One who was sitting on the throne said,
"Look! I am making everything new!"
Then he said, "Write this, because these words are true
and can be trusted."

REVELATION 21:5 NCV

Take another look at the verse. What exactly did Jesus say he's making new? Everything. All things. There will be nothing left out, nothing forgotten. He's not hiding some stuff away in a closet, hoping people will forget about it.

No, this is a clean sweep. All things become new. Our powerful King, who has conquered sin and death and sits on the throne now says, "Look! Look at the work I am doing. I am making all things new." There is nothing outside of his reach or abilities. What a powerful, amazing God we serve. Let wonder and praise fill you as you see new things that God is doing.

Jesus, you are my glorious King. Thank you for making things new! Help me to focus on that and not on despair.

He Knows

He was despised and rejected by men,
a man of sorrows and acquainted with grief;
and as one from whom men hide their faces he was despised,
and we esteemed him not.

ISAIAH 53:3 ESV

Do you want a more attractive Jesus? We would never admit it out loud, but many of us subscribe to a faith that wants to clean up Jesus. We love the concert style of worship with its flashing lights, full band, and catchy lyrics, but we shy away from our prayer closets. We position our pretty art Bibles just so, with a candle and a latte, to post on social media—but we don't dive into Scripture. We make or buy wooden signs with beautiful calligraphy that have a popular verse (or half of one) about hospitality. We hang them in our dining rooms, and yet we fail to open our homes to the broken and needy. We tell people we will pray for them but never utter a word to the Savior.

In these and many more ways, we want the attractive Jesus, and not the Jesus described to us in the verse above. Let's drop the facade of attractive Christianity and humbly kneel before the cross. Seeing his feet, his hands, his side, and the thorns in his crown, let us follow the way of our Savior, who gave his very life for us.

Where are you guilty of subscribing to the attractive Jesus and denying the despised Savior?

He was despised and rejected—
a man of sorrows, acquainted with deepest grief.
We turned our backs on him and looked the other way.
He was despised, and we did not care.

ISAIAH 53:3 NLT

If you are suffering as you walk with Jesus, take heart. You are not alone. Jesus was well acquainted with the difficulties that come with choosing the Father's will. He is familiar with grief, rejection, betrayal, and suffering. None of the things you go through are unfamiliar to him.

While it might seem odd, let that encourage you. You do not have a God who cannot relate to your sufferings. Your God came down and took on humanity so that you could dwell with him forever. Let it encourage you that Jesus can empathize with you, and he also has the power to overcome all you are going through.

Jesus, thank you for dying on the cross for me. I am humbled that you are so acquainted with grief. Help me to walk in the way of the cross.

Encouragement for Today

Everything that was written in the past was written to teach us.
The Scriptures give us patience and encouragement
so that we can have hope.

ROMANS 15:4 NCV

Ask most believers how to grow in faith and they will answer:
read your Bible, pray, and go to church. Yet why is it so hard
for us to open our Bibles? We might say it matters while not
truly believing it does. Maybe it is a nagging feeling that time
spent reading the ancient text is not productive. Perhaps we
tend to trust popular speakers, pastors, or authors instead of
trusting that the Holy Spirit speaks to us.

This is part of spiritual warfare. We have an enemy who
will do anything to keep us hopeless. Take some time this
morning to pray specifically about what hinders you from
studying God's Word. The Word needs to become a necessity
and lifeline in our daily lives, not a book of suggestions we
turn to occasionally.

What's holding you back from accessing the patience,
encouragement, and hope of the Scriptures that
you need for daily living?

Whatever things were written before were written for our learning, that we through the patience and comfort of the Scriptures might have hope.

ROMANS 15:4 NKJV

You can get a new manicure every week. You can get in a good workout and drink all green juices and take vitamins. Go to college, get a masters, get a PHD. You can snag that promotion and make those zeros line up in your bank account. You can outfit your kids in the cutest clothes, stick cute notes in their healthy lunches, and show up for every PTA event. You can hustle and work and achieve like mad, but if you aren't rooted in the Word of God, what are you doing?

Everything that the world hands to us as hope will crumble into ash and blow away. All that remains is his Word, his promises, himself. Yesterday, today, and forever. That is the greatest pursuit and achievement you can gain.

God, help me to dig deep into your Word. Remove roadblocks that keep me from it, and let your Word come alive in me as it becomes my lifeline.

Not in Vain

Lord, you know the hopes of the helpless.
Surely you will hear their cries and comfort them.

PSALM 10:17 NLT

Who comes to mind when you read this passage? We don't
to think of ourselves as helpless. The reality is that, without
Christ, we are all helpless in our sin. The Bible often refers to
us as dead. Dead in our sins, we have no power or ability that
can move us closer to peace with God and freedom from sin
and death. We are completely helpless.

This news is not to bring you to a state of despair. It's meant to
lead you into awe of your Savior. Jesus made a way. Jesus saw
us in our helpless state, took compassion on us, and brought
us into a right relationship with God—and he continues to do
so. The process of restoration and making things new is the
process of Jesus freeing us from our helpless position and
fulfilling all our hopes. Take heart; he hears you, and he is
working in your life today.

Have you stopped to consider
the great work of our Savior recently?

Lord, you know and understand all the hopes of the humble
and will hear their cries and comfort their hearts,
helping them all!

PSALM 10:17 TPT

God wants us to communicate with him in prayer. When we cry out to him, it is never in vain. He is willing and able to answer your prayers. The problem is that we don't pray! Is your first thought when you need help to cry out to Jesus? That is a habit all Christians need to develop, because he is near to those who cry out to him.

Prayer is important because it develops our relationship with God, and it shows us more and more of his character. It displays a posture of submission, one that tells God the believer wants to partner with him in this life instead of pushing through on their own. Try to start making it a habit of praying wherever you are, and you'll be amazed as God hears your cries.

Jesus, thank you for being near to me. Thank you for hearing my prayers. I come to you in my helpless state and ask you to draw near.

Over and Over

*Our fathers who were delivered from Egypt
didn't fully understand your wonders,
and they took you for granted.
Over and over you showed them
such tender love and mercy!*

PSALM 106:7 TPT

When life is going pretty well, it can be easy to forget the tough times. In hard times, we know we need help. We cry out to God for deliverance just as the Israelites did for freedom from Egypt. We cry out, and he responds to us. He works in our life, performs miracles, brings freedom; it's a wild ride!

But then the good times come. While we aren't sad about that, it can make us forgetful. As the psalmist puts it, we take God for granted. We get used to the calm, and we are blind to his mercy. We forget who is handing us blessings. But don't despair! God's not going to snatch some good gift out of your hand because of this. He's not going to rain down tribulation on you. All he wants is for you to remember. Remember what he has done for you. See the steady stream of mercy that supplies your life, and never cease to give thanks for it. Give thanks in good and bad times. Don't grow blind when times are good; lift your voice up to Jesus.

What steady stream of mercy can you thank Jesus for today?

Our ancestors in Egypt
were not impressed by the LORD's miraculous deeds.
They soon forgot his many acts of kindness to them.
Instead, they rebelled against him at the Red Sea.

PSALM 106:7 NLT

Don't worry, there is plenty of God to go around. Do you see
the hand of God moving in your friend's life? Are you amazed
at how your pastor's wife always seems to glow with the love
of Christ? Do you long to feel the connection your roommate
has with Jesus?

You have the same amount of access as anyone else. Don't
compare your journey with others' paths. God is just as
benevolent with his love, grace, time, and mercy toward you
as he is toward others. He does not withhold from you. There
is enough to go around! Drink deep of the well tonight.

Jesus, thank you for your abundance and generosity. Help me
to remember where all my gifts come from, even when times
are good.

Come Again

You who are my Comforter in sorrow,
my heart is faint within me.

JEREMIAH 8:18 NIV

Have you ever faced a grieving friend, unsure of what to say?
We can be paralyzed by fear of saying the wrong thing. The
solution is not to stay away or not show up at all. Your friend
needs you. There is comfort to be found in the Word of God
and in pointing a friend to Jesus. While verses about God
being sovereign or working things together for good might
not be healing when a grief first happens, the nearness of
Jesus is a comfort that needs to be communicated.

It is okay to grieve, to be sad, to cry, to mourn over the pains
and hard things in this world. When you or a loved one is
facing deep grief, remind them (and yourself) that Jesus
wept. Jesus had sorrow as well. And on top of that, he is near.
The greatest comfort is that Jesus has never abandoned or left
because things were hard or sad. Jesus is near, and that is all
you need.

What comfort do you get from knowing Jesus is near?

My grief is beyond healing;
my heart is broken.

JEREMIAH 8:18

Though you might not know what to do or say in times of grief, the Holy Spirit does. In Jeremiah, our verse says that he is our comforter in sorrow. That means the Holy Spirit knows how to comfort in this particular sorrow. It is possible. The Holy Spirit can move in ways that we don't understand. He knows the depths of our spirits and hurts.

Let us not shy away from his comfort, bottling up our feelings and hurts. Let us run to the open arms of Jesus and tell him our sorrows. He cares for us. Only he can bring healing and peace.

Jesus, be near to me. My heart has sorrow today. Here are my woes. I need you to show yourself; I need your presence. Thank you for comforting me.

Unimaginable Power

He will take our weak mortal bodies and change them into glorious bodies like his own, using the same power with which he will bring everything under his control.

PHILIPPIANS 3:21 NLT

Resurrection power. Bringing-people-back-from-the-dead power. Descend-into-hell, conquer-sin-and-death kind of power. No-weapon-of-the-enemy-can-prosper power. Words-that-create-galaxies power. Naming-stars kind of power. Knows-every-hair-on-your-head power.

This is our King. When the headlines scream of turbulence, this is our King. When politics fail us, this is our King. When we feel helpless in the face of evil in this world, this is our Savior who is in charge and in control. He's got the plan. He knows how the story ends. You too know how the story wins. Jesus wins, love wins, the enemy is defeated, and we are transformed to be like him and be with him forever. Restoration comes, peace resides, and Jesus reigns on the throne forever and ever. Amen! What a Savior!

Do things feel out of control in the world?
Dwell on the power of God this morning.

*By his power to rule all things, he will change our humble bodies
and make them like his own glorious body.*

PHILIPPIANS 3:21 NCV

The verse preceding this one states that our citizenship is in
heaven. Though God has placed each of us in a specific time
and place in history for his glory, we cannot our identities
get wrapped up in the here and now. We have to avoid the
allure of power for earthly country of citizenship, our political
affiliation, or our positions in our society. Our focus needs to
be on eternity, where our inheritance and citizenship await.

That makes us refugees on this earth, travelers passing
through on the way home. Our home is prepared and awaiting
us, so why settle for temporary security here when what we
look forward to so exceeds anything we could gain here? Let
us be citizens of heaven on a journey to our home, eager to
have all those around us join in.

God, you are so mighty and so powerful. I praise your robust
nature and the fact that you are in complete control. Help me
to find my identity as a citizen of heaven and live with eternity
in mind.

Spirit Thoughts

To set the mind on the flesh is death,
but to set the mind on the Spirit is life and peace.

ROMANS 8:6 ESV

How can we set our minds on the Spirit? You're starting off well by reading this devotion and being in God's Word first thing in the morning. However, our devotions cannot stop here. We can't read God's Word, pray, check off the box, and be on our way.

If you pray for help this morning to be kinder to your co-worker, and then you find yourself struggling with how to treat them at one pm, pray again! Set your mind on the things of the Spirit moment by moment. You don't have to be in your prayer closet to communicate with the Spirit. He will help you and meet you all throughout your day, giving you peace. We need to set our minds on the Spirit throughout the day. Praying at all times will transform your mind and set it on the Spirit.

How can you remind yourself to
turn your mind toward God throughout today?

To be carnally minded is death,
but to be spiritually minded is life and peace.

ROMANS 8:6 NKJV

Another way we can set our minds on the Spirit is by keeping truth in front of us. This morning, we looked at how to turn our minds toward God. Imagine yourself driving a car. In order to turn the car, you look in the direction you want to go and turn the wheel. We need to be looking to the Spirit for guidance and keep our eyes focused on him. We need to keep truth in front of us by memorizing Scripture and knowing the Bible. Then we need to take action on the truth that we know.

You can look in the direction you want to go all you want, but if you don't turn the wheel, you won't end up there. By the power of the Holy Spirit, let's set our minds on him. Let's turn toward truth and get back our lives and our peace.

Holy Spirit, will you guide me toward truth? I want to set my mind on the things of the Spirit.

Always Known

I will be glad and rejoice in Your mercy,
For You have considered my trouble;
You have known my soul in adversities.

PSALM 31:7 NKJV

Have you heard the term "fair-weather friend?" It refers to
a person who only sticks around when things are going well.
This friend is there for parties, celebrations, and sunshine—
the good weather in life. They stick around when you are
successful, accomplished, and doing things they deem as
right. One sign of trouble, though, and they are out the door.

Jesus is not that kind of friend. He is there in the good times,
but he is even nearer in adversity. He is near for both fair and
foul weather. He never abandons you when things get hard.
To Jesus, you are always known. He knows the depths of your
sin, forgives you, and loves you unconditionally. He sees your
suffering and draws in closer. He doesn't run in fear. You are
always known by the God of the universe. Let that truth be
balm to your soul today.

How has Jesus stuck by you in fair weather and in foul?

*In mercy you have seen my troubles and you have cared for me;
even during this crisis in my soul I will be radiant with joy,
filled with praise for your love and mercy.*

PSALM 31:7 TPT

It is so hard when friends betray us. Friends can inflict some
of the deepest hurts in our lives because of the nature of the
relationship. We share so much with them, and we venture to
let down our guards. When a friend betrays us, it cuts deep.
Jesus knows this pain too because he has been betrayed in
this way.

Isn't it interesting how you bond quicker with those who
can empathize with you? They have been through a similar
situation. Jesus knows your pain. He knows your hurt. He's
been there. He empathizes with you. He can extend the most
personal, tender mercy because of this. Let his mercy wash
over you and bring joy to your soul. Let the friendship of
Christ encourage you today.

Jesus, my friend, thank you for your mercy and for
empathizing with my pain. Thank you for knowing me and
loving me.

Abundant Provision

May mercy, peace, and love
be yours in abundance.

JUDE 1:2 NRSV

What do you need? We serve a generous God who has abundant provision. God has everything you need and is willing to meet every need. Imagine yourself without payment and in need. You go to God and ask. He has exactly what you need, and he gives it. All you had to do was ask!

Are you in need of compassion and forgiveness this morning? Turn to Jesus. Is there turmoil in your soul and life, and you long for peace? God's got that; just ask. Are you hurting and in need of tender love today? God's got that for you. There is no end to the provisions he has for you! Why do we continue to turn to empty places, seeking out what we need? Why do we scrape and toil to make payment on things that Jesus offers us for free? Mercy, peace, love—it's all abundantly yours in Christ.

What do you need this morning? Ask for it now.

May God give you more and more
mercy, peace, and love.

JUDE 1:2 NLT

Jude writes these words at the very beginning of his letter. He wastes no time in getting into the deep truths. He knows that those he is writing to need access to mercy, peace, and love. Those who have been given mercy are more likely to extend mercy to others. Those who are at peace are secure when times get hard. Love for God and his people would spur the readers on toward good works and toward telling others about Jesus.

The people Jude wrote to may have been living in a precarious time, but Jude knew that God could provide exactly what they needed for their specific situation. How can God's abundant mercy, peace, and love meet you where you are tonight?

Jesus, thank you for your love. Thank you for extending mercy to me. Thank you for your abundant peace that washes over me. You love me, and you are generous. Give me boldness to ask for what I need.

Wholeness in Him

May the God who gives us his peace and wholeness be with you all.
Yes, Lord, so let it be!

Romans 15:33 TPT

What does it mean for God to make us whole? When God first created mankind, he declared us good. Before the fall, mankind was whole. Adam walked in the garden with God. Man was whole and at peace with God. Then sin came in, destroying the relationship between God and man and breaking man's perfection.

Now, Jesus has made a way for peace with God, and God is working to restore us. We won't be made completely whole until we are united with Christ in heaven, when the process of sanctification is complete. However, we can daily move toward wholeness by letting God move in our lives and sanctify us. We need complete renewal: mental, physical, spiritual. We can honor the process by working with God as he sanctifies us. For some, that might mean pursuing Biblical counseling to work on past wounds. It means honoring God with how we treat our physical bodies. It means using Scripture to renew our minds.

Where is God asking you to partner with him
to work toward wholeness in your life?

The God of peace be with all of you.
Amen.

ROMANS 15:33 NRSV

Have you ever dropped a glass on a tile floor? It shatters into what seems like a million unfixable pieces. It's impossible to restore, so we sweep it up and throw it away. Our lives are like that shattered glass. Sin has left us shattered. Without an outside power, we have no hope of being whole again.

Jesus enters our brokenness. He is the only one with the power to make all those little pieces fit back together. He makes us whole again. The parts of your life that you just want to throw away and forget about, he will restore. The parts of your life that feel lost or beyond repair, Jesus will heal. What a mighty God we serve!

God, I want to partner with you to work toward wholeness. Thank you for your awesome power. May my shattered parts heal and point to your glory.

Life Forever

*That faith and that knowledge come from the hope for life forever,
which God promised to us before time began.*

TITUS 1:2 NCV

Is eternal life impacting your current life? It should! It's called
having an eternal perspective. There are several ways it should
be changing your life. Eternal life means we have changed into
beings that know God himself. Jesus gave us peace with God,
and now we can truly know the character of God.

This is why what you are doing right now is so important:
taking time first thing in the morning to meet with God and
read his Word. Eternal life begins with knowing God. There is
great reward for those who choose to live their life according
to God's Word and submit to him. Eternity should impact how
we live here and now.

How does eternity impact your life?
What can you change in your life to reflect eternity?

The hope of eternal life, which God, who does not lie,
promised before the beginning of time.

TITUS 1:2 NIV

Eternal life impacts our current life with hope. We have hope in life forever with Christ. This means that the second death, which is judgment after physical death, has no power over us because of Christ. By choosing to follow Jesus here, we are forever secured in his kingdom. We are free from the power of sin and death over us.

Having eternal hope helps us live with heaven on our minds. That doesn't mean we stare out the window all day, waiting for Jesus to return, or that we wish for death. It means that our priorities and how we spend our time, money, and resources are changed. We go from living for ourselves to living with the hope of the kingdom to come.

Jesus, thank you for the hope you give me! Give me an eternal perspective, today and every day.

Seeds Sown

*Those who sow in tears
shall reap with shouts of joy.*

PSALM 126:5 ESV

Verse five comes to us right in the middle of a psalm of celebration. There is a party going on! Why is the psalmist bringing up tears and sadness? How does that fit? Sowing and reaping goes back to gardening terms. What you plant, you harvest. If you plant sunflowers, you'll get sunflowers, right? So, how can you sow sadness and get joy? By the power of Christ.

He sees your tears and hard times. Those moments that you feel like you can't go on, but you do. You do the next right thing. You put in another load of laundry and do the dishes. You go to work. You walk your dog. Some of these tasks you do in tears, but the tears are sowing something. You might want to quit, but you keep going. As your tears wet the ground of your life, and what does God promise? Joy. Not just a tiny bit, but shouts of it. Abundant joy! It will come. Just continue to your best, humbly and with repentance. Don't quit. Don't bottle up your tears. Let them water and do their part for the joy that is to come.

Are you in a season of tears or joy?

Those who plant in tears
will harvest with shouts of joy.

PSALM 126:5 NLT

If you are feeling discouraged and down, if things are not going how you planned, go ahead and cry. God is big enough for your feelings, and he expects your sorrows. Then, continue on. Keep doing the hard work God has called you to do and wait on him. He will reap your reward. He will give you joy.

It's a promise! And God is always faithful to his promises. Know that this despair comes for a time, but joy comes in the morning. Keep on, dear believer.

Jesus, I feel discouraged. Please comfort me in my tears. I cling to the promise of the joy that will come.

Out of My Hands

We can make our plans,
but the LORD determines our steps.

PROVERBS 16:9 NLT

What's the point of making plans if the Lord is going to change the plan? Isn't the writer of proverbs setting us a futile task? It's easy to make our own plans, locking our eyes on that specific future idea. The difference between these two plans is who has the aerial view.

God is the one who can see far down the road. He knows the ins and outs of every part of our lives, and he wants to be in each moment. That doesn't mean he wants us to sit back and let everything happen to us. This proverb is asking, who has control? We make plans, but God gives the days. Are you open to the days he gives? He is the God who goes ahead of us. He knows the best path and what will grow your character and sanctify you on the journey.

When have you felt like God direct your steps differently than how you had planned? How did you react?

Within your heart you can make plans for your future,
but the Lord chooses the steps you take to get there.

PROVERBS 16:9 TPT

Let the pressure roll off you. You don't have to walk this path
alone. God has promised to never leave you, and to go before
you to prepare the way. He has determined your steps, and
you have his Holy Spirit as a constant help and comfort, no
matter what road you walk.

There is no part of your journey that is too dark, too hard, or
too simplistic for his care. Will you open yourself up to his
companionship? Don't try to walk through life alone. To have
friend we can be completely vulnerable with, who knows the
future and has our very best in mind? Sounds like a dream,
but it's a Christian's reality.

Thank you, God, for going before me. You have numbered my
days. I am honored that you want to be in every moment of
my life. I lay my plans at your feet, and with open palms,
I look for your direction.

Taken Care Of

"People everywhere seem to worry about making a living, but your heavenly Father knows your every need and will take care of you."

LUKE 12:30 TPT

People everywhere seem to worry about little things. It makes sense because the human struggle with sin is rooted in pride. When we worry, we pridefully show that we choose to trust in our own strength. We greedily grab for control. Pride manifested in anxiety is an expression of disbelief that God controls our future.

So how do we remedy this? With humility. We must humble ourselves and admit that the Father knows and will take care of our every need. We must cry out to him with our concerns instead of carrying them on our own. We must drive forward in prayer instead of in anxious thought. We have strong promise that he will care for us in today's verse and in many, many places in Scripture. Cling to the promise of his care, humble yourself before the Lord, and unload your fears and anxious worries onto the shoulders of Jesus.

What do you think about the link between worry and pride?

> *"For all these things the nations of the world seek after,
> and your Father knows that you need these things."*
>
> LUKE 12:30 NKJV

When you think of the phrase "will take care of you," it
probably brings a certain picture to mind. One might think
of a parent's care: how they cooked your meals, packed
your school lunches, washed your clothes, and kissed your
forehead when you were sick. When you think of being cared
for, it is usually a restful picture. Someone else is meeting
your needs. When we hand over our cares to Jesus and let him
take care of us, it brings rest.

We can fall into the trap of productivity that makes us believe
if we are resting, we are useless to God and society. This just
breeds anxiety within us, because the opposite of anxiety
is being cared for, which implies rest. Did you know God
commands us to rest? That he himself rested? It is Biblical
to do so. And it's Biblical to lay down your worries and cares.
Let's follow in the way of Jesus and allow him to care for us
tenderly, just like our parents used to do.

Jesus, forgive me of my pride. I give you my burdens. Help me
to rest in you.

Strong in Joy

Don't be sad, because the joy of the LORD
will make you strong.

NEHEMIAH 8:10 NCV

In the book of Nehemiah, there is a first-person account by
a Jewish man who was a high-ranking Persian officer. Many
years after the destruction of Jerusalem and the exile of the
people to Babylon, the people were finally able to return and
rebuild their city. Nehemiah came, and they began rebuilding
the walls of the city. As they worked, they found the law of
God (chapter 8), and it was brought out and read before all
the people.

And they were crushed. They were sad, which is the context
behind our verse today. The reading of the Word made them
sad because they saw how far they had strayed from God.
The Word of God was doing its job. In 2 Timothy, it says
that Scripture is used for reproof and correction. Reproof
and correction will often lead to sorrow over our sins, but
this isn't a bad thing! Sorrow leads to repentance, and
repentance to forgiveness, and forgiveness to joy at restoring
relationship with God.

Have you felt sorrow over your sins lately?

Do not sorrow, for the joy of the LORD
is your strength.
NEHEMIAH 8:10 NKJV

Our knowledge of our sin should never be bigger than our knowledge of our Savior. Though it is good to weep over sin, it is just as good to rejoice in forgiveness. We are all great sinners. It's our nature to sin. Before Christ, we are dead in our sin. But once we are in Christ, we are new creations. While we still sin, we cannot forget that our Savior is bigger than any sin. He is stronger than sin and death. And he has conquered them both.

When we are convicted of our sin, we can find joy even there, because it means the Holy Spirit is working in us. It means that God is working in our lives to make us more like him—the very outcome we want. Don't let condemnation and guilt steal the joy that can come with conviction.

Jesus, thank you for forgiving me of my sins. Thank you for conviction and thank you for your strength.

Generations of Mercy

*"His mercy is for those who fear him
from generation to generation."*

LUKE 1:50 NRSV

Legacy is important. Leaving a legacy for the next generation
is for every person, not just those with children. There is
blessing and bounty in store for the next generation when it
rises up and takes this one's place. Praying for disciples in
the next generation of Christians is a way to leave a legacy.
What bounty is in store for those who have prayerful parents,
parents who brought them before the Lord constantly!

We are called to be spiritual parents to those who need it.
No matter your age right now, there is someone out there
who could learn, grow, and benefit from your prayers. Let us
not keep blessings to ourselves. Let us look out on the sea of
younger faces and ask God to lead us to those he wants us to
disciple. Then, make a move toward them! Ask them out for
coffee, send them a note saying you are praying for them, or
offer to lead a Bible study. Let us be spiritual parents who are
conduits of his mercy to the generations that encounter us.

Is there a young person that you could pray for and disciple?

"He shows mercy from generation to generation to all who fear him."

LUKE 1:50 NLT

His mercy is for you. It is accessible to you and available to you. You are a person who fears God. Therefore, his mercy is yours. Are you running hard, attempting to keep it all together and not mess up? In the modern age, so many people struggle with perfectionism.

Let this truth—that his mercy is for you—slow you down and wrap its arms around you. There is more than enough. Jesus does not expect you to be perfect. He wants you to come to him with all your imperfection and allow him to wrap you in his merciful embrace.

Jesus, thank you for your mercy. I know it is always there for me. Lead me to those with whom you want me to share your mercy.

Steady Support

If I say, "My foot slips,"
Your mercy, O Lord, will hold me up.

PSALM 94:18 NKJV

The Bible is our main resource for understanding the character of God. In the Bible, we are given the picture of a God who is very understanding. God doesn't ask us to pretend to be strong when we are weak. He knows our weaknesses and doesn't turn us away because of them. What God does ask is that we submit our weaknesses to him and let him work through us.

The psalmist is crying out his weakness. "My foot slips!" He was going to fall, and he recognized the fact that he couldn't save himself. It is in that moment that the Lord met him with mercy and strength. Let us follow in the same pattern. When we feel a foot slip, when we feel weak, let us cry out to Jesus. He will meet us in our moments of weakness and provide steady support.

How have you seen God meet your needs
when you cried out to him?

When I screamed out, "Lord, I'm doomed!"
your fiery love was stirred and you raced to my rescue.

PSALM 94:18 TPT

This concept is not just reserved for the psalmist. We see it presented many times in the Bible, the weak voicing their needs to God. Jesus healed so many people who reached out to him in their weakness. He made blind people see, lame walk, the dead rise, all because people admitted their weakness to him.

Paul confesses his weakness by listing off the trials he has been through and talking about a thorn in his side. Paul concludes that "in my weakness, then I am strong." How does he conclude this? It comes back to what our psalmist, those Jesus healed, and Paul all know. The Lord's mercy will strengthen us and hold us up.

God, thank you for not rejecting me because of my weakness. Continue to strengthen me.

How Much More

I am weary with my sighing;
Every night I make my bed swim,
I dissolve my couch with my tears.
My eye has wasted away with grief;
It has become old because of all my adversaries.

PSALM 6:6-8 NASB

Have you ever felt abandoned, left to face a hard situation on your own? Jesus experienced this too. He lost friends and family several times, but the most prominent example is when Jesus went to the cross. As he hung there to die for our sins, the presence of the heavenly Father, the one he constantly relied on while on earth, escaped him. The pain was agonizing. Jesus cried out in Matthew 27:46, "My God, My God, why have you forsaken me?"

Here in Psalms, David is talking about a similar, lonely pain. Jesus underwent the pain of crucifixion for you, but he also embodied the ultimate level of loneliness—separation from the Father—so that you never have to. It was because of this that he now promises us his presence. Peace himself will never leave you. You are never alone.

Do you find comfort in the fact that Jesus and David also experienced loneliness?

I'm exhausted and worn out with my weeping.
I endure weary, sleepless nights filled with moaning,
soaking my pillow with my tears.
My eyes of faith won't focus anymore, for sorrow fills my heart.
There are so many enemies who come against me!
Go away! Leave me, all you troublemakers!
For the Lord has turned to listen to my thunderous cry.

PSALM 6:6-8 TPT

The actions that David writes about in this psalm seem very
private and personal. They are things that most of us do in
secret. We might not want to be alone, but heavy grief is hard
to show others. It makes us vulnerable, and in our minds, it
makes us weak.

Jesus laid everything out on the cross. He exposed his most
vulnerable moment for friends and enemies alike to see.
But the story does not end there. Jesus rose again. He is now
seated at the right hand of the Father. David's story doesn't
stop here in his grief, either. Grief will come like waves, but
this is not the end of your story. Take heart in knowing that
you will rise from this bed of tears.

Jesus, you can relate to my pain and suffering, and I love that
about you. Be near to me in my grief.

Unifying Love

*If there is any encouragement in Christ, any comfort from love,
any participation in the Spirit, any affection and sympathy,
complete my joy by being of the same mind, having the same love,
being in full accord and of one mind.*

PHILIPPIANS 2:1-2 ESV

Let's talk about hospitality. People often think of hospitality as a 50s-style homemaker, pulling a roast from the oven in a sparkling kitchen and pouring cocktails for her husband's boss. To many people, hospitality is meant to impress. Biblical hospitality is the opposite. It's about considering others as more important than yourself. That means not putting on an impressive front, but just being welcoming. That means meeting people where they are, offering a smile and a listening ear.

When we try to impress, it sucks the life and the meaning out of hospitality. It doesn't foster real community and relationships. When we drop the pretenses and allow people into our messy lives with love, then the Spirit really starts to move among us. Hospitality is life on life with the mindset of serving others well. It can be practiced at home, at work, or anywhere you are.

How can you practice godly hospitality today?

Is there any encouragement from belonging to Christ? Any comfort from his love? Any fellowship together in the Spirit? Are your hearts tender and compassionate? Then make me truly happy by agreeing wholeheartedly with each other, loving one another, and working together with one mind and purpose.

PHILIPPIANS 2:1-2 NLT

We hate to admit it, but the popular phrase "every man for himself" is often how we like to live. You see it even in church communities, where we have been given specific instructions to live in unity and community with one another. We show up on Sunday mornings, looking nice, to have small talk over coffee for ten minutes, listen to a sermon, and then head home.

Dear Christian, that is not how God intended his church to behave! Church is not a Sunday morning cocktail hour or a Groundhog Day meet-and-greet that repeats itself every week. The church is meant to live together. Life on life. Messy, broken, imperfect. It means bearing one another, praying with one another, encouraging one another. Is this what your church life looks like? If so, praise God! If not, how could you be the first one to take steps toward change?

Jesus, thank you for creating the body of Christ. Please, give me the courage to live in hospitality toward others.

Consider It

*If you are truly wise, you'll learn from what I've told you.
It's time for you to consider these profound lessons
of God's great love and mercy.*

PSALM 107:43 TPT

This morning, grab your Bible and read all of Psalm 107.
The psalmist tells us of four different peoples: some who
wandered with no home, some in prison because they
rebelled against God, some who sinned and found affliction,
and some who went out to sea to work. The point of
recounting all these stories is in verse 2, "Let the redeemed
tell their story."

What story do you need to tell? Are you hiding your story in
shame, not wanting anyone to know about your sin? Are you
keeping silent because your story seems mundane, just like
everyone else's? Has God freed you from the chains of an
addiction, but society silences you? Don't let shame and fear
keep you from proclaiming God's marvelous work in your life
today. If you are breathing and you have faith in Christ, you
have hope to share, and God has a purpose for you to share it.
Let your story be a lesson for others to consider God's great love
and great mercy toward you, and in turn, find it for themselves.

What redemptive story can you share with someone today
to bring glory to God?

Let the one who is wise heed these things
and ponder the loving deeds of the LORD.

PSALM 107:43 NIV

Maybe you aren't at the point of seeing your life as redeemed. It can be an important and helpful activity to take time to consider your walk with Jesus. How can you trace his faithfulness to you? Where can you see his hand in your life? What are his mercies toward you?

Remembering his past faithfulness is encouraging. It helps us to see his work in our lives, and it empowers us to share the true character of God with other people. We can also find healing when we look back and see it from the different perspective of God working in our lives instead of just chance incidents. Take time to write out a few examples tonight, and praise God for his love and mercy toward you.

God, thank you for the love that's written all over my story. Thank you for your mercy and for holding me together. Show me your handiwork etched all over my life. Make clear your presence as I consider your ways.

Keep

Keep yourselves in the love of God, waiting for the mercy of our Lord Jesus Christ that leads to eternal life.

JUDE 1:21 ESV

Imagine someone getting married. The couple says their vows, makes the promise to dwell together for the rest of their lives, and has a wedding feast. Then, when all that is done, he goes back to his apartment on one side of town, and she goes to her apartment. On Sundays, they meet at the house they bought together for a cup of coffee. But after that, back to their own apartments they go. Occasionally one will send a text message to the other, asking for advice.

Sounds ridiculous, right? Yet this is how we Christians often live with Christ. When Jude writes to keep yourselves in, he is not speaking of working for your salvation. That is already done by Christ. He's talking about dwelling with Christ. That means you got to let Jesus move in.

Do you live adjacent to Christ like the couple above, or would you say you abide with Christ?

Await the mercy of our Lord Jesus Christ, who will bring you eternal life. In this way, you will keep yourselves safe in God's love.

JUDE 1:21 NLT

When Jesus moves in, he isn't going to let you keep things how they are. Before Christ, you are dead in sin, and your life shows that. He's going to move in and change things. He will bring light into the dark, dusty places. He will rearrange the furniture of your heart, maybe even throw some things out. Your style and Jesus' style are not going to always align, because how Jesus does things is so different from our nature.

But imagine the home, the life, that Jesus wants to give you. He wants to restore the broken parts. He wants to bring brilliant, healing light into those areas you thought could never illuminate. He wants to bring warmth and comfort to what was cold and dead. When you abide with Jesus and submit to the Holy Spirit, it is possible for your life to be full of light and love, shining in a world that is plunged in darkness. Keep abiding with God. Keep letting Jesus remodel. It won't always be easy, but it leads to the contented life we all desire.

Jesus, I don't want to live like strangers, meeting with you only on Sunday mornings. I want to abide with you. Keep me in your love and let me dwell in it. Move in, that my life may be a shining beacon of hope.

Calling

We keep on praying for you, asking our God to enable you to live a life worthy of his call. May he give you the power to accomplish all the good things your faith prompts you to do.

2 THESSALONIANS 1:11 NLT

Each of us has something that God has planned for us to do. Have you ever felt like yours was too big? To be honest, you are exactly right. It is too big for you to do on your own. God doesn't give us callings we could accomplish without him. He gives us big tasks and God-sized dreams, so that when they come to pass, there is no way anyone could point to you and say, "Woah! Look what they did!" Instead, all the glory goes to God and his power working in your life.

And isn't that what we want? When we have big dreams, we need people in our corner, praying for us and supporting us. If you're attempting to go at something alone, maybe hit the pause button. Reach out to some friends, your pastor, or some brothers and sisters in Christ at church, and ask them to support you in prayer. Surrounding yourself with a praying community and communicating your God-sized dreams to others is the perfect way to get started.

What God-sized dreams do you have that you need to share with someone else today?

We constantly pray that our God will empower you to live worthy of all that he has invited you to experience. And we pray that by his power all the pleasures of goodness and all works inspired by faith would fill you completely.

2 Thessalonians 1:11 TPT

There are two things we need to do if we are going to seek God's glory while chasing our dreams. First, live in faith. God loves faith. He rewards those who step out in faith and who trust in him. It pleases your Father in heaven when you have faith, and his pleasure never takes a downward spiral if you mess up while pursuing him.

Secondly, we need to practice self-control. Saying yes to God and stepping out in faith in one area will usually result in needing to say no to things that would get you off track. We must cut out the static of other things if we are going to whole-heartedly pursue our calling from God.

God, I want to know what you have planned for me. I'm ready to step out in faith. Help me to say no to the things that are distracting me and take a leap of faith with you today.

Pure Motives

The Lord wants to show his mercy to you.
He wants to rise and comfort you.
The Lord is a fair God,
and everyone who waits for his help will be happy.

ISAIAH 30:18 NCV

One of the worst feelings in a relationship is feeling like a burden. This feeling can cause you to hide how you really feel because you don't want to trouble the other person. It can lead you to always walking on eggshells and even working too much because you just don't want to be that extra baggage. Worse, you don't want them to get tired of you and dump the "baggage".

Consciously or subconsciously, we sometimes think God considers us a burden as well. Read this verse again and notice the words. The Lord wants. He *wants*. The Lord does not consider you a burden. Say it out loud. He wants to show you mercy. He wants to comfort you, which means he wants to know what your feelings are. You don't need to walk on eggshells around him, and you are no trouble to him. You don't need to work harder or do certain things to make him show you love and mercy. It's there, a free gift. Won't you come to him today?

Do you feel like a burden to someone?
How does this affect relationship with God?

*The Lord must wait for you to come to him
so he can show you his love and compassion.
For the Lord is a faithful God.
Blessed are those who wait for his help.*

ISAIAH 30:18 NLT

A happy life is not an independent life. A happy life is a life
supported by Christ. The last line of our verse tells us that
those who wait for God's help will be happy. Sounds like
great promise, but we aren't good at waiting. We are good at
pushing ahead, moving things around to get our way, and
making things work.

Waiting is hard. It involves patience and stillness. But
the reward is a happy life, a life dependent on Christ and
powered by the Holy Spirit.

Jesus, help me to wait for you. I want to live a happy life, and
I want to wait. Please, free me from feeling like a burden. Be
near to me. Thank you for your free gifts of mercy and grace.

Every Morning

The Sovereign Lord has given me his words of wisdom,
so that I know how to comfort the weary.
Morning by morning he wakens me
and opens my understanding to his will.

ISAIAH 50:4 NLT

What does this day hold? No one knows the answer to that question. What we do know is that we are here, August 11, and a brand-new day has been given to us. What better way to find out what the day holds than meeting with Jesus? God has so much in store for each one of us every day. Some of us go to a job, some of us work in the home, but all of us have divine appointments from God waiting for us.

The best way to be prepared for those is to do what you're doing. Start your days in God's Word, learning from his words of wisdom. His Word will give you the knowledge you need to comfort the weary around you. His Word will give you the understanding to preach the gospel and the discernment to know who needs to hear it. His Word provides rich guidance. Dive in deep this morning!

Has spending your mornings in the Word
changed your outlook?

The Lord Yahweh has equipped me
with the anointed, skillful tongue of a teacher—
to know how to speak a timely word to the weary.
Morning by morning, he awakens my heart.
He opens my ears to hear his voice, to be trained to teach.

ISAIAH 50:4 TPT

We all need a refill, and it's not coffee! We need a refill of the living water. You will be asked to pour out every day. The question is, are you getting a refill afterwards? It's not weak to need to spend time with Jesus every day. It's wise! It's the mark of a true disciple, and the empowerment for that disciple to make other disciples.

You can't lead people to fullness if you yourself are empty. Make it a priority to fill up every single day. Spend time in the Word and spend time in prayer, asking God to give you discernment. Imagine the hope you carry in your cup, and the thirsty, waiting world that needs to hear it.

Jesus, thank you for giving me wisdom daily. Help me to not neglect my time with you.

A Season

"Now is your time of grief, but I will see you again and you will rejoice, and no one will take away your joy."

JOHN 16:22 NIV

Farmers know how to read the seasons; it's vital to their livelihood. As Christians, we also must learn to read the seasons of life that we walk. We must accept and listen to Jesus when he tells us that we will have seasons of grief and hardship, and painful things will come our way. This does not mean that God is punishing us or that we don't have enough faith.

It is, however, an opportunity to press into God. He gives us grace for each season that we are in. We have the opportunity to praise him in times that feel like mountaintops and in times that feel like valleys. Though we go through different seasons in our life, God is constant and never changes. Where do you find yourself in life today? Know your season, whatever it is, and use it as an opportunity to find new grace in God.

What season are you in?
How can you praise God in this season?

"You also pass through a time of intense sorrow when I am taken from you, but you will see me again! And then your hearts will burst with joy, with no one being able to take it from you!"

JOHN 16:22 TPT

A continuous season that every believer shares in is mentioned in our passage above. We are in what is called the church age. This is the time in history after Christ has first come, died on the cross, rose again and ascended into heaven. He promises here, and elsewhere in Scripture, that he is coming again. That day of our glorious reunion has not yet come, but it could happen at any time.

When we are reunited with Christ, it will be the most glorious occasion, the most ecstatic rejoicing. This is the future hope of our coming King, a truth that can spur us on in the most difficult of times. Keep your eyes focused on the eternal perspective, the joy that is to come to us, and our reuniting with our Savior. Let it create in you an unquenchable joy!

Jesus, you are coming again. Hallelujah! I praise you for being with me in all seasons. Thank you for sending the Holy Spirit and being so near. Help me to know what season I am in and give me new measures of grace for the things I face.

Rejoicing in Comfort

*Sing for joy, O heavens, and exult, O Earth;
break forth, O mountains, into singing!
For the LORD has comforted his people,
and will have compassion on his suffering one.*

ISAIAH 49:13 NRSV

Our greatest certainty in life is the presence of the living God. Still, you may join with many who have asked how suffering and God's goodness can co-exist. This is something that every believer wrestles with. When circumstances don't align, we find ourselves stripped bare of all we find comfort in.

This fall, the trees will start to shed their leaves and stand barren. This is the same posture we take, one of surrender and waiting on God. Though we all must wrestle through the facts of suffering in this world, we have a God who suffered with us and suffered for us. Let's not get stuck on repeat. Let our song ring out about the comfort that the Lord gives us, about the compassion that he wraps around us. The song of suffering might seem loud, but the earth is declaring louder the comfort and compassion of our risen Savior. Join in the singing!

How can you praise God today
for his comfort and compassion?

Sing, O heavens!
Be joyful, O earth!
And break out in singing, O mountains!
For the LORD has comforted His people,
And will have mercy on His afflicted.

ISAIAH 49:13 NKJV

God has promised to comfort you, but maybe you aren't in need of comfort right now. In the same way that God shows empathy toward us in our times of need, how can you be a vessel for his empathy and compassion for someone else? God loves to move and work through his people. There are many in your life today who need to hear the song of God's compassion but can't. They need you to show up for them and play the song.

Jesus displayed a great example to us in the gospel, giving compassion to others and loving well those who were suffering. We need to follow in his example and mourn with those who are mourning, lending a hand to our brothers and sisters in need. This knits us together even closer as the body of Christ.

Lord, thank you for always extending your compassion and comfort to me. Show me who needs to hear your words of life and peace today.

My Protection

The name of the Lord is blessed and lifted high!
For his marvelous miracle of mercy protected me
when I was overwhelmed by my enemies.

PSALM 31:21 TPT

To those who have suffered, it can be difficult to reconcile our reality with Scriptures like these. Our minds lean toward cynicism as we scoff, "Protection? Where was God when…" Fill in the blank. It doesn't take many years on this earth for us to have a blank to fill in. The question is, can we really expect God to protect us?

These grief-filled questions are welcome at the foot of the cross, but we must also realize that God cares more for our eternal souls than our temporary, physical bodies. Not that he doesn't care for our bodies; he is out to redeem both. It can be difficult for us as finite humans to align our values with God, to get our eyes off of this short-term physical life and onto the glory of eternity. We want to apply all the promises of protection to the here and now, but God has so much more in mind. The most beautiful protection we have is in the essence of his holy Word—the Holy Spirit. By this, we know that we are sealed forever into God's kingdom.

Do you feel like you can bring
your grief-filled questions to God?

Praise the LORD,
for he has shown me the wonders of his unfailing love.
He kept me safe when my city was under attack.

PSALM 31:21 NLT

If we can shift our perspective to the eternal, we no longer have to worry about self-protection. We can throw our lives into the gospel with the guarantee that we will one day be resurrected like Jesus. It means that we can see that suffering and loss here pale in comparison to the richness that awaits us.

Our time is now free from the anxiety of getting the most we can from this life. Our focus has shifted to the next one. God has a big, wide redemptive plan for all of creation. He invites us to participate in this plan, rely on him to protect what matters, and lose our lives for the very sake of finding them.

Jesus, give me a deeper understanding of protection. Help me to have an eternal perspective. My life for the gospel, Lord. May you be glorified!

Guilt Free

Whatever is good and perfect is a gift coming down to us from God our Father, who created all the lights in the heavens. He never changes or casts a shifting shadow.

JAMES 1:17 NLT

Have you ever felt guilty for goodness? There is no condemnation for believers, we learn in Romans, and we should apply it often when Satan tries to make us feel guilty over our forgiven sins. But what about feeling guilty for the goodness and blessings that God rains down on his children? Have you ever had a prayer answered, and yet seen someone else seemingly left in silence? Perhaps you praise God secretly for his blessings, but feel too ashamed to share with others, for fear of judgment.

Beloved, don't be subject to guilt over God's goodness. Every gift in your life is from him. The goodness is from him, and he wants you to rejoice in it. You can be a beacon of hope in the lives of other people by sharing what he has done and is doing for you. Don't apologize for God's provision in your life or try and hide away his power. Respond in love to those around you, sharing that they too can receive the blessing of God that is for all who believe.

Do you feel guilty for any blessings?
Praise him for them today and free yourself of the guilt.

Every good gift and every perfect gift is from above, and comes down from the Father of lights, with whom there is no variation or shadow of turning.

JAMES 1:17 NKJV

What has God saved you from? This is called a testimony. Everyone has one. They are our personal stories of God's redemption and power in our lives. Another guilt trap that we can sometimes fall into is thinking our story is not enough. Maybe if you didn't live a long, previous life of sin or come out of dark addiction, your story of God's saving power in your life is not enough. That's a lie! The moments you've been given are a gift.

Don't allow this lie to lessen the powerful movement that God has had in your story. It's there. It won't look like the story of the person to your right or to your left, but if you are a believer in Jesus Christ, then you have a grace story to share. God gives some the gifts of meeting with him early in life or growing up in faith-based homes. Each story is unique, and God is so grand that each story can bring him glory in different ways. Don't dishonor the gift you have been given. Share his grace story with the world.

God, thank you for giving good gifts. Thank you for all your blessings. Help me to not succumb to guilt, but to praise you loud and proud for all of them.

More Than Able

> *"I know that You can do all things,*
> *And that no purpose of Yours can be thwarted."*
>
> JOB 42:2 NASB

If God has a plan (and he does), nothing can stop it. Absolutely nothing. Do you believe that? We waste so much of our time and energy worrying. We worry about headlines, our families, our jobs, and things that haven't even happened yet. Stop worry and start considering. Our almighty, all-powerful God has a plan. We serve a miracle-working God! He wants to take your best effort, your offering of faith, and do miraculous things with it.

God requires your participation, but he doesn't ask for your performance. Consider the time Jesus was getting ready to feed the masses. He asked the disciples how much bread they had. He didn't require them to go buy or bake enough for the thousands. What they had didn't seem like anything of significance, but to Jesus, it was about the faith that it took to hand the bread over and let him work. Instead of participating in the work of worry, hand over what you have to God. He is more than able to work the miracle you need today.

What can you offer Jesus today?
How can you participate instead of trying to perform?

> *"I know that you can do anything,*
> *and no one can stop you."*
>
> JOB 42:2 NLT

We read these words from Job at the end of the book. It's not the end of his story, but it comes to us after page upon page of Job's suffering. How could he possibly still have confidence that God had a purpose and a plan after so much suffering? Isn't that the question we ask when suffering comes, and things seem out of control?

The presence of suffering is not the absence of God's plan. Jesus tells us that in this world, we will face trials and suffering. It's to be expected from a fallen world. Our hope lies in the plan. God's got this. His purpose is to restore creation and all of humanity to himself. He set in motion a plan from before the beginning of time to redeem us. His Son came, gave his life, and conquered death—right on schedule. God's not unaware. He's in control. Trust him!

God, I praise you for your miracles and planning. Remind me that you are in control and help me to trust you.

Not Forgotten

> *"Can a woman forget the baby she nurses?*
> *Can she feel no kindness for the child to which she gave birth?*
> *Even if she could forget her children, I will not forget you."*

ISAIAH 49:15 NCV

Parental relationships can be complicated, but there is one thing every single one of us have had—a biological mother and a father. It's no surprise that God would bring human life into the world is through relationships. God has created us to need one another from the very beginning. Children and parents are wired to be attached to one another.

In our fallen world, that relationship with a parental figure does not always pan out the way God intended. But the fallen nature that strains and breaks human relationships has no power over our relationship with God. Human love will fall short every time, but God's love for us surpasses that of the best human parent. Picture someone that you would describe as an excellent parent. Think of how they care for their children, knowing that God's care goes extravagantly beyond that for you.

What good parental care do you need today?
List them and ask for them in prayer.

*"How could a loving mother forget her nursing child
and not deeply love the one she bore?
Even if a there is a mother who forgets her child,
I could never, no never, forget you."*

ISAIAH 49:15 TPT

Our relationships with our parents reflect our relationship with God. Lack of attachment and a negative childhood environment can skew how we view God. People often compare earthly fathers to God the Father, but God relates to us through mothers and motherhood as well.

This verse might bring up pain to those of us who have been or feel abandoned by our mothers, pointing out the fact that they did indeed forget us. It takes intentional effort to untangle our views of God from our experiences with earthly parents. Seek out a mentor or counselor to help you on this journey. Be honest and vulnerable. Hold fast to the character of God, knowing that there are no lies in him. When he says he will never forget you, you will know it's true.

God, thank you for your nurturing nature. You are kind and never forget us, and you exceed even the best earthly parents in everything you do. Today, I need your care. Help me to see you in truth, not skewed by my own painful experiences.

Discernment

The wise see danger ahead and avoid it,
but fools keep going and get into trouble.

PROVERBS 27:12 NCV

When you first learn to drive, there is a whole book of road signs that you must learn to recognize. These signs tell you what lane to use, if a road is closed ahead, when to stop, and many more essential signals, all needed to safely operate a motor vehicle. A good driver notes the signs and heeds them. Likewise, a wise person practices what is called discernment.

Discernment is partnering with God to make a decision. It's when we observe the road signs God gives us, either through prayer or through the reading of Scripture, and make decisions based off of that. The beautiful thing about Christian discernment is God that has the map. He has the bird's-eye view of the journey ahead, and he knows every pothole in the road. He is our perfect guide, and the Bible that he has many road signs to inform and warn us. Let us be wise, asking God to give us discernment and listening to his voice along the way.

Do you seek first God's wisdom by coming to him in prayer and in Scripture, or do you push for your own way?

The prudent sees danger and hides himself,
but the simple go on and suffer for it.

PROVERBS 27:12 ESV

In order to see, you need to have eyes that work. What causes spiritual blindness? If we are spiritually blind, we are unable to see the danger ahead, and we act foolishly. Three things come to mind as causes for spiritual blindness. First, cynicism. Cynicism is a poison that's out to get goodness. You may have been hurt in the church before or have unanswered questions about God that have soured your judgment into cynicism. Cynicism will blind you to the goodness of God and make you unable to see dangers ahead.

The second cause is a hard heart. This one is a partner to cynicism. Hard hearts have let bitterness and other kinds of evil take root deep into our souls, making us unwilling to submit to God. If we don't submit ourselves to God, our hardness blinds us from his grace. Lastly, being unfamiliar with or ignorant of the Word of God will blind us. We need to soak in the Scriptures if we wish to gain wisdom.

God, help me not to fall prey to any of these three blind spots. If I have, I repent. Show me your goodness. Lead me in your wisdom.

Growing

Let us stop going over the basic teachings about Christ again and again. Let us go on instead and become mature in our understanding. Surely we don't need to start again with the fundamental importance of repenting from evil deeds and placing our faith in God.

HEBREWS 6:1 NLT

Has your appetite changed since you were a kid? Most of us would say so. It seems like kids can live on a steady diet of mac and cheese and hot dogs. Teenagers are unfazed by what they consume at their favorite fast-food joints. As we mature, our tastes change, our bodies change, and we don't desire or find appetizing the same foods we loved as kids.

The author of Hebrews is asking his readers to grow up in their faith. Elementary teachings aren't bad, but as people mature in their faith, they will have an appetite for more complex food in Christ. A steak dinner doesn't work for a baby, but it's very satisfying for an adult. Likewise, your faith should grow and change with your understanding of Scripture, deepening as you go along.

Are you maturing in your faith or staying in the same spot?

Now is the time for us to progress beyond the basic message of Christ and advance into perfection. The foundation has already been laid for us to build upon: turning away from our dead works to embrace faith in God.

HEBREWS 6:1 TPT

The writer of Hebrews is not saying that simple teachings, like repentance and faith, need to be abolished in the church. There is nothing new under the sun; no new revelation is going to come down. The writer is making a case for believers to strengthen what they know about these matters, and then continue learning Scripture.

Sometimes, we can mistake new enlightenment with maturity. There is the temptation to create something new out of Scripture, to find a new way or a new revelation and follow it. This makes people appear mature and knowledgeable about the Bible. Though we are called to grow and mature, be wary of teachings that offer something new. Scripture is alive, and it doesn't need to be reborn. Become mature in the wise teachings of Scripture.

God, help me to mature in my faith. May I grow up strong on a steady diet of your Word.

Pressing On

You need to persevere so that when you have done the will of God,
you will receive what he has promised.

HEBREWS 10:36 NIV

Running a marathon is not a decision you make on the day of the event. Marathon runners know that training for the marathon takes a large portion of their time. First, there is the training. Running many miles can take up a whole morning. Second, there is nutrition. Runners spend a lot of time refueling the calories their bodies burned. A long run might deplete their energy for a whole weekend. But the runners have the end goal in sight—triumphantly finishing the race—so they continue. It is different from the sprints of childhood, which were spontaneous, unplanned, and quickly over.

Life is a marathon. It is not a sprint. The Christian walk is not one-and-done after a single prayer. It requires you to press on. If you are breathing this morning, God still has a will for you on this earth. He has things for you to train for, to accomplish, and to work on. Keep going! Don't give up. God is always true to his promises.

What do you need to not give up on today?

Patient endurance is what you need now, so that you will continue to do God's will. Then you will receive all that he has promised.

HEBREWS 10:36 NLT

How does a runner keep going when they feel tired? Have you ever wondered or experienced this yourself? There must be some motivation for them to rise to their alarms every morning and run. They know how to keep going when there is pain, how to persevere they don't get the time they wanted or suffer an injury setback.

The motivation is the dream of crossing that finish line. The reward doesn't have to be a tangible one; the self-satisfaction of conquering and accomplishing pushes them forward. When you want to give up, cling to the promise of eternal life and reward with Jesus. What a great finish line we will cross when we hear him say, "Well done, good and faithful servant."

Jesus, help me to persevere. I want to press on and not give up. Keep my eyes focused on you.

Greater Love

Don't set the affections of your heart on this world or in loving the things of the world. The love of the Father and the love of the world are incompatible.

1 JOHN 2:15 TPT

Affections. The Greek word used in this verse implies treasuring something. It means to have great attachment to something, to build one's life around it or give priority to it. At the exclusion of other things, your sights are set exclusively on this one thing.

John is telling us we can't serve two masters. We can't be full of two different substances. It's either love from the Holy Spirit or love for the things of this world. But what does he mean by things of this world? These things can trace back to prideful love and assertion of self. Things like money, sex, family relationships, career, creativity, and status can all take center stage instead of Christ. Many of these pursuits are not bad on their own; it is fallen nature that skews them. Where do your devotions lie? What are you dedicating your life to, even subconsciously? Search your heart and see if God is your true source of affection.

What might be taking your affections away from Christ?

Do not love the world or anything in the world.
If anyone loves the world, love for the Father is not in them.

1 JOHN 2:15 NIV

The love of the world and the love of the Father are incompatible because they are opposites. The love of God has holy, perfect characteristics and attributes that worldly love will never have. Worldly love takes and skews good things to become sinful.

God redeems and renews. His love reflects his goodness. How love operates in the kingdom of God is different than the system we are used to. He is so vast that we can spend our whole lives diving into the ocean of God's love and how he does things. We can dive deep into the grace that he offers, sinking deeper and deeper and never touching the bottom.

God, you are so good! I am in awe of how different your ways are, how beautiful and pure. More than anything else, teach me to love like you.

Made New

Create in me a clean heart, O God,
and put a new and right spirit within me.

PSALM 51:10 NRSV

Have you ever watched one of those home makeover shows? You hear the story of how deserving the people are, and then watch as a talented team transforms their humble home into something spectacular. There's usually a lot of tears and gratitude, and it's a feel-good moment.

Transformation is a beautiful thing, but it requires hard work. Another God-given example from nature is the caterpillar. It spends a lot of time in preparation: eating milkweed, growing to the proper size, and then searching for the perfect spot to hang upside down. But the one day, it stops eating, hangs upside down, and disappears into the cocoon it makes for itself. The caterpillar literally turns to mush and begins to create new matter. When it's finished, the new creature is no longer chained to the earth; it can soar high. The same is true of our transformation in Christ. The whole process is important. Don't try to skip any of it! Jesus is working and moving, creating clean and new things in your life. Let the Spirit move and go with the change.

Is God trying to create something new in your life
that you are currently resisting?

Create a new, clean heart within me.
Fill me with pure thoughts and holy desires,
ready to please you.

PSALM 51:10 TPT

This morning's examples of the new home and the butterfly are beautiful, and we also need to remember that God does not force any of us into this transition. In fact, in our verse above, the psalmist is asking for the clean heart and the new spirit. He knows and trusts that God's ways are higher and better.

New can be scary sometimes, the unknown unnerving. But the beautiful part is that you can trust God. He's going to do something beautiful with your life.

Jesus, thank you for transforming me. I submit my life to you. Make me more like you!

Source

All things are of God, who has reconciled us to Himself through Jesus Christ, and has given us the ministry of reconciliation.

2 CORINTHIANS 5:18 NKJV

We've got work to do! God has invited us to partner with him by giving us the ministry of reconciliation. What does that mean? It means there is a world out there aching to know the love of Jesus. It's a whole world that needs to know reconciliation with God is possible, that peace with God is accessible, and that God is real and loves them. And it's your job to get the word out! It is your job to proclaim the gospel and the beautiful assurance it brings of forgiveness of sin.

We are Christ's ambassadors to the world. An ambassador to a foreign country goes to that country and represents their nation's interests to the one they are in. As citizens of heaven, we are ambassadors to this world. We represent the interests of God to the world around us, for instance, his interest in telling everyone that peace with God has been made available to them through Christ. What are you waiting for?

Who can you share this good news with today?

All of this is a gift from God, who brought us back to himself
through Christ. And God has given us this task
of reconciling people to him.

2 CORINTHIANS 5:18 NLT

You may be wondering why we need reconciliation. The good news is that you do not need to do the work of reconciling yourself or others to God, Jesus has done it for you. Your only job is to spread his good news. We need reconciliation with God because our relationship with God is broken by sin. God is holy and righteous, and sin created the divide between us.

Jesus' work on the cross bridged that divide as he bore the weight of our sins. Now, reconciliation with God is possible to every single human through Christ. What good news! We need to get out and share it. It is not our job to do the reconciling, or even the convicting, but it is our job to share.

Jesus, lead me to those who need to hear the amazing news of the peace with God that is available to them.

Good Food

"Don't work for the food that spoils. Work for the food that stays good always and gives eternal life. The Son of Man will give you this food, because on him God the Father has put his power."

JOHN 6:27 NCV

For many in the world, the end of August means the beginning of harvest. From patio planters to green acres in Iowa, gardeners and farmers know that the fruit of their labors is nearly ready. Maybe you are familiar with countertops lined with tomatoes, cucumbers, zucchini—more than can be consumed before they spoil.

This passage in John is right after Jesus feeds the five thousand and walks on water. He gets in a boat and crosses over, and when the people find him, they want more miraculous bread. More bounty, please! This is when Jesus speaks the above verse to them. He makes it even clearer a few verses later: the work of God they do is believing in Christ. Jesus came to turn our worlds upside down. He is the never-ending harvest, the bounty, the bread of life that fills us up. Belief in Christ will never lead to a spoiled or unfruitful life. Praise God for the gift of his Son.

How have you seen the benefits of belief
in Christ in your life?

Why would you strive for food that is perishable and not be passionate to seek the food of eternal life, which never spoils? I, the Son of Man, am ready to give you what matters most, for God the Father has destined me for this purpose.

JOHN 6:27 TPT

When you go to Jesus in prayer, are you more like the crowd that demanded more food from him? Or are you a true disciple, coming to him for the bread that will satisfy? Though we don't want to admit it, it's easy to be like the crowd. We come before Jesus and ask for temporary things, for things that spoil.

It can be hard to ask for thankfulness and contentment in Him, truly believing that he is all we need to be satisfied. It's difficult to see that, in the circumstances you want removed or the thing you think you need, Jesus has your character in mind and knows what is best for you. Spend time in prayer tonight thanking Jesus for being enough for you.

Jesus, thank you for being enough! Thank you for being my complete satisfaction. You are a gift from the Father. Thank you for your work on the cross, which has brought me into right relationship with you. Help me to be satisfied with you, not pursuing the bread that spoils, trusting that you are the bread of life.

Greater Understanding

How blessed is the man who finds wisdom
And the man who gains understanding.

PROVERBS 3:13 NASB

How would you define wisdom? Wisdom can be defined as the ability to make godly choices. The Bible refers to this kind of wisdom. It comes only from God, through faith in Christ, and it has the end goal of glorifying God. Godly wisdom submits itself to God and his authority. It means using the resources God has given you, such as his Word, to make choices that are for his glory.

When you spell it out, wisdom doesn't seem hard to find, does it? Wisdom is right here in front of you, in the Bible. Choosing to read it this morning, beginning your day with a proverb, is the perfect start to finding wisdom and gaining understanding. Consider yourself blessed as you pursue a life that puts God first and makes choices based on his Word.

How can you use your knowledge of God's Word
to make godly choices today?

*Joyful is the person who finds wisdom,
the one who gains understanding.*

PROVERBS 3:13 NLT

We are not in a giant game of hide-and-seek. What a relief! Wisdom is not hiding from you. If you feel you are lacking in wisdom, or if you don't know where to find it, the answer is right here. If you need wisdom, James tells us to ask for it.

Have you asked God for the wisdom you need lately? Have you listened for an answer? The wisdom you need is often right in front of you. If you have a Bible, it holds the wisdom you need. Spending time in God's Word is a great way to stock up on wisdom. Then, when you ask, the Holy Spirit can draw from the deep reservoir you have created within yourself of God's Word and remind you of the truth. It's a double whammy to the insecurity and lies that the enemy tries to give us.

God, thank you for your Word. Thank you for your wisdom. Thank you for answering me when I ask for wisdom. Help me to grow in understanding tonight.

Not My Way

Going a little farther, he fell on the ground and prayed that, if it were possible, the hour might pass from him. And he said, "Abba, Father, all things are possible for you. Remove this cup from me. Yet not what I will, but what you will."

MARK 14:35-36 ESV

What a prayer. Here we find Jesus, who has been obedient in every single step, who set aside all the privileges and grandeur of being God and stepped into a tiny embryo form of man. He grew inside the womb of a woman, being born in flesh. He lived in the humblest of circumstances, not in a palace but in small homes. He grew up obscure and unknown, fully God and yet fully human. Connected to the Father along every step of the plan, he heard in his baptism that the Father was pleased with him. He was God for every miracle, for every healing.

And here, he is still connected to the Father, praying for the pain and agony and separation that he knows lies in front of him to be removed. But most of all, he prays for the will of God to be done. May we follow in the example of our dear Jesus, who did not push, bargain, or barter for his own will to be done, but in humility, submitted himself to the Father's will.

What area of your life are you having a hard time submitting to the Father's will?

He walked a short distance away, and being overcome with grief, he threw himself face down on the ground. He prayed that if it were possible, he would not have to experience this hour of suffering. He prayed, "Abba, my Father, all things are possible for you. Please— don't allow me to drink this cup of suffering! Yet what I want is not important, for I only desire to fulfill your plan for me."

MARK 14:35-36 TPT

Jesus faced the worse situation any of us could imagine facing. He went from being in complete unity with God, to having God turn his face completely away from him on the cross. Here, Jesus is asking that the cross be taken from him. "If there is any other way," he prays. Yet in the end, he submits. He does this out of trust of the Father's plan, and out of love for you.

What vast love both the Father and the Son display for you, that the cross was endured for you! What do you face that seems unbearable? What are you asking God to remove from your life? Can you trust the will of God through suffering, just like Jesus did? Know that his will is always for your good.

Jesus, thank you for enduring the cross for me. Thank you for that vast love. Father, help me to submit to your will, even when it's not aligned with mine.

Victorious Life

Be supernaturally infused with strength through your life-union with the Lord Jesus. Stand victorious with the force of his explosive power flowing in and through you.

EPHESIANS 6:10 TPT

Who doesn't want to be considered the winner? Whether you're competitive or not, we all want to end up on the winning side of any endeavor we pursue. The Bible tells us how to be victors in the most important endeavor of all: life!

A life connected to Christ is a life of victory. There is no human being, no matter how weak or feeble, who is powerless if their life is connected to Christ. As believers, we have the Holy Spirit. That same Spirit raised Christ from the dead and split the Red Sea, freeing the Israelites from captivity. That power is with us. Let that sink in. Do not listen to the lies of powerlessness that the enemy tells. In the name of Jesus, stand.

In what area of your life do you feel
most powerless or helpless?

*Be strong in the Lord
and in his mighty power.*

EPHESIANS 6:10 NIV

Today's verse is at the beginning of a very prominent section of Scripture: the armor of God. This portion of Scripture is a wealth of information on how to live victoriously in the battle against the enemy, Satan. Go ahead and read through verses 13-18 that speak of the armor pieces.

It is important to note a couple of things. First, strength is a gift. It is something you receive. How do you receive strength? Through relationship with Jesus. Secondly, this supernatural, explosive power comes from using the spiritual protection that is offered to you in verses 13-18. Take heart! Christ has provided you with everything you need to be protected and to win in life.

Holy Spirit, thank you for your power in my life. Help me to put on the armor of God and fight my battles. Show me where I have neglected my armor and give me strength when I feel powerless.

Leader of My Life

*Whether you turn to the right or to the left,
your ears will hear a voice behind you, saying,
"This is the way; walk in it."*

ISAIAH 30:21 NIV

Have you ever been lost while driving in a big city? With so many pedestrians, unfamiliar streets, one-ways, bikers, and other distractions, it can be overwhelming and confusing. Twenty years ago, you might have wandered around for hours or ended up in a part of town you did not want to be. Now, with the help of GPS on our phones, we can simply ask the device to take us home, and a friendly voice will help us navigate the chaos.

Life can be the exact same way—overwhelming, noisy, and sometimes leaving you with the feeling that you are headed in a direction you don't want to go. Turn to Jesus. Better than any GPS, he can quiet your soul and guide you in the right direction. He will lovingly lead you along the way. He knows the plan; ask him for directions this morning.

What do you need to ask Jesus to guide you through today?

When you turn to the right or turn to the left,
you will hear his voice behind you to guide you, saying,
"This is the right path; follow it."

ISAIAH 30:21 TPT

The world is a noisy place. Jesus promises to guide and lead us along the way. But how do we know his voice from the others? At a playground, there can be lots of parents there watching their children. When a child calls for their parent, how does the parent just know it's them? With nearly everyone answering to "mom" and "dad," isn't it fascinating that the parent can pick their child's voice out from the crowd?

One could argue that the familiarity built between parent and child is why they can do this. The more you listen for God's voice, and the more you tune your ear to hear it, the better you will become at picking him out among the noise. Start in the quiet place, in prayer, listening for his voice. That's your training ground for the noisy world. Become familiar with the kind voice of Christ tonight.

Jesus, thank you for speaking to me. You are so kind. Help me to tune my ear to your voice.

To Dwell

"Those who love me will keep my word, and my Father will love them, and we will come to them and make our home with them."

JOHN 14:23 NRSV

"There is no place like home," the old saying goes. Most people would agree on that. The question is more, "Well, what makes a place a home?" Overwhelmingly, the response is that what makes a place a home is your comfort level. Can you be yourself there? Let down your guard? That seems to be what people would define as a home more than a particular type of dwelling.

God wants to dwell with you. He wants to make his home with you. This means God wants to be on a certain level of comfort and warmth with you. He wants you to let your guard down when you are around him. He wants you to feel welcome. He wants to know you for who you truly are, and he desires intimacy with you. And in the greatest story ever told, God became man so he could make his home among us.

How does it make you feel to know that God wants you to be at home with him?

"Anyone who loves me will obey my teaching. My Father will love them, and we will come to them and make our home with them."

JOHN 14:23 NIV

Some of us might not know what it means to have a home. The warm, comfortable feelings described this morning might be unfamiliar. How can we possibly let our guard down with God when we never have been able to in real life?

Dear Christian, if this is you, God wants to transform your idea of home. He wants you to have a good Father. He wants you to experience unconditional love. He wants you to know what it is to be known. But you can keep the door locked. Jesus is waiting at the door, ever the gentlemen, never going to force his way and start remodeling. Won't you trust him? Won't you open the door and let Jesus dwell with you, guard down and fully known, tonight?

Jesus, will you come dwell with me? I want to be known by you. I want to experience your love. Thank you for your promise to dwell with me.

Follow Through

The plans of the diligent lead surely to plenty,
But those of everyone who is hasty, surely to poverty.

PROVERBS 21:5 NKJV

The virtue in this proverb is faithfulness. Faithfulness is
a character trait of God, and one of the fruits of the Spirit.
Some might read this verse and think that God is promising
them success as they hope to achieve it. The truth, however,
is that God is far more concerned with you being faithful than
he ever has been with you achieving success.

A person who plans diligently prays over their actions. They
wait and listen for the Lord's leading and timing. They use
godly wisdom to discern when to stick with something and
when to let something go. This characteristic is not one
you achieve overnight. Faithfulness takes time to grow and
mature. What is God calling you to be faithful and diligent
in today? What must you do your best in, even if you don't
see its significance? God has rewards in store for those who
continue in the hard work.

What do you need to follow through on today?

Brilliant ideas pay off and bring you prosperity,
but making hasty, impatient decisions
will only lead to financial loss.

PROVERBS 21:5 TPT

Do you ever feel like you don't know what God's will is
for you? Like you feel stagnant and at a standstill? It's our
society's impulse to make quick decisions and just move on to
the next thing. It's easy to abandon ship due to boredom, fear,
excitement for something new, or discouragement. If you feel
unsure of what to do, ask yourself; what is the last thing you
can remember God telling you to do? Then do that.

His timing is not like our timing, and while we may feel like
we are in a season of his silence, perhaps God is saying, "I
already gave you the command and instruction. Now, be
faithful!" Did God urge you to go to school? Then keep at
it! Did God ask you to serve in the kids' ministry at church?
Then keep at it. There are so many areas where we feel lost or
want to rush ahead to the next thing. In reality, God is asking
us to follow through with what he has already called us to.

God, help me to be faithful to what you have given me. Thank
you for your faithfulness.

Architect

*It is by faith we understand that
the whole world was made by God's
command so what we see was made
by something that cannot be seen.*

HEBREWS 11:3 NCV

Faith can be a difficult, abstract concept. What are we really saying when we say we have faith? At the beginning of Hebrews 11, we are not told what faith is, but rather what faith does. It fortifies what we hope for. It is the foundation of our relationship with God. When you are building, you start with a foundation and work your way up, much like God started with nothing and built the heavens and the earth with his spoken Word. We start with faith, the belief of Jesus Christ's work on the cross.

But it doesn't stop there! Your faith should continue to build from belief into confidence as you enter into a deeper relationship. As your relationship matures, confidence deepens trust. Different aspects of faith can be at different levels, for the character of God is vast and unmeasurable. You can trust that he is good while just beginning to believe that he is just.

Which aspect of the character of God evades your hope?
How can you come to right understanding of that aspect?

Faith empowers us to see that the universe was created and beautifully coordinated by the power of God's words! He spoke and the invisible realm gave birth to all that is seen.

HEBREWS 11:3 TPT

Hebrews 11 is often referred to as the chapter of faith. Our verse today is the beginning of a long list of "by faith" statements that the author uses to build his case. Faith is foundation of our Christian character, and our view of it can affect our daily, physical life, what is called our worldview.

Many will say that believing God spoke everything into being, formed man from dust, rested on the sixth day, and so on, is lunacy. How you feel about the creation account can shape your views on the rest of the Bible. Straying from God as creator is a slippery slope to dismantling the work that faith has already done in your life. Stick to the Scriptures as the true and trusted Word of God, being wary of any teachers who lead you elsewhere.

God, thank you for creating our world. Thank you for creating me, for making me in your image. Build my faith and help me to see through any argument of man that would lead me away from you.

Patience

The Lord is not slow about His promise, as some count slowness,
but is patient toward you, not wishing for any to perish but for all
to come to repentance.

2 PETER 3:9 NASB

Looking around, headlines tell us that the world is not getting
any better. Wars, famines, great violence between people—can
can feel like someone has the world by both sides and is
ripping it in two. This might lead you to ask, "God, where are
you?" Many Christians say they wish he would just come back
already. How could it get any worse?

Thank God that his timing is not our timing. He sees
everything around us, better than we can. He sees all of
time laid out before him like a scroll. He is sovereign and
in control. He is not unaware or uncaring of the pain felt on
earth. He has a plan, and in his massive graciousness, he does
not want one person to be separated from him for eternity.
He gives all of us living the opportunity to choose him and
live. What a merciful God we serve! So be patient, believer.
As you wait for his return, remember that he has so many he
wants to join you in eternal life.

What are your thoughts on why God prolongs Jesus' return?

Contrary to man's perspective, the Lord is not late with his promise to return, as some measure lateness. But rather, his "delay" simply reveals his loving patience toward you, because he does not want any to perish but all to come to repentance.

2 PETER 3:9 TPT

Should we be idle while we wait? Is that the meaning of having patience for Christ's return? Certainly not! You have been placed at this point in history, in your town, with your sphere of influence, for a reason. God wants you to share the good news of Christ to all those around you.

Patience does not mean sitting idly by and staring at the sky. Though we all long for Christ's return, he wants us to live our lives in a way that reflects our eternal mindsets. That means he wants us to join in on his mission that none should perish. You have a job to do. Go and share the love of Christ!

Jesus, set a fire in my soul to share your love with all those around me. Thank you for your patience toward humanity.

Don't Give Up

We say that they are happy because they did not give up. You have heard about Job's patience, and you know the Lord's purpose for him in the end. You know the Lord is full of mercy and is kind.

JAMES 5:11 NCV

Running a race takes a vast amount of preparation. You set up a running schedule, making improvements by increasing lengths and times. You buy good running shoes and a water bottle. You make playlists, set your alarm, and lay your clothes out. There are plenty of training days that you won't want to get up and get going, but you do anyway. You'll face so many obstacles, including rainy days, aching muscles, broken equipment, and your own will.

When you finally reach the day of your marathon, you go, because you've spent all your time getting ready for it. You run hard to get across that line. It wasn't just a morning you gave up to run it. It was many days of preparation. You want to know your hard work has paid off. And when you cross that finish line, you have the deepest satisfaction and joy. You made it! What happiness can be found in not giving up in a pursuit. It's the same way with life. We find happiness when we journey with Jesus and when we have patience with ourselves and with God. You can trust God.

Do you find happiness in completed things?

We count as blessed those who have persevered. You have heard of Job's perseverance and have seen what the Lord finally brought about. The Lord is full of compassion and mercy.

JAMES 5:11 NIV

This devotional book is titled "God Is My Happy Place." You bought this book because that appeals to you, or because a friend thought it would. The happiness to be found in God appeals to you. What a great happiness to pursue!

God is a loving and merciful Father. He will never abandon you or leave you. He has a purpose for your life, and you will receive great happiness in walking with him to fulfill that purpose. Don't give up. See this one through. This is one race you don't want to miss out on.

Jesus, help me to be patient in this life. Thank you for sticking by me. Help me to not give up. May I find happiness in my journey with you.

Unshakable

Let us be thankful, because we have a kingdom that cannot be shaken. We should worship God in a way that pleases him with respect and fear.

It is pretty incredible that we can walk among history. Tour companies take thousands of people every year to see the ruins of great civilizations of the past, from Italy and Greece to China and Peru. In Israel, you can walk on bricks and inside broken synagogues where Jesus himself may have taught.

If you ever get the chance to do this, let the crumbled walls and derelict buildings serve as a reminder that the empires of the world are shakable. The nations and governments of this world will rise and fall. Everything in this world, in fact, will come to an end. But as Christians, we can be thankful that we have a kingdom that has no end. We operate in God's kingdom, and it cannot be shaken. The kingdom of God will always be, and no ruler or natural disaster can destroy it. What an amazing God we serve!

What comfort do you have in the knowledge that God's kingdom cannot be destroyed?

Since we are receiving our rights to an unshakeable kingdom we should be extremely thankful and offer God the purest worship that delights his heart as we lay down our lives in absolute surrender, filled with awe.

This knowledge of the unshakeable kingdom demands one response: pure worship. We are saying that our God is so powerful, nothing can destroy his kingdom. That, live or die, we have an inheritance in heaven. We know that his reign and rule is both now and forevermore.

It should stir awe inside your soul. Your temporary dwellings or country of residence could be in turmoil or in peace. Either way, God's kingdom does not change. This can encourage you to approach him with awe and reverence. Worship your mighty King tonight!

God, I worship you. You are mighty in power! Your kingdom has no end. I praise you! Thank you for welcoming me into your kingdom and calling me your child. Thank you for my inheritance.

Be Open

*Whoever conceals his transgressions will not prosper,
but he who confesses and forsakes them will obtain mercy.*

PROVERBS 28:13 ESV

Do you feel the pressure? As believers, we often fall into the
pressure-filled trap of perfection. We want to live for Christ
and display the change he has made in our life to the world
around us. We don't want people to see us sin and mess up.
But we do sin, because the only person who was every perfect
is Jesus. What now? Do we continue on the pressure path and
try to hide our mistakes? Or do we own up to them?

Dear Christian, the best example of a true Christian that you
can give to the unbelieving world is a repentant believer, not
a perfect one. When children see their parents confess their
sins and ask for forgiveness, they see the mercy of Christ at
work in. When spouses or friends receive forgiveness, they
are covered by the same mercy God uses to cover us. When
our neighbors, co-workers, and friends watch us admit
to our mistakes, ask for mercy, and walk out in confident
forgiveness, they will be in awe of the power at work in us.
The best witness you can give is not a perfect life; it's the life
of a believer who confesses mistakes.

Do you find it hard to ask for forgiveness
and display your mistakes?

One who conceals his wrongdoings will not prosper,
But one who confesses and abandons them will find compassion.

PROVERBS 28:13 NASB

When we sin, we have options. We can try to cover it up, we can try to forget about it, or we can confess. Covering up sin is futile because there is nothing hidden from God. When we try to forget about it, we find that it refuses to disappear. But oh, what joy is to be found in confessing it!

When we confess and repent of our sins, we see our sins from God's point of view. We agree with him that they are wrong. Then, we are given immediate mercy. Instant forgiveness. Yes, there are still consequences, but the freedom that is found in confessing sins to God and having him walk with us through those consequences is a beautiful thing.

Jesus, I confess my sins to you tonight. Thank you for your forgiveness and mercy. Make me whole again.

Treasure

Your laws are my treasure;
they are my heart's delight.

PSALM 119:111 NLT

In every city in the world today, there are hundreds of thousands of laws. Mankind has been making up laws and rules from the very beginning. It's not a bad thing, usually. How can anyone know them all? Do you know all the laws of your town? Some of them are common sense, and some of them are obscure. Others, people have never heard of. Some people dedicate their lives to studying the law; we call them lawyers. But you would be hard-pressed to find anyone who always treasures and delights in the laws of the land.

And yet, this is exactly how David described his feelings toward God's law. A treasure is something you hold in high esteem, and it is of great value to you. This is how David felt about God's commands. They aren't a burden, they aren't a puzzle, and they aren't obscure. They are a delight.

Do you feel as David does about God's commands
for your life? Are they a burden or a delight?

Your testimonies I have taken as a heritage forever,
For they are the rejoicing of my heart.

PSALM 119:111 NKJV

How can we know all of God's laws? The answers are all in the Bible. God's Word is an educational gift. It contains poetry, history, and prophecy, and it also holds instructions and warnings for earthly life. It also holds greatest gift of all: the road to salvation.

When you read the Bible, don't fly through it. It can be especially tempting to skip sections of God's law. Try meditating on God's laws. Think about them, memorize them, and take them to heart. They will then become a delight to you as you find yourself pulling them up from your mind, with the help of the Holy Spirit, and applying them to your daily life. When you find yourself in hard situations, you will be amazed at the treasures of Scripture that will come to mind and encourage you. God will also use these nuggets to encourage and bless others through you as well.

God, help me to know you and your Word better. Help me to delight and treasure your commands. Hide your Word in my heart.

Compassionate Heart

"Show mercy and compassion for others, just as your heavenly Father overflows with mercy and compassion for all."
LUKE 6:36 TPT

What a vessel is full of is what will spill out. If a mug is full of coffee, and you keep pouring coffee into it, the overflow will be coffee. Simple, right? What you say and how you act toward others is an overflow of what is in your heart. When you speak words that will heal someone's soul, when you offer them the words of Christ, that is the overflow of an empathetic heart.

Speaking empathy is an overflow of a heart that is full of mercy and compassion. Mercy and compassion find their source in the heart of Christ. The closer we are to Christ, the more our overflow will look like his overflow. Oh, to be believers who overflow with rivers of mercy for loved ones to find refreshment in! Ask God to fill you with his mercy and compassion today.

What is your overflow right now?

*"Be merciful,
just as your Father is merciful."*

LUKE 6:36 NIV

In the same manner that goodness can be traced to the overflowing heart of Christ, our negative traits also reflect the overflow of our heart. What you fill up on is important. Do you have countless hours to binge-watch the latest sitcom but precious few minutes for Jesus? Do you spend your commute saturated in the ramblings of talk radio or the expletives of the local radio station, unable to create an appetite for worship music or spiritual podcasts?

What fills you is what will flow out to you. You cannot expect yourself to be full of mercy and compassion for others if you don't fill yourself with mercy from God. Maybe you refuse to accept his mercy, working and striving to save yourself. What goes in must come out. Won't you let God fill you today?

Jesus, will you fill me? Thank you for showing me the importance of what I put in my mind and soul. Let me be full of compassion and mercy, so that I can give those gifts to those around me.

Law of Love

"Do to others what you want them to do to you. This is the meaning of the law of Moses and the teaching of the prophets."

MATTHEW 7:12 NCV

This passage comes at the end of Jesus' famous Sermon on the Mount. It is often referred to as "the golden rule." You may have heard it most often when growing up, but this passage is so much more than a quote for kids. It is a summary of the law, Jesus' teaching to his disciples, and the words of the prophets for how we are to live in relationship with one another.

We are not here to live for ourselves. We worship God by living a life that is a blessing to others, that serves those around us. These eleven words are easy to say but much harder to live. Think about your relationships—online, in real life, at work, and at home.

Are you living a golden life toward those around you?

> *"Whatever you want men to do to you, do also to them,*
> *for this is the Law and the Prophets."*
>
> MATTHEW 7:12 NKJV

If you heard this phrase growing up, or you say it often to your own children, it can be easy to say it to others without thinking about how to apply it in your own life. Are you stumped about a relationship that has hit a dead end? Have you tried applying this law of love?

It takes a large dose of humility to live this way, and Jesus knew that. When he calls us to treat others the way we want to be treated, he is fully prepared to equip us to do so. He can empower us to live in humility and love in all of our relationships. Don't be afraid of getting trampled if you humble yourself to lift others up. Jesus will protect you and keep you safe. He is not unaware of how against our nature this law goes. He is fully prepared to equip you to live toward others according to the law of love.

Jesus, thank you for giving me everything I need to show your honor and love in my relationships. Show me where I can extend my practice of this golden rule.

It's Certain

Certainly, God has heard me;
He has attended to the voice of my prayer.

PSALM 66:19 NKJV

There is something so comforting about a sure thing. It is rare in life, as the idea of failing often haunts and halts so many of our endeavors. If you could use a slam dunk fact today, know this: God hears you when you pray. Examine the many religions of the world, and you will see people going to extreme lengths to communicate with their gods and to find out what they are communicating to them. Further your study, and you will see that no one has certainty that their god has heard them like we Christians do.

Our God is alive. He has written us a love letter that is 66 books long. He exposes his character to us in the creation around us. He sent his only Son to secure our eternal future with him, and he gives us his very Spirit to comfort, guide, and teach us. He is powerful enough to move mountains and involved enough to answer prayers through the people around us. With all this in mind, with the sure-fire knowledge that God hears you, what does that change for you today?

What would you pray if you felt certain
that God would answer and move? Pray that.

*Praises rise to God,
for he paid attention to my prayer
and answered my cry to him!*

PSALM 66:19 TPT

When you attend to something, you show it your care and
concern. God is attending to your prayers tonight. He is
giving them his attention, he cares for them, and he is
concerned over what concerns you. He is not an absent-
minded listener, hoping you will stop talking and forgetting
anything you say. God hears you.

In fact, even when we don't know what to pray, the Bible
tells us that the Holy Spirit is praying for us. It also tells us
that Jesus is interceding for us before the throne. The lines
of communication are open wide. All you have to do is pray.
Won't you take time tonight to speak to the one who wants to
hear your heart as you listen to his?

Jesus, here I am. Share your heart with me. I'm listening. Thank
you for hearing me and caring about the things I care about.

Expectations

The news about him spread all the more, so that crowds of people came to hear him and to be healed of their sicknesses. But Jesus often withdrew to lonely places and prayed.

LUKE 5:15-16 NIV

Do you think Jesus ever disappointed people? We are given many examples of it in Scripture. He disappointed the religious leaders by not being who they wanted him to be. They often thought he extended far too much grace to people. Once, the people asked for more miracles, and Jesus didn't perform. Some of the disciples thought he should be a political leader, and instead he died at the hands of Romans and Jews.

Not living up to expectations or disappointing people is not a sin. Jesus was about his Father's business, and he knew what was most important. We aren't perfect like Jesus, and there will be times when we disappoint people because of sin. But there will be other times when we are doing what our Father has asked, and it will be disappointing. Take heart! You are in good company, because Jesus experienced this too. Jesus showed his love to others by not doing everything they wanted him to do and not being everything they wanted him to be. He loved them by doing what he was called to do.

How can you love by doing what you have been asked by God to do, regardless of others' expectations?

The report of his power spread even faster, and vast crowds came to hear him preach and to be healed of their diseases. But Jesus often withdrew to the wilderness for prayer.

LUKE 5:15-16 NLT

Your job is to keep your eyes on God and to seek first his kingdom. If you are living in the pressure-filled place of trying to fulfill everyone's expectations for you, you will end up worn out and certain you aren't enough. Let us take after the example of Jesus and do what our Father has told us to do, regardless of the expectations of the world.

Jesus lived his mission, all the way to dying on the cross (something no one expected to happen). He knew the importance of being connected to the Father and doing his work. Let us be believers who stay on track, loving others by serving God and his call first and foremost.

Jesus, thank you for the example you set while on earth. Help me not to fall into the trap of living to make others happy. Though their disappointment can hurt, I know my life is yours. Search my heart and show me when sin is causing disappointment; show me when I'm living for others instead of you. Thank you for your wisdom!

Rest in Hope

"You will have confidence, because there is hope;
you will be protected and take your rest in safety."

JOB 11:18 NRSV

There is always hope for a Christian. The nations may rage, politicians may be corrupt, and the climate may destroy our possessions. The world may feel like a snow globe in the hands of a two-year-old, but there will always be hope for the believer. How is that possible? It's possible because we are a people whose hope lies in the unshakeable.

Our hope lies in Jesus Christ and all that he has promised us. And he has promised us an unshakable, immovable kingdom. Our confidence is not in worldly systems or things. With Jesus as our hope, we can live our lives boldly, proclaiming his good news no matter what comes our way. We can sleep without anxiety. We can walk in confidence of what he has called us to do, knowing he will protect us. Dear believer, where does your hope rest? Are you suffering from misplaced hope? Ask Jesus to reveal your heart this morning and realign your hope with him.

Where is your hope?
Do some soul searching this morning.

Having hope will give you courage.
You will be protected and will rest in safety.

JOB 11:18 NLT

A hope aligned on Christ will change your entire life. The perfect parable of this is of the men who built their homes. Jesus tells us about two men who built houses, one upon the sand and one upon the rock. If you have ever been to the ocean, you know that the sand is constantly shifting due to wind and waves. That's just daily life, never mind the power of a catastrophic hurricane. Jesus points out that the house built upon the rock survived the storm, but the one on the sand did not.

We are building our houses on rock when we center our lives and hopes around Christ. It is he who gives us strength to withstand daily shifts and powerful storms. Jesus is the only firm foundation upon which to base your life. With him as your rock, you cannot lose.

Jesus, be my rock and my solid ground. My hope is in you.

Forever Good

*Jesus Christ is the same
yesterday and today and forever.*

HEBREWS 13:8 NASB

Change is inevitable in our world. We are all growing older, and we can't stop it. The seasons change from spring to summer, fall to winter. We'd be hard-pressed to think of anything of value in our material world that will not change.

Maybe you don't do well with change. Maybe the lack of control scares you. Take comfort in the fact that Jesus is the same. From before the beginning of time, he was who he is, and he will remain that way forever. Is God good? Yes, and he always will be. Is he compassionate? Yes, and he always will be. Is he in control? Yes, and he always will be. His character is forever. This reliability brings us great reassurance when we face the change. Lean completely on God, for he never changes.

What comfort do you get from the unchanging nature of God?

Jesus Christ is the same
yesterday, today, and forever.
HEBREWS 13:8 NLT

Why does this verse list three separate sections of time—yesterday, today, and forever? Jesus of yesterday is important because he is the act of God throughout history. It's recorded in the Bible, and it is a large way of how we get to know who God is. Today is important because this is the when we interact with God. The here and now is our personal experience with him. What We know about him from yesterday enables us to know him today.

Lastly, it is important that he is the same in the future because he is the hanger upon which our hope rests. Our hope does not disappoint because we can be confident that he is the same God in the future, and his promises are sure.

Jesus, thank you for being the same yesterday, today and forever. Thank you that I can cast all my hope upon you because of these facts. Thank you for being forever good.

Tenacity

Remember to stay alert and hold firmly to all that you believe.
Be mighty and full of courage.

1 CORINTHIANS 16:13 TPT

From the moment you awoke this morning until you close
your eyes tonight, choices will bombard you. These choices
will be simple and mostly inconsequential, like what to have
for breakfast. But others will be defining and testing, asking
you to sway away from the convictions that God has given you.
Starting your day here in God's Word is an example of the
first battle. You didn't skip out on what God has for you this
morning—good work! Continue in this pattern for the rest of
your day. Hold onto the things that the Holy Spirit has spoken
to you in prayer and through God's Word. At times, it will
require great courage. Ask God to fill you up with it. Tests will
prove if you're mighty enough, and you are most mighty when
you get your strength from God. Choose to rely on him, and it
will lead to a day full of choices that give God the glory.

Do you foresee a particular area of your day that will be
challenging? How can you be alert to the enemy's schemes?

Be on your guard; stand firm in the faith;
be courageous; be strong.

1 CORINTHIANS 16:13 NIV

Have you ever kicked up some deer while walking on a trail?
God has given many animals, like deer, the ability to hear
the slightest noise. When you come upon the deer in the
distance, and they hear you, what do they do? They stand up
straight, perk their ears, and lean in to listen more. This is
how they detect danger and decide if they should bolt or not.

In today's verse from Corinthians, Paul is telling us to be
like those deer. To be alert. Being alert doesn't mean you
are living in fear; it means that you are aware that there is
an enemy who schemes against you. If you are alert, you can
identify areas in your life that may be under attack and ask
God to fight for you. Wise is the believer who is on guard,
suited up in the armor of God and aware of what is going on
in the spiritual realm.

God, help me to be alert. Thank you for fighting for me. Fill
me with courage and strength today and speak to me through
your Word.

Lean on Others

Confess your sins to each other and pray for each other so that you may be healed. The earnest prayer of a righteous person has great power and produces wonderful results.

JAMES 5:16 NLT

God works in many ways. There is much to be done in the privacy of prayer, when God intimately works on our hearts. But God created us to live in community, and he also has mighty plans to work through earthly relationships with others. When we keep our sins to ourselves, confessing them to God alone, it's easy to maintain a mask that everything is fine in your life. Confession is never fun but wearing masks in front of God and others will lever lead to a fruit-filled life.

It's okay to say you're not okay. God is abundant in grace, and you can also ask him for a place in a community that will model that same love and grace. Things that feel overwhelming or chains that feel like they will never be broken loose power when confessed to others. Speaking out loud to another believer brings the issue into the light of Christ, exposes it for what it is (powerless before the throne of God), and brings freedom to your life.

Are you in a community that encourages confession?
If not, pray for God to bring you into one today.

Confess and acknowledge how you have offended one another
and then pray for one another to be instantly healed,
for tremendous power is released through the passionate,
heartfelt prayer of a godly believer!

JAMES 5:16 TPT

"I thought I was the only one!" has been exclaimed by people over and over. This is a lie that the enemy tries to feed us. If he can make us feel like we are the only ones with this problem, we feel like a failure and continue to struggle with our sins. Worse, he has us cornered and alone.

Don't let it happen! You are not alone, and you are not the only one. There is so much power in community with fellow brothers and sisters in Christ. When you share your life with them, you are no longer cornered—you have a whole community in your corner. This isn't just any community, either. It's the body of Christ, full of the Holy Spirit and the healing power he brings. Not only do you need them, but they also need you! God has given you a unique story and gifts to be an active part in someone else's healing. Stop hiding, step out in faith, and rise with the body of Christ.

God, thank you for the body of Christ. Thank you for healing me of my sins. I am so grateful that I'm not alone. Help me to find a group of believers who seek your face and don't want to live trapped in sin.

Fullness of Life

You make known to me the path of life;
in your presence there is fullness of joy;
at your right hand are pleasures forevermore.

PSALM 16:11 ESV

We've grown up on a diet of mantras like "carpe diem." You only get one life, so make the most of it! While this is true, it's also a trap that can paralyze us. Imagine if you gave an artist only one piece of paper on which to create their life's masterpiece, or a musician one run-through on a new piece of music? Seems absurd, doesn't it?

We don't need to live our lives like God has one piece of paper to hand to us and then he will run out. We have a God who offers life in abundance. He's got sheets upon sheets of grace, ready to be handed to us. He's got enough love to forgive any mistakes we make. We need not live in fear that he is going to run out of what we need. Unlimited provision. How could that change your life? There is fullness with Christ awaiting you. Go ahead and take the step of faith and grace that God has been beckoning you to take.

Would you describe yourself as having a scarcity mentality or an abundance mentality?

You will show me the way of life,
granting me the joy of your presence
and the pleasures of living with you forever.

PSALM 16:11 NLT

To find the abundant life David is speaking about in this psalm, we have to lift our eyes above this physical realm to the world beyond. We must lift our eyes to Christ and have an eternal perspective. God wants us to move away from living with a mindset that says there will never be enough to go around. He gives a life of abundance. We have all we need in God, and he is enough.

He provides for our needs. He is the God of cattle on a thousand hills. What God wants us to do is not focused on how much we have, but rather about being good stewards of what we have. To do this, we must hand it all over to Jesus. See what fullness and pleasures he can give out of what you have to offer. Entrust your life to him.

Father God, I praise you, for you are the God of abundance. In you is fullness, and there is no lack. Help me to be a good steward of the gifts you have given me.

Vulnerability

For Christ's sake, I delight in weaknesses,
in insults, in hardships, in persecutions, in difficulties.
For when I am weak, then I am strong.

2 CORINTHIANS 12:10 NIV

Here, we find a lesson about God's upside-down kingdom. Weakness is a negative term in most cultures. It is ingrained in us to love strength. Muscular athletes, tough soldiers, clever businesspersons; the list goes on. We cheer and applaud, putting those who are this way on pedestals and in leadership positions. Even at birth, when a child is born, you will often hear someone say, "the baby is strong and healthy!" Which is a good thing, right?

Paul and Jesus aren't telling us here to bemoan our health, abilities, or the good things that come in our lives. The message of the upside-down kingdom is that of dependency. Weaknesses force us to depend on others, and we need to live every moment of our life dependent on Christ. In health and in hardship, with talent or with lack, make Christ the source of your strength. Depend on God like your life depends on it—because it does. It's the posture of our hearts in this upside-down kingdom, and it's the way of the King.

Do you have a hard time accepting weakness
as an opportunity to depend on God?

*That's why I take pleasure in my weaknesses, and in the insults,
hardships, persecutions, and troubles that I suffer for Christ.
For when I am weak, then I am strong.*

2 CORINTHIANS 12:10 NLT

Do you try to hide your weaknesses? The Christian life calls
us to vulnerability, both with God and with others. If we
try to put on masks and not show our weaknesses, we miss
out on the opportunity to flourish in Christ. We hinder our
relationships with other people by not revealing our true
selves. It can be scary, but God wants to reach others through
you. He wants to heal your family, your friends, and your
co-workers, and he's going to work through your life's story,
if you depend on him. Opening up to others, allowing them
to mourn with you and share joy with you, enriches both your
life and theirs.

And if we try to hide from God, we are only fooling ourselves.
Showing him our weakness is gold in the kingdom of God.
He is the banker who takes your pennies and turns them
into gold. It's an investment you can't pass up! What are you
holding back on and trying to fix with your own strength?
Turn it over to God. Be vulnerable with him and with others
and watch him use your weakness for glory.

God, train me in your upside-down ways. Help me to be open
with you. Teach me to be vulnerable in my relationships. Take
my weakness, that I may depend on your strength.

In the Meantime

It is not yet time for the message to come true,
but that time is coming soon; the message will come true.
It may seem like a long time, but be patient and wait for it,
because it will surely come; it will not be delayed.

HABAKKUK 2:3 NCV

Do you remember being a kid and thinking that anything that took a few minutes, like waiting in line, seemed to take forever? The waiting game isn't a fun one, no matter what age you are. As adults, we have more understanding of time when it comes to things like waiting in line at the grocery store, but we can still be impatient with God when it comes to bigger things in life.

Waiting for that job opportunity. Waiting for a spouse. Waiting for a child. Waiting for healing. Waiting for a dream to come to fruition. Some waiting rooms are a lot more painful than others, aren't they? Just because you are waiting doesn't mean God is not working. Don't pull away from him because the season hasn't come, or the days feel mundane. Let the waiting room draw you closer into the presence of God. He's got the plan, he knows the outcome, and he has the answers to all your questions. Draw near to him and ask him for patience to sustain you.

What are you waiting for?
What waits have pulled you away from God?

The revelation awaits an appointed time;
it speaks of the end
and will not prove false.
Though it linger, wait for it;
it will certainly come
and will not delay.

HABAKKUK 2:3 NIV

God is a good Father who knows your needs and desires to give good things to you. Every good gift you receive is from him. While you are waiting for something, does it blind your eyes to all the "in the meantime" gifts God bestows on you?

His hand does not close because the timing isn't right on certain things. He doesn't turn his back on you because you are waiting. You haven't been benched in the kingdom of God. He wants to work through you in every season. He wants to give you gifts; you just have to open your eyes to them. They might not look the way you think they should, but trust that God has your best in mind and knows what you need.

God, thank you for not forgetting me. I know you don't bench me. As I wait, draw me closer to you.

Pursue Peace

*Let us pursue the things which make for peace
and the things by which one may edify another.*

ROMANS 14:19 NKJV

There is a difference between a peacekeeper and a peacemaker. Which one do you think Jesus calls us to be? Spiritual peacekeepers maintain the veneer of peace at all costs. They refuse to confront sin, avoid conflict, and often sweep things under the rug to have peace. Proverbs 10:10 tells us that these people are just winking at wrongdoing.

Peacemakers, on the other hand, know that peace is not a given. They know that peace does not come without work and that a lack of conflict does not indicate true peace. Peacemakers see the job that needs to be done. They work to build bridges, facilitate reconciliation, and acknowledge that conflict will come. Jesus did not lead a conflict-free life, and neither did his disciples or Paul. Jesus was a peacemaker, going to great lengths, including death, to reconcile man to God and give us the tools to be reconciled with each other.

Are you a peacekeeper or a peacemaker?

*Let us aim for harmony in the church
and try to build each other up.*

ROMANS 14:19 NLT

There are several steps we can take to see to it that we are
peacemakers. First off, we need to glorify God. We need to
follow in his footsteps of forgiveness and mercy. Next, we need
to make sure we are taking responsibility for our own actions
when conflict arises. It's easy to shift blame and to justify; it's
harder to look at ourselves in humility and recognize where we
have gone astray. We should be women who lead by example
in repentance and self-awareness. Next, when an offense
does happen, we seek to restore, not condemn. We don't dwell
on petty differences but offer grace in these circumstances.
In more serious matters, we take the matter straight to the
offender, following the protocol of Matthew 18. And lastly,
we pursue peace. We work for it, pray for it, actively pursue
it. Jesus gave his life so you could have peace with the Father.
Won't you serve your fellow brothers and sisters in the same
manner, being a peacemaker among them?

Jesus, you are peace. Thank you for dying to restore peace
between me and the Father. Make me a peacemaker. Help
me to not fall into the trap of being a peacekeeper, instead
seeking reconciliation and restoration, just like you do.

Reliability Matters

"He who is faithful in a very little thing is faithful also in much; and he who is unrighteous in a very little thing is unrighteous also in much."

LUKE 16:10 NASB

We delight in the fact that God cares about the little details of our life when it benefits us. But do we have that same delight when God asks us to be faithful in little things, to feel remorse over seemingly small sins? We can't measure our sins on a scale of consequences. We tell a small lie, and there is no consequence. It can't matter to God, right? We fudge the rules and do things when we think no one notices, and if it doesn't hurt anyone, what does it matter?

It matters to God. It matters because it reflects our integrity, which speaks to who we are as people. It's easy to get legalistic and even bitter about these tiny things. But God's way is not meant to be burdensome; it's meant to bring freedom. Each time you choose God's way, it's one more strand in your rope of trust in him. God is asking us to do things his way so we can watch all the little moments build up into a monument of praise to God and his kingdom.

Pray and ask God to convict you of any small sins that you have been ignoring.

> *"Whoever can be trusted with very little can also be trusted with much, and whoever is dishonest with very little will also be dishonest with much."*
>
> LUKE 16:10 NIV

In these words from our Savior, other aspect we can consider is the mundane factor of our everyday lives. Life cannot be one long mountaintop experience, and it also will not be only in a deep, hard valley. There are thousands of moments in between: washing dishes, finishing a work report, checking the mail, taking care of animals, having coffee. Does God care about these moments?

Yes, he does, for these are the moments that make up our life. As we referenced this morning, we can build a life that is a monument of praise to our Creator one brick, or one moment, at a time. Each moment does matter to God. Even when we're using it to do ordinary things, he wants to share in them. He wants us to daily rely on him for the small things in life. We can experience God no matter where we are or what we are doing. Folding laundry, you can praise him. Sitting in line in your car, he is there. He doesn't expect constant service from us, but he does desire consistent communion with us.

God, thank you for being a God of details. Convict me of those things in my life that I may view as too small. Help me to glorify you in the big and the small moments.

Invitation

He said, "Come." And when Peter had come down out of the boat,
he walked on the water to go to Jesus.

MATTHEW 14:29 NKJV

Life is not a steady stream. It comes at us in waves. Waves of achievement, of grief, of joy, of pain. Just like waves sweep in and out of the ocean, life ebbs and flows around us. Life is like the waves that crashed up against the rocking boat where Peter sat.

You have an invitation this morning to surrender your boat. You can step out of whatever earthly thing your security is in as you navigate the waves coming at you. You can step out in faith in the one who can calm those waves. As you come out of your boat, look into the eyes of Jesus. Those who step out of their boats keep their eyes focused on Jesus, not on the waves around them.

What is Jesus asking you to let go of this morning? Follow him, and let courage rise in you as you keep your eyes on him.

"Come and join me," Jesus replied.
So Peter stepped out onto the water
and began to walk toward Jesus.

MATTHEW 14:29 TPT

Jesus spoke one word, one command. *Come.* If Jesus says come, believer, know that he will provide a way. You might be looking at the impossible, at the storm crashing and swirling around you, but Jesus is beckoning you to come because only he can provide the way.

He is the way. There is nothing too hard for him. He is making a way for you. He is forging paths and moving mountains, and you are asked to do just one thing—come. Take that step!

Jesus, I see the waves, I feel the waves, and I hear the waves, but I choose to set my senses only on you. As you invite me, help me to boldly step out in faith and leave the boat behind. Help me to follow you. Will you make a way for me through this storm? Guide me and lead me. I want only you.

Heavenly Citizens

We are citizens of heaven, where the Lord Jesus Christ lives.
And we are eagerly waiting for him to return as our Savior.

PHILIPPIANS 3:20 NLT

Citizenship is a hot button topic in politics today. Debates range on topics from immigration to national pride. Christians are faced with the distinct choice to either put their country and politics first, or to remember where their true citizenship lies.

What does this mean? It means that Jesus is on the throne. He is king, and we are citizens in his kingdom. We ourselves are pilgrims on a journey to our true home. This earth, with your country and town of citizenship, is not your final home. We must operate as such. We must put our allegiance to Jesus above our allegiance to any flag we sit beneath. This means living our lives by his Word, the Bible, first.

Do you struggle to see yourself as a pilgrim?
What does having citizenship in heaven change for you?

Our citizenship is in heaven, from which we also eagerly wait for the Savior, the Lord Jesus Christ.

PHILIPPIANS 3:20 NKJV

Another aspect of our lives that citizenship affects is that sometimes, we will be asked to lay down our rights. If you are a citizen of a freer country, this can be especially hard. We think it is our right to punish our enemies, to have wealth, to be able to say whatever we want—even to practice our religion without persecution. While these aren't strictly bad things, they are things the Bible says we will need to lay down. You can probably think of other examples that are more personal to you.

Why do we assume we have the right to religious freedom? The early church did not, and they flourished. Why do we assume that we can kill our enemies? Doesn't Jesus tell us to love them? Making yourself first a citizen in the kingdom can turn your life upside down as you begin to live by kingdom principles. Let Jesus guide you on this journey, dear pilgrim, for he will be the one to welcome you home.

Jesus, your ways are radical and different. Help me to live on earth as a citizen of heaven.

Rejoice

Rejoice in the Lord always,
again I say, Rejoice.

PHILIPPIANS 4:4 NKJV

How do you turn the feelings found in your happy place into an ongoing thing? You chase after joy. Joy and happiness can sometimes be used interchangeably, but it can be a mistake. Happiness tends to be temporary and based on circumstances. Joy is far more solid and steadier, but it also must be pursued. Rarely does joy just fall into your lap.

You must choose, no matter what the circumstances around you, to chase after joy. Joy is selfless, internal, and always based around connection with God. When you connect with God, he doesn't just become your happy place. He becomes your source of joy, which is a river that can carry you through so many life situations.

Have you considered before
the difference between happiness and joy?

Be full of joy in the Lord always.
I will say again, be full of joy.

PHILIPPIANS 4:4 NCV

Want to start a revolution? Start chasing relentlessly after
joy. With all you've got, pursue it. Jump on the bandwagon of
gratitude and ride it all the way as you go after joy. This will
start a revolution, for joy is contagious. When true joy enters
a room, it spreads quickly. It cannot be stopped.

Having a rough day? Stop pushing and trying harder and take
a pause. Find three things you are grateful for. Turn up some
praise music and dance. Dance before the Lord and let him
fill you with joy and watch as others around you join or try to
resist being a part of the joy. Joy is contagious and God calls
us to spread it. Do you know someone could use some joy?
How could you encourage your pastor, your fellow believer,
or your neighbor with joy? Let love take the reins as you race
down this wild path, and don't be surprised if it takes you to
some pretty great God moments. Joy is the revolution this
world needs tonight.

Jesus, will you fill me joy? Be my source and help me to
spread it to all those around me.

Passionate Love

Christ proved God's passionate love for us by dying in our place while we were still lost and ungodly!

ROMANS 5:8 TPT

We have a tendency to assign people worth based on what they do. This tendency leaks into our Christianity, teaching us to work for our salvation by being good or following legalistic rituals. But that's not how God works. God's love chased after us while we were still lost and dead in our sins, completely powerless to change anything ourselves. Christ displayed this for all the world to see by his death on the cross.

We can be scandalized by this grace when we think about God forgiving those we find unforgivable, those whose sins we couldn't imagine committing. God's forgiveness is just as much for them as it is for you. His love is that strong. When you find yourself unable to forgive someone, appalled at someone else's actions, or just judging others, try to remember that they too are a person for whom Christ died. None of us are above reproach. All of us equally need God's grace.

Who is hard to love in your life?

God showed his great love for us by sending Christ to
die for us while we were still sinners.

ROMANS 5:8 NLT

There is wild freedom to be found in the good news of Jesus dying for us. It's amazing, the freedom you have when you recognize that nothing you did saved you. It's a weight lifted off your shoulders. It's the freedom of grace. Nothing you did saved you, and nothing you do can separate you from his love. That's no pressure on you!

This freedom of grace and peace with God has the power to change your life. Stop trying harder, hustling, and pushing for salvation. Rest in his grace. Run through the wide-open fields of his love, and breath deep of the peace you now have with God. Freedom is so sweet.

Jesus, I am in awe of the price you paid for grace. Thank you for your work on the cross. Thank you for your love.

No Surprise

Do not be surprised at the fiery ordeal among you, which comes upon you for your testing, as though some strange thing were happening to you; but to the degree that you share the sufferings of Christ, keep on rejoicing, so that also at the revelation of His glory you may rejoice with exultation.

1 PETER 4:12-13 NASB

Somewhere along the Christian way, most of us get into our heads that the Christian life means the easy life. After all, the Bible is full of promises about goodness and plenty and love and promised lands. Surely that means here and now, right? Not necessarily. In the Bible, we are told to expect to suffer as Christ did. We are told to expect the world to hate us as it did Christ. Even the mouth of Jesus is full of warnings about hard things.

How do we blend blessings and warnings? The truth is that our promise land is heaven. Our citizenship lies there. Our hope is eternal. We cannot expect all the promises to manifest themselves right now in our lives. There is still a battle raging with sin, even though we know who the victor is. There are still people who need to hear the good news of Jesus, and evil forces do not want that to happen. Take heart, dear believer, that God has not abandoned you because you are facing hard times. He mourns with you, he hurts with you, and he is still sovereign.

Do you feel abandoned by God
when hard times come your way?

Do not be surprised at the fiery ordeal that has come on you to test you, as though something strange were happening to you. But rejoice in as much as you participate in the sufferings of Christ, so that you may be overjoyed when his glory is revealed.

1 PETER 4:12-13 NIV

What are we being tested on? Here in 1 Peter, it states that some of the situations we go through are tests. It asks a question. Where does your hope lie? On whom do you depend? Where have you put your allegiance? Is your hope fully in Christ when hard times come? Do you lean on God when the fires get hot? Are you quick to curse God or abandon his will when things get hard?

These are questions all of us need to ponder. When trials come, they can produce good fruit in us, if we keep our eyes on Christ. Let God work all things for good in your life, even when you don't see the good in them.

Jesus, keep my eyes focused on you during hard times. Thank you for being my hope.

Humble Heart

He poured water into the basin and began to wash the disciples'
feet and to wipe them with the towel with which He was girded.

JOHN 13:5 NASB

If you search for images of kings on the internet, you will get a
vast array of pictures, most of them of men in ornate crowns.
Their garments are fine fabrics usually in shades of red and
purple, symbolizing royalty. They are surrounded by material
possessions and wealth. They have bodyguards and personal
carriages (or jet planes), servants and news staff following
them around. But the picture we get of the King of kings is
opposite.

Reread today's verse. Jesus removed his outer garments,
kneeled on the floor, poured water, and began to do the job
of a servant. It was a job that none of his other disciples
thought to do, even though feet washing was customary.
Jesus humbled himself as a servant. The highest king in all of
history, kneeling on the floor before some fishermen and tax
collectors. Who would have thought? This is the example that
Jesus gives to us for our leadership and our lives. He calls us
to live humbly and to serve.

How will you answer the call of humility today?

He poured water into a basin. Then he began to wash the disciples'
feet, drying them with the towel he had around him.

JOHN 13:5 NLT

When was the last time you prayed for humility? There is
an old saying that you need to be careful what you pray for,
because God will give you situations to hone that character
trait! The feeling behind this sentiment makes God out to
be a stern teacher, waiting to give harsh lessons to naughty
students.

God wants you to walk in humility because it is the kingdom
way, and anything that is the kingdom way is the best way.
He doesn't want to punish you. He wants the best for you. He
wants to make you like Christ, to refine you. Don't fall into
the trap of not praying for kingdom traits because you are
afraid you will get hard situations. Pray for humility, so that
God may refine you and make you more like him.

Jesus, make me humble. Make me more like you. Teach me
humility.

Closer

One who has unreliable friends soon comes to ruin,
but there is a friend who sticks closer than a brother.

PROVERBS 18:24, NIV

Who is this friend that sticks closer than a brother? Jesus, of course! He displays for us one of the most important qualities in a friendship: loyalty. To be a good friend is to be loyal through good times and hard times.

This does not mean you need to be a doormat for abuse. It does mean that, as much as you can, you work for peace in your relationships. You are quick to ask forgiveness and seek understanding. You bear the tension of rejoicing when they rejoice and weeping when they weep. You are available with your time and resources to this person, even when it costs you. Jesus displays this kind of loyalty toward us. His loyalty creates a security net for us, allowing us to be truly known and loved.

How can you be a loyal friend today?
What friendship needs repair?
Ask God for guidance in your friendships today.

Some friendships don't last for long,
but there is one loving friend who is joined to your heart
closer than any other!

PROVERBS 18:24 TPT

Why is making friends so hard? We crave that kind of relationship, but it often eludes us. Gone are the days of finding someone on the swing set who has the same color shirt as you and becoming instant buddies. Gone are the days where college roommates or high school clubs automatically put people with like interests into our lives.

Jesus doesn't want us to live in loneliness. He made us for relationships. He wants to work through you as a good friend in someone else's life, and he has friends in mind for you too. Pray about who you could pursue in friendship, and then take the leap. There is a beautiful relationship waiting for you.

Jesus, thank you for being a good friend, my perfect friend. Help me to be a conduit for your love to others in friendship.

Submitted

Instead, you ought to say,
"If the Lord wills, we will live and also do this or that."

JAMES 4:15 NCV

God hates your day planner. That's a joke, but isn't it the feeling you get from this passage in James? Does God not want us to plan things? Before you chuck that calendar in the trash, consider the point James is actually making here. He is not saying that God is against us planning out our days. The question is about who is in control.

To whom is your life submitted? Does your confidence lie in your plans? Do you think that if you work hard and make the right moves, everything will go your way? Or is your confidence in God, your plans humbly submitted to his lordship? A Christian after God's heart will be one who asks God to participate in planning. This believer gets God's input before stepping forward and trusts that he is in control of life. God wants to be involved in the big and little of your life. He wants to display his power to others through you. Submit your plans to God and let him work mightily in your life.

Do you include God in your planning?

Instead you should say,
"Our tomorrows are in the Lord's hands
and if he is willing we will live life to its fullest
and do this or that."

JAMES 4:15 TPT

Our perspective matters. Our lives are short, which is what James speaks on here in chapter four. Should we plan things at all? The answer is yes, but your perspective matters. It matters that you are aware that your life is just a breath. Though it is a short amount of time, God is not saying to sit around and wait for it to be over. God wants you to submit it to him and see what he can do.

Live with eternity in perspective, so that the things that you do and how you spend your time are about the things that matter and not those that burned up on judgment day. Live a life of deep impact by submitting your plans to the Lord and letting him lead.

Jesus, I give you control of my life. Thank you for giving me life. Use it for your glory.

Sharpened

As iron sharpens iron,
so a friend sharpens a friend.
PROVERBS 27:17 NLT

Have you ever felt like you are not doing much for the kingdom of God? You look around and see others who are called to full time ministry, like pastors, missionaries, authors, and theologians. There are those running homeless shelters and others meeting all sorts of needs. Where do you fit in if ministry is not in your job description?

Proverbs tells us that there is full time ministry to be found in friendship. Are you the type of iron-sharpening friend that spurs on other believers toward Christ? That's ministry. Jesus lived his life with twelve close disciples and three even closer friends. Ministry does not have to look like feeding thousands or preaching on a stage. Most true ministry is done in flesh to flesh, life to life, in the mundane ways of showing up for other people. Look at the people already around you, the friendships you have. Ask God to use you to lead someone closer to him today.

Who does God want you to encourage or sharpen today?

It takes a grinding wheel to sharpen a blade,
and so one person sharpens the character of another.

PROVERBS 27:17 TPT

Loneliness is difficult. An iron-sharpening friendship can be a sweet aroma that drifts through the stale smell of isolation. Loneliness causes many of us to retreat, build up walls, and suffer in silence. It's a horrible captor, and it is not how God intended us to live our lives.

An iron-sharpening friend can point you to truth when you are surrounded by lies. They can pray for you when you can't muster the words yourself. They always lead you back to Jesus. This is the friend we need to be to the people around us. Then, our lives are a fragrant aroma of Christ's love. This attracts more people, and this is how discipleship works. Don't let fear and loneliness trap you. Take a bold step toward a sharpening friendship today.

Jesus, lead me to those you want me to befriend. Free me from the bondage of loneliness.

Eyes Open

Since we are approaching the end of all things, be intentional, purposeful, and self-controlled so that you can be given to prayer.

1 PETER 4:7 TPT

Imagine yourself in the church that received this letter from Peter. You are all seated on the floor, listening attentively to the instructions this man, who walked with Jesus, was sharing for your life. Your ears perk up when you hear the phrase, "We are approaching the end of all things." The end! you think. How would you act if you knew the end was near?

Peter tells us exactly how to act, and it is unlike anything in a bucket list movie or a touching country music song. Peter tells us to devote ourselves to prayer. Prayer? Prayer is usually the last, most inactive thing we could do. Why spend the last days doing that? Peter disagrees. Prayer deserves intention, a scheduled time. A prayer plan brings purpose with specific things to pray for. And it takes self-control to make time for prayer. If it was the last year of your life, would you frantically try to accomplish more? Or would you give yourself to prayer? It's an interesting question, and it reveals a heart's attitude about prayer. Let's make a solid effort to prioritize prayer, starting this morning.

Does it surprise you that Peter brings up prayer?
How often do you pray?

The end of all things is near.
Therefore, be alert and of sober mind so that you may pray.

1 PETER 4:7 NIV

Why is prayer so important? Prayer is our direct line to God. It's how we connect with him. It's how we bring our needs to him. It's one way he speaks to us. It has the power to quiet our souls, to give us direction and revelation, and to change our lives and others.

The prayers of a righteous man affect many, says James, and that goes for righteous women as well. In Christ, you are righteous. Bring your prayers to the throne room, and watch God do the mighty work that only he can.

Jesus, thank you for hearing and moving in my prayers. Help me to pray often and with purpose.

A Way Prepared

"Build up, build up, prepare the road!
Remove the obstacles out of the way of my people."

ISAIAH 57:14 NIV

When read in the context, Isaiah 56 tells of Israel's corruption. Their leadership had turned away from God and toward idolatry, child sacrifice, sexual sin, sorcery, and cruelty. Sounds pretty grim, right? But God does not abandon his people. Here, in Isaiah 57, hope begins to rise. He says to clear the road for his people because they will return to him. What a picture of redemption and forgiveness.

Believer, the road is clear between you and God. There is no sin too horrendous that the road is now blocked. Jesus, with his death on the cross, permanently established the bridge between you and God. Peace has come to stay. Does it feel like there are obstacles between you and God? Is the way unclear? That is a lie from the enemy. The path is clear, straight, and narrow. Let Jesus show you the way home.

Do you feel like there is a roadblock between you and God?
What is it?

> *"Let the people return to me.*
> *Build! Build up the road, clear the way, and get it ready!*
> *Remove every obstacle from their path."*

ISAIAH 57:14 TPT

This morning, we considered how our sin can make us feel like there are roadblocks between us and God. Consider this evening how your actions and responses might become a roadblock between someone else and God. Have you heard the verse that says it is worse for the person who leads a little one astray? It's called being a stumbling block, and Jesus takes it pretty seriously.

While we cannot live our lives in fear of what others think, we must live our lives in fear of God, that or actions and words honor him and do not cause others to stray from him. If we don't act in this manner, we need to be quick to ask for forgiveness and make reconciliation. Examine your life and heart tonight and let the Holy Spirit convict you of any ways you might be a roadblock to those around you. Let Jesus' path be free and open to all.

Jesus, search my heart. See if there are any stumbling blocks within me. Thank you for making peace with God possible.

Even So

"As for you, you meant evil against me;
but God meant it for good,
in order to bring it about as it is this day,
to save many people alive."

GENESIS 50:20 NKJV

"That's unfair!" If you've been around kids for even a few minutes, you have heard this phrase before. We want justice, or what we think is justice, from a very young age. The reality is that there will be harm done to us in life. Life won't be fair; things won't always go our way. When this happens, we have two choices. We can choose to get loud, get bitter, scream that it's not fair, and push for our rights. Or, we can grieve the situation, submit it to God, and hold fast to his promise to work all things for good.

There are evil schemes plotted against you by the enemy, maybe even through others. But you serve a powerful God who is in control. He will not abandon you, and he will bring justice. He has the power to bring about good and to redeem all things. Whatever the situation is, trust God to fight for you and do the good work today.

What area of your life do you need God to redeem for good?

> *"You intended to harm me,*
> *but God intended it all for good.*
> *He brought me to this position*
> *so I could save the lives of many people."*

GENESIS 50:20 NLT

What a mighty God we serve! There is nothing outside of his power to redeem. Consider the story of Joseph. He was betrayed by his brothers, sold, kept in prison, accused of rape, and the list goes on. But God had a plan the whole time. He did not abandon Joseph or forget about him.

God's timing is not our own. Surely, Joseph would have preferred to hit fast forward and get out of prison. He had to submit himself to God and his timing, trusting that God had good in mind. Whatever you are waiting for, God has good in mind for you. He will never forget about you or abandon you. You can trust him.

God, I trust you to work all things for good in my life. Help me to hold on to your promises.

Better Than Life

Because Your lovingkindness is better than life,
My lips will praise You.

PSALM 63:3 NASB

We are quick to share what we love with our friends. If we find a new restaurant that is delicious, we recommend it to others. If we find a skincare product that finally works for us, we rave about it on social media. It is not difficult to get people talking about the good things, because they are so good you want your joy to spread to others! And, if it was so good and life-changing for you, wouldn't you want them to experience the same joy?

In the same way, God is so good. His love is better than life itself. That's a pretty rave review! Our natural reaction to the love of God should be to share it and to share our joy with others. If it is so good, how can we hold it inside?

How have you experienced God's great love?
Who do you need to share it with?

Your tender mercies mean more to me than life itself.
How I love and praise you, God!

PSALM 63:3 TPT

What does it mean to praise God? First, let's go over what praise is not. Praise is not a Sunday morning, church-only activity. Praise is not always a scheduled activity. It can be spontaneous. Praise isn't always a loud expression. It is often seen in Scripture with quiet and waiting. Lastly, and most importantly, our praise and worship shouldn't be for anyone but God.

Now, what does it mean to praise God? It means that you are expressing honor and adoration for God. It is based in his Word, as it starts with a right understanding of God's place and our place. Praise is often coupled with an intense desire for the Lord. And lastly, praise grows reverence for God in us, which in turn, helps us to grow in wisdom. Isn't that amazing? Through song, spoken word, or quiet waiting, praise God, for his love is so good!

Jesus, your love is amazing! Thank you so much. It makes my heart burst with love. Help me to see those with whom to share your love.

Encouragement

Anxiety weighs down the human heart,
but a good word cheers it up.

PROVERBS 12:25 NRSV

We all deal with anxiety at some point. This doesn't mean we all have an anxiety disorder diagnosed by a doctor. It simply means anyone can get anxious. Even Paul wrote about having anxiety in the book of Philippians, and he told the church to be anxious for nothing. We have everyday anxieties and fears that plague us and can make hearts heavy. Often, we try to fix the problem ourselves. Maybe if we had more self-care, or if we got more sleep or worked out more, we wouldn't have this anxiety.

While those are all good things, the Bible adds another aspect to the equation: relationships. Good words usually come from one of two places, the Word of God or the word of a friend. We are not meant to carry our burdens alone. Give them to God and share them with another person. God made us to live in relationship with other people. When we bear each other's burdens, it can help lift the weight of anxiety on our hearts.

Do you bottle up your anxieties, or do you share them
with a friend and pray over them?

Anxious fear brings depression,
but a life-giving word of encouragement
can do wonders to restore joy to the heart.

PROVERBS 12:25 TPT

Have you ever sat across from a friend at Starbucks who is pouring out their woes quicker than the barista poured your coffee? As you sit there listening, you might be wishing you had just the right thing to say to make everything better. People will often share with us things that we can't fix and things for which we find no solution.

First off, just show up for them, and keep showing up. Being there is a large part of encouragement. Secondly, say something kind. Pray to the Holy Spirit to give you wisdom on what to say. Let him speak kindness to their souls through you. It doesn't have to be profound; it just needs to show care and compassion.

Jesus, show me where to share my burdens. Thank you for sharing my burdens with me. Help me to be a good friend and to show kindness to those who entrust me with their pain.

Only One

God is the only Lawmaker and Judge. He is the only One who can save and destroy. So it is not right for you to judge your neighbor.

JAMES 4:12 NCV

Imagine a courtroom scene. In front is the stern-faced judge in long, black robe. Standing in front of the judge is the defendant, someone you know. They are solemnly awaiting the decision. The judge's mouth opens and declares pardon to your acquaintance. Indignant, you rush to the front of the room and grab the gavel, trying to wrestle it away from the judge. This person deserves judgment!

Do you think that scene would fly in a human court of law? No? Then why do we do this to God all the time? We think we know best. We want this wrongdoer to stand trial and pay for what they've done, so we try to take over as judge. In life, this means condemning our neighbor by rumors and gossip, sentencing our co-workers with harsh treatment, making our spouses suffer with the silent treatment, or excluding that visitor at church because of how she dresses. We love to be the judge, but that role is not ours. Repent of the times you have tried to grab the gavel from God. Let him be the only true and right judge.

Do you find it hard to withhold judgment and condemnation on those you feel deserve it?

God alone, who gave the law, is the Judge.
He alone has the power to save or to destroy.
So what right do you have to judge your neighbor?

JAMES 4:12 NLT

God is just. You might be right in your judgment of someone else, meaning what you think about the situation is true. However, that doesn't mean you get to be the judge. God is just and fully capable of handling all of humanity and the grievances we commit against one another. He sees them all. He knows the pain and hurt that person has inflicted on you. He knows what they deserve, but he also knows what you deserve.

Every single one of us is deserving of death. But God has extended great love and forgiveness to us in our darkest place, and he will act in the same manner to everyone. You might not think they deserve it, or you might have a hard time forgiving them, but God is willing to forgive anyone who humbly confesses their sin and asks for forgiveness. If we want to judge like God, may we also be willing to die for our neighbors, as God did in love. Ask God to plant in your heart his mercy and forgiveness today.

God, you are just. I don't want to judge others anymore. I give control to you. Help me to forgive as you forgive.

Qualified

It is not that we think we are qualified to do anything on our own.
Our qualification comes from God.

2 CORINTHIANS 3:5 NLT

Grab your football helmet and let's go! You've got a spot on
your favorite NFL team as their starting quarterback. Can
you imagine? How laughable is this? Very few of us would
consider ourselves qualified to walk out our front doors and
onto a professional football field right now.

In the same manner, there is nothing about us that qualifies
us for grace. It doesn't matter how much money you make.
It doesn't matter what church you go to. It doesn't matter
if you've been baptized in the Jordan or sprinkled with the
holiest of water. Go on, list them. List all of the ways and
things we do to get ourselves right with God. Then, boast in
this fact; none of them matter. All that matters is grace, faith,
and the blood of Jesus Christ. That's how you are qualified.
That's it.

Are you trying to qualify yourself for heaven today?
What "qualifying" task do you need to stop taking pride in?

*Not that we are competent in ourselves to claim anything
for ourselves, but our competence comes from God.*

2 CORINTHIANS 3:5 NIV

We established this morning that there is nothing we can do
to qualify ourselves for grace. But did you also know that you
need no qualifications to be God's instrument? You don't
need to go to Bible school. You don't need to be a pastor. You
don't need to memorize a whole book of the Bible or wear
your hair in a certain style. You don't need to be male. You
don't need to be old and experienced.

God wants to use you, dear believer of God! He has chosen
this time in history, this place on the globe, and your unique
talents and gifts, all for his glory. You are qualified to serve
because you are in Christ. Don't let anyone tell you otherwise.
Walk in the boldness of your calling today!

Jesus, I know that I don't have to qualify in any fashion to
receive grace. Thank you for qualifying me to be useful for
your kingdom. Give me courage to walk boldly in the calling
you have given me.

Higher Thoughts

Set your minds on things that are above,
not on things that are on earth.

COLOSSIANS 3:2 NASB

Ever heard the phrase, "You are what you eat?" We could
also say, "You are what you think." It is important to analyze
what occupies your thoughts. If our minds are focused on the
things of this world—longings of the flesh, lust of the eyes,
dangerous pride in life—then that's what we will become.
But if we renew our minds to be in Christ, submitting our
thoughts to the Holy Spirit, then we will become like Christ.

The point is not just to think about Christ, but to take his Word
and let it transform your life. The Bible is key to the renewal of
your mind. When you memorize Scripture, you create a deep
well of wealth for the Holy Spirit to pull from when you're
attacked by negative thoughts and lies from the enemy. When
you know Scripture, you can pray Scripture, reminding God
of his promises and his words and finding new depth in your
prayer life. When you know God's Word, you can share it with
others far more easily. The benefits are endless.

Who do you want to be like today?

*Think about the things of heaven,
not the things of earth.*

COLOSSIANS 3:2 NLT

There are four benefits to having a mind set on Christ. First, you gain an eternal perspective. Instead of being distracted by temporary things, your focus and drive are on eternal things. Second, the things of this world lose their appeal. It's hard to know you stink if everything around you does too, isn't it? But if you step outside and get fresh air, suddenly you are aware of the smell, and you don't want to be in there anymore.

It's the same with the world. The more you saturate yourself in Christ and breath the fresh air he provides, the less you'll want the world. Third, you will find security in Christ. Nothing can separate you from him; you are safe. Lastly, we will realize what waits for us in glory. With something so beautiful to look forward to, your search for temporary pleasures will fade.

Jesus, help me renew my mind and focus on things above, rather than on the things of this earth.

Holy Union

"I am the Way, I am the Truth, and I am the Life.
No one comes next to the Father except through union with me.
To know me is to know my Father too."

JOHN 14:6 TPT

"Turn right in .5 miles. Your destination is on the left." With the development of GPS, we are used to following the voice coming out of our phones, trusting it will get us where we need to go. In fact, studies have shown that the use of GPS is altering our brains. We no longer make mental maps of our surroundings, because we aren't paying attention as keenly as we did when we followed an actual map or had to do the navigating ourselves.

While that's not good news for our geographical intelligence, it makes for a great analogy about us and Jesus. Jesus said he is the way. The one way, the only way. Often, we try to navigate the course ourselves, but we have no idea where we are going or how to get there. Jesus has all the information. He knows where the roadblocks are and when construction or weather is going to slow you down. He is the only way to get to the Father, which is exactly where we need to be. Trust in his voice and leading.

What does Jesus being the way to the Father mean to you?

> *"I am the way, the truth, and the life.*
> *No one can come to the Father except through me."*

What does Jesus mean by union with him? When sin entered the world, death entered the world. This all happened through Adam. Now, we as humans have what is called a sinful nature, meaning we are born with and dead in sin from birth. Our sin separates us from the Father. Because of his vast holiness, sin cannot be in his presence. Therefore, we are separated.

But our holy God was not satisfied with that separation or content to scrap the whole of humankind and start over. Instead, he laid into motion a plan to bring us back into union with himself. He sent his Son, Jesus, in a form that was fully man and fully God, to live a perfect, sinless life on earth. The punishment for a sinful person (which is all of us) is death and eternal separation from God. When the right time come, Jesus went to the cross, bearing that punishment for our sins. He was perfect, overcame sin and death in his dying, and rose again on the third day. This bridged the gap between us and the Father and created the only way to union with the Father forever. In Jesus, we know the Father. Praise God for this truth!

Jesus, your work on the cross always amazes me. Thank you for being the way, the truth, and the life. Thank you for reuniting me with the Father.

Untold Secrets

*"Call to me and I will answer you and will tell you great
and hidden things that you have not known."*

JEREMIAH 33:3 NRSV

How can we show great love toward someone? By listening to
them. In the gospels, Jesus says that we need to pray always.
Paul expounds on this in the epistles, where he says that we
should pray without ceasing. God the Father, many times
in the Old Testament and blatantly here in Jeremiah, is
personalizing it. Call me! God says.

Do you have a close friend or family member that you call to
talk about everything? It's an intimate, personal relationship,
right? That's what God is asking for here. He wants to hear
from you. He wants to speak to you. He is not put off or
annoyed by you. Don't believe the lie that God doesn't care.
Over and over, he tells us to talk to him. Start today and spend
some extra time in prayer. Call out to the God of the universe
and be blessed when he answers you.

What do you need to call God about today?

*"Ask me and I will tell you remarkable secrets
you do not know about things to come."*

JEREMIAH 33:3 NLT

In order to live a happy life, prayer needs to be a priority for us. Here are a few tips to help you call out to God. First, make it a habit. Just like any other healthy habit, if you miss a day or forget, start again, and again, until it becomes a habitual part of your life. Second, keep a record of your requests and things prayed about. It's so encouraging when you can tangibly look back and see God answering your prayers.

Third, pray out loud when you can. Verbalizing your prayers can help you focus. Lastly, learn to pray often—when your mind wanders to a specific person, when you are met with frustration, even when you are doing dishes. These are all opportunities to call out to God. What he has in store for you is better than anything else you could occupy your time with.

God, I call out to you! Show me the great and hidden things. Speak to me tonight. Thank you for always being available and willing to answer me.

Known

You discern my going out and my lying down;
you are familiar with all my ways.

PSALM 139:3 NIV

God is meticulous when it comes to your life. He is a God of the big picture and a God of the details. He has collected every tear, heard every prayer, seen every road, and recognized every need. Prayers you once earnestly prayed and have now forgotten, he remembers. Answers he's given that you didn't notice, he remembers. Dreams you abandoned, he still holds in his hand.

He is kinder than you can imagine and better to you than you dare to realize. You are known to God, fully and absolutely. He is working in your life right now, with your best interest and his glory in mind. Is that not the deepest longing of our souls, to be known fully? He knows you. He created you, and most importantly, he loves you, no strings attached. Find joy in this truth this morning.

What revelation do you get from thinking
about being fully known by God?

You see me when I travel
and when I rest at home.
You know everything I do.

PSALM 139:3 NLT

Is there a greater love story than this one? There is nothing we do that makes us stand out. Isaiah tells us that all our works, even our righteous ones, are like filthy rags. This is the ultimate glass slipper story. Unimportant people, with nothing to offer or bring to the table, noticed by the King of the universe. And not just noticed—chosen. Taken in. Loved. Brought into his kingdom and made heirs to the king.

It is a lie of the enemy that we are not loved. Darkness tells us that we can't be known. Loneliness will pervade our lives forever. Verses like Psalm 139 remind us just how precious we are to God. When you are struggling with the lie, take these verses to heart. Memorize them and post them in your home. The truth is that you are known and loved.

God, thank you for loving me and knowing me fully. Thank you for choosing me before the foundation of the world and for bringing me into your kingdom. I rejoice in this truth!

Trust Him

"You have also given me the shield of Your salvation;
your gentleness has made me great."

2 SAMUEL 22:36 NKJV

What makes greatness? Countless inspirational movies about underdogs rising to success come to mind. Football teams, boxing stars, battalions of soldiers. These great groups are not often shown with leaders who are gentle to them. That's why it's interesting that, at the end of David's life, he writes a psalm that tells us the characteristic of God that made him great, that gave him success, was gentleness. Talk about a complete contradiction to how our society likes to motivate!

There is a new dimension of God that we need to take to heart here. God is not a stern father, counseling you to pull yourself up by your bootstraps. If your walk has fallen to a crawl or halted altogether, he's a gentle father, wanting to scoop you up in his arms and carry you. Next time you hear the stern voice telling you to get your act together, remind yourself of this Scripture. It is his gentleness that will lead you to true success.

Why is it surprising that this is from David?
How have you been motivated to greatness
by people in the past?

"You protect me with your saving shield.
You have stooped to make me great."

2 SAMUEL 22:36 NCV

Your answer to this morning's second question was probably
not sternness or cruelty. If that is true, perhaps we can
become people who find out how to encourage and motivate
those around us with gentleness. In doing this, we will reflect
the character of Christ and probably get far better results
than anger or harshness would.

Think about how you have responded to those around you
going through a hard time. Is it with empathy? Empathy is
gentleness, and it is what our friends in pain need. Proverbs
15:1 comes to mind. You have influence on so many people
around you, and you are a leader even if you don't have a title.
Try using gentleness when responding to friends, co-workers,
spouses, and children, and watch greatness rise in them.

Father, thank you for being gentle toward me. Help me to
reflect your gentleness to those in my influence. May I be a
catalyst of change in the lives of those around me.

Perfect Power

*"My grace is sufficient for you, for power is perfected in weakness."
Most gladly, therefore, I will rather boast about my weaknesses,
so that the power of Christ may dwell in me.*

2 CORINTHIANS 12:9 NASB

When it comes to social media, people have said over and over that the images we see on our screens are the highlight reels of people's lives. You see their far-off vacations, their pretty homes, their matching Christmas pajamas. Online, we inadvertently boast about all of our material things. We post the parts of our life we want people to see. Do people know and see only this side of you, or do they see the power of Christ shining through your weakness?

There is nothing wrong with sharing the fun or victorious moments of our lives with others. But we need to make sure that we are showing others the power of Christ at work in our lives. Christ's power shines most brightly through our weakness. Don't hide your weakness from the world. Don't shy away. Don't participate in the highlights-only life that we have become accustomed to. Show the world the power of Christ by sharing the testimony of your weakness.

What fear is keeping you from sharing
the display of Christ's power in your life?

"My grace is all you need. My power works best in weakness."
So now I am glad to boast about my weaknesses,
so that the power of Christ can work through me.

2 CORINTHIANS 12:9 NLT

Why didn't God take away Paul's weakness? Why didn't God honor Paul's request when he begged to have the thorn removed? God gently explains to Paul why he kept the thorn in Paul's side. In Paul's weakness, Christ's power would be displayed in his life.

If you feel self-sufficient, the power of God is not being displayed in your life. If you look independent, the power of God is not shining through your life. It's a startling thought, isn't it? If you feel and act this way, you are the one getting the glory, not Christ. Sometimes, God chooses to leave thorns in our lives so that it's not our strength that is seen, but Christ's. Can you, like Paul, rejoice in this? Or does it make you bitter? Search your heart and see.

Jesus, it can be difficult to admit my weaknesses. Use my life for your glory. Make me weak so your power may be displayed, and may I rejoice in it!

Proven Character

We also have joy with our troubles because we know that these troubles produce patience. And patience produces character, and character produces hope.

ROMANS 5:3-4 NCV

In this section of Romans, Paul penned a sure statement for us. Consider it a math formula or a recipe. He's not saying that God might; he is saying that God certainly will. We can rejoice right now, right in the midst of troubles, because of what God will do. God wastes nothing.

God will use this trial, big or small, to produce patience in you. That patience grows your character, and that character grows hope in you. You can rejoice in the fact that no matter what suffering you face, God will see you through it. That's where the endurance comes in, the constant leaning on Jesus. Character becomes a tested and strengthened character. It's a refining of yourself to become more Christ-like. Through all this, God creates a masterpiece of hope in us. All of that from a situation we don't even want! Rejoice today as God works in your life, even the hard parts.

How does Paul's recipe change your perspective on suffering?

We also glory in our sufferings, because we know that suffering produces perseverance; perseverance, character; and character, hope.

ROMANS 5:3-4 NIV

Though we are told to rejoice in our sufferings, it isn't an easy thing to do. It seems contradictory. Joy implies happiness, and we associate happiness with the opposite of pain, sadness, and hard times. The key is changing our perspective. When we have it in our minds that God is in control, that he is working all things for our good, that he is making us more like him, then we can begin to rejoice. When we learn to surrender to Jesus, we find joy in hard times because he is our strength.

As we discovered this morning, God wastes nothing. What a promise! He is using the big, hard things and the small, trying things alike to refine our characters and bring him glory. Praise God that he wastes nothing!

Jesus, thank you for using everything and wasting nothing as you work in my life. Help me to rejoice even when things are hard.

OCTOBER 12

Tended

He heals the brokenhearted
and bandages their wounds.

PSALM 147:3 NLT

God made our bodies complex and crammed with amazing abilities. One of these abilities is how the body works to heal itself. For instance, if you break your arm, your body starts the healing process. There are many steps in the process, and it takes time, but the body has already begun to go through the motions before you visit a doctor.

In this life, we are all broken in some manner, especially in our sinful natures. You might feel it more in your mind, your body, or your relationships, but we all have brokenness and that needs attention and care. Just as our bones go through a process of healing, our spiritual brokenness takes time as well. As much as we would like God to one and done it, there is often a road to healing that we are required to walk. The good news is, your good physician is the one in charge, and he is walking that road with you, every step of the way.

What brokenness needs to start its healing journey today?

He heals the wounds
of every shattered heart.

PSALM 147:3 TPT

The journey can be long, and it may not look the way we want it to. It might feel like God isn't healing you fast enough or doing anything at all. But he is moving in your life. He is working. If you have asked God to heal you, he is faithful.

Don't fall into the temptation of dealing with your brokenness alone. This might look like turning to other things for quick relief, burying it deep so you don't have to deal with it, or finding a distraction. These provide temporary relief for a long-term problem. Only God and the road he has for you will make an eternal difference, healing you completely. Trust God to heal you, and don't stray from the road he has laid out for you.

Great Physician, thank you for all you have healed. I know you can heal all that is broken. I submit my life to you, and I acknowledge that your ways are best.

Tapestry of Grace

We are convinced that every detail of our lives is continually woven together to fit into God's perfect plan of bringing good into our lives, for we are his lovers who have been called to fulfill his designed purpose.

ROMANS 8:28 TPT

When you begin a quilt, the materials that are in front of you aren't anything special. You have some thread, patches of fabric, pins, needles, and batting. Separate, they don't look like something that should be displayed or could possibly keep you warm. If you watch someone make a quilt, the process can look daunting, cutting out squares and squares of fabric and putting it together piece by piece. It takes vision and planning for it to end up like the beautiful heirlooms we see displayed in people's homes.

It is the same with God and his plan for your life. You may look at your life and see only seemingly insignificant moments and patches of time where you wonder if any good will come from them. Don't give up hope. God is weaving together the life of your quilt, and he's got the sewing plan. He's promised to turn it into a masterpiece; trust him with the materials of your life.

How can you find encouragement from the fact that God is in the details of your life, working them together for good?

*We know that God causes everything to work together
for the good of those who love God and are called
according to his purpose for them.*

ROMANS 8:28 NLT

There is nothing in our lives that God cannot use for his glory.
However, we need to live with our palms open to our Savior.
That means that we daily submit our lives and plans to Christ.

The quilt God is working on of your life will not look exactly
like how you would plan it out. It will take humility to say,
"Your will, your way, Lord!" We want to be believer in whom
God moves mightily and displays his glory brightly. A key to
this is humility and submission to the will of the Father.

Father God, I submit my life to you. Thank you for working in
the details of my life. Please, move in my life and use me for
your glory.

His Work

The LORD will fulfill his purpose for me;
your steadfast love, O LORD, endures forever.
Do not forsake the work of your hands.

PSALM 138:8 ESV

As any creative will know, there is a process to making a piece of art. It starts with plans and ideas of how you want it to look. Then, it goes through a lot of mess, work, and patience to come out the other end, and it may look different from what you expected. It's like that with our lives too. God is the one who sees the whole plan. He has a perfect plan for the messy parts, the parts we would scrap. He has a masterpiece in mind for us, and we have to be patient and trust the process.

Before the beginning of time, he had planned for you and knew the moments you would live. He knows how to use each mess for his glory, if you will trust him with them. Keep in mind that God is the one at work—always at work—in your life. He sees things we can't, and we must be confident in him that he will produce a masterpiece out of us. Have faith and trust in his promises.

Can you trust God with the messy moments this morning?

You keep every promise you've ever made to me!
Since your love for me is constant and endless,
I ask you, Lord, to finish every good thing that you've begun in me!

PSALM 138:8 TPT

Steadfast means faithful. Isn't it beautiful that God is faithful to never give up on us? He is faithful to give us good gifts and abilities to use for his glory as well. Growing and developing them are one way that he fulfills his purpose through us. God doesn't waste a thing, and he gave you the gifts you have to edify the church and bring glory to his name.

How beautiful that we get to partner with our creative God to work in, create, and change this world! His purpose for you is intertwined with the gifts he has given you. Don't hide them; use them.

God, you are the source of creativity. Thank you for working in my life. I know that you will be faithful to complete this work and that you will produce good things from life. Help me to bring you glory through the gifts you have given me.

More

In all these things we are more than conquerors through Him who loved us. For I am persuaded that neither death nor life, nor angels nor principalities nor powers, nor things present nor things to come, nor height nor depth, nor any other created thing, shall be able to separate us from the love of God which is in Christ Jesus our Lord.

ROMANS 8:37–39 NKJV

Enough. Many days, we struggle to even feel like we are enough. The enemy has clever lies for our hearts, convincing us that our every shortcoming and failing keeps us from adding up. Or, he places an impossible standard in front of us, one that we feel like we have to achieve but will never quite reach. And if we one day do feel enough, it doesn't sound much like a victory, does it?

Beloved, what if someone told you that you are not just enough, you are more than enough? In our verse above, we are more than. Not once are we referred to as just enough in Scripture. God always comes after us with abundance in so many ways. He refers to us as loved, as chosen, and as worthy of the life of his Son. We are wholly forgiven, not in part. Let God's truth have more power in your life than the lies of the evil one.

Do you struggle with feeling like you're enough?
How can you apply the truth that you are more than?

Despite all these things, overwhelming victory is ours through Christ, who loved us. And I am convinced that nothing can ever separate us from God's love. Neither death nor life, neither angels nor demons, neither our fears for today nor our worries about tomorrow—not even the powers of hell can separate us from God's love. No power in the sky above or in the earth below—indeed, nothing in all creation will ever be able to separate us from the love of God that is revealed in Christ Jesus our Lord.

ROMANS 8:37-39 NLT

What do we do with this newfound confidence in being more? The hope is that you will know that you are more, and in thus knowing, you will be more in Christ. Not asking you to do more, but to settle deeper into your identity in Christ.

When you realize that you are more loved, you show more love to others. When you realize you are uniquely chosen, you communicate that same worth to those around you who have also been chosen. When you realize God found you worthy of the life of his Son, you extend that heavenly mercy and forgiveness more to those around you. Let being more in Christ spur you to show more to others. If nothing possibly can separate you from God's love, wouldn't you want to share that kind of security with others?

God, thank you for saying that I am more. You are such a good father. I am so grateful that nothing can separate me from your love.

Spirit Power

The Spirit of the LORD will rest on Him,
The spirit of wisdom and understanding,
The spirit of counsel and strength,
The spirit of knowledge and the fear of the LORD.

ISAIAH 11:2 NASB

Have you ever wished Jesus could have just stayed on the earth? His disciples sure did. By the time they got to the end of Jesus' time on earth, they realized that without him, they didn't have much at all. Jesus knew this too, and he knew that the tasks he wanted his disciples to carry out would be impossible with the power of God.

That's why God gave his disciples his Spirit in the book of Acts. The gift of the Holy Spirit was not a one-time deal, though. Every believer has the Holy Spirit. Every believer has the power of God in them to accomplish what God has asked them to do. You haven't been abandoned. You've been empowered!

How does the power of the Holy Spirit
change your life choices?

The Spirit of Yahweh will rest upon him,
the Spirit of Extraordinary Wisdom,
the Spirit of Perfect Understanding
the Spirit of Wise Strategy,
the Spirit of Mighty Power,
the Spirit of Revelation,
and the Spirit of the Fear of Yahweh.

ISAIAH 11:2 TPT

What do you need? The Spirit that is talked about in this verse is the Spirit that lives inside of you. Do you feel void of wisdom? You've got the Spirit that is wisdom itself. Do you need understanding? The Spirit of God has understanding that surpasses all human understanding.

What about counsel? Looking for some advice? Your just God gave you the Spirit that can aid you in any matter. Feeling weak and unsure? The Holy Spirit inside of you is full of strength. Wishing the Bible made more sense to you? You've got the Spirit of knowledge that longs to teach you. Wondering if the decision you need to make honors God? The Holy Spirit is full of the fear of the Lord. For anything you need, the Holy Spirit is alive inside of you. Just ask!

Holy Spirit, thank you for being near. Thank you for all you offer to me. Will you fill me with the fear of the Lord tonight and guide me in truth?

Saturated

Let every activity of your lives and every word that comes from your lips be drenched with the beauty of our Lord Jesus, the Anointed One. And bring your constant praise to God the Father because of what Christ has done for you!

COLOSSIANS 3:17 TPT

What makes us as humans unique on earth? Many have speculated over this question. A quick response could be to say that we bear the image of God, but diving deeper, what does that really mean? Some point to the fact that humans have a desire for truth, goodness, and beauty. Christians often are strong in areas of goodness and truth, but what is to be said for beauty? What place does beauty have in our Christian lives? Some men and women struggle with the concept of beauty. The world tries to tell them that it means to look a certain way or to fit into jeans of a certain size.

But beauty leads to Christ in several ways when handled properly. True beauty attracts. Why do we climb mountains, go to the ocean, or relish in the fall leaves around us? Because we are attracted to them. Let the beauty you see attract you to Christ. Here in Colossians, Jesus himself is described as beautiful.

How does the beauty of Christ attract you to him?

Whatever you do, whether in word or deed, do it all in the name of the Lord Jesus, giving thanks to God the Father through him.

COLOSSIANS 3:17 NIV

Beauty can stir up belief in us. Isn't nature beautiful? Isn't a relationship restored beautiful? Isn't seeing true love, or mercy on display, or grace given out, beautiful? It is a tool of God to call to our hearts out of the darkness of this world and into his reality. Beauty also inspires. Artists are always copying one another or pulling inspiration from things around them. Beauty inspires us to create, imitating our creator God.

Our society is can be quite pragmatic and practical. We esteem function and productivity, especially since the industrial revolution. Do you like scented candles? Some might see them as wasteful, but they release a light and scent into the room that can change the whole atmosphere. Their purpose is to awaken our senses and bring peace. God does the same by creating beauty that he didn't have to. For instance, he didn't have to make the leaves brilliant shades of red, oranges, and yellows as they die this fall. But he did. In doing so, it awakens us. May beauty awaken us to the presence of our beautiful Savior.

Beautiful Savior, thank you for this world full of beauty. Help me to see it with fresh eyes, and may it always remind me of you.

Delivered Again

The righteous person may have many troubles,
but the LORD delivers him from them all.

PSALM 34:19 NIV

Many action genre TV shows have one person always getting
in trouble and the hero always getting them out of it. It makes
for good entertainment, and it's also true for us in real life.
As Christians, we are not promised a life that is trouble-free.
Here in Psalm 34, the person is called righteous, which you
think would make them above having any hard times here
on earth. Good behavior equals pleasant, easy life, right?
That's not always the case. We live in a fallen world, and we
ourselves are fallen people. The ripple effects of sin echo
throughout our world.

But we have a hero who promises to save us. Jesus will deliver
us, no matter the troubles we face. Trials and tribulation
are sure to come, and we aren't always sure why they are
happening to us. We can know for certain that God is with us
through every single one. He will never abandon us in our
time of need. What a Savior. What a hero!

Do you think that being righteous should
automatically qualify you for a trouble-free life?
How is that thinking contradictory to the Bible?

Even when bad things happen to the good and godly ones,
the Lord will save them and not let them be defeated
by what they face.

PSALM 34:19 TPT

In a TV show, when a person is saved over and over again, they begin to realize that their hero is reliable. They can act courageously because they know the hero will have their back when things get sticky.

Let courage rise in you to take a risk of faith, because the Lord has your back. We aren't talking about doing something sinful or stupid. This is about those things God has put on your heart to do to further his kingdom—the ones that you think about often, but they scare you. Have courage! The Lord is loyal to you. He will not ask you to step out only to watch you fall on your face. You always have the guarantee of his presence and deliverance. What do you have to lose? Ask God how he wants you to take a leap of faith and partner with him today.

God, thank you for being loyal to me. I know that you will never abandon me. Please, deliver me from all the troubles that come my way.

Led to Life

Godly grief produces a repentance that leads to salvation and brings no regret, but worldly grief produces death.

2 CORINTHIANS 7:10 NRSV

This verse compares godly sorrow and worldly sorrow. What is the difference? Godly sorrow is when the Holy Spirit brings conviction into your heart. It is when you are brought to the realization by the Holy Spirit that you have harmed or hurt someone or yourself and have sinned against God. Once the Holy Spirit shows us our grievance, we are then to repent and ask for God's forgiveness. Our sin has already been dealt with at the cross, and repenting before God leads him to restore us, cleanse us, and let us feel again the power of the forgiveness we have in Christ.

Worldly sorrow, on the other hand, drudges up past sins. Even after you ask for forgiveness, it continues to berate you and beat you down. Sometimes, it tries to trap you into feeling guilty for things that aren't even sin against others. Worldly sorrow is based on lies, and it will never grant you freedom and peace like the Holy Spirit will. It's important for us to know how to discern between the two.

Can you name some moments of godly and worldly sorrow in your life? Do you recognize the difference between them?

God designed us to feel remorse over sin in order to produce
repentance that leads to victory. This leaves us with no regrets.
But the sorrow of the world works death.

2 CORINTHIANS 7:10 TPT

How could repentance lead to life? Only in the upside-down kingdom of Christ does this work. Often, we view mistakes and sin as the end of the road. But with Christ, it can be just the beginning. There is no depth too deep that Christ can't save you from. Godly repentance sets us free and lets the power of the Holy Spirit move in our lives, bringing us to fullness in Christ.

Won't you come to him in repentance today and let his power work in your life? Won't you let him lead you to abundance?

Jesus, thank you for making all things new. Thank you for dying on the cross and forgiving me of my sins. Help me to be quick to repent. I want to walk in right step with you.

Have Mercy

Answer me when I pray to you,
my God who does what is right.
Make things easier for me when I am in trouble.
Have mercy on me and hear my prayer.

PSALM 4:1 NCV

Have you ever heard someone say, "I don't know how I would have done it without Christ?" What a blessing it is to be a child of God in this world. We have the protection of God with us at every turn. Those who don't believe in Christ live in a dim reality in that when hard times and trials come their way, they are alone.

You, dear believer, are never alone. You live in the fullness of his mercy. David calls to God, and God answers him. What an example we have through their relationship. David knows that God's mercy is readily available to him. All he has to do is ask. The same is true for us.

What do you need mercy for this morning?
Bring it to God in prayer.

Answer me when I call, O God of my righteousness!
You have given me relief when I was in distress.
Be gracious to me and hear my prayer!

PSALM 4:1 ESV

Tensions seem to be high for our psalmist, with stress mounting up all around him. How does the king deal with the stress? He turns to prayer. Prayer is the greatest stress reliever in our lives. It's not so much what happens after we pray, but rather the presence of the one to whom we pray. The relief comes when we notice that we have God's attention. He hears, he answers, and he cares.

You have God's attention; does he have yours? We tend to want to do more when we are stressed. We want to keep checking off the boxes on the to-do list, to keep moving at a pace that isn't healthy. Bu if you want true stress relief, peace, and mercy, turn your full attention to Jesus. Cry out to him and know that you have God's attention. Let peace come from his presence.

Jesus, I am in a stressful time. Help me to slow down and notice you. Help me to give you my full attention. Show me mercy and be near to me.

No One Else

No one is holy like the Lord!
There is no one besides you;
there is no Rock like our God.

1 Samuel 2:2 NLT

When you consider the word *holy*, does the word *happiness* come to mind as well? Holiness and happiness are not usually often in our current world. We often attribute holiness to outdated rituals or a list of manmade, tedious rules. But can these negative connotations ring true when the word *holy* is used in the Bible over five hundred times? "Holy" is also the only attribute of God used three times in a row to describe Him, in Isaiah and in Revelation.

It is what He is! We have been taught to think that happiness cannot be holy. We sin when we seek out other things to satisfy us that we think will bring us more pleasure than God. But we are created to find true joy and happiness in the presence of the Holy Lord himself.

Do you think that happiness and holiness go together?
Where do you have the wrong views of holiness?

No one is holy like the LORD,
For there is none besides You,
Nor is there any rock like our God.

1 SAMUEL 2:2 NKJV

Here, the author of 1 Samuel is declaring a positive thing when he writes that no one is holy like the Lord. Do we have it wrong about what true holiness is? To be holy means to be set apart, sanctified, or sacred.

In declaring that our God is holy, we also declare that his set apart ways are best. His sanctification of us will make us holy and bring us happiness. His sacred sacrifice is the only true way to access the abundant pleasure found in the holy presence of God.

Holy God, there is no one like you. Show me the negative ways that I think and feel about holiness. Show me that holiness is who you are and the basis of all your wonderful attributes. Help me to find happiness in your presence alone and stop seeking pleasure in other things.

Shared Burden

If one part suffers, every part suffers with it;
if one part is honored, every part rejoices with it.

1 CORINTHIANS 12:26 NIV

The body of Christ is a gift from God. We are not made to do life on our own. Though we get our strength from the Holy Spirit, God created us to also be in relationship with other Christians as well. He created us to operate in unity with those around us to bring him glory.

The body of Christ is made up of people from different backgrounds, genders, ethnicities, and socio-economic classes. We all have different gifts to give to the body too. Today's verse is asking brothers and sisters in Christ to share with each other. If someone in the body of Christ is suffering, do you share in that? Do you pray with them, support them, and find ways to lift them up? We have to get away from our individualistic Christianity. There is so much joy to be found in communion with the body of Christ.

How can you encourage a fellow believer
in the body of Christ today?

Whatever happens to one member happens to all.
If one suffers, everyone suffers. If one is honored, everyone rejoices.

1 CORINTHIANS 12:26 TPT

Let's take up the challenge from Paul to shift our relationships with the body of Christ from Sunday morning handshakes to Thursday evening dinners, Tuesday morning coffees, and nighttime texts for prayer. The people you attend church with are not supposed to be just acquaintances who happen to enjoy a similar style of worship music and preaching as you do. They are your body. They are a part of you, and all of you together make up the hands and feet of Jesus to your local community.

It is vital that we get past superficial relationships and get into real life together. It's there, in suffering with each other and rejoicing with each other, that God gets glory and your community notices. It's also a source of support and strength that we desperately need. What are you waiting for? Invite someone from your church into your home.

God, thank you for giving us each other in the body of Christ. Please, help me to reach out and support others. Show me who could use my gifts, time, and friendship.

Test It Out

Do not believe every spirit, but test the spirits, whether they are of God; because many false prophets have gone out into the world.

1 JOHN 4:1 NKJV

This verse can be confusing without some context. John was writing to a church that was dealing with the false teachings of Gnosticism. This belief claimed that anything that was physical was evil; therefore, if Jesus came in the flesh, he was tainted. This group also said that Jesus never came in the flesh. He just seemed to. An easy solution, right? No harm, no foul?

John was writing because this twist of the truth threatened to split the church apart. Today, there are so many slight twists of the truth that threaten to tear the body of Christ to pieces. Fellow believers, we must not believe everything that is presented to us, and we must test out what we hear. We must be buried deep in the Scriptures to know the truth from a lie. Study the actual truth, and you will be able to spot a counterfeit.

Have you been tempted to follow a false gospel?

Do not believe every spirit, but test the spirits to see whether they are from God, because many false prophets have gone out into the world.

1 JOHN 4:1 NIV

One false gospel from past few years is the idea that your happiness depends on you. If you are reading this devotional, then you are a person who has recognized that God is the only place to find true happiness. The lie that the world will try to feed you is that you need Jesus plus other things to be happy. It will claim that your happiness must come from your hard work and dedication.

Self-love and self-care champion this movement and turn us into self-centered heroes who pull themselves up by the bootstraps and use Jesus as a nice banner to help them achieve their goals. When this "gospel" is presented, run! And take every person you know with you. You need Jesus. That's it. Pray for protection and wisdom against false gospels.

Jesus, expose false gospels to me. Help me not to follow false teachers. Lead me in your truth.

Counseled by Wisdom

*"I will instruct you and teach you the way you should go;
I will counsel you with my eye upon you."*

PSALM 32:8 NRSV

Growing up, did you have a teacher who had a great influence on you? As we grow, our parents are our first major influence, but as we get older, our circle widens to include other important adult relationships. Teachers and coaches are often high on that list.

As a believer, think of wisdom like that favorite teacher. As you grow in your faith, wisdom teaches and leads us. Wisdom reinforces all the things our Father has made known to us already. Many people strive to learn under a famous professor or teacher in their field. They want to learn from the best. In other religions, people seek out wise men and the highest authority for learning. Every single Christian has access to the best life education through the wisdom of God's Word and a relationship with the Holy Spirit. You have God himself living inside of you, teaching, counseling, and instructing you. You've been given the best of the best! Don't take that for granted today.

In what area of your life do you need
wisdom's teaching today?

> *"I will stay close to you,*
> *instructing and guiding you along the pathway for your life.*
> *I will advise you along the way*
> *and lead you forth with my eyes as your guide."*

PSALM 32:8 TPT

Have you ever been in a situation where you had to teach a class or a group of people and no one was listening? You just could not grab their attention. The class obviously did not have very teachable hearts, and you probably doubted that any of them walked away with any of the information you were trying to convey.

Unfortunately, we can be like this with Jesus. We believers need to check our hearts to make sure we have what is called a teachable spirit. A teachable spirit is a heart that is willing to hear correction and instruction. It submits itself to the Bible and its standards, and it doesn't buck its head in pride when corrected. Do you have a teachable heart?

Jesus, create in me a teachable heart. Thank you for giving me your Holy Spirit to guide and lead me. Help me to listen.

In Process

I pray with great faith for you, because I'm fully convinced that the One who began this glorious work in you will faithfully continue the process of maturing you and will put his finishing touches to it until the unveiling of our Lord Jesus Christ!

PHILIPPIANS 1:6 TPT

Ponder the phrase "work in progress." Can you imagine getting frustrated with a store that is only half stocked while there signs everywhere that say they are under construction? How about telling a painter to give up when he's only a partway through his masterpiece because it looks ugly? That seems crazy! Then why do we not extend the same amount of grace to ourselves?

You are a work in progress. That process is called sanctification. Jesus did not expect you to be perfect the minute you prayed for repentance. He knew that the glorious work of maturing you and making you Christ-like would last your whole lifetime. He's not disappointed in the progress or frustrated by the in-between. Give yourself some grace. You are a work in progress, and that is exactly what you are meant to be.

Where do you expect perfection in yourself?
How can you extend some grace there today?

Being confident of this very thing, that He who has begun a good work in you will complete it until the day of Jesus Christ.

PHILIPPIANS 1:6 NKJV

Artists have a vision for their painting, but they cannot be completely sure how it will turn out. Though we often hear the analogy of God the potter and we the clay, or the God the artist and we the canvas, the analogy falls short because Jesus is 100% confident in your glorification.

Being a work in progress may not seem like much fun. We want to see the finished result. We get glimpses of it throughout our lifetime, but we won't see full glorification until we see Christ. We can know for certain that it's going to be a masterpiece! No guessing, no letdowns. What God is working in you today will for sure work out for glory. Praise him!

Jesus, thank you for working in my life. Help me to give myself grace and remember that I am a work in progress.

Eternal Life

> *"God so loved the world that he gave his one and only Son, that whoever believes in him shall not perish but have eternal life."*
>
> JOHN 3:16 NIV

The success of millions of dollars' worth of movies, books, and TV shows just goes to show—who doesn't love a good love story? Imagine a gentleman with a heart of gold who pursues a lovely, intelligent, and brave woman. Their story always starts out differently but ends the same. He finds ways to woo and win her and they share in an adventure. Perhaps they have some rocky moments in the middle, but in the end, they are together. He asks her to marry them, sparklers are lit, rice is thrown, and they live happily ever after. The end.

You might be really into stories like these or they might make you gag, but did you know that you are in the middle of the greatest love story of all time? God has loved you from before you were even born. Before time began, he put into motion the plan of his Son to win you back. From the moment you were born, he has been calling to you and wooing you, giving you chance after chance to know him. Won't you take a chance to know him this morning?

Where do you have a hard time
seeing the love story of God pursuing you?

> *"This is how God loved the world:*
> *He gave his one and only Son,*
> *so that everyone who believes in him*
> *will not perish but have eternal life."*

JOHN 3:16 NLT

When you say yes to Jesus, you become his bride. He delights in you and lavishes love on you. He celebrates at your union. He has written you a love letter throughout all of Scripture. He wants to be with you and spend time with you, listen to your hopes and dreams, and hold you when you cry. He serves you in love and his face shines with love toward you. He gave up everything to be with you.

What extravagant love Jesus has for you! Do you believe it? It can feel too good to be true at times. But the greatest love story ever told is about Jesus, our Savior, dying on the cross to reunite us with God forever. He longs to make you pure and clean, part of the body of Christ, presented to him as his bride. Take his hand, and let his love change your life.

Jesus, help me to see myself as you see me. Help me to accept your love. I love you! Show me how to love you more.

Capable

Using the Scriptures, the person who serves God will be capable, having all that is needed to do every good work.

2 TIMOTHY 3:17 NCV

There is nothing worse than being sent to do a job unprepared. You start a recipe in the kitchen and find you are out of milk. You get geared up to tidy the lawn, and your leaf blower is missing. Sometimes, we act like we are unprepared for the work God has called us to do. But if he has called us to it, he will give us what we need to accomplish the task.

Fear of being unprepared or of not having enough can stop us from stepping out in faith. What is God calling you to this morning? What does he want you to take action on? Don't let fear disable you. God will fully equip you for every good work that he calls you to do. Trust in him!

What is God calling you to do?
What steps can to take today to begin?

You will be God's servant, fully mature and perfectly prepared to fulfill any assignment God gives you.

2 TIMOTHY 3:17 TPT

There is nothing like the Word of God. In these troubled times, as false gospels and false teachers run around deceiving people of the truth, hold fast to the Word of God. Stick to the truth that you have learned and believed so far. The Scripture is profitable and useful in all areas of our life.

Don't deny yourself the reading of the Scripture. Eat God's Word every day. Let it work in your life. Pray for teachers who teach with integrity and stick to what Scripture says, not following the whims of their own hearts. Be a teacher of integrity, using the Scripture to correct others. Instruct them, guide them, and point out their rebellious ways with gentleness. We must be in the Scripture if we want to stand in this evil day. We must know the Word of God. Don't give up! Keep diving deep into God's Word.

God, thank you for giving me your Word. Thank you for all the benefits it brings to my life. Keep me from false teachings.

Mandate

Bear one another's burdens,
and thereby fulfill the law of Christ.

GALATIANS 6:2 NASB

This verse is eleven simple words packed with a lifetime of work. It is no easy task to live out this line of Scripture, but as today's title implies, it is a mandate. What does it realistically mean to bear one another's burdens? In our self-consumed culture, this is where the church can shine. When we see a brother or a sister in Christ stumbling under the weight of a trial or a temptation, it's our job to come alongside them and help them. We can pray for them, encourage them, point them to Scripture, hold them accountable, and love them through the hardship.

This added strength from the body of Christ is often a make-or-break point for a believer. Without the community shining light in their dark times, they break under the pressure of the burden. What a beautiful and grand responsibility we have been given for those around us.

Who can you encourage in the body of Christ today?

*Love empowers us to fulfill the law of the Anointed One
as we carry each other's troubles.*

GALATIANS 6:2 TPT

This is an "easier said than done" type of Scripture for an individualistic society like our own. We are used to showing up on Sunday mornings, maybe Wednesday nights, and keeping it pretty surface level with the church. Many believers would not say that those they go to church with are their closest community. It's easier to hear of a need and say "Oh, I'll pray for you," rather than stopping what we are doing and praying right then for that person.

We make excuses that our own loads are too heavy (wouldn't they be lighter if we shared too?). We blame others for not doing their jobs and shift responsibility around. But Paul is clear; the church needs to step up. This is a major way that we display Christ's love to one another.

Jesus, show me where I'm neglecting the burdens of others and where I should share my own troubles. Help me to love and lift up the body of Christ.

Continual Surrender

By the help of your God, return;
Observe mercy and justice,
And wait on your God continually.

HOSEA 12:6 NKJV

At this point, Israel was a nation that no longer knew God. Israel had crumbled, sinking into a state of lawlessness. After Hosea gives his final prophecy to Israel, Assyria takes over, and the Israelites are led into captivity. Y could say that Israel did not know who God was. This is why they needed God's help to return to him. They had become unfamiliar with his ways.

It is said that righteousness and justice are the foundations of God's throne. A society that does not know God does not know what mercy and justice look like, hence their need to observe it. The ways of God, like justice and mercy, had become strange to the Israelites as they served other gods. If we desire to have a society that returns to justice and embraces mercy, we must return to God. We must turn from our sins, our idolatries, and our own ways, and turn to God.

What similarities do you see between this time for Israel and our current time in history?

Come back to your God.
Act with love and justice,
and always depend on him.

HOSEA 12:6 NLT

Is observing justice and mercy a passive thing or an active thing? When we return to God, we are active in pursuing these things. To observe justice is to do right by your fellow man, to award the dignity that each human being deserves, and to treat them as those made in the image of God. It means we do not owe another person anything and do not cause harm to their person or possessions.

To show mercy is to show forgiveness to others, extending to them what God extended to you in your most vile state. These are hard works, muscles in our life that need exercising. As you work in these manners, waiting on God in prayer is vital. This will be your source and guidance to love in mercy and to act in justice. God delights in the one who does these things.

Jesus, I know you delight in mercy and justice. I trust you with my life. Be near to me and help me to walk with mercy and justice for those around me.

Justice

The LORD waits to be gracious to you,
and therefore he exalts himself to show mercy to you.
For the LORD is a God of justice;
blessed are all those who wait for him.

ISAIAH 30:18 ESV

God knows how evil, how awful, is the fate of those who choose to follow their own pride instead of him. And because of this, God waits. Time goes on, God not willing that one of us should perish, wanting all of us to find repentance. That is the Lord, extending grace to us. God reveals himself to us, through his Word, through creation, and through his church. He reveals himself and shows us glimpses of his glory as a merciful act to lead us to himself.

Are you ignoring his mercy? He is showing himself to you because he knows that the world will not satisfy you. It will not go well for the one who chooses darkness over light, and this grieves the heart of God. He is extending mercy and grace to all of us. Won't you respond? He is a God of justice, and he cannot turn a blind eye to the destructive nature and the horrors of sin. Why would we want him to? Still, he also wants all to turn to him.

In what ways are you pursuing the world
and ignoring the mercy and grace of God?

The Lord is still waiting to show his favor to you
so he can show you his marvelous love.
He waits to be gracious to you.
He sits on his throne ready to show mercy to you.
For Yahweh is the Lord of justice,
faithful to keep his promises.
Overwhelmed with bliss are all
who will entwine their hearts in him,
waiting for him to help them.

ISAIAH 30:18 TPT

Waiting for God is hard, especially if it is tied to waiting for justice. We see injustice in our world, and we cry out, "How long, oh Lord!" Our bodies groan.

God has not turned a deaf ear to our cries. He is not blind to the injustice we see around us. We continue to wait for him because he will move. Because he will make it right. He sees you in your groaning and extends mercy, endurance, and grace to you.

God, you are the God who sees me. You are a God of justice as well as mercy and grace. Hear my cries for justice and answer my pleas, Lord. Show me where I might be ignoring your mercy. Help me repent and turn quickly to you.

Worn Down

> LORD, have mercy, because I am in misery.
> My eyes are weak from so much crying,
> and my whole being is tired from grief.
>
> PSALM 31:9 NCV

Live any number of years on this earth, and there will no doubt be griefs that empty us. Living in a fallen world inevitably exposes us to misery. The question "why do bad things happen" is one of the biggest objections to the existence of God. If he exists, why would David have to experience such misery? Why do these bad things happen to us? Shouldn't being saved mean being free from suffering of this kind? Does God even care?

The questions swirl. Stop the whirlwind by following the psalmist. Pour everything out. He lays every emotion before God. His distress, his honest pain, his disappointment, his wondering at where God is—it's all there. But he also finds the path to redirect his eyes to God because God is merciful, present, and good. Read all of Psalm 31 and see how David still clings to God, despite his whirling emotions. God is alive, God is near, and he is big enough to handle your griefs.

What grief do you need to hand to Jesus?

O Lord, help me again! Keep showing me such mercy.
For I am in anguish, always in tears,
and I'm worn out with weeping.
I'm becoming old because of grief; my health is broken.

PSALM 31:9 TPT

Don't hold it in. If you are feeling grief, don't give into the temptation to shove it away. Lamentation and grief are an essential part of our Christian faith. You can see them all throughout the Bible. You are not supposed to be okay with the way things are. There are hard and horrible things going on in our world, in our lives, that cause us grief.

Living in a fallen world should cause us grief. God doesn't ask us to bottle it up, put it away, and tape on a happy face. He wants to hear from you what you truly feel. It does not make you less of a Christian to have grief. In fact, expressing our grief is a way that God can meet us and heal us. Don't bottle it up. Run into the open arms of Jesus tonight and cry.

Jesus, my heart hurts. Will you help me with this burden? This is how I feel tonight. These are my griefs. I'm so tired, Lord.

Dwell Among Us

The Living Expression became a man and lived among us!
And we gazed upon the splendor of his glory,
the glory of the One and Only who came from the Father
overflowing with tender mercy and truth!

JOHN 1:14 TPT

Have you ever been camping before? Perhaps just in your backyard, or away in a gorgeous location, you pitched a tent, threw some sleeping bags inside, and camped. This verse is about God going camping. The word here for living among us literally translates to "pitched his tent among us."

Back in Exodus, the Israelites had the tabernacle of God in a tent, and it went with them everywhere they went, until about 586 BC, when the Babylonians destroyed Jerusalem. Then, 600 years later, we have this writing from John, proclaiming the good news that God was going to camp among us again—only this time, the tent was the body of Christ. And now, God wants to camp with each of us. He wants to dwell inside us, empower us with the Holy Spirit, and use us as tents that spread his glory to the nations. Praise to God who dwells with his people and is not far away!

Does God dwell in you today?

The Word became flesh and made his dwelling among us.
We have seen his glory, the glory of the one and only Son,
who came from the Father, full of grace and truth.

JOHN 1:14 NIV

Can you think of another religion that says their God shows humility and intimacy in dwelling among his people? In Philippians 2, it describes the humility Jesus had in coming to this earth to dwell among us. He laid aside his God status to become fully man. Why would he do such a thing? Because of his tender mercy for you, dear believer.

He saw you, in your sin and your distance from him, shackled in darkness. He humbled himself to die on that cross because he had mercy on you. He wanted to do whatever it took to rebuild that bridge between humanity and God so that we could dwell together, forever. He pursued you. He wanted you. That is the truth wrapped in mercy and presented to you today. Can you believe it?

God, I am humbled by the lengths you went to pursue me and bring me to yourself. Thank you! I give my life to you. Thank you for dwelling among us, always so near.

Transformed

We all, with unveiled face, beholding as in a mirror the glory of the Lord, are being transformed into the same image from glory to glory, just as by the Spirit of the Lord.

2 CORINTHIANS 3:18 NKJV

If you have lived in cold climates or camped in the fall or winter, you know the importance of a fire and the delight and warmth that it brings. When you feel spiritually cold and distant, it's time to retreat to the fireplace of God's Word and allow the intensity of his face to restore your fervency again.

The key to keeping our hearts warm to God is not a secret. It is not responding to endless altar calls, though God can work through them. It's not having other people pray over you, though that is encouraging and valid. It's not found in listening to a famous sermon or pumping up the volume on a new worship album, though these things can point our hearts to Christ. If you want to stay hot in your fervor for Christ, you must get into your prayer space. You have to shut your door and gaze on the face of God. One-on-one time is key. It's where the fire is blazing hot. Draw near to God in this place and be transformed this morning.

Does your heart feel cold this morning?

We can all draw close to him with the veil removed from our faces. And with no veil we all become like mirrors who brightly reflect the glory of the Lord Jesus. We are being transfigured into his very image as we move from one brighter level of glory to another. And this glorious transfiguration comes from the Lord, who is the Spirit.

2 CORINTHIANS 3:18 TPT

It is a daily act, dragging our cold hearts before the fireplace of God and allowing him to warm our souls and ignite our spirits. If you leave a fire unattended for a long period of time, it goes out. Not that God will leave, but the point is that you are spending your time elsewhere and not prioritizing coming to God daily, our fires go out.

But God is always present and willing to ignite. He wants to burn away all the parts of us that don't reflect his image and leave us pure and blameless. This takes time in his presence. Make it a priority to come before God. Watch his transforming power change your life for the better.

God, will you melt away all the parts of me that aren't holy? Make me holy as you are holy. Ignite my soul again; build up my passion for you.

Work for the Lord

Whatever you do, work at it with all your heart,
as working unto the Lord, not for human masters.

COLOSSIANS 3:23 ESV

What work is set in front of you? We all face times when the job set before us seems boring. Teaching Sunday school. Doing the laundry. Finishing spread sheets. Taking care of the toddler. Even in these tasks, you have the opportunity to bring your best to the job the Lord has given you.

You can put your best into the lessons Sunday morning, no matter how old your class is, and expect the Holy Spirit to show up. You can sing praises and do your laundry with a good attitude. You can work with diligence on those spreadsheets. You can pray over your toddler and engage with them in meaningful ways. You can take a task that seems mundane and find a way to use it for the glory of God.

What tasks are in front of you today?
How can you glorify God in the mundane?

Work willingly at whatever you do,
as though you were working for the Lord
rather than for people.

COLOSSIANS 3:23 NLT

Often, a stumbling block in facing our work is comparison.
God gives us a vision and we are excited, but then we look
over and see what other people are doing, and we get
distressed. We let feelings of inadequacy and foolishness rob
us of the joy of working for the Lord.

We aren't asked to do things for man; we are asked to do
things for God. If he has called you to something, given you
the necessary gifts and the vision, he doesn't want a carbon
copy of what that girl on Instagram is doing. He knows and
wants what you have to offer. You bring a unique aspect and
beauty to the situations where God has called you. Don't shy
away by falling into comparisons. Do your job, rock it, and
give God the glory for working through you.

Jesus, thank you for calling me to work for you. No matter
what I am doing, I know it can be done for your glory. Help
me to seize those moments.

Clothed in Love

Beyond all these things put on love, which is the perfect bond of unity. Let the peace of Christ rule in your hearts, to which indeed you were called in one body; and be thankful.

Colossians 3:14-15 nasb

What is it that ties together the perfect outfit for you? Is it a piece of statement jewelry? A fashionable belt? That matching handbag? The last piece we put on usually completes our outfit and really makes it pop. In today's clothing analogy, last thing Paul lists is love.

Above everything else you are clothing yourself with in Christ, put on love. Love will pull it off, tie it together, and make it all pop. He goes on to describe love as the perfect bond of unity. We can have so much in the body of Christ: right doctrine, a good worship team, engaging outreach events, and vibrant small groups. But if any of it is not fueled by love, then what is it for? Make sure you put on love. It's the one accessory you shouldn't live without.

How do love-filled actions change things?
What action can you do with love today?

Love is supreme and must flow through each of these virtues. Love becomes the mark of true maturity. Let your heart be always guided by the peace of the Anointed One, who called you to peace as part of his one body. And always be thankful.

COLOSSIANS 3:14-15 TPT

Paul is really hitting home the case for unity here. Unity is vital in the body of Christ. Paul gives us a few tips on unity. First, as we talked about this morning, we must be sure our motivation is rooted in Christ-like love. Second is to have the peace of Christ ruling in our hearts. This is made possible by keeping our hearts in check and making sure no bitterness or discord is taking root. By communicating with others and using the Matthew 18 model to work out our problems, we let peace rule in our hearts.

And the last key is gratitude. Gratitude is a subject that comes up a lot in November, but why not make it a year-round focus? Hearts that are thankful find it much harder to be hearts that complain about each other.

Jesus, help me grow in love, peace, and thankfulness. Examine my heart and show me if there is any dissent or bitterness.

It Belongs to Him

*Yours, LORD, is the greatness and the power and the glory
and the majesty and the splendor, for everything
in heaven and earth is yours.*

1 CHRONICLES 29:11 NIV

You will never see a U-Haul behind a hearse. When we die, we can't take anything with us. Though we have things here and now, the reality is that everything belongs to God. Still, let's not take up a renter's mentality, losing interest in what we have and not taking care of it. We can use what God has entrusted to us for his glory. He has given to you generously because he is generous, and because he wants to model to you what he expects of you.

If God has blessed you with a vehicle, how can you use it for his glory? Does your neighbor need a ride to work? Does your friend need help moving to a new home? If God has blessed you with land, who can you invite to come enjoy the beauty of God's creation? What has God blessed you with? How can you use that to bring him glory? He gives us things so we might take ownership of them, using them to advance his kingdom and bring him glory.

What is God calling you to be generous with today?
Where has he been generous with you?

*Yours, O Lord, is the greatness and the power and the glory
and the victory and the majesty, for all that is in the heavens
and in the earth is yours. Yours is the kingdom, O Lord,
and you are exalted as head above all.*

1 Chronicles 29:11 ESV

Let's give credit where credit is due. Read the first line of the verse again. What is the Lord's? Five things are listed, and they all belong to the Lord. Are we giving them to him? It's hard to take credit for anything good in life when you read this list. We need to be a people who proclaim the good things the Lord has done from the rooftops.

It's easy to bypass praising God and give the credit to yourself or to others. The doctors healed your sickness. The check that appeared in the mailbox at just the right time was from the government or a friend. God is working miracles around us constantly; we just need to have eyes to see how he is working and moving. Let us look for ways to praise him and attribute things to him, because they are right in front of us.

God, to you be the greatness, power, glory, majesty, and splendor, forever and ever. Show me how I can use the resources you have given me for your glory.

Medicine for the Heart

A joyful, cheerful heart brings healing to both body and soul.
But the one whose heart is crushed
struggles with sickness and depression.

PROVERBS 17:22 TPT

Sara had gone through a very rough year. Turmoil in extended family had landed a family member in prison. A terrifying season of strong hurricanes threatened to take her home. It was a divisive election year. A dear friend received a scary diagnosis from the doctor. The griefs seemed to pile high. Sara cried, gave her grief to God, mourned, and prayed. She read the Bible and clung to promises from his Scripture. Sara found comfort in these things, but she longed for something else—a birth or a wedding. She remembered the joy she had felt at her own wedding and the births of her three children. In the midst of trouble, she longed for a moment when she could lay aside the weight on her shoulders and cry tears of happiness, not sadness.

Believer, sometimes we need to sit, cry, and grieve with those who are crushed. Other times, we need to lift them up by bringing them somewhere they can taste the sweetness of joy again. May God give us discernment to know what we need to share with those around us.

How can a cheerful heart give good medicine
to someone who feels crushed?

A cheerful heart is good medicine,
but a broken spirit saps a person's strength.

PROVERBS 17:22 NLT

After you read the story of Sara this morning, we asked
for discernment. Sometimes, a joyful heart will rub salt in
the wound of someone who is grieving. But other times,
especially when the grieving process has been long, or if the
griever is supported by Jesus, a cheerful heart can bring the
healing that they need.

When entering a situation with a grieving person, be sure
to pray for discernment from the Holy Spirit for how to
respond. He will guide you to help in the proper way for
healing to come to this person, and he will use you in their
life. And don't forget; the worst thing you can do is not show
up at all.

God, give me a discerning heart to interact with the grieving.
Use me in the lives of those around me.

At a Loss

*The Spirit also helps our weakness; for we do not know how
to pray as we should, but the Spirit Himself intercedes for us
with groanings too deep for words.*

ROMANS 8:26 NASB

There are situations, in either our lives or in the ones we love,
that will feel like you are watching an accident happen in slow
motion. You are helpless to stop the destruction. What can
you do? You always can pray.

Why do we use prayer as our last resort when it should be our
first line of defense? Often, it is not until we feel our weakness
and reach the end of our ropes that we realize we need to
hand the situation over to God. Praise God for working in our
weakness! He is not hindered by our shortcomings. It was
never you that needed to stop the avalanche or redeem the
aftermath. It has always been God. Turn to him, even when
you don't know what to say. Call out to God, and let the Spirit
move in you and your loved ones' lives.

Do you tend to use prayer as a last resort?

The Holy Spirit helps us in our weakness. For example, we don't know what God wants us to pray for. But the Holy Spirit prays for us with groanings that cannot be expressed in words.

ROMANS 8:26 NLT

It is in your DNA to want to protect and keep safe those you love, be they friends, spouses, children, or siblings. It can be difficult not to overreach and try to control the outcome of their stories. But friend, it is not your job to be the Holy Spirit.

You can't soften someone's heart to accept the Word of God, but you can pray to the one who can. You can't force someone to change, but you can pray to the God who moves stubborn hearts. You can't see what the future has for all of us, but you can pray to the one who knows. You can't heal someone's heart, but God promises to heal, and you have direct access to his healing. Get the picture? Let's stop trying to do the job of the Holy Spirit. Instead, let's take up our shield of faith and intercede for those we want to protect.

Holy Spirit, you know the groanings of my heart, the ones about situations in my life and in those that I love, the ones I don't know how to talk about. Would you move in my heart tonight?

Real Rest

All who have entered into God's rest have rested from their labors,
just as God did after creating the world.

HEBREWS 4:10 NLT

Are we busy out of necessity or busy out of avoidance? Our culture gobbles up stress like a Thanksgiving pie—quickly, and always asking for more. The pace we keep in our lives, however, is not always out of necessity. God knows, and wants, for us to work. Work is not a bad thing. Taking care of your family is not bad; doing things is not bad. But sometimes, we can be keeping busy to avoid pain. When we finally slow down, reality crashes into us. For some, that may be too much to handle.

So, we keep going, faster and faster. Beloved, this is not the life that God created you for. If the truth and the pain catch up with you when you rest, then rest is exactly what you need. God does not want you to run and avoid. He wants you to heal. Though it can be scary, slow down to deal with the pain. Enter into true, healing rest, and let God tend to your wounds.

Are you living life in the fast lane to avoid something?
Pray through this question today.

As we enter into God's faith-rest life we cease from our own works,
just as God celebrates his finished works and rests in them.

HEBREWS 4:10 TPT

For God to be our happy place, he needs to be the one in charge. In the Bible, God explicitly commands us to rest. Not only does he put it in the ten commandments, also he tells us to imitate Christ, and Christ rested. Today's verse from Hebrews shows that God did his work. He was creative and productive, but then he rested.

As you desire to become more like Christ, resist the temptation to do more. We tend to add more and more. Even more and more spiritual things can be too much. You will find happiness in God when you simply follow his commands, and he commands rest. Follow his lead by taking time out of your routine to chill, eat, sleep, get outside, spend time with Jesus, and be yourself with friends. There are many ways to find real sabbath in Christ. Let's imitate Christ and pursue rest this week.

God, thank you so much for providing me with an opportunity to rest. Help me to live by your example and create a habit out of resting. You know my limitations better than anyone and you tell me to rest. I want to obey you with a happy heart that trusts in you.

Covenant Promise

My covenant I will not break,
Nor alter the word that has gone out of My lips.

PSALM 89:34 NKJV

One of the most beautiful things about God is his faithfulness. He never breaks a promise to us. In your Christian walk, you are sure to meet disappointment. There will be times when you feel stagnant in your faith. Stagnant water is water that isn't moving. It usually carries the connotation of being smelly and not good to drink.

When you feel stuck like this, remember the last thing God spoke to you. What was the last thing he asked you to do? Was there a promise that stands out to you that you remember? He is faithful to those promises. He hasn't forgotten them. He can't break them. Remembering this about him and what he told you will be like fresh water to your soul. Jesus says he is the living water, not stagnant water. Let your soul be refreshed by dwelling on his faithfulness this morning.

What was the last promise God spoke to you?

How could I revoke my covenant of love that I promised David?
For I have given him my word, my holy, irrevocable word.
How could I lie to my loving servant David?

PSALM 89:34 TPT

When we cling to the promises of God, we cultivate perseverance. Perseverance is an important quality to have as a believer because our race is a marathon, not a sprint. As we run, the promises of God, like the illustration shared this morning, are cups of cool water for your soul. It's important to be aware of them.

You can look on the internet for lists of the promises of God found in Scripture. You could also start a journal where you write out what God speaks to you, answered prayers, and important Scriptures. Then, when you feel like you just can't keep going, you have a resource to help you remember, a cup of water to give you the strength to continue on.

God, thank you for being faithful to me. I know you keep your promises; you never break them. I am amazed by you! Refresh my soul today. Give me perseverance and remind me what you have said to me in the past.

Abundant Goodness

How abundant are the good things
that you have stored up for those who fear you,
that you bestow in the sight of all,
on those who take refuge in you.

PSALM 31:19 NIV

If you talk to someone who has spent a lot of their life in an undeveloped country before moving to America, one difference that is often mentioned is the grocery stores. It's hard to get over entire aisles dedicated to just breakfast cereal or fresh vegetables, the abundance and variation of selection. To some, it can be very overwhelming!

Think of this analogy in terms of becoming an heir of the King. You go from having a cereal box that you fought and scraped for, to having aisles of boxes at your disposal. God has an abundance, aisles and aisles, of good things stored up for you. He wants to give them to you, to lavish you with these good gifts. When we open our eyes to the abundance of our King, it can be overwhelming to behold even a small portion of his goodness. Let it overflow your heart with praise and thanksgiving toward him.

Do you believe in the abundance
of God's goodness toward you?
How have you experienced it?

Lord, how wonderful you are!
You have stored up so many good things for us,
like a treasure chest heaped up and spilling over with blessings—
all for those who honor and worship you!
Everybody knows what you can do
for those who turn and hide themselves in you.

PSALM 31:19 TPT

Comparisons can rob us of joy in the goodness that God has stored up for us. Dear believer, there is enough for her and him, and there is enough for you. If you look to your left, see a fellow believer in Christ, and envy the abundance she seems to have, you are operating out of a mindset of poverty. If you look around and see only her gifts, her position, his family, his personality—on and on the list goes.

You wonder why these people have so much and you don't have enough. You are letting envy rob you of the abundant goodness that God has in store for you. There is more than enough, and it will never run out. Ask God to refocus your sights and help you see his goodness in your life.

God, your goodness is abundant. Help me to recognize and rejoice in the overflow of your goodness in my life.

Favor in Hard Times

In the light of a king's face is life,
And his favor is like a cloud with the spring rain.

PROVERBS 16:15 NASB

Have you seen those cartoons of a person walking around with a rain cloud over their head? Usually, this depicts their sadness and discomfort. Not exactly favorable, right? But here in Proverbs, the clouds are shown as favor.

Can you see hard things in your life as favor? Do you believe that God can turn the bitter into sweet? It takes faith to wait and sit with the clouds. It takes faith to cling to Jesus as a bitter situation unfolds, remembering what he has promised. We serve a powerful God, powerful enough to make every bitter thing sweet in our lives, every hard thing for good, and every disappointment for his glory. Nothing is exempt from the leading of God. He doesn't waste, and he doesn't miss things. He restores, and his favor is on you.

Do you believe that God can meet you in your bitter places? Identify and pray over these places today.

When the king smiles, there is life;
his favor refreshes like a spring rain.

PROVERBS 16:15 NLT

The rain can be healing. When clouds loom grey and large, we trust in God, and then the rain comes. The rain can wash us clean and change our perspective. Have you ever gone outside after a good rain when air is crisp and fresh? God can do this with our perspective on hard things as well.

He is the cleansing force we need. We need to be healed by his rain, to let the pain lead us into the arms of our Savior. We need to take the spots of our life that we see as bitter or riddled with clouds and ask him to make them sweet to us. That doesn't necessarily mean he will take the hard thing away or change the outcome to what you want, but he will bring goodness out of tough spots. It takes a lot of faith, but God will build up your faith and give you eyes to see.

Jesus, help me give over the hard spots in my life to you. Will you turn my bitter clouds into sweet rain?

Ready Help

God, hurry to help me, run to my rescue!
For you're my Savior and my only hope!

PSALM 38:22 TPT

Let's be honest. Is God the first person you turn to for help? If you answered yes, you are the right track! If you answered no, take a moment to reflect on what it is you usually turn to for help. Sometimes, even good things can get in the way of us fully turning to and relying on God for help. Maybe we turn to shopping for relief from the pain. Maybe we throw ourselves into our work. Or perhaps if our house was nice and clean, it might give us a false sense of control.

These are just three examples, and the Holy Spirit can search our hearts if we ask, showing us how we are turning to earthly things to help instead of God. God is patient with us. He's willing to save us and comfort us, if only we turn to him first.

Ask the Holy Spirit to search your heart.
What do you turn to for help or comfort?

Come quickly to help me,
my Lᴏʀᴅ and my Savior.

Pѕᴀʟᴍ 38:22 ɴɪᴠ

Sometimes, we don't turn to other things to help us get through. Instead, we turn to ourselves! Our own pride can get in the way of letting God help us. For some of us, it's not easy to ask for help. We are used to pulling ourselves up by our bootstraps and being independent.

God won't force you to do things his way, but his way is always better. We need to choose humility and ask him to help us. The psalmist, David, was not a weak man. He was a king! But here, he shows that even kings of great nations need to humble themselves and ask for help from the one true King of the universe. Let us follow in that example, showing those around us that our help and hope is found in God.

God, be my only help. You are my Savior! Show me those places where I turn to things that are not you. May I not turn to worldly things for help or rely on my own strength.

Chosen

You are a chosen generation, a royal priesthood, a holy nation, His own special people, that you may proclaim the praises of Him who called you out of darkness into His marvelous light.

1 PETER 2:9 NKJV

Inside all of us is the deep desire to be known, wanted, and loved in spite of being fully known. We sometimes turn to fashion, romance, alcohol, career accolades or a myriad of other things to feel accepted, loved, and known. These things, however, always leave us empty. They never fully satisfy the problem.

Good news! God has chosen you. He chose you when he made you, delighting over each detail of your unborn form. He placed you in this era and this place for a reason. He sees every detail of your life and is proud of you. He delights to see you walking in the light and reaches for you when you're lost in the dark. He never forgets you or abandons you, and nothing you do will make him say, "Well, that was the last straw."

How would your life look different if you always lived as a chosen and known child of God?

You are not like that, for you are a chosen people. You are royal priests, a holy nation, God's very own possession. As a result, you can show others the goodness of God, for he called you out of the darkness into his wonderful light.

1 Peter 2:9 nlt

To answer this morning's question, one important way our lives would be different if we lived as chosen ones is that we would praise God more. When you have good news, it can be almost impossible to keep it to yourself. Good news is meant to be shared.

We have the good news that we are chosen by God, plus the even better news that this is not an exclusive club. When you proclaim his goodness in your life, be sure to tell others that they too are loved by God, that he wants to welcome them into his family and know them fully. How can we keep this glorious light to ourselves? We can't! Proclaim his praise to all who will hear.

God, thank you for choosing me. May this truth sink deep into my soul. Help me to live as your chosen child and to proclaim your goodness to all around me.

Sought and Found

*"You will seek me and find me
when you seek me with all your heart."*

JEREMIAH 29:13 NIV

Have you ever asked, "Where is God?" Most people have at some point in their lives. Asking this shows an underlying fear that God is unavailable, uninterested, or too busy. But our perception is wrong, because God is none of those things.

Our Christian walk will have highs and lows, mountains and valleys. On top of the mountain, we feel like we see God so spectacularly, and in the valleys, we can cry out in despair as to where he might be. In reality, God is not that hard to find. Here in Jeremiah, he promises that if you seek him, he will be there. Elsewhere, it says that he is near. God is ever-present; we just have to make a perspective shift so that we can recognize him around us. This isn't a game of hide and seek. He is near. Trust in his promise and seek him with your whole heart today.

Do you believe that God is near you today?

*"If you look for me wholeheartedly,
you will find me."*

JEREMIAH 29:13 NLT

Let's go over a few roadblocks that might be making it more difficult for you to find God, thus making you think that he is not near. First, maybe your life is too fast paced. When we live in the fast lane, always getting to the next thing in our maxed-out schedule, we miss out on opportunities to hear God speak. God asks us to be still sometimes, to make room for rest, and he often speaks in a gentle whisper. Are we moving too fast and loud and to hear?

Next, are we too focused on ourselves? It's important to check your heart regularly. Are you building God's kingdom or your own? Or perhaps we are just too lazy. Jeremiah writes that we are to seek, and that takes action. Are you willing to change your lifestyle? To spend time in prayer, to actively seek in order to find? Lastly, perhaps a certain sin is in your way. God is a perfect and holy God, and though he will never abandon you, unconfessed sin can be a roadblock that keeps you away. Turn to God in repentance and let him restore your relationship again.

God, I seek you. I want to know you are near. I want to have fellowship with you. Reveal to me any of the roadblocks that might be hindering me from seeing or finding you.

Stick It Out

Blessed is the one who perseveres under trial because,
having stood the test, that person will receive the crown of life
that the Lord has promised to those who love him.

JAMES 1:12 NIV

Before GPS and smart phones, people had to use atlases. They would keep these big paper maps in their cars. When they went on a road trip, they pulled out the map, using highlighters to mark out the route. Now, technology maps it out for us, warning us about roadblocks, construction, and even hazards ahead. What luxury!

In this journey of faith, we all experience trials and tribulations. Like a GPS, James is warning us that there will be hazards and roadblocks ahead. The destination? Spiritual maturity. Going through tough things doesn't mean you've strayed onto a backroad, leaving God's mapped out plan for your life. Though sin can do that to us, we often face the very trials God has placed for us to persevere through on these supposed backroads. These things will build your faith and make you more mature in Christ, helping you get to your final destination. Take heart and be blessed as you persevere.

How could the trial you are facing be an opportunity
to move toward spiritual maturity?

*Blessed is the man who endures temptation;
for when he has been approved, he will receive the crown of life
which the Lord has promised to those who love Him.*

JAMES 1:12 NKJV

The crown of life is mentioned twice in Scripture, here and in Revelation 2:10. The word in Greek is similar to the wording used for the laurel wreaths that were handed out at sporting events like the Olympic games. The winner of the event gets the wreath placed on their head.

It's important to not confuse the crown of life with eternal life. Eternal life will always be a gift to humanity from God. It isn't earned by going through the trials or standing through tests. It has nothing to do with our merit and everything to do with God's grace toward us. The crown of life, however, is a crown for those Christians who stick it out through the hard times on this earth. For those who, like athletes, kept going and finished their race. Paul talks about finishing his race and finishing it well. He faced many difficult things in his life, but he finished well because he kept his eyes on Christ. May we learn from his example and keep our eyes focused on Christ, that we might wear the crown of life in eternity.

Jesus, thank you for your promises. Help me to persevere and run my race while keeping my eyes focused on you.

Draw Near

I am praying to you because I know you will answer, O God.
Bend down and listen as I pray.

PSALM 17:6 NLT

Kids are short. You can communicate with them while
standing, but it usually works best if you come down to their
level and look them in the eye. Imagine a six-foot father
towering over his three-foot toddler. Now, picture a father
bending down on one knee, drawing the child in and looking
them in the eyes.

Which one do you think is the better form of communication?
The latter, of course! This is how your Father God postures
himself toward you. He isn't upright or three strides ahead of
you, talking as you lag behind. As the best Father, he bends
down to you, his child, and draws you near, looks you in
the eye, and lovingly speaks to you. Do you see this as God's
posture toward you? Depending on our interactions with
our earthly fathers, our perspectives of our heavenly Father
can be skewed. During your time of prayer this morning, try
praying through this, asking God to change your perspective
if needed and accepting his loving embrace.

Do you view God as a kind father, drawing you near?
Or is your view different?

I call upon you, for you will answer me, O God;
incline your ear to me, hear my words.

PSALM 17:6 NRSV

There's nothing worse than asking someone a question and having them not respond. Maybe it's the gray box with three blinking dots on a text message, the "read" notification with no reply, or the silence of a phone that doesn't ring. It is painful when people don't respond. It feels like rejection, and rejection cuts deep.

God is not like our earthly relations. God answers. He's always available, and he will answer you. That's the beauty of our restored relationship through Christ. The lines of communication are wide open, and the Father is waiting for you to call. Call out to him and be reassured by his voice tonight.

God, I know you are a God who hears. You answer me and you love me. You are my kind Father, bending down to hear me. I love you!

My Praise

Heal me, O LORD, and I will be healed;
Save me and I will be saved,
For You are my praise.

JEREMIAH 17:14, NASB

Jeremiah had the tough job of being a prophet to the people of Israel. His message was one of coming judgment if the king and the people of Israel did not turn from their wickedness. His message was not well received by the king or the people. This taught Jeremiah a hard lesson: God's opinion is the only one that matters.

He wasn't accepted by the king or the people. They scorned him and laughed at him. He learned that the only one who would be faithful to keep his word was the Lord. If God said that Jeremiah would be saved, Jeremiah knew he would. If God said that healing would come, Jeremiah had confidence that it would. It didn't matter what those around him thought, and he wasn't swayed by their opinions. God was faithful to fulfill his Word, and Jeremiah kept preaching, even when no one else affirmed him. Believer, keep on serving the Lord, even if your ministry seems unfruitful and isn't garnering the praise of the masses. Be faithful to God, for he is faithful to you.

What is God asking you to be faithful in today?

O LORD, if you heal me, I will be truly healed;
if you save me, I will be truly saved.
My praises are for you alone!

JEREMIAH 17:14 NLT

It can be hard to trust God when the Bible tells us he is one way, but we see him in a different way. God says he will heal us, but perhaps the healing doesn't come the way we think it should. He says that he is faithful, but we feel abandoned.

There are so many scenarios that God's character doesn't seem to align with what we are experiencing. This is where we should cry out to him in unashamed trust. If God says he will heal you, he will. It's a sure thing. We must trust him when the healing doesn't come or look like how we think it should. If God says he will deliver you out of a situation, he will. Our perception can be deceiving, but our God is pure and true. He is the solid line; there is no wavering. Hold on to what he has told you tonight.

God, help me to hold onto your unwavering promises.

Move My Heart

Jesus, when He came out, saw a great multitude and was moved with compassion for them, because they were like sheep not having a shepherd. So He began to teach them many things.

MARK 6:34 NKJV

If you look into sheep, the farm animal kind, you will see that they are not survivors. They don't hunt and take care of their young, and they aren't considered strong and independent. Without a shepherd, domestic sheep just die. Sheep need a shepherd because they are directionless. You can put them in the exact spot they need to be, but without someone to supervise they are still prone to wander. Likewise, without the guidance of Jesus on this path of life, without the gift of his Word, we will stray.

Sheep are also quite defenseless. While other animals have sharp teeth, claws, or some form of self-defense, sheep have none of these things. They can't really run away either, as speed isn't their strong suit. They need someone to defend them. Like the sheep, we have no real defenses. Jesus, however, offers to defend us against the enemy. If we live our lives in complete dependence on the Good Shepherd, we will thrive.

How do you need Jesus to be your good shepherd today?

By the time Jesus came ashore, a massive crowd was waiting.
At the sight of them, his heart was filled with compassion,
because they seemed like wandering sheep who had no shepherd.
So he taught them many things.

MARK 6:34 TPT

When Jesus came and saw the crowds, he didn't get angry
at them. He wasn't annoyed or frustrated. He didn't take to
the podium and tell them to get over it and get their lives
together. No, when Jesus saw this mass of people, he was
moved with compassion. Doesn't that strike awe in your
heart? Often, our response is much different from that of our
Savior's. To be moved by compassion is to have empathy for
others. He recognized their hurt and need and met them in it,
and he began by teaching them.

When you come across people who are different from
you, do you have a haughty attitude? Think of people with
different political views, or those who hold beliefs different
than yours. Consider people who struggle with addiction,
those with physical or mental illness, or people who have a
lot of wealth or none at all. Are you frustrated by their very
existence? Will you allow God to make you more like Christ
and move you to compassion and empathy toward them?

Jesus, thank you for being my good shepherd. I want to be
more like you. Will you help me to be humble and move
with compassion?

Here's My Heart

My child, give me your heart,
and let your eyes find happiness in my ways.

PROVERBS 23:26 NRSV

It can be scary to give our hearts away. Past experiences may tell us to put up walls at all costs. Once you have been hurt, it feels necessary to become a bricklayer. Parents let you down—lay a brick. Your romantic partner deals wrongly with you—lay a few more. A friend betrays you, so you build further up and add the mortar.

Pretty soon, your heart is completely safe. Or is it? The walls that we erect with our own hands are not the right way to guard our hearts in this world. The best protection we have is in the Savior who gave his life for us. He is completely trustworthy. You can give him your heart, and he promises that he will protect it and keep it safe. Won't you trust him to be your protector today?

Where have you built walls in your life?
How can you learn to trust Jesus in those areas?

Give me your heart, my son,
And let your eyes delight in my ways.

PROVERBS 23:26 NASB

The second part of this verse falls in line quite nicely with the overarching theme of this book. The believer who entrusts their heart to Jesus will find happiness. This is because he is faithful and true. He is trustworthy and valiant, and he will care for you like no one on earth can. He knows you through and through, and he wants to restore to you the things that have been stolen.

Dear believer, a heart in the hands of Christ is the heart of a person who has found their happy spot. With Jesus as your protector, you can be vulnerable and authentic to those around you without fear of being torn apart. Trust in him.

God, I give you my heart. Tear down these walls that I built all around it. I entrust it completely to you.

If You Would

*I begged the Lord three times
to take this problem away from me.*

2 CORINTHIANS 12:8 NCV

Paul has been through a lot. In the chapter before this one, he lists many of the things he has faced. Beatings, whippings, shipwrecks, near-death experiences, persecution from both Jews and gentiles, coldness and nakedness, hunger and thirst, robbery—the list just goes on and on. It makes you wonder what this one specific thing was that Paul asked to be taken away. However, that it is not the point of the passage.

The point is that this man, who knows what suffering is and has faced so much, is still asking God to take some of it away. All the things he has been through have not made him bitter. He has not left God because God hasn't delivered him as expected. Instead, the apostle comes to God again, and again, and again. Paul takes shelter in his Lord and in prayer.

Has bitterness caused you to shy away from prayer?

Concerning this thing I pleaded with the Lord three times
that it might depart from me.

2 CORINTHIANS 12:8 NKJV

This morning, we went back to chapter eleven to see everything Paul had gone through. If you go forward in chapter twelve, you will see how God answers Paul's petitions. The answer is no. He doesn't heal it, and he doesn't take it away. Wouldn't Paul, of all people, be deserving of a miracle? After all he has done for Christ, after all he has been through!

Thankfully, that's not how God works. His goodness is not based on our merit, purity, or works. God has a different purpose and plan for each of our lives, and he is working faithfully to carry that plan out. In Paul's case, God chose to display his strength through Paul's learning to rely on the strength of God. Paul learned that in his weakness, Christ's strength shines through. There's nothing you can do to twist God's arm and get the outcome or miracle you desire. The best thing you can do is ask him what he wants with your life, trusting in him.

God, help me to rely on you. Even when it's hard and it hurts, teach me to trust you. Remove bitterness from my heart and show me your strength through my weakness.

Construction Workers

Encourage one another and build one another up,
just as you are doing.

1 THESSALONIANS 5:11 NASB

Do you like to build things? Most kids love tiny, colorful building blocks, and they create all sorts of wonderful worlds out of them. Some of us grew up to make building our profession, constructing houses, roads, and skyscrapers. In the Christian faith, God asks all of us to be builders.

When we participate in the growth of another believer, we build. You are called a temple of God when you become a believer. You are a temple alone, but also a part of the whole body of Christ, a sanctuary being built with Christ as the cornerstone. When we encourage each other in the faith, we are building a better house. The temple is where the Holy Spirit dwells. He dwells in you and in other believers. We can use our words and our actions to build up a better house for the Holy Spirit, one of unity and love. It's amazing how God works through his people. Won't you join him in building today?

How can you encourage other believers?

Encourage the hearts of your fellow believers and support one another, just as you have already been doing.

1 THESSALONIANS 5:11 TPT

Everything we do should be for the glory of God. When you share your testimony of how God has moved in your life, it can encourage others. There is a brick laid. When you pray for someone, a brick is laid. When you grab a coffee and pour over the Word of God with another believer in Christ, sharing your insights and lessons, there is a brick laid.

When you serve in the nursery and pray over the kids, usher in church, or volunteer for a church position, there is a brick laid. When you order takeout for a friend who just moved, visit a church member in a nursing home, and jot a note to your pastor to encourage him, that's brick after brick laid. Keep finding creative ways to encourage the body of Christ!

Lord, thank you for the encouragement I receive through the body of Christ. Help me extend that encouragement to those around me.

Holy Helper

"The Helper, the Holy Spirit, whom the Father will send in My name, He will teach you all things, and bring to your remembrance all that I said to you."

JOHN 14:26 NASB

The Holy Spirit can often be overlooked in Scripture, and our understanding of who he is can be sorely lacking. Let's take some time to dive into the helper that the Father has sent us. The Holy Spirit is just as much God as Jesus and the Father are. "Three in one" means that they are equal and one, singular God. The Holy Spirit has done a lot in the Bible, but let's focus on this verse.

After Jesus ascended into heaven, he and the Father gave believers the gift of the Holy Spirit. The Holy Spirit dwells inside those of us who believe in Jesus, and he has the role of teaching, convicting, giving wisdom, giving power, and empowering our spiritual gifts. He seals us in Christ, intercedes for us, sanctifies us, bears fruit through us, helps us in weakness, and more. As the Father desired to dwell with his people in the Old Testament and took up tabernacle among them, and as Jesus came as a baby in the New Testament to dwell among us, now the Holy Spirit dwells inside of us, making us temples to God.

Which of the Spirit's offerings stands out to you the most?

"When the Father sends the Spirit of Holiness, the One like me who sets you free, he will teach you all things in my name. And he will inspire you to remember every word that I've told you."

JOHN 14:26 TPT

Tonight, let's again focus on the role of the Holy Spirit as mentioned in our verse in John. The Spirit will teach you all things. Facing the Bible can be a daunting task. Good work, making it so far in this devotional! It shows your desire to know God's Word better. We don't have to attend Bible college to know the Scriptures well. We don't need a theology teacher or even a pastor to open up the Scriptures and understand God. We have the best teacher of all in the Holy Spirit.

Though it is important to be in a body of believers and to hear from others about the Scriptures, in your personal, daily time with God, the Holy Spirit is extremely qualified to teach you about the Word. If you are ever confused about a passage, first turn to him for help. After all, he dwells inside you! If studying the Bible feels overwhelming, make sure you are starting your Scripture time in prayer. You'll be surprised at what you can learn when you submit your daily reading to the Holy Spirit.

Holy Spirit, empower me with courage and help me to dive into the Word. Teach me!

Cheered On

Since we are surrounded by so great a cloud of witnesses,
let us also lay aside every weight, and sin which clings so closely,
and let us run with endurance the race that is set before us.

HEBREWS 12:1 ESV

In the year 2020, the world faced a pandemic that shut down many large gatherings, including sports events. When sporting events did reopen, they had to do most of their seasons without fans. Many athletes commented on how difficult this was. It was hard to perform their best without the cheering and support of their fans.

Here, the writer of Hebrews is describing our Christian faith like a marathon. In this event, we are not like the athletes of 2020 who had to play without the cheers of their fans. Those who have gone before us in the faith, from the beginning till now, are all telling their stories as a sort of cheering section for us. The great men and women of faith who have gone before us are waving banners that say, "Keep your eyes on Christ!" "Run with perseverance!" "It's worth it!" You can find their testimonies in Scripture, in books, and from the mouths of those around you. Hear their encouraging shouts. Keep running.

Do you have a favorite testimony?
What encouragement can you draw from it today?

We are surrounded by a great cloud of people whose lives tell us what faith means. So let us run the race that is before us and never give up. We should remove from our lives anything that would get in the way and the sin that so easily holds us back.

HEBREWS 12:1 NCV

Another thing that testimonies tell us is that we need to let go. We tend to cling to a particular sin, fear, or worldly comfort. We get it in our heads that we are functioning just fine with our burden. But it is so much easier and so much better when we let it go. Lay it aside. It is possible. God can give you the power you need to lay it down.

Surrender. Lay it at the feet of Jesus. Then, continue your race with a lightened heart. Doesn't that sound like the life you want to live? Picture two horses. One has packs, bags, and all sorts of things on its back. The other is free and has nothing attached. Who do you see as a picture of freedom? Run free, dear believer. Lay it at the feet of Jesus.

Jesus, I lay my weights and burdens at your feet. Thank you for the testimony of those who have gone before me. Help me to run my race with endurance.

Big Picture

A thousand years in your sight
are like a day that has just gone by,
or like a watch in the night.

PSALM 90:4 NIV

The more instant our society is, the easier it becomes to get too focused on the moment. We get really caught up in the day-to-day things, living in a reactionary way, always trying to be the first one. We want to be the first to respond, to hear the news, or to get the invite. Our world is running at a dizzying speed that we just can't keep up with.

Jesus offers us a way to get off the crazy train by slowing down and letting him take control. He sees the big picture. Jesus sees our whole lives played out from a bird's-eye view. While he usually doesn't share exactly what life entails for us, it's important to remember that he's not living at our pace. It's okay to get off the train and live at his pace. It's wiser to take time to pray over things before you react. Submit your plans to Jesus. Wait on the Lord. Don't be afraid of missing out; your life is in the hands of the one who sees it all. Just continue to live in submission to him.

Do you need to slow down and submit to Jesus?
In what areas?

One thousand years pass before your eyes
like yesterday that quickly faded away,
like a night's sleep soon forgotten.

PSALM 90:4 TPT

God's timing is not like our timing. He's not in a rush or a hurry. Everything is going how he planned, and it's not out of control in the least. Sometimes, we get the calling right, but the timing off. We hear God asking us to do something or promising us something, and we get really excited. Then, in a few days, when our timetable has expired, we get discouraged.

We must keep in mind that God's timing is not like ours. He may have given you the vision, but the timetable is his doing. Be faithful, seek him, and wait for him to show you when the time is right. Don't push a round peg into a square hole. Let God guide you in the calling and in the timeline.

Jesus, help me be patient with your timeline. Teach me to wait on you. Help me to know when the time is right.

Sound Mind

God has not given us a spirit of fear,
but of power and of love and of a sound mind.

2 TIMOTHY 1:7 NKJV

God is a generous God. What has he given you? He has given you the Holy Spirit, who bestows on you power, love, and a sound mind. Trust and fear often wrestle in our souls. In today's verse, Timothy tells us whose side we should be on. Fear is not from God and is on the side of the enemy. With that being said, which one are you cheering on?

We might not think we are cheering on fear, but feeding fear is the same as cheering it on. Are you full of worry about larger events happening in the world? Take a break from TV and social media, which constantly stream doom and gloom into your soul. Are you afraid of repeating the past, or the past being repeated on you? Stop visualizing it over and over and dwelling on past mistakes. This wrestling match is going on in the battlefield of our minds, and we must play close attention to where our encouragement goes. Encourage truth in your life by steeping in the Word of God, memorizing Scripture, listening to worship music, and praying your fears and worries to God. Repeat to yourself the character traits of God. Cheer on trust in your life!

What area of fear might you be encouraging?
What are some practical ways to stop doing so?

God will never give you the spirit of fear,
but the Holy Spirit who gives you mighty power,
love, and self-control.

2 TIMOTHY 1:7 TPT

What does it mean to have a spirit of power, love, and a self-control? The means that the gift itself is a sound mind. It means a mind that takes every thought captive and submits it to Christ. This gift comes with power—the power to have a sound mind. That power comes through the Holy Spirit. Without the Holy Spirit, we would not be able to fight against fear. He gives us the power to do it.

And lastly, it comes with love. Perfect love gets rid of fear. It's the weapon that dispels it. God's love is perfect. We renew our minds by dispelling fear and refilling on the love of God and the truth of his Word.

God, help me not to give into fear. I want to have a self-controlled mind, focused on your love, by the power of the Holy Spirit.

Keep Asking

*"If in my name you ask me for anything,
I will do it."*

JOHN 14:14 NRSV

"Stop! In the name of the law!" This phrase is in many old movies. It's shouted by law enforcement officers to show by what authority they yell. It is also presented as "stop, in the name of love" in a popular pop song. As with the law version, the idea is that the person is asking for someone to stop based on the authority of love. It's the same when we pray "in the name of Jesus."

When we ask for things in Jesus' name, it is not like rubbing a magic genie lamp, saying the right words, and then poof! You get what you want. When we pray in the name of Jesus, we invoke the authority that Jesus has. We are saying, "let this thing be done, by the power of God." Obviously, God will not honor prayers that go against his nature or his will. If you pray for an expensive sports car, you are asking for a genie and not the authority of God. This is an important clarification for our prayers. When we pray, let us ask in the power and will of God for him to move mountains and work in our lives. Let us pray that His will be done. In Jesus' name, let his will be done.

Does this understanding bring clarity
as to why we pray in Jesus' name?

*"Ask me anything in my name,
and I will do it for you!"*

JOHN 14:14 TPT

Imagine you go into a bank for a loan. They won't give it to
you without a cosigner. The co-signer says they will be held
responsible, and they provide security on your loan in case
you can't pay the bank back.

Jesus co-signs on our prayers when we pray in his name. We
don't march into the throne of God, demanding things of our
own authority and power. We have that access through Christ.
He extends his authority to us when we believe in him. He
intercedes for us and co-signs on what we ask for. Prayer is
a partnership, a relationship. How does this change the way
you pray?

Jesus, bring me into the right understanding of prayer.
In your name, let your will be done.

Better Desire

They desire a better, that is, a heavenly country.
Therefore, God is not ashamed to be called their God,
for He has prepared a city for them.

HEBREWS 11:16 NKJV

Have you ever felt a longing deep within you that couldn't explain? A desire for a place you have never been but long to be? These desires can be stirred up when we watch movies about other worlds, or when we see a brilliant sunset. This longing is for our heavenly country. Believers can identify it spot-on. It's the struggle with the feeling that you don't belong here, that this is not your home.

If you feel like a sojourner or a pilgrim, then your feelings are right. We shouldn't be too comfortable here on our earthy home. We should wrestle with a deep longing to be home with Jesus. That is a good thing! It's a sweet sorrow, because we know and believe in the goodness that is to come, but we also know that God still has work for us to do here. When the longing comes, sit with it. Know that it's a good thing. It means you have recognized this place as not your home and have the proper eternal perspective on life. Say a prayer for Jesus to come quickly, and then get back at it. God is on the move, and we are partnering with him.

Have you felt this desire before?
Have you been able to pinpoint what it is?

They were longing for a better country—a heavenly one.
Therefore, God is not ashamed to be called their God,
for he has prepared a city for them.

HEBREWS 11:16 NIV

Nonbelievers feel the longing too, creating an excellent opportunity for you to identify with them what they are feeling. Every single person was made to be united with Christ, to be one with the Father. Those that don't know Jesus are lacking in this area. The longings are strong within them; they just might not know what they are.

Expressing how you long to be with Jesus is not wishing for death. It's showing where your hope lies. Once you know this, you can help your non-Christian friends identify this longing in their lives too, and gently point them to Jesus, the only one that satisfies that desire.

Jesus, I long to be home with you. Help me to be a witness to others of your goodness.

Satisfied

Even lions may get weak and hungry,
but those who look to the LORD will have every good thing.

PSALM 34:10 NCV

Do you question this statement from David? Do you look around and think that you, or a Christian you know, is lacking and has needs? This statement is not a blanket statement that Christians will have every little thing our hearts desire and ask for. As believers, there will be those of us that face hardship and even physical poverty.

No matter the situation we find ourselves in, we are always promised spiritual nourishment on this earth. When you are found in Christ, you have everything you need available to you. He is enough for you. David is praising God for that fact. David had times in his story that we would say he was in great need. Where was God then? God knew and was near. God sees our lives as a whole picture. He meets needs and gives us good things, but he isn't limited to what we see temporarily. He knows what is best for our good and his glory. What more could we want?

What goodness do you see in your life?
Where do you see need?

Even the strong and the wealthy grow weak and hungry,
but those who passionately pursue the Lord
will never lack any good thing.

PSALM 34:10 TPT

Lions are fierce. They are often called the kings and queens of the animal kingdom. They are not known being unable to hunt or going hungry. While even the fiercest hunters in the animal kingdom cannot guarantee their kill, nourishment, and security, those who hunger for God will always be nourished and sustained.

Are you too full to hunger for God? Have you satisfied yourself with the things of the world and filled up on empty pleasures? In order to be satisfied, we must first be hungry. That means we must sit with the lack in our lives and stop trying to fill it with things that will never satisfy. Only God satisfies the hungry soul. What empty things have you been turning to instead? Try to identify what those things are and repent of them today. Ask God to make you hungry for more of him. He is sweet and filling, goodness for your soul. He will nourish you and sustain you.

Jesus, help me to hunger for more of you. I know the empty things of this world can't truly satisfy. Nourish me with your presence today.

Goodness in Store

*"No eye has seen, no ear has heard,
and no mind has imagined
what God has prepared
for those who love him."*

1 CORINTHIANS 2:9 NLT

Have you ever been the recipient a surprise party or planned one for someone else? It's easy to get caught up in the fun and excitement of planning out the party to extravagantly express your love for someone else. Now, think about the most unexpected, lavish gift you have received. Someone put thought and care into picking that out for you.

This is the life of a believer. With a twinkle in his eye, God has prepared a life for you that is a gift. Look around you and you can see his love laced into even the simplest details of your life. It's important to cultivate eyes that want to see and ears that stretch to hear the gifts that God has placed all around you.

What parts of your life feel like gifts to you?
Can you think of any surprising ones?

"What no eye has seen,
what no ear has heard,
and what no human mind has conceived
the things God has prepared for those who love him."

1 CORINTHIANS 2:9 NIV

As a child, it can seem like good things just magically happen. A long day at the beach, full of sun, play, snacks, and laughter is like magic. As an adult, you come to realize that those days take planning. Someone has to find the beach, a place to stay, pack snacks, bring toys and swimsuits, and so on. There is a lot of preparation behind many magical moments.

It's the same with a good movie. We sit and enjoy the two hours of good storyline and visual stimulation, but in reality, it took years and lots of people to make those two hours worthwhile. Preparation is the key. And you have someone preparing for you, someone better than a company or a caring family member. God is working in unseen ways, preparing for you. Rest in the fact that you are cared for.

Jesus, thank you for this life you have gifted to me. Thank you for preparing this life for me and being involved in every detail. I know you love me, and I can rest in your care.

Governed by Grace

Remember this: sin will not conquer you, for God already has!
You are not governed by law but governed by
the reign of the grace of God.

ROMANS 6:14 TPT

What is the job of a governor? A governor has authority over a certain area. This person gives direction and guidance to the land appointed to them. They work with others to enforce laws, making sure people live by them. When we become believers, we transfer from the kingdom of the world, which is governed by the law, to the kingdom of God which is governed by his grace. No longer does sin have rule and place in your life, because you are covered by grace.

What does this mean for our life practically? It means that sin will try to shame you, accuse you, and condemn you. Every single time, you can point to the cross. You can say that you are covered by the blood of Jesus, and by his grace you are clean and new. Grace rules in your life. Be free of the shackles of sin and shame and rejoice! You, once a captive, have been set free.

What grace have you seen in your life
that you can rejoice over today?

Sin shall no longer be your master
because you are not under the law,
but under grace.

ROMANS 6:14, NIV

There are times when sin can really get us down. It feels like a battle we can't win. We feel like a people conquered. Defeated, we hang our heads in shame as we come to God and ask for forgiveness again. If this is you, raise your head. Sin has not conquered you! God has set you free. You may be in a battle against a stronghold or an addiction, but God does not despise your repentant heart. He honors it. He longs to see you live in the land of freedom and to bring healing to you.

Do not give up in shame; do not let sin defeat you. Remember that you are loved by God. He has conquered sin, and he has not abandoned you in this fight. Continue to pursue godliness by the power of the Holy Spirit tonight.

Jesus, let me be conquered by your grace, not by sin. Free me from bondage. I submit my life to you. Remind me that shame doesn't rule over me.

Peace Here

"Glory to God in the highest,
and on earth peace among those with whom he is pleased!"

LUKE 2:14 ESV

The Christmas season is upon us! Let's whip out the to-do list and cram as much into the next twenty-five days as possible! Cookies, parties, ballets, gift shopping, hot cocoa, candlelight services, family pictures, putting up the tree...

Okay, that's a lot. Slow down for a minute. Sure, most of these things are fun celebrations of the Christmas season. But why do we pack the season so full? Is our busyness an antidote for loneliness, emptiness, or lack of peace? We must be careful with our over-packed day planner. We must be sure we are spending our mornings here, in God's Word, first. Giving him glory, hearing his voice. He might ask you to slow down a bit or cut a few things out, even though you feel afraid of missing out. "Do not fear," the angels said, so do not fear. God wants us to experience his glory this season, and it's something far more exciting and fulfilling than anything we could pencil in.

Do you use your busyness to cover up
what is really going on in your heart?

> *"Glory to God in the highest realms of heaven!*
> *For there is peace and a good hope given to the sons of men."*

LUKE 2:14 TPT

The angels told the shepherds exactly what was going to happen. "On earth, peace." Peace among us. We often overlook it when we are reading the Christmas story, but here, the angels are being quite literal. Peace himself came to live among us. Peace, personified, came down as a baby, grew up, did ministry, and then died on a cross, all while among us.

This is the embodiment of God's deep desire to dwell among us. Peace came to dwell among us. Jesus is that peace. Peace is not a particular place or a chant or a candlelight service. Peace is Jesus. His presence is peace. This Christmas, take time to dwell with God, to dwell with peace.

Jesus, you are peace. What a beautiful realization! When the angels said peace among us, they meant you. Be near to me today. Help me to slow down and enjoy your peace.

Journey of Faith

When they saw the star,
they rejoiced exceedingly with great joy.

MATTHEW 2:10 ESV

There are some extreme, descriptive words here. "Rejoiced exceedingly" with "great joy?" We know without a doubt how the wise men reacted! They had spent their whole lives, maybe even trained from the time they were kids, studying the stars. Imagine the patience and diligence that art takes. Then, they found a new star and left their homelands, traveling miles and miles, believing that the star would lead them where they wanted to go. When the star finally stopped, they believed that this was it—this was the place of the new king! What faith and belief they display to us.

God has a calling for your life, and he may be asking you to step out in faith and follow him. Then, when the journey is done, he might ask for even more belief from you. Perhaps the destination doesn't look like you thought. Did the magi expect a humble house and a poor child? God wants you to trust him all the same. Prepare, have faith, and believe.

What is God asking for your faith in today?

When they saw that the star had stopped,
they were overwhelmed with joy.

MATTHEW 2:10 NRSV

Let's circle back to those extra descriptive words Matthew
uses to describe the emotions of the wise men. This morning,
we covered the faith they had in following the star and finding
the King. Once they had completed their mission, there was
an abundance of joy. They knew they had found a king.

As you go out into the world this month, you can give great
joy to those around you. The holiday season can be marred
by pain and loneliness for so many. But you carry the light of
Jesus in you. He wants you to shine his love to all those around
you. Will you shine like a star and announce God's presence to
those in your presence? Let his joy shine through you.

God, I praise you! You bring such joy to me. Let me be a light
to others and step out in faith, following you today.

An Open Book

All my longings lie open before you, Lord;
my sighing is not hidden from you.

PSALM 38:9 NIV

It's called being passive aggressive when you huff and puff around the house, trying to communicate to your roommate, spouse, or parent that you are upset without outright telling them. Most of us act in a passive aggressive manner at some time or another in our lives, and we all know it is not a good way to communicate.

Sometimes, we act that way toward God, huffing and puffing, maybe talking to others about him, feeling all upset about something, but never really coming to him with our issue. Don't beat around the bush; come to Jesus. Bring your frustrations and hurts to him. You can't hide from God. You are an open book before him already. He knows you inside and out. Come to Jesus with your pain and work through the healing together.

What do you need to bring to Jesus this morning?

Lord, you know all my desires and deepest longings.
My tears are liquid words and you can read them all.

PSALM 38:9 TPT

Like we said this morning, you can't hide from God. Why do
we try? We are upset over something, or troubles don't go
away, so we try to hide from God. It looks different for each of
us. Some keep going through the motions while their hearts
have checked out. That is just hollow religion. Others return
to old, sinful patterns for healing when they know only Jesus
will heal truly. Others try to speed life up, staying busy until
the hard part passes.

Which category do you fall in? Hopefully, none of them.
Hopefully, whatever is tempting you to hide from God instead
makes you run that much faster into his arms. You cannot
hide from God. You cannot run from him. There is nowhere
you can go to get away from him. Confess your sins and your
hurt and draw near to him tonight.

God, there is nowhere I can run from you. I want to draw
closer to you. Thank you for forgiving me and knowing me
so thoroughly.

Today

This is the day the Lord has made;
We will rejoice and be glad in it.

PSALM 118:24 NKJV

Did you grow up singing a song based on this verse? Maybe you can hear the tune in your head already, picturing little five-year-olds singing it in rounds. Maybe you've heard this phrase so many times, you are tempted to skip over today's reading. It's a little too perky for you, a little too cliché. Actually, it's God's living Word, and he wants to minister to your heart through it today.

This is miracle that he has handed to you when your eyes first fluttered open this morning. It is a gift he gave you as your feet touched the floor beside your bed and you padded toward the bathroom. The joy is ringing through the air as you grab your hot beverage, your Bible, and this book. It is a great day to be alive! Why? Not because of any earthly circumstance, but because this very day is a gift from your Father. He's handing it to you, a whole day, ready like that first blank, crisp page in a journal. He can't wait to see what you will write on it. Fill it with his glory. Fill it with his joy. Rejoice!

Spend a few moments dwelling on the fact that this day is a gift. How has God already blessed you today?

This is the very day of the Lord that brings
gladness and joy, filling our hearts with glee.

PSALM 118:24 TPT

Here you are, at the end of the day that was given to you as a gift. Maybe it was a good day by your standards. Maybe you now scoff at your naive eagerness from this morning. Jesus is not sitting here with a scoreboard, rating how well you did on the gift he gave you. It's a no strings attached kind of deal. Instead, imagine Jesus sitting here with a cup of tea, saying you've done a good job.

Do you have a burden? Come take the load off. Did you accomplish something today? Come tell him about it. Did you get hurt? Let him heal you. He is full of love toward you, no matter how your day went. And that's what makes it a day to rejoice in, not just to be happy in. Joy is a lasting thing, given to us by God. Happiness is fleeting. No matter the circumstances of the day, you can rejoice, because your eyes are focused on your Savior.

Jesus, thank you for the gift of this day. Thank you for taking all my day's burdens onto yourself. Fill me with joy!

Highest Law

"Love the LORD your God with all your heart,
all your soul, all your strength, and all your mind."
Also, "Love your neighbor as you love yourself."

LUKE 10:27 NCV

You could dedicate your life to embodying just this verse.
Though only a few words, this is the summary of the law and
God's will for our lives. As followers of Jesus, we are called to
love. Everything that God does is motivated by love. Love is
who he is. Jesus is asking us to follow in his example.

When love is our action, any sinful motive or attitude is
dispelled. But love does not come to us naturally. We must
draw from the source. When we display true love to those
around us, we display Christ. In John 13:35, it says that others
will know you are Jesus' disciples by your love. Not by your
big, fancy building. Not by your political stances. Not by your
wealth. Love is the marker that declares to the world that we
are his.

How is God calling you to act in love today?

> *"You shall love the Lord your God with all your heart,*
> *with all your soul, with all your strength,*
> *and with all your mind," and "your neighbor as yourself."*
>
> LUKE 10:27 NKJV

When you read the word *love*, do you automatically equate it
with romance? There are many different types of love: love
between friends, family, and yes, romantic relationships.
How do you learn about how those types of love act? Did
you learn from movies, books, or TV? Was it through those
around you? Those are all sources where we learn what love
looks like, but often they are wrong.

The best source to learn about what love looks like is God's
Word. Try starting in 1 Corinthians 13, the chapter of love.
What you read there will probably be very different from what
you've seen in movies! God's love is different from the cheap,
imitation love the world tries to feed us. People are starving
for true love, the 1 Corinthians kind. Don't follow in the
example of the imitation; take your cues from the source of
true love himself, Jesus Christ.

Jesus, teach me how to love. Teach me what true love is. Help
me to love those you put into my sphere of influence.

Abide

Let what you heard from the beginning abide in you.
If what you heard from the beginning abides in you,
then you will abide in the Son and in the Father.

1 JOHN 2:24 NRSV

Doctors will tell you it's important to stay active. Even a simple walk around the block is good for your health. We don't walk as much as people used to because of bikes, cars, and other modes of transportation. In the Bible, walking is a common theme. We see in the very beginning that Adam and Eve walked in the garden with God. There was intimacy in those walks, the Creator of the universe and the first humans together. In the Old Testament, with examples like Noah and Enoch, those with a close relationship with God "walked with God."

Jesus walked all over Israel with his disciples, teaching about the kingdom. Some of their discussions happened while walking along and are recorded in the gospels. Jesus walked up the hill at Calvary, bearing the cross so that you could walk with him as Adam and Eve did in the garden. Walking is a form of abiding by stepping together. Jesus is inviting you to walk with him. Won't you step out in faith today?

Do you think you are walking in step with Jesus?
Where are your feet straying?

Be sure to keep the message burning in your hearts;
that is, the message of life you heard from the beginning.
If you do, you will always be living in close fellowship
with the Son and with the Father.

1 JOHN 2:24, TPT

People who walk or run for exercise know that they travel best at a set pace. In order to not sprint your whole run, you need something to set the pace. It could be the beat of your music or the gait of person next to you.

In the journey of your life, you need someone to set the pace. Jesus wants to walk with you; are you letting him set the pace? Do you tend to sprint ahead of him? Do you tend to drag your feet and lag behind? Abiding with Jesus means falling in line with his step, letting him set the pace and course of your life. How can you change to fall in step with him tonight?

Jesus, thank you for walking with me and abiding with me. Help me to match my pace to yours.

Get Back Up

The godly may trip seven times, but they will get up again.
But one disaster is enough to overthrow the wicked.

PROVERBS 24:16 NLT

What animal are Christians often compared to in Scripture? Sheep! Psalm 23, Isaiah 53, and John 10, to name a few, make a comparison between sheep and followers of God. Did you know that if a sheep rolls onto its back with all four legs in the air, it cannot get back up on its own? Shepherds call this being "cast down." Without a shepherd, or some form of outside help, the sheep will suffocate in that position and die. After they fall, an experienced shepherd must turn them over, help them regain their balance and footing, and even massage their legs to reawaken them.

This is how Jesus, the Good Shepherd, is toward us, his flock. When we fall, he restores us to an upright position. We can only get back up again because of him.

Have you fallen recently?
Have you tried calling out to God to help you stand?

The righteous falls seven times and rises again,
but the wicked stumble in times of calamity.

PROVERBS 24:16 ESV

In this verse, both the godly and the wicked fall. Elsewhere in Scripture, we are told that the rain falls on the righteous and the wicked alike. Having hard things happen to you, meeting troubles, and even struggling with sin are not signs that you don't have enough faith.

What is the one key difference between the wicked and the godly in this passage? The Holy Spirit. You, as a believer, have God on your side. The Spirit of God dwells in you. He fights for you, comforts you, empowers you, and wants to make you more like Christ. He gives you freedom, peace, and abundant living. Hard times are not a sign of no faith; hard times will come to all. But you have Christ on your side and getting back up means turning to him for all that you need.

Holy Spirit, thank you for all you do in my life. Thank you for helping me up when I fall. Jesus, thank you for being the Good Shepherd and restorer of my soul.

Yours

*"Whatever you ask in prayer,
believe that you have received it,
and it will be yours."*

MARK 11:24, ESV

Isn't it easier when A equals B? Some believers try to take Scriptures, like this one, in that way. If you ask God, and believe hard enough, he will give you what you want. A equals B. Easy math! The danger in this is we might miss what Jesus is really teaching here by not accounting the Bible's teachings as a whole. This view of prayer compromises the sovereignty of God and ignores other parts of Scripture.

Then it gets confusing. Did Jesus not just give us a clear imperative to have faith? Doesn't Jesus want us to pray and pray in faith? Of course he does! But he is not asking you to force yourself into belief. He's asking you to submit your needs and lay them before God. Faith comes from the Spirit as a gift. The very act of prayer gives you the gift of faith. It's in the drawing near, the asking, the submitting, that faith works in you. It becomes less about getting a specific thing as God makes known to you his will and his way.

Is faith something you feel you've had to work for,
or do you view it as a gift?

"This is the reason I urge you to boldly believe for whatever you ask for in prayer—believe that you have received it and it will be yours."

MARK 11:24 TPT

Here is another question for you to ponder. When you doubt, do you still pray? We often don't leave room in our prayers for our doubts, as if expressing them to God will come across negatively or hinder what we are asking for.

But God welcomes your doubts because he is bigger than them. He knows you so thoroughly that he already knows them. Those doubts lose power, find answers, or just are quieted when brought to God. If you are only presenting the good side in your prayers tonight, stop for a moment and whisper some doubts to God. See if he is not big enough to handle them and love you through it all.

Jesus, thank you for teaching me how to pray. I know you want to talk with me. Let faith rise in me. Help me to submit all to you, from my highest aspirations to my darkest doubts.

Perfect Pattern

I want you to pattern your lives after me,
just as I pattern mine after Christ.

1 CORINTHIANS 11:1 TPT

When constructing a garment, you could try to make it just by guessing and cutting. However, most good seamstresses follow a pattern. Patterns are thin sheets of paper that you lay over your fabric, using their shapes to cut out the fabric exactly how you need it. If you follow the pattern, you can be fairly sure the outcome will look like what you are going for.

In the same manner, Paul wrote this verse to the church in Corinthians. He patterned his life after Christ, so they could pattern their lives after him. What or who are you patterning your life after? If we attempt to wing it, we are going to end up with a pretty messed up end piece. We could also pattern our lives after the world, but then we will end up sharing the world's fate. As Christians, the best way to live a life that brings glory to God is to pattern your life after Christ.

Who is the pattern for your life?
What worldly patterns keep sneaking in?

You should imitate me,
just as I imitate Christ.

1 CORINTHIANS 11:1 NLT

Paul speaks with confidence when he tells the church that he has patterned his life after Christ, and they can pattern their lives after him. Can you speak with the same confidence? We all have people under our influence, those that God has given us to shepherd and advise. We are all leaders in some form. Where are you leading those around you?

Let's be people who pattern our lives after love, servanthood, humility, mercy and grace. As we pattern our lives after Jesus and walk with him, it encourages those in our influence to do the same. This is disciple-making in a nutshell. Walk with each other in Christ. Every one of us is called to make disciples. Take into consideration those in your influence tonight.

Jesus, I want to pattern my life after yours. I want to be a good leader. Help me to lead people to you and show me who those people are.

Free from Guilt

*There is now no condemnation
for those who are in Christ Jesus.*

ROMANS 8:1 NASB

Guilt can feel like drowning. With the heavy bricks of condemnation tied to your feet, often by our own two hands, guilt can pull you deeper and deeper until you can't breathe. Let Jesus bend down and untie the knot. Let this verse pierce your soul. Turn it and toss it in your head until it's the one sinking into your very soul.

There is no condemnation for you. There is nothing you have done, nothing you will do, that is too much for Christ's blood. He died for every single sin and mistake, and he covers them all. God is compassionate toward you, and the last thing he wants is for you to drown in guilt. He has set you free to swim to the surface, to gulp the fresh breath of grace every day. When you cut ties with guilt, you are free to learn from your mistakes, grow, and change.

What guilt is tied to your feet?
Can you let God cut the rope?

There remains no accusing voice of condemnation against those who are joined in life-union with Jesus, the Anointed One.

ROMANS 8:1 TPT

When we dwell in guilt and shame, it is essentially saying that the blood of Jesus was not enough. When we submit to the lies of condemnation that drag us down, we are refusing to accept the forgiveness that Jesus freely offers. It's dishonorable to our Savior to continue to live in this way, and it offers no benefits.

Often, the battle is in our minds. If that is where the battle is, that is where we need to fight. Try using Scripture to fight by looking up verses about your freedom and forgiveness in Christ. Post them around your house, memorize them, and take them to heart. When the lies come knocking, when guilt threatens to drown you, you have a weapon to fight back. Speak Scripture to the lies, and watch the victory unfold.

Jesus, you are my beautiful Savior. Thank you for extending your grace to me. It runs deeper than my deepest shame. Free me from guilt and shame today.

Courageous

"Have I not commanded you? Be strong and of good courage;
do not be afraid, nor be dismayed, for the LORD your God
is with you wherever you go."

JOSHUA 1:9 NKJV

Picture a classic war or action film. Right before the battle, the commander trots back and forth on horseback in front of his troops, giving an impassioned speech that he hopes will build their confidence to fight the battle. Sometimes, it's in front of the strongest and most agile warriors. Sometimes, it's for a chosen and elite group. But it stirs our hearts the most when it's in front of a group of underdogs, those with the odds stacked against them. On their own, they really don't have a chance. They aren't the most skilled, talented, or strong. In fact, most would describe them as weak and incapable.

Isn't it the same for us? God calls us to be courageous and strong, to not be afraid. He knows we are in the underdog group—weak and incapable of winning the battle on our own. But God also knows that the key to the victory lies in those last ten words of today's verse. "The Lord your God is with you wherever you go." With God for you, who can be against you? Take courage!

What battle is God encouraging you for this morning?

"This is my command—be strong and courageous!
Do not be afraid or discouraged.
For the LORD your God is with you wherever you go."

JOSHUA 1:9 NLT

God isn't giving suggestions or commentary in this verse. He is giving a commandment. Be brave! In the army, you don't disobey direct commands from officers. What they say, you do. Let us be Christians who are like this with God. If God commands us something, we do it. We take up courage and march right out in bravery, confident in the one who goes with us.

You were always meant to be brave. Sometimes, it can be scary to be who you are meant to be, to step into a role already prepared for you. God has prepared a brave and courageous road for you today. When you step into bravery, it changes the lives of those around you, and it changes your life.

Jesus, you make me brave! Help me to step out in courage into my God-given calling today.

Growth

Grow in the grace and knowledge of our Lord and Savior Jesus Christ. To him be glory both now and forever! Amen.

2 PETER 3:18 NIV

December is a time of reflection. The close of a year gives most of us the urge to look back over the year that has passed. As you look back, did you grow spiritually? Your walk with Christ is the most important relationship and aspect of your life. Our lives should be centered around Christ and bringing him glory; it's the purpose of every human being. With this in mind, how did you see growth in your relationship this year?

The point is not to look for perfection. None of us will be perfect this side of heaven. It is also not to measure how many good works you did to see if you qualify for salvation. No, the point is to take an honest look at the state of your heart. Are your life choices helping you to grow in Christ, or are you wilting?

How do your time, priorities, and lifestyle reflect growth and give glory to God?

*Grow in the grace and knowledge of our Lord and Savior
Jesus Christ. Glory be to him now and forever! Amen.*

2 PETER 3:18 NCV

Peter admonishes his readers to grow in two areas, grace and
knowledge. What does that mean practically? Many believers
accept God's grace when they first come to faith, and then
fail to thrive in grace throughout their lives. A good example
of how to grow in grace and knowledge comes to us from
the lives of early believers, displayed in Acts 2:42. It says
that they gave themselves wholeheartedly to four specific
practices.

First was listening to the teachings of the apostles or the
leadership of the early church. This could be equated
to attending a church and soaking up the Bible-based
teachings it offers. Second is fellowship. They lived with
other believers. They had close fellowship, sharing in joy,
in sorrow, inviting each other into their homes, and sharing
daily life together. Third, they broke bread together or took
communion and shared a meal. Again, it shows the power of
living in relationship with one another. Lastly, they practiced
prayer, a vital tool for spiritual growth.

God, thank you for the learning example of early believers.
Show me areas of my life where I am lacking. As I reflect,
help me to make a plan for change.

Still Trust

When I am afraid,
I will put my trust in you.

PSALM 56:3 NLT

It's ok to be afraid. God never asks us to become emotionally sterile when we become Christians. There can be a misconception that if you feel certain feelings, you don't have enough faith, or you aren't walking closely enough with God. This is more of a works-based love mentality, and it is not how God operates. Of course, he doesn't want you to live in fear or any negative emotion, but he doesn't expect you to never have them. He is big enough for all your big emotions.

What he wants more than anything is that when the fear, or the anxiety, or the sadness comes, you turn to him. That is what it means to put your trust in him. Let the big emotions turn you toward God, not away from him, and watch as he meets you in your greatest need.

Do you try to hide your emotions from God sometimes? What hinders you from coming to him just as you are?

In the day that I'm afraid, I lay all my fears before you
and trust in you with all my heart.

PSALM 56:3 TPT

There are some things that trusting in God is not. Trusting in God does not mean that every little thing will go your way and in the way you planned it out. Some people are tempted to believe that trusting in God means a problem-free life. Look at the many examples we are given in Scripture, like Job and Joseph, and you will find that simply isn't true.

Trusting in God also does not mean that God is going to tell you exactly why everything will happen in your life. God doesn't owe us a why, though it's okay to ask for one. Sometimes he will tell you, and other times he won't. Trusting in God means turning toward him in every situation. Which type of trust do you tend to practice? How can you turn toward God this evening in trust?

God, thank you for being trustworthy. I know that you are big enough for all my emotions. You won't run away from them. Help me to trust in that fact, even at my lowest points.

Healed

"Behold, I will bring to it health and healing,
and I will heal them and reveal
to them abundance of prosperity and security."

JEREMIAH 33:6 ESV

Jeremiah penned these words from prison as Jerusalem lay
in waste and destruction because of the wicked acts of the
people. A pretty despairing and desolate picture, isn't it? How
can you possibly follow that reality with words like abundance,
prosperity, security, health, and healing? It's like throwing
a basketball in the middle of a kid's one-of-a-kind Lego
creation—how could we possibly make that look the same?

God's not looking to make it the same. He's looking to do
more. He's wants to fashion a life of eternal value, full of
the riches of heaven, secure in his grace and whole in his
presence. Restoration is the name of his game, and he wants
to do a mighty work in your life just like he did for his people
in Jeremiah's time. If your life looks like a wasteland, take
heart that God is going to move mightily in you today.

What areas of your life need restoration today?

> *"I will bring it health and healing;*
> *I will heal them and reveal to them*
> *the abundance of peace and truth."*
>
> JEREMIAH 33:6 NKJV

Have you heard of the marvelous works that God has done? If you need healing tonight, emotionally, spiritually, relationally, or physically, turn to your Bible to find testimony of our God who heals. Making things new is what he does, and he does not want you to stay stuck in the brokenness you are experiencing.

As you find accounts of the blind seeing, the lame walking, and the dead coming alive again, let them encourage your soul. He is not done doing these things. The work he did in Jeremiah's time of restoration, the work he did in the lives of so many throughout the Bible, is not a closed case. His healing power is alive for you today. Find encouragement from their testimonies and let faith arise in you.

Jesus, thank you for being my healer. Even if I doubt, you are still in the business of healing today. Will you heal me tonight?

Mindset

Think about the things that are good and worthy of praise.
Think about the things that are true and honorable and right
and pure and beautiful and respected.

PHILIPPIANS 4:8 NCV

Modern technology allowed many of us to become aspiring photographers just with the use of our phones. There is a setting on most of these phone cameras called portrait mode. Portrait mode takes whatever you have as the subject into crisp focus and blurs out the background. Doing this draws the viewer's eye to focus on whatever it is you, the photographer, want them to focus on.

Wouldn't it be awesome if we came with a portrait mode? Our minds can easily be distracted by things that aren't helpful. Constant worries, past mistakes, and wrong choices all try to consume our attention when our focus should be on Christ. Through the power of Christ, let's turn on our portrait mode and bring into focus the list of things that Paul gives us above.

What threatens to consume your focus instead of Christ?

*Fix your thoughts on what is true, and honorable,
and right, and pure, and lovely, and admirable.
Think about things that are excellent and worthy of praise.*

PHILIPPIANS 4:8 NLT

Oftentimes, a happy place is just a place in your mind that you go to by using your imagination. Some say the ocean is their happy place, even if they can only physically get there once or twice a year. If we are to be people who have God as our happy place, then we must focus our minds on him.

He is all the things listed above: true, honorable, right, pure, beautiful, and respected. When we dwell on the character of God and the attributes of Christ, it transforms us. When we practice dwelling on these things, these things manifest in our lives. Suddenly, we find ourselves in the presence of God, no matter where we physically are, and we find ourselves in our happy place.

God, shift my mind from things below to things above. Help me to dwell on you and the things that are worthy of praise. Push away everything else that pulls my attention. Help me to dwell in you.

Motivation

Every man's way is right in his own eyes,
But the LORD weighs the hearts.

PROVERBS 21:2 NASB

Every action we take has an underlying motive. If we choose to help a neighbor move, we might look like we are helpful on the outside, but inside, our motive is looking for appreciation. Some of us might describe ourselves as hard-working, but underneath hides a struggle with perfectionism. Maybe you are known as a peaceful, easy-going friend but, in reality, you are unwilling to confront problems when it is necessary. Our actions can be good or seemingly harmless, but our motives can reveal many root struggles, and sometimes sin.

God knows the motivations of your heart. Even if you're trying to cover up your need to be wanted or your struggle with feeling like a failure, God sees it. We are exposed completely before him. Sometimes, we don't like that! It takes moments of silence and self-reflection in prayer to realize these issues, but God is right there to walk with you through them. Though you are exposed to him, he does not reject or shame you. He wants to heal you.

How can you submit to the gentle correction
of the Savior today?

People may be right in their own eyes,
but the Lord examines their heart.

PROVERBS 21:2 NLT

Not only does God want to show you your motives and help
you heal; he can also give you the right motivation. He can
bring restoration and so much more. And those times in the
past where maybe you acted out of wrong motivation? He can
redeem those and use them for good.

Nothing is wasted in the kingdom of God. You don't need to
pendulum swing into inaction because you are afraid of doing
something with a wrong motive. God's grace covers that. The
key is submitting to him, letting him guide you and restore
your heart. If you're walking with God, he can move even
when your motive might be wrong. You don't limit him, and
he empowers you.

Jesus, in you, I am not limited by my inability. Search my
heart. Show me any wrong motives and help me change.
Thank you for your grace in my life.

Blessing

"The LORD bless you and keep you;
the LORD make his face shine on you and be gracious to you;
the LORD turn his face toward you and give you peace."

NUMBERS 6:24-26 NIV

Communication is both verbal and nonverbal. What does a smile communicate to you? When someone smiles, they are usually trying to convey peace, pleasure, or delight. A simple smile can transform someone's day, communicating to them that they are noticed and appreciated.

God is smiling upon you. Let this promise in Numbers communicate to you that God loves you. Let it sink deep into your bones that he approves of you and delights in you. Let this smile open the floodgates and bring peace to wash over you. God is pleased with you. Root yourself in that truth this morning. Let it change your day.

Have you taken time to consider
how deep the Father's love is for you?
Picture his smile.

"May the LORD bless you and keep you.
May the LORD show you his kindness
and have mercy on you.
May the LORD watch over you
and give you peace."

NUMBERS 6:24-26 NCV

There is nonverbal communication that the Lord is giving us in this verse, but the person speaking is using verbal communication to his audience as well. The message of God's love for his people is one we need to open our mouths and proclaim. There are so many in our spheres of influence who haven't felt the warmth of the Lord's smile. For whatever reason, they are living under guilt and condemnation, unaware that they have a father in heaven who wants a relationship with them.

As much as we need to let it sink into our own souls that God loves us and is vastly pleased with us, let us also share this truth with the world as well. Let us speak this blessing over our friends, our family, our children, our neighbors, and our fellow church members.

God, I know you are smiling at me. Thank you for the love and warmth that that conveys. I love you! Help me to spread your love and peace to those around me who could really use some encouragement. I want to be a conduit of your grace to a hurting world.

Father's Help

Give us a Father's help when we face our enemies.
For to trust in any man is an empty hope.

PSALM 108:12 TPT

What are the traits of a good father? We have various experiences with our earthly fathers, and none of them were or are perfect. But we all share a perfect heavenly Father, and here are some of the things that make him good. First, a good father protects. He does what he can to keep his family out of harm's way. Your Father God has immeasurable strength to protect you from any plot of the enemy. A good father spends time with his kids. He listens to them and treats them with dignity. Your Father in heaven delights in you when you come to him. He longs to spend time with you and hears every prayer.

A good father also challenges his kids and teaches them lessons. Scripture tells us that God disciplines those he loves. God disciplines us and uses various means to teach us the things we need to know to walk in godliness. Lastly, a good father shows unconditional love. You can rely on him to love you and be there for you, no matter how badly you screw up. God is exactly like that, with oceans of forgiveness and mercy for you. We have a good, heavenly father in God.

Which aspect of the perfect heavenly Father
are you most appreciative of this morning?

Oh, please help us against our enemies,
for all human help is useless.

PSALM 108:12 NLT

When you were a kid, there were probably some tasks were got regulated to dad. Need help putting a toy together or getting your bike fixed? That's dad's job. Need the gutters cleaned out? Dad's job. Got to learn how to change your oil? Dad will teach you. Not all of us grew up in two-parent household, or even with a dad who was willing to take on a helping role, but we all understand the cultural stereotype of what jobs go to dad and how he can help.

A father's help. We need Father's help when we face the enemy, Satan. We need a strong defender, someone full of wisdom, one who knows the enemy's tactics and has already won the battle. We need someone who can protect us completely and build up our weaknesses. We need our Father God. He will fight for you. You need only come to him and cry out for help. God will never let you down. Where do you need some fatherly help tonight? Pray to God to meet you in that need.

Father God, thank you for being a good father. Thank you for meeting my every need. I ask for your help tonight. Will you be my defender?

No Comparison

I consider that our present sufferings are not worth comparing with the glory that will be revealed in us.

ROMANS 8:18 NIV

For the word *consider*, picture two scales, like the scales of justice. You place things on the scales and you observe to see which one has more weight. The one that has more weight isn't subject to how you are feeling that day, It's a fact that is nonnegotiable.

This is the picture that you can reference when you read this verse from Paul. Paul says to imagine life—our whole, eternal life—as the scales. On one side, we put the present sufferings that we face. On the other rests the weight of glory in eternity. It's not even a contest! The weight of glory would be like a brick hitting the ground against a feather of suffering we placed in the other pan. This can help us keep things in perspective. Glory unimaginable and reality so sweet awaits us. Persevere, dear believer, through whatever trial you are facing, and let the weight of glory ground you in the truth.

When was the last time you considered the weight of glory?

*The sufferings we have now are nothing compared
to the great glory that will be shown to us.*

ROMANS 8:18 NCV

We tend to fixate on our sufferings, only affording a brief
glance to the glory to come. We need to flip this practice on
its head and fixate on glory while glancing at sufferings. How
do we fixate on glory? One way is by giving the things we are
going through an eternal perspective. What does the Bible
say about them? Are there rewards in heaven for what you are
going through? Has Jesus made specific promises regarding
your situation? Is the greatness of God more than what your
trial is?

The answer is yes. When we try to comprehend the long scope
of eternity and the wonders that await us, it helps us to see
that the fleeting moments on earth, though important and
real, will all be worth it when we reach the other side.

Jesus, thank you for promising to be near in my suffering.
Help me to weigh it out and to focus more on eternity and
your glory than on my present circumstances.

Gift of God

By grace you have been saved through faith;
and that not of yourselves, it is the gift of God;
not as a result of works, so that no one may boast.

EPHESIANS 2:8-9 NASB

We are five days away from Christmas, in the thick of the
season of gift-giving. Maybe you're curled up in a favorite
chair this morning, a cup of eggnog in hand, right next to
your tree. Under the tree there are probably a few packages
of different sizes, wrapped in bows and pretty paper. The
gifts, paper, bows, decorations, even the eggnog—most of it
was bought using your hard-earned money. Christmas is a
bit different as an adult, isn't it? You realize the cost involved
behind all the magic, especially the presents.

Though you won't find much advice here about finding the
magic again from a financial standpoint, let's look at the
spiritual standpoint. Let's unwrap grace again and let our souls
be in awe of a gift that cost more than we could ever imagine.
There is a special wonder attached to receiving gifts as a child.
You have no comprehension of how much work and money
went into the gift. There's just that unbridled joy at receiving
exactly what you wanted. God has paid the greatest price to
give us a gift that is exactly what we want and need. Won't you
receive it this morning?

When was the last time you felt wonder over the gift of grace?

It was only through this wonderful grace that we believed in him. Nothing we did could ever earn this salvation, for it was the gracious gift from God that brought us to Christ! So no one will ever be able to boast, for salvation is never a reward for good works or human striving.

<small>EPHESIANS 2:8-9 TPT</small>

It's pretty annoying when you run into that one family member or friend that always has to outdo everyone, isn't it? They love to boast about the things they are able to purchase and do, and though their charity isn't a bad thing, their attitude of bragging gives it a negative edge.

Let's check ourselves. Are we Christians who speak as though the grace we in our lives is a result of our own doing? Any grace we have, any blessing, is 100% the work of our Father in heaven. Let us be careful to give credit and praise where it is due and not try to obtain it for ourselves.

God, check my heart. Am I taking credit for your work in my life? I want to give you all the praise, all the glory. Thank you for this gift that I never deserved. You are amazing!

A Father's Compassion

As a father has compassion on his children,
so the LORD has compassion on those who fear him.

PSALM 103:13 NIV

There is a parable of Jesus' that correlates to this passage.
Jesus tells the story of the prodigal son in Luke 15. It's about
a son who takes his inheritance early from his father and
leaves. He goes and parties it up hard, forsaking all his father
stood for. In the end, he runs out of money and ends up living
with some pigs. When he goes back to his father to beg for
mercy, the father runs to greet him and throws him a huge
party, reinstating him to the status of son. He is overjoyed
that his son has returned!

This story is a beautiful example of a father having
compassion on his child. Some of us need an outside picture
because we didn't have very compassionate fathers growing
up. When you read this verse, consider the prodigal son's
father running toward him, embracing him and loving him.
Imagine the forgiveness and acceptance the father showed.
That's the love your Father in heaven has for you. If you feel
like you are too much or not enough, your Father God wants to
show you with compassionate love that he accepts you today.

What are you running from and who are you running toward?
Choose to run to the Father today.

*The LORD has mercy on those who respect him,
as a father has mercy on his children.*

PSALM 103:13 NCV

If you started this book in January and are still reading, chances are you are a person who fears God. You care enough to get up and read and study his Word every day. Have you ever read statements like the second part of this verse and seen it as a clause to the first? The enemy then whispers in your ear that you don't qualify for the clause.

Dear believer, that is a lie. If you believe in Jesus and desire to follow him, you fear God. The Lord is a compassionate father, not one waiting for you to trip up. Hold onto the promise of his true character tonight.

Father, thank you for showing me compassion. Thank you for running toward me with open arms and for forgiving me.

Humble Love

Love is patient, love is kind.
It does not envy, it does not boast,
it is not proud.

1 CORINTHIANS 13:4 NIV

"Oh good, another list that I will fall short of." Do you ever feel this way when you read the Bible? With lists like the one in today's verse, it can be easy to feel like a failure when you try to measure up. We might start our days trying our best, but if we use the Bible like a checklist, we will have empty boxes every time. Paul never meant that you should conjure up this kind of love on your own strength. That's impossible! We will all fall short of these standards at some point. Paul knew this.

This list is less of a to-do list for you and more of an achievement list of the Holy Spirit. We cannot be patient enough on our own strength. We cannot muster up kindness out of our selfishness. We cannot deny envy, squelch pride, or silence boasting. But for believers who love through the power of the Holy Spirit, this list becomes a list of how we love, because it's how he loves. When we ask the Holy Spirit to empower our love, we can check off the boxes in 1 Corinthians because God is moving through us. Don't be defeated when your love doesn't look perfect. Instead, ask the Holy Spirit to give you the power to love the way only he can.

How can you let the Holy Spirit empower your love today?

Love is large and incredibly patient. Love is gentle and consistently kind to all. It refuses to be jealous when blessing comes to someone else. Love does not brag about one's achievements nor inflate its own importance.

1 Corinthians 13:4 tpt

The holidays are almost over, and maybe you're breathing a sigh of relief. Maybe that sigh comes with a twinge of regret too. It's easy to get caught up in pride and envy over the holidays. It can become all about the best gifts, the prettiest parties, the cutest family Christmas cards.

Don't let these things steal from your holiday season. A December full of gifts but lacking in love is a sad picture. If need be, repent of the ways you have fallen into these snares, and let these last days of the year be a gift of love, 1 Corinthians style, to those around you.

God, forgive me of the ways I've tried to love on my own strength or turned to other things. Empower me to love like you today.

Perfect Timing

For everything there is a season,
and a time for every matter under heaven.

ECCLESIASTES 3:1 NRSV

What you do with your minutes is what you do with your days. What you do with your days is what you do with your years, and your years make up your life. We are told in the Bible that life is but a vapor. It is short and our days are numbered.

How have you been filling your time? Time is passing, and none of us can stop it. But you can choose to be a person who lives with intentionality—someone who numbers their moments, who considers their time, and who seeks to bring God glory from every moment he has gifted them. If you are intentional about doing the things God has gifted you in, the desires he has placed inside you, how would your days look different?

Will you partner with God to fulfill his plan?
How can you act on his plans today?

There is a time for everything,
and a season for every activity under the heavens.

ECCLESIASTES 3:1 NIV

December is a reflective time of year. Many of us look back over the year that has gone by and contemplate past events. Most of us can agree that, though there are moments that feel long, the days are passing fast. It is imperative that as children of God, we read the seasons. God is faithful to lead us, but not every season looks the same. It's like the way we have recently exchanged the brilliant colors of fall for the hushed carols and green pines of winter.

Maybe you are stuck in a past season, unwilling to let go. Maybe you are fearful of the next one, feeling unprepared. Beloved, God is not unaware. What is most important is that you are following him from one season to the next. He gives us the grace we need for each season. Let go, press in, and find the beauty in your current season.

God, help me to make the most of each season I am in. I want to move from season to season in your timing and with your grace. Thank you for continuing to work in my life. I want you to fulfill your plan for me.

Wonderful Counselor

A child has been born to us; God has given a son to us.
He will be responsible for leading the people.
His name will be Wonderful Counselor, Powerful God,
Father Who Lives Forever, Prince of Peace.

ISAIAH 9:6 NCV

Let's slow down the Christmas rush. Light a candle this morning, grab a hot beverage, and read this Scripture out loud. There was a period of time, for Isaiah especially, of prophecy abounding. Many of the prophecies had to do with the coming Messiah, the one everyone was waiting for. After all these prophecies, it was 400 years of silence.

The people waited. Some forgot. Some misinterpreted and expected a military powerhouse or an educated scholar, someone who would quickly and swiftly overthrow the government that oppressed them. Jesus came with a power that no one expected, and frankly, not many wanted. He came with a meekness that was about the Father's business alone. Many did not understand, and many were disappointed. But in this manner, he saved the whole world.

Where can you see the unconventional power
of God in the Christmas story?

For unto us a Child is born,
Unto us a Son is given;
And the government will be upon His shoulder.
And His name will be called
Wonderful, Counselor, Mighty God,
Everlasting Father, Prince of Peace.

ISAIAH 9:6 NKJV

He is the King with four names. Wonderful counselor. What do you think of when you hear the word *counselor*? A person who listens, who gives advice? He is a king who is wonderful in wisdom, guidance, and advice, and he shares it with us. Next is mighty God, which we touched on a bit this morning. God's power knows no end. It is displayed throughout the whole Bible. Eternal Father speaks to the nature of God—how he was, is, and is to come. How there is no end to his reign and kingdom? Our God controls eternity.

Lastly, the Prince of peace. Peace itself came down in the form of a baby. He established peace with God, and now we can live at peace with God forever. What beautiful news!

Jesus, you are the king with four names, and all your attributes are great. Thank you for coming as a baby and dying to set me free.

Messiah

*"Today in the town of David a Savior has been born to you;
he is the Messiah, the Lord."*

LUKE 2:11 NIV

Merry Christmas! The Messiah has come. Most of us can probably agree that one thing we love about Christmas is the gifts. Colorful packages wrapped in beautiful paper, festive bags, lovely bows. Then, there is the anticipation of what is in those boxes. What if you bought someone a great gift and they didn't open it? They just left it in the box. Sure, the box was pretty, but what good is the gift if it's wrapped up and left in the box?

We do this with God. We come to him, and he seems great, all wrapped up in the box of what we know. But we never go deeper. We never unwrap the box. Maybe some of us are afraid of what we will get if we do. Maybe God will be different than we expect. What if he doesn't show up and the box is empty? What if he isn't what was hoped for? We have to trust God to be God. We have to let him out of the boxes we keep him in. In *The Chronicles of Narnia*, Aslan, the lion version of Jesus, is described as, "He's King. He's not a tame lion, but he is good." Beloved, God is not tame, and we need to stop trying to tame him. But he is good, and that is something you can count on.

Do you need to unbox God and let him be God?
Start untying the ribbons today.

*"Today in Bethlehem a rescuer was born for you.
He is the Lord Yahweh, the Messiah."*

LUKE 2:11 TPT

At the end of this busy day, pull up a chair and contemplate
what it means that Jesus is Lord. To paraphrase this morning's
Narnia author, C.S. Lewis once said that Jesus can be one of
three things: he can be a liar, he can be a lunatic, or he can be
our Lord. Each human must wrestle with this. Either Jesus
was lying the whole time about being God, he was straight up
crazy, or he really is the Messiah, then and today.

Most of us who are reading this have concluded that he is
Lord. If Jesus is Lord, how does that change your life? How
do you need to bow your knee to the King of kings? How can
you submit your life to his lordship this coming year? These
are all questions to contemplate this Christmas evening as we
finish celebrating the first coming of our Messiah.

Jesus, thank you for becoming flesh and dwelling with us.
Be Lord of my life.

Overflow

"He who believes in Me, as the Scripture has said,
out of his heart will flow rivers of living water."

JOHN 7:38 NKJV

Water is crucial to human life. Did you know that 70% of our world is covered by water? Even more fascinating, only 1% of that is drinkable by humans. Did you know that our bodies are made up of almost 60% water? Think about this. There is water all around us, 70%, but so little of it can give us life and will quench our thirst.

Spiritually, there are options abounding in our world. But only Jesus will quench the thirst of the world. You know the living water himself. You believe in Jesus. Out of you can flow rivers of living water for a thirsty world. How are you taking the gospel to the world? Those who don't know Jesus are swimming in the 70%, and they are so thirsty. You have access to the 1% of life-giving, drinkable water that they need. What are you going to do about it? Fellow believer, share the gospel!

Who do you need to offer living water to today?

"Believe in me so that rivers of living water will burst out from within you, flowing from your innermost being, just like the Scripture says!"

JOHN 7:38 TPT

Water is refreshing. This morning, hopefully you thought about someone you know who needs that refreshment. Who needs Jesus? Did you take action to communicate the gospel to them today? Maybe God stirred in your heart even more. What about those in the world who don't have access to the living water, the life-giving message of the gospel? Is God calling you to reach them?

Maybe he is asking you to move. Maybe he is asking you to give financially. Maybe he is asking you to fast and pray and intercede. How is he asking you to bring water to those who have no access to it?

Jesus, show me those who need your living water. Reveal how you want me to reach them in your timing. Give me courage to take action.

Forgiveness

"If you forgive those who sin against you, your heavenly Father will forgive you. But if you refuse to forgive others, your Father will not forgive your sins."

MATTHEW 6:14-15 NLT

Why is forgiveness so important? Forgiveness stands between us and God. God has forgiven us in the depths of our sin. If we have come to realize our sinful state, and have seen how God has forgiven us even then, how can we say we want to be like Christ while withholding forgiveness from others? Unforgiveness does not make us Christ-like.

Secondly, unforgiveness does not harm the person who you won't forgive as much as it harms you. It creates bitterness in your heart, which takes root and wreaks havoc on your life. If you live in unforgiveness, you are the one stuck in the past. You are the one carrying around the heavy load. The damage you are doing is always to yourself. Thirdly, forgiveness helps you grow. When you forgive, it enables you to let go, grow, change, and move on.

Are you harboring unforgiveness
toward anyone in your heart?

> *"When you pray, make sure you forgive the faults of others so that your Father in heaven will also forgive you. But if you withhold forgiveness from others, your Father withholds forgiveness from you."*
>
> MATTHEW 6:14-15 TPT

Jesus knows it isn't easy to forgive other people. He is not asking you to ignore the pain that has been inflicted upon you. But he is asking you to live according to kingdom principles and to forgive. He wants what is best for you, and he knows that forgiveness will only benefit you.

It should be said, however, that forgiving someone does not mean that the relationship is restored. You can forgive someone and still not be restored to them. There are relationships that will need to end. There are things that will take time to mend. There are boundaries that are healthy. Forgiveness does not mean everything is swept under the rug and we pretend it never happened. Forgiveness is necessary, and restoration is a process. The distinction is important.

Jesus, thank you for forgiving me. Help me to forgive those who have hurt me. Give me wisdom in how to forgive and how to live in the difficult nature of this relationship with this person who has hurt me.

Great Confidence

The LORD will be your confidence,
And will keep your foot from being caught.

PROVERBS 3:26 NASB

It is doubtful that many of us have ever physically been caught
in a trap, but let's explore what we know of them from TV
and books for a minute. Traps are usually hidden. Traps
can hurt you. Traps keep you in bondage so that the trapper
can capture you. Traps are often set with ill intent. When
we set traps in our kitchen to catch mice, we bait them with
something yummy that the mice like.

Now, think of all these things in relation to the enemy. His
traps will be hidden. He is the father of lies. His lies are
meant to hurt you, to turn you against God. His traps, though
alluring with worldly desires, lead to bondage and death.
His definitely has bad intentions. This is your enemy. Now,
consider your God. If God is your hope and confidence, he
will keep you from falling into the enemy's traps. Stick close
to Jesus and hope in him. He will protect you.

Identify some of the ways the enemy tries to trap you.
What bait does he use? What camouflage?

The LORD will keep you safe.
He will keep you from being trapped.

PROVERBS 3:26 NCV

What do you do if you fall into a trap? Are you done for? No!
Jesus is mighty and powerful. He will not abandon you to the
enemy. He will save you. Cry out to Jesus for freedom from
the bondage you face. He doesn't give up on us just because
we make mistakes and fall into traps. He rescues us. What a
great God we serve!

Afterwards, let your fall turn to wisdom in your life. Now you
know how to identify the traps of the enemy. You know that
they are there. And you can use your story to warn others and to
encourage them to put their confidence in Jesus. He is mighty
to save, our great defender. Put your confidence in him.

Jesus, help me to use wisdom to see the traps of the enemy.
Keep my foot from being caught.

Making Things Right

After you suffer for a short time, God, who gives all grace, will make everything right. He will make you strong and support you and keep you from falling. He called you to share in his glory in Christ, a glory that will continue forever.

1 PETER 5:10 NCV

Has it been a rough year? This beautiful verse encourages those of us who may have had a difficult go of it this year. Suffering is for a short time. Read that again. This will not last forever, Christian. There is an end in sight. Suffering is not eternal for believers—glory is. We get to share in the glory of Christ that is eternal and wonderful!

Even though suffering rarely feels short, we must put our confidence and hope in Christ, who promises to give us grace through it all. We must trust him when he tells us that, in light of eternity, this suffering is short and worth it. God is on the move, and he is working his redemption power. He is healing. He is saving. He is making things right and restoring them to himself. Through it all, he supports you and never leaves you. Take heart. Jesus has overcome the world.

How has Jesus overcome the world in your life?

After your brief suffering, the God of all loving grace, who has called you to share in his eternal glory in Christ, will personally and powerfully restore you and make you stronger than ever. Yes, he will set you firmly in place and build you up.

1 Peter 5:10 TPT

Think about childbirth. Have you heard the joke that if women remembered the full pain and suffering they went through in childbirth, then we would have no more humans? Most women who have had babies will attest to the fact that the pain is very real, and very present, and it feels like it lasts for lifetimes. They also admit that afterwards, when they are holding their child, the pain is not what they recall; it's the beauty of their child.

In a similar fashion, the pain and suffering of this world is real. It hurts. Peter is not downplaying that here. But he is telling you that it's worth it for the glory that is to come. When you have reached the glory that you will share with Christ, the suffering will fade in comparison. Let this truth spark hope within us to persevere.

Jesus, the suffering is real. Thank you for being near me. Thank you for sharing your eternal glory with me. I look forward to it!

Wisdom's Instruction

*Teach us to number our days,
that we may gain a heart of wisdom.*

PSALM 90:12 NIV

At the end of the year, you can look back and see that God gifted you with 364 days thus far. Each day has twenty-four hours, which equals about 8,760 hours for the year. Did you know most people spend 2,920 of those hours sleeping? If you work forty hours a week, you also spend around that amount at work. The number of free hours is dwindling down, isn't it?

This is not written to discourage you or scare you, but to make you mindful of what you are doing with the hours that God has given you. Today's psalm says that by analyzing our days and taking them into account, we gain wisdom. Take some time to look over your life this morning and analyze your minutes and hours. Are a few too many given to endless scrolling? Could you look up from a screen and into the eyes of those around you more? Maybe you are a workaholic and need to add more hours to resting or being with family. We can all gain wisdom for living in godliness by looking at your life. Ask Jesus to guide you as you analyze this.

What wisdom do you gain from looking at your days?
Where should you put more or fewer hours?

*Help us to remember that our days are numbered,
and help us to interpret our lives correctly.
Set your wisdom deeply in our hearts
so that we may accept your correction.*

PSALM 90:12 TPT

In analyzing our days, we gain wisdom from seeing things we can change. Let's also take a moment to celebrate the things we did right—the ways God used us this year, the moments we dedicated to him. It's not all "work harder, do more, or change this" in the life of a Christian. There is always room for celebration.

All those moments you spent with a friend, investing in the relationship. The times you served your family by doing dishes or your church community by sweeping floors. The phone calls you took and the people you prayed with. The encouraging verses you shared on social media. The sabbath days you spent resting and meditating on God's Word. The cheerful laughter you shared with a clerk at a store.

Jesus, help me to number my days, that I might gain wisdom. Thank you for the victories in my life. Let's celebrate them together right now.

A Fresh Start

"Behold, I am doing a new thing;
now it springs forth, do you not perceive it?
I will make a way in the wilderness
and rivers in the desert."

ISAIAH 43:19 ESV

It's the last day of this devotional and this year, and what a verse! Newness is in the air. Can you feel it? Most of us can feel the hope of a new calendar laid out before us, the anticipation of things to come. Maybe this past year has been a desert. You've felt dry and far from God. You've kept going, but things aren't flourishing how you would like. Or maybe your year has been a wilderness, and you've felt lost and alone.

Whatever your year has been like, let us give thanks to God for the fact that he makes all things new. He will make a way in the wilderness. He will bring fresh water into our deserts. He will bring beauty from ashes and rejoicing from pain. Even stronger than the hope of a new calendar year is the hope we have in Jesus Christ, who is making all things new. Rejoice, dear believer. God is not done yet. He is moving mightily!

What new thing do you hope to see God do
in your life this next year?

"I am about to do something new.
See, I have already begun! Do you not see it?
I will make a pathway through the wilderness.
I will create rivers in the dry wasteland."

ISAIAH 43:19 NLT

Whatever new things may come, don't let go of the good thing you have developed this year, and that is being in God's Word daily. The habit that you cultivated over this year is the most important one you will use in your life. Don't forsake the daily reading of God's Word. Don't stop praying to him every morning and every evening. Remember that in order to live a blessed, full, happy life, we must find God as our happy place every single day. We must bring our cold, hard hearts before the warm flames of his Spirit and ask him to revive us again.

May this next year bring you closer to Jesus more than anything else. May this next year be one where you see his Spirit move mightily in your life. May this next year be a continuation of you finding your true happy place in Christ.

Jesus, thank you for the gift of this year. Help me to remember that you are my joy and my happy place, today and in the whole new year ahead.